FREE Test Taking Tips DVD Offer

To help us better serve you, we have developed a Test Taking Tips DVD that we would like to give you for FREE. **This DVD covers world-class test taking tips that you can use to be even more successful when you are taking your test.**

All that we ask is that you email us your feedback about your study guide. Please let us know what you thought about it – whether that is good, bad or indifferent.

To get your **FREE Test Taking Tips DVD**, email freedvd@studyguideteam.com with "FREE DVD" in the subject line and the following information in the body of the email:

    a. The title of your study guide.

    b. Your product rating on a scale of 1-5, with 5 being the highest rating.

    c. Your feedback about the study guide. What did you think of it?

    d. Your full name and shipping address to send your free DVD.

If you have any questions or concerns, please don't hesitate to contact us at freedvd@studyguideteam.com.

Thanks again!

ACT Prep Book 2019 & 2020

ACT Test Prep Study Guide 2019-2020 & Practice Test Questions

Test Prep Books

Table of Contents

Quick Overview

As you draw closer to taking your exam, effective preparation becomes more and more important. Thankfully, you have this study guide to help you get ready. Use this guide to help keep your studying on track and refer to it often.

This study guide contains several key sections that will help you be successful on your exam. The guide contains tips for what you should do the night before and the day of the test. Also included are test-taking tips. Knowing the right information is not always enough. Many well-prepared test takers struggle with exams. These tips will help equip you to accurately read, assess, and answer test questions.

A large part of the guide is devoted to showing you what content to expect on the exam and to helping you better understand that content. In this guide are practice test questions so that you can see how well you have grasped the content. Then, answer explanations are provided so that you can understand why you missed certain questions.

Don't try to cram the night before you take your exam. This is not a wise strategy for a few reasons. First, your retention of the information will be low. Your time would be better used by reviewing information you already know rather than trying to learn a lot of new information. Second, you will likely become stressed as you try to gain a large amount of knowledge in a short amount of time. Third, you will be depriving yourself of sleep. So be sure to go to bed at a reasonable time the night before. Being well-rested helps you focus and remain calm.

Be sure to eat a substantial breakfast the morning of the exam. If you are taking the exam in the afternoon, be sure to have a good lunch as well. Being hungry is distracting and can make it difficult to focus. You have hopefully spent lots of time preparing for the exam. Don't let an empty stomach get in the way of success!

When travelling to the testing center, leave earlier than needed. That way, you have a buffer in case you experience any delays. This will help you remain calm and will keep you from missing your appointment time at the testing center.

Be sure to pace yourself during the exam. Don't try to rush through the exam. There is no need to risk performing poorly on the exam just so you can leave the testing center early. Allow yourself to use all of the allotted time if needed.

Remain positive while taking the exam even if you feel like you are performing poorly. Thinking about the content you should have mastered will not help you perform better on the exam.

Once the exam is complete, take some time to relax. Even if you feel that you need to take the exam again, you will be well served by some down time before you begin studying again. It's often easier to convince yourself to study if you know that it will come with a reward!

Test-Taking Strategies

1. Predicting the Answer

When you feel confident in your preparation for a multiple-choice test, try predicting the answer before reading the answer choices. This is especially useful on questions that test objective factual knowledge or that ask you to fill in a blank. By predicting the answer before reading the available choices, you eliminate the possibility that you will be distracted or led astray by an incorrect answer choice. You will feel more confident in your selection if you read the question, predict the answer, and then find your prediction among the answer choices. After using this strategy, be sure to still read all of the answer choices carefully and completely. If you feel unprepared, you should not attempt to predict the answers. This would be a waste of time and an opportunity for your mind to wander in the wrong direction.

2. Reading the Whole Question

Too often, test takers scan a multiple-choice question, recognize a few familiar words, and immediately jump to the answer choices. Test authors are aware of this common impatience, and they will sometimes prey upon it. For instance, a test author might subtly turn the question into a negative, or he or she might redirect the focus of the question right at the end. The only way to avoid falling into these traps is to read the entirety of the question carefully before reading the answer choices.

3. Looking for Wrong Answers

Long and complicated multiple-choice questions can be intimidating. One way to simplify a difficult multiple-choice question is to eliminate all of the answer choices that are clearly wrong. In most sets of answers, there will be at least one selection that can be dismissed right away. If the test is administered on paper, the test taker could draw a line through it to indicate that it may be ignored; otherwise, the test taker will have to perform this operation mentally or on scratch paper. In either case, once the obviously incorrect answers have been eliminated, the remaining choices may be considered. Sometimes identifying the clearly wrong answers will give the test taker some information about the correct answer. For instance, if one of the remaining answer choices is a direct opposite of one of the eliminated answer choices, it may well be the correct answer. The opposite of obviously wrong is obviously right! Of course, this is not always the case. Some answers are obviously incorrect simply because they are irrelevant to the question being asked. Still, identifying and eliminating some incorrect answer choices is a good way to simplify a multiple-choice question.

4. Don't Overanalyze

Anxious test takers often overanalyze questions. When you are nervous, your brain will often run wild, causing you to make associations and discover clues that don't actually exist. If you feel that this may be a problem for you, do whatever you can to slow down during the test. Try taking a deep breath or counting to ten. As you read and consider the question, restrict yourself to the particular words used by the author. Avoid thought tangents about what the author *really* meant, or what he or she was *trying* to say. The only things that matter on a multiple-choice test are the words that are actually in the question. You must avoid reading too much into a multiple-choice question, or supposing that the writer meant something other than what he or she wrote.

5. No Need for Panic

It is wise to learn as many strategies as possible before taking a multiple-choice test, but it is likely that you will come across a few questions for which you simply don't know the answer. In this situation, avoid panicking. Because most multiple-choice tests include dozens of questions, the relative value of a single wrong answer is small. Moreover, your failure on one question has no effect on your success elsewhere on the test. As much as possible, you should compartmentalize each question on a multiple-choice test. In other words, you should not allow your feelings about one question to affect your success on the others. When you find a question that you either don't understand or don't know how to answer, just take a deep breath and do your best. Read the entire question slowly and carefully. Try rephrasing the question a couple of different ways. Then, read all of the answer choices carefully. After eliminating obviously wrong answers, make a selection and move on to the next question.

6. Confusing Answer Choices

When working on a difficult multiple-choice question, there may be a tendency to focus on the answer choices that are the easiest to understand. Many people, whether consciously or not, gravitate to the answer choices that require the least concentration, knowledge, and memory. This is a mistake. When you come across an answer choice that is confusing, you should give it extra attention. A question might be confusing because you do not know the subject matter to which it refers. If this is the case, don't eliminate the answer before you have affirmatively settled on another. When you come across an answer choice of this type, set it aside as you look at the remaining choices. If you can confidently assert that one of the other choices is correct, you can leave the confusing answer aside. Otherwise, you will need to take a moment to try to better understand the confusing answer choice. Rephrasing is one way to tease out the sense of a confusing answer choice.

7. Your First Instinct

Many people struggle with multiple-choice tests because they overthink the questions. If you have studied sufficiently for the test, you should be prepared to trust your first instinct once you have carefully and completely read the question and all of the answer choices. There is a great deal of research suggesting that the mind can come to the correct conclusion very quickly once it has obtained all of the relevant information. At times, it may seem to you as if your intuition is working faster even than your reasoning mind. This may in fact be true. The knowledge you obtain while studying may be retrieved from your subconscious before you have a chance to work out the associations that support it. Verify your instinct by working out the reasons that it should be trusted.

8. Key Words

Many test takers struggle with multiple-choice questions because they have poor reading comprehension skills. Quickly reading and understanding a multiple-choice question requires a mixture of skill and experience. To help with this, try jotting down a few key words and phrases on a piece of scrap paper. Doing this concentrates the process of reading and forces the mind to weigh the relative importance of the question's parts. In selecting words and phrases to write down, the test taker thinks about the question more deeply and carefully. This is especially true for multiple-choice questions that are preceded by a long prompt.

9. Subtle Negatives

One of the oldest tricks in the multiple-choice test writer's book is to subtly reverse the meaning of a question with a word like *not* or *except*. If you are not paying attention to each word in the question, you can easily be led astray by this trick. For instance, a common question format is, "Which of the following is…?" Obviously, if the question instead is, "Which of the following is not…?," then the answer will be quite different. Even worse, the test makers are aware of the potential for this mistake and will include one answer choice that would be correct if the question were not negated or reversed. A test taker who misses the reversal will find what he or she believes to be a correct answer and will be so confident that he or she will fail to reread the question and discover the original error. The only way to avoid this is to practice a wide variety of multiple-choice questions and to pay close attention to each and every word.

10. Reading Every Answer Choice

It may seem obvious, but you should always read every one of the answer choices! Too many test takers fall into the habit of scanning the question and assuming that they understand the question because they recognize a few key words. From there, they pick the first answer choice that answers the question they believe they have read. Test takers who read all of the answer choices might discover that one of the latter answer choices is actually *more* correct. Moreover, reading all of the answer choices can remind you of facts related to the question that can help you arrive at the correct answer. Sometimes, a misstatement or incorrect detail in one of the latter answer choices will trigger your memory of the subject and will enable you to find the right answer. Failing to read all of the answer choices is like not reading all of the items on a restaurant menu: you might miss out on the perfect choice.

11. Spot the Hedges

One of the keys to success on multiple-choice tests is paying close attention to every word. This is never truer than with words like almost, most, some, and sometimes. These words are called "hedges" because they indicate that a statement is not totally true or not true in every place and time. An absolute statement will contain no hedges, but in many subjects, like literature and history, the answers are not always straightforward or absolute. There are always exceptions to the rules in these subjects. For this reason, you should favor those multiple-choice questions that contain hedging language. The presence of qualifying words indicates that the author is taking special care with his or her words, which is certainly important when composing the right answer. After all, there are many ways to be wrong, but there is only one way to be right! For this reason, it is wise to avoid answers that are absolute when taking a multiple-choice test. An absolute answer is one that says things are either all one way or all another. They often include words like *every*, *always*, *best*, and *never*. If you are taking a multiple-choice test in a subject that doesn't lend itself to absolute answers, be on your guard if you see any of these words.

12. Long Answers

In many subject areas, the answers are not simple. As already mentioned, the right answer often requires hedges. Another common feature of the answers to a complex or subjective question are qualifying clauses, which are groups of words that subtly modify the meaning of the sentence. If the question or answer choice describes a rule to which there are exceptions or the subject matter is complicated, ambiguous, or confusing, the correct answer will require many words in order to be expressed clearly and accurately. In essence, you should not be deterred by answer choices that seem excessively long. Oftentimes, the author of the text will not be able to write the correct answer without offering some qualifications and modifications. Your job is to read the answer choices thoroughly and completely and to select the one that most accurately and precisely answers the question.

13. Restating to Understand

Sometimes, a question on a multiple-choice test is difficult not because of what it asks but because of how it is written. If this is the case, restate the question or answer choice in different words. This process serves a couple of important purposes. First, it forces you to concentrate on the core of the question. In order to rephrase the question accurately, you have to understand it well. Rephrasing the question will concentrate your mind on the key words and ideas. Second, it will present the information to your mind in a fresh way. This process may trigger your memory and render some useful scrap of information picked up while studying.

14. True Statements

Sometimes an answer choice will be true in itself, but it does not answer the question. This is one of the main reasons why it is essential to read the question carefully and completely before proceeding to the answer choices. Too often, test takers skip ahead to the answer choices and look for true statements. Having found one of these, they are content to select it without reference to the question above. Obviously, this provides an easy way for test makers to play tricks. The savvy test taker will always read the entire question before turning to the answer choices. Then, having settled on a correct answer choice, he or she will refer to the original question and ensure that the selected answer is relevant. The mistake of choosing a correct-but-irrelevant answer choice is especially common on questions related to specific pieces of objective knowledge, like historical or scientific facts. A prepared test taker will have a wealth of factual knowledge at his or her disposal and should not be careless in its application.

15. No Patterns

One of the more dangerous ideas that circulates about multiple-choice tests is that the correct answers tend to fall into patterns. These erroneous ideas range from a belief that B and C are the most common right answers, to the idea that an unprepared test-taker should answer "A-B-A-C-A-D-A-B-A." It cannot be emphasized enough that pattern-seeking of this type is exactly the WRONG way to approach a multiple-choice test. To begin with, it is highly unlikely that the test maker will plot the correct answers according to some predetermined pattern. The questions are scrambled and delivered in a random order. Furthermore, even if the test maker was following a pattern in the assignation of correct answers, there is no reason why the test taker would know which pattern he or she was using. Any attempt to discern a pattern in the answer choices is a waste of time and a distraction from the real work of taking the test. A test taker would be much better served by extra preparation before the test than by reliance on a pattern in the answers.

FREE DVD OFFER

Don't forget that doing well on your exam includes both understanding the test content and understanding how to use what you know to do well on the test. We offer a completely FREE Test Taking Tips DVD that covers world class test taking tips that you can use to be even more successful when you are taking your test.

All that we ask is that you email us your feedback about your study guide. To get your **FREE Test Taking Tips DVD**, email freedvd@studyguideteam.com with "FREE DVD" in the subject line and the following information in the body of the email:

- The title of your study guide.
- Your product rating on a scale of 1-5, with 5 being the highest rating.
- Your feedback about the study guide. What did you think of it?
- Your full name and shipping address to send your free DVD.

Introduction to the ACT

Function of the Test

The ACT is one of two national standardized college entrance examinations (the SAT being the other). Most prospective college students take the ACT or the SAT, and it is increasingly common for students to take both. All four-year colleges and universities in the United States accept the ACT for admissions purposes, and some require it. Some of those schools also use ACT subject scores for placement purposes. Sixteen states also require all high school juniors to take the ACT as part of the states' school evaluation efforts.

The vast majority of people taking the ACT are high school juniors and seniors who intend to apply to college. Traditionally, the SAT was more commonly taken than the ACT, particularly among students on the East and West coasts. However, the popularity of the ACT has grown dramatically in recent years and is now commonly taken by students in all fifty states. In fact, starting in 2013, more test takers took the ACT than the SAT. In 2015, 1.92 million students took the ACT. About 28 percent of 2015 high school graduates taking the ACT met the test's college-readiness benchmarks in all four subjects, while 31 percent met none of the benchmarks.

Test Administration

The ACT is offered on six dates throughout the year in the U.S. and Canada, and on five of those same dates in other countries. The registration fee includes score reports for four colleges, with additional reports available for purchase. There is a separate registration fee for the optional writing section.

On test dates, the ACT is administered at test centers throughout the world. The test centers are usually high schools or colleges, with several locations usually available in significant population centers.

Test takers can retake the ACT as frequently as the test is offered, up to a maximum of twelve times; although, individual colleges may have limits on how many retakes they will consider. Scores from the various sections cannot be combined from different sessions. The ACT does provide reasonable accommodations to test takers with professionally-documented disabilities.

Test Format

The ACT consists of 215 multiple-choice questions in four subject areas (English, mathematics, reading, and science) and takes about three hours and thirty minutes to complete. It also has an optional writing test, which takes an additional forty minutes.

The English section is 45 minutes long and contains 75 questions on usage, language mechanics, and rhetorical skills. The Mathematics section is 60 minutes long and contains 60 questions on algebra, geometry, and elementary trigonometry. Calculators that meet the ACT's calculator policy are permitted on the Mathematics section. The Reading section is 35 minutes long and contains four written passages with ten questions per passage. The Science section is 35 minutes long and contains 40 questions.

The Writing section is forty minutes long and is always given at the end so that test takers not wishing to take it may leave after completing the other four sections. This section consists of one essay in which students must analyze three different perspectives on a broad social issue. Although the Writing section is optional, some colleges do require it.

Section	Length	Questions
English	45 minutes	75
Mathematics	60 minutes	60
Reading	35 minutes	40
Science	35 minutes	40
Writing (optional)	40 minutes	1 essay

Scoring

Test takers receive a score between 1 and 36 for each of the four subject areas. Those scores are averaged together to give a Composite Score, which is the primary score reported as an "ACT score." The most prestigious schools typically admit students with Composite ACT Scores in the low 30's. Other selective schools typically admit students with scores in the high 20's. Traditional colleges more likely admit students with scores in the low 20's, while community colleges and other more open schools typically accept students with scores in the high teens. In 2015, the average composite score among all test takers (including those not applying to college) was 21.

Recent/Future Developments

In 2015, the Writing section underwent several changes. The allotted time extended 10 minutes (from 30 to 40 minutes) and the scoring changed to a scale from 1 to 36 (as with the other subject and Composite scores), rather than the previous scale from 2 to 12. The test also began asking test takers to give an opinion on a subject in light of three different perspectives provided by the test prompt, Lastly, the ACT began reporting four new "subscores," providing different ways to combine and evaluate the results of the various sections.

Beginning in September 2016, the scoring of the writing section changed back to a 2 to 12 scale.

ACT English Test

What to Expect

The English test contains five passages that are each followed by fifteen multiple-choice questions. Therefore, overall, the section contains 75 questions, which much be answered in the allotted 45 minutes. The passages contain underlined portions (words, phrases, or sentences) that are numbered. The questions that follow the passage will pertain to the correspondingly-numbered underlined portion (for example, question 5 would pertain to the underlined text labeled 5). However, some questions pertain to the passage as a whole or a particular section of it. The answer options will provide alternatives to what is written in the underlined text in the passage; typically, answer choice A will say "NO CHANGE" and should be selected when the initial text is correct as is. The content of the passages vary, but they are designed to be pulled from a variety of disciplines and topics that should interest test takers. Familiarity with the content is not important; instead, the function of the English test is to assess the candidate's editing skills and command of the English language.

Tips for the English Test

- Consider the context. When answering a question, it's important to think about how the underlined portion fits into the sentence, paragraph, and passage at large. In this way, the writing style and tone should be consistent in a given passage. Test takers should consider how the potential choices do or do not fit well within the section of the passage. For this reason, it's important to read the entire paragraph surrounding the underlined portion before jumping in and answering a given question. Failing to do so might result in context mistakes.

- Carefully read the questions to identify what element of writing is being addressed in the question. Verb tense, sentence structure, tone, etc. might all be problematic in a given underlined portion, but the question might prioritize the revision of one aspect over another. With that said, do not choose an answer choice that solves one error but creates a different one. The "correct" choice should be the best option overall.

- Double-check your choice. After selecting your answer, reread the portion of the passage with the new change to ensure it is indeed correct.

Production of Writing

Topic Development

<u>Identifying the Position and Purpose</u>
When it comes to an author's writing, readers should always identify a **position** or **stance**. No matter how objective a text may seem, readers should assume the author has preconceived beliefs. One can reduce the likelihood of accepting an invalid argument by looking for multiple articles on the topic, including those with varying opinions. If several opinions point in the same direction and are backed by reputable peer-reviewed sources, it's more likely that the author has a valid argument. Positions that run contrary to widely held beliefs and existing data should invite scrutiny. There are exceptions to the rule, so readers should be careful consumers of information.

While themes, symbols, and motifs are buried deep within the text and can sometimes be difficult to infer, an author's **purpose** is usually obvious from the beginning. There are four purposes of writing: to inform, to persuade, to describe, and to entertain. **Informative** writing presents facts in an accessible way. **Persuasive** writing appeals to emotions and logic to inspire the reader to adopt a specific stance. Readers should be wary of this type of writing, as it can mask a lack of objectivity with powerful emotion. **Descriptive** writing is designed to paint a picture in the reader's mind, while texts that **entertain** are often narratives designed to engage and delight the reader.

The various writing styles are usually blended, with one purpose dominating the rest. A persuasive text, for example, might begin with a humorous tale to make readers more receptive to the persuasive message, or a recipe in a cookbook designed to inform might be preceded by an entertaining anecdote that makes the recipes more appealing.

Identifying the Purposes of Parts of Texts

Writing can be classified under four passage types: narrative, expository, descriptive (sometimes called technical), and persuasive. Although these types are not mutually exclusive, one form tends to dominate the rest. By recognizing the type of passage being read, readers gain insight into how they should read. A narrative passage intended to entertain can sometimes be read more quickly if the details are discernible. A technical document, on the other hand, might require a close read, because skimming the passage might cause the reader to miss salient details.

Narrative, at its core, is the art of storytelling. For a narrative to exist, certain elements must be present. It must have characters. While many characters are human, characters can be defined as anything that thinks, acts, and talks like a human. For example, many recent movies, such as *Lord of the Rings* and *The Chronicles of Narnia*, include animals, fantastical creatures, and even trees that behave like humans. Narratives also must have a plot or sequence of events. Typically, those events follow a standard plot diagram, but recent trends start *in medias res* or in the middle (nearer the climax). In this instance, foreshadowing and flashbacks often fill in plot details. Along with characters and a plot, there must also be conflict. **Conflict** is usually divided into two types: internal and external. **Internal conflict** indicates the character is in turmoil. One can imagine an angel on one shoulder and the devil on the other, arguing it out. Internal conflicts are presented through the character's thoughts. **External conflicts** are visible. Types of external conflict include person versus person, person versus nature, person versus technology, person versus the supernatural, or a person versus fate.

Expository texts are detached and to the point, while other types of writing—persuasive, narrative, and descriptive—are livelier. Since expository writing is designed to instruct or inform, it usually involves directions and steps written in second person (the "you" voice) and lacks any persuasive or narrative elements. Sequence words such as *first*, *second*, and *third*, or *in the first place*, *secondly*, and *lastly* are often given to add fluency and cohesion. Common examples of expository writing include instructor's lessons, cookbook recipes, and repair manuals.

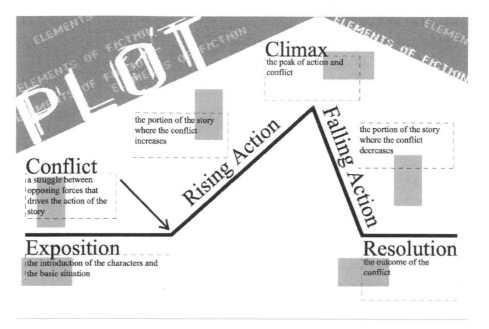

Due to its empirical nature, **technical** writing is filled with steps, charts, graphs, data, and statistics. The goal of technical writing is to advance understanding in a field through the scientific method. Experts such as teachers, doctors, or mechanics use words unique to the profession in which they operate. These words, which often incorporate acronyms, are called **jargon**. Technical writing is a type of expository writing but is not meant to be understood by the general public. Instead, technical writers assume readers have received a formal education in a particular field of study and need no explanation as to what the jargon means. One can imagine a doctor trying to understand a diagnostic reading for a car or a mechanic trying to interpret lab results. Only professionals with proper training will fully comprehend the text.

Persuasive texts are designed to change opinions and attitudes. The topic, stance, and arguments are found in the thesis, which is positioned near the end of the introduction. Later supporting paragraphs offer relevant quotations, paraphrases, and summaries from primary or secondary sources, which are then interpreted, analyzed, and evaluated. The goal of persuasive writers is not to stack quotes, but to develop original ideas by using sources as a starting point. Good persuasive writing makes powerful arguments with valid sources and thoughtful analyses. Poor persuasive writing is riddled with bias and logical fallacies. Sometimes, logical and illogical arguments are sandwiched together in the same text. Therefore, readers should employ skepticism when reading persuasive arguments.

Determining Whether a Text Has Met Its Intended Goal
Authors typically make it very easy for readers to identify the purpose of a passage: to entertain, inform, or persuade. The author's purpose might be determined through the formatting or organization of the text (such as through headings or a thesis statement), or through the presentation of ideas.

For example, if the author's purpose is to entertain, he or she might use humorous language or share a personal story. The use of personal anecdotes or experiences indicates that the intent is probably to entertain. Description is also often used in writing that seeks to entertain, although some authors choose this as a distinctive purpose. Descriptive writing paints a picture with words, and an author will use various adjectives and adverbs that entail the five senses (sight, sound, touch, smell, and taste) to do this.

If the author's purpose is to inform, the passage will likely contain facts, figures, and studies. The goal in such a passage is to educate readers; therefore, authors typically do this in a very straightforward way. The informative passage uses a clear thesis statement, which usually appears at the end of the introduction. The information will be presented in a fair, balanced manner, without the use of the author's opinion. There may be some elements of entertaining language or even a bias in the way the information is presented, but overall, the informative passage will be a clear presentation of facts.

When the author's intent is to persuade, he or she may employ other types of writing to engage the reader. There may be personal details or humorous language used to draw on the emotions of the reader. The persuasive writer might also include facts and figures to drive a point home. A persuasive passage might also present the point at the beginning, but it will most likely be in the form of a claim.

It's important for readers to be able to identify an author's purpose and determine whether the author has achieved that purpose effectively and consistently.

Evaluating the Relevance of Material in Terms of a Text's Focus
Critical reading strategies are critical for assessing what a text is saying and why the author has written it. The first step of critical reading is to determine why you are reading the text: do you need general information about a topic or are you looking for specific details? Once you determine the purpose, it will be easier to find the relevant material within the text. For example, a text that focuses on the formation of the solar system would not be particularly relevant for a research project delving into lunar eclipses here on Earth. Reading a text should bring up factual and analytical questions. The factual questions inquire about the content and details of the text. The analytical questions should make readers think about what they learned from the text and draw conclusions about the facts they learned. The relevant material can also be understood by looking at the structure of the text. Headings, subheadings, tables, graphs, and captions can all provide information about the focus of the text. The reader should also look at whether the text is in written to describe cause and effect, a problem and a solution, or in a descriptive pattern as each method can help elucidate the important information. Lastly, the reader should summarize the material in his or her own words to further enhance comprehension of the text and the main takeaways from the particular text.

Organization, Unity, and Cohesion

Main Ideas and Supporting Details
Topics and main ideas are critical parts of writing. The **topic** is the subject matter of the piece. An example of a topic would be *global warming*.

The **main idea** is what the writer wants to say about that topic. A writer may make the point that global warming is a growing problem that must be addressed in order to save the planet. Therefore, the topic is global warming, and the main idea is that it's *a serious problem needing to be addressed*. The topic can be expressed in a word or two, but the main idea should be a complete thought.

An author will likely identify the topic immediately within the title or the first sentence of the passage. The main idea is usually presented in the introduction. In a single passage, the main idea may be identified in the first or last sentence, but it will most likely be directly stated and easily recognized by the reader. Because it is not always stated immediately in a passage, it's important that readers carefully read the entire passage to identify the main idea.

The main idea should not be confused with the thesis statement. A **thesis statement** is a clear statement of the writer's specific stance and can often be found in the introduction of a nonfiction piece. The thesis is a specific sentence (or two) that offers the direction and focus of the discussion.

In order to illustrate the main idea, a writer will use **supporting details**, which provide evidence or examples to help make a point. Supporting details are typically found in nonfiction pieces that seek to inform or persuade the reader.

For example, in the example of global warming, where the author's main idea is to show the seriousness of this growing problem and the need for change, supporting details would be critical for effectively making that point. Supporting details used here might include *statistics* on an increase in global temperatures and **studies** showing the impact of global warming on the planet. The author could also include **projections** for future climate change in order to illustrate potential lasting effects of global warming.

It's important that readers evaluate the author's supporting details to be sure that they are credible, provide evidence of the author's point, and directly support the main idea. Although shocking statistics grab readers' attention, their use may provide ineffective information in the piece. Details like this are crucial to understanding the passage and evaluating how well the author presents his or her argument and evidence.

Parts of the Essay

The **introduction** of an essay has to do a few important things:

- Establish the topic of the essay in original wording
- Clarify the significance/importance of the topic or the purpose for writing
- Offer a thesis statement that identifies the writer's own viewpoint on the topic (typically one or two brief sentences as a clear, concise explanation of the main point on the topic)

Body paragraphs reflect the ideas developed in the middle of an essay. Body paragraphs should include the following:

- A **topic sentence** that identifies the sub-point (e.g., a reason why, a way how, a cause or effect)
- A detailed **explanation** of the point, explaining why the writer thinks the point is valid
- Illustrative **examples**, such as personal examples or real-world examples, that support and validate the point (i.e., "prove" the point)
- A **concluding sentence** that connects the examples, reasoning, and analysis of the point being made

The **conclusion,** or final paragraph, should be brief and should reiterate the focus, clarifying why the discussion is significant or important. It is important that writers avoid adding specific details or new ideas to this paragraph. The purpose of the conclusion is to sum up what has been said to bring the discussion to a close.

<u>Ensuring a Text Is Logically Organized and Flows Smoothly</u>

A text should be organized in a logical way so that it flows smoothly; ideas should be connected so that readers can follow along. In essence, the text must be coherent. Coherence is simply defined as the quality of being logical and consistent. In order to have coherent sentences, paragraphs, and completed texts, therefore, authors must be logical and consistent in their writing, whatever the document might be. Two words are helpful to understanding coherence: flow and relationship. Transitions are often referred to as being the "glue" to put organized thoughts together. Now, let's look at the topic sentence from which flow and relationship originate.

The topic sentence, usually the first in a paragraph, holds the essential features that will be brought forth in the paragraph. It is also here that authors either grab or lose readers. It may be the only writing that a reader encounters from that writer, so it is a good idea to summarize and represent ideas accurately.

The coherent paragraph has a logical order. It utilizes transitional words and phrases, parallel sentence structure, clear pronoun references, and reasonable repetition of key words and phrases. It is important to use common sense for repetition, consider synonyms for variety, and be consistent in verb tense whenever possible.

When writers have accomplished their paragraph's purpose, they prepare it to receive the next paragraph. While writing, read the paragraph over, edit, examine, evaluate, and make changes accordingly. Possibly, a paragraph has gone on too long. If that occurs, it needs to be broken up into other paragraphs, or the length should be reduced. If a paragraph didn't fully accomplish its purpose, consider revising it.

Within a paragraph, the ideal sentence length—the number of words in a sentence—depends upon the sentence's purpose.

It's okay for a sentence to be brief, and it's fine for a sentence to be lengthy. It's just important to make sure that long sentences do not become run-on sentences or too long to keep up with.

To keep writing interesting, authors should vary sentence lengths, using a mixture of short, medium and long sentences.

Finally, when considering the logical flow and organization of a text, readers should ensure that the author has made appropriate comparisons in their writing. It's easy to make mistakes in sentences that involve comparisons, and those mistakes are difficult to spot. Try to find the error in the following sentence:

> Senator Wilson's proposed seat belt legislation was similar to Senator Abernathy.

Can't find it? First, ask what two things are actually being compared. It seems like the writer *wants* to compare two different types of legislation, but the sentence actually compares legislation ("Senator Wilson's proposed seat belt legislation") to a person ("Senator Abernathy"). This is a strange and illogical comparison to make.

So how can the writer correct this mistake? The answer is to make sure that the second half of the sentence logically refers back to the first half. The most obvious way to do this is to repeat words:

> Senator Wilson's proposed seat belt legislation was similar to Senator Abernathy's seat belt legislation.

Now the sentence is logically correct, but it's a little wordy and awkward. A better solution is to eliminate the word-for-word repetition by using suitable replacement words:

> Senator Wilson's proposed seat belt legislation was similar to that of Senator Abernathy.

> Senator Wilson's proposed seat belt legislation was similar to the bill offered by Senator Abernathy.

Here's another similar example:

> More lives in the U.S. are saved by seat belts than Japan.

The writer probably means to compare lives saved by seat belts in the U.S. to lives saved by seat belts in Japan. Unfortunately, the sentence's meaning is garbled by an illogical comparison, and instead refers to U.S. lives saved *by Japan* rather than *in Japan.* To resolve this issue, first repeat the words and phrases needed to make an identical comparison:

> More lives in the U.S. are saved by seat belts than lives in Japan are saved by seat belts.

Then, use a replacement word to clean up the repetitive text:

> More lives in the U.S. are saved by seat belts than in Japan.

Knowledge of Language

Precision

People often think of precision in terms of math, but precise word choice is another key to successful writing. Since language itself is imprecise, it's important for the writer to find the exact word or words to convey the full, intended meaning of a given situation. For example:

> The number of deaths has gone down since seat belt laws started.

There are several problems with this sentence. First, the word *deaths* is too general. From the context, it's assumed that the writer is referring only to deaths caused by car accidents. However, without clarification, the sentence lacks impact and is probably untrue. The phrase *gone down* might be accurate, but a more precise word would provide more information and greater accuracy. Did the numbers show a slow and steady decrease in highway fatalities or a sudden drop? If the latter is true, the writer is missing a chance to make his or her point more dramatically. Instead of *gone down* the author could substitute *plummeted, fallen drastically,* or *rapidly diminished* to bring the information to life. Also, the phrase *seat belt laws* is unclear. Does it refer to laws requiring cars to include seat belts or to laws requiring drivers and passengers to use them? Finally, *started* is not a strong verb. Words like *enacted* or *adopted* are more direct and make the content more real. When put together, these changes create a far more powerful sentence:

> The number of highway fatalities has plummeted since laws requiring seat belt usage were enacted.

However, it's important to note that precise word choice can sometimes be taken too far. If the writer of the sentence above takes precision to an extreme, it might result in the following:

> The incidence of high-speed, automobile accident-related fatalities has decreased 75% and continued to remain at historical lows since the initial set of federal legislations requiring seat belt use were enacted in 1992.

This sentence is extremely precise, but it takes so long to achieve that precision that it suffers from a lack of clarity. Precise writing is about finding the right balance between information and flow. This is also an issue of conciseness (discussed in the next section).

The last thing for writers to consider with precision is a word choice that's not only unclear or uninteresting, but also confusing or misleading. For example:

> The number of highway fatalities has become hugely lower since laws requiring seat belt use were enacted.

In this case, the reader might be confused by the word *hugely*. Huge means large, but here the writer uses *hugely* in an incorrect and awkward manner. Although most readers can decipher this, doing so disconnects them from the flow of the writing and makes the writer's point less effective.

Concision

"Less is more" is a good rule for writers to follow when composing a sentence. Unfortunately, writers often include extra words and phrases that seem necessary at the time but add nothing to the main idea. This confuses the reader and creates unnecessary repetition. Writing that lacks conciseness is usually guilty of excessive wordiness and redundant phrases. Here's an example containing both of these issues:

> When legislators decided to begin creating legislation making it mandatory for automobile drivers and passengers to make use of seat belts while in cars, a large number of them made those laws for reasons that were political reasons.

There are several empty or "fluff" words here that take up too much space. These can be eliminated while still maintaining the writer's meaning. For example:

- *decided to begin* could be shortened to *began*
- *making it mandatory for* could be shortened to *requiring*
- *make use of* could be shortened to *use*
- *a large number* could be shortened to *many*

In addition, there are several examples of redundancy that can be eliminated:

- legislators decided to begin creating legislation and made those laws
- automobile drivers and passengers and while in cars
- reasons that were political reasons

These changes are incorporated as follows:

> When legislators began requiring drivers and passengers to use seat belts, many of them did so for political reasons.

There are many general examples of redundant phrases, such as *add an additional, complete and total, time schedule*, and *transportation vehicle*. If asked to identify a redundant phrase on the exam, test takers should look for words that are close together with the same (or similar) meanings.

Consistency in Style and Tone

Style and tone are often thought to be the same thing. Though they're closely related, there are important differences to keep in mind. The easiest way to do this is to remember that **style** creates and affects **tone**. More specifically, style is *how the writer uses words* to create the desired tone for his or her writing.

Style
Style can include any number of technical writing choices, and some may have to be analyzed on the test. A few examples of style choices include:

- Sentence Construction: When presenting facts, does the writer use shorter sentences to create a quicker sense of the supporting evidence, or does he or she use longer sentences to elaborate and explain the information?

- Technical Language: Does the writer use jargon to demonstrate his or her expertise in the subject, or do the writer use ordinary language to help the reader understand things in simple terms?

- Formal Language: Does the writer refrain from using contractions such as *won't* or *can't* to create a more formal tone, or does he or she use a colloquial, conversational style to connect to the reader?

- Formatting: Does the writer use a series of shorter paragraphs to help the reader follow a line of argument, or does he or she use longer paragraphs to examine an issue in great detail and demonstrate his or her knowledge of the topic?

On the exam, test takers should examine the writer's style and how his or her writing choices affect the way the text comes across.

Tone
Tone refers to the writer's attitude toward the subject matter. Tone is usually explained in terms of a work of fiction. For example, the tone conveys how the writer feels about the characters and the situations in which they're involved. Nonfiction writing is sometimes thought to have no tone at all; however, this is incorrect.

A lot of nonfiction writing has a neutral tone, which is an important one for the writer to use. A neutral tone demonstrates that the writer is presenting a topic impartially and letting the information speak for itself. On the other hand, nonfiction writing can be just as effective and appropriate if the tone isn't neutral. The following short passage provides an example of tone in nonfiction writing:

> Seat belts save more lives than any other automobile safety feature. Many studies show that airbags save lives as well; however, not all cars have airbags. For instance, some older cars don't. Furthermore, air bags aren't entirely reliable. For example, studies show that in 15% of accidents airbags don't deploy as designed, but, on the other hand, seat belt malfunctions are extremely rare. The number of highway fatalities has plummeted since laws requiring seat belt usage were enacted.

In this passage, the writer mostly chooses to retain a neutral tone when presenting information. If instead, the author chose to include his or her own personal experience of losing a friend or family member in a car accident, the tone would change dramatically. The tone would no longer be neutral and would show that the writer has a personal stake in the content, allowing him or her to interpret the information in a different way. When analyzing tone, the reader should consider what the writer is trying to achieve in the text and how they *create* the tone using style.

Word Parts

By analyzing and understanding Latin, Greek, and Anglo-Saxon word roots, prefixes, and suffixes, one can better understand word meanings. Of course, people can always look words up if a dictionary or thesaurus if available, but meaning can often be gleaned on the spot if the reader learns to dissect and examine words.

A word can consist of the following combinations:

- root
- root + suffix
- prefix + root
- prefix + root + suffix

For example, if someone was unfamiliar with the word *submarine* they could break the word into its parts.

prefix + root

sub + marine

It can be determined that *sub* means *below* as in *subway* and *subpar*. Additionally, one can determine that *marine* refers to *the sea* as in *marine life*. Thus, it can be figured that *submarine* refers to something below the water.

Roots
Roots are the basic components of words. Many roots can stand alone as individual words, but others must be combined with a prefix or suffix to be a word. For example, *calc* is a root but it needs a suffix to be an actual word (*calcium*).

Prefixes

A **prefix** is a word, letter, or number that is placed before another. It adjusts or qualifies the root word's meaning. When written alone, prefixes are followed by a dash to indicate that the root word follows. Some of the most common prefixes are the following:

Prefix	Meaning	Example
dis-	not or opposite of	disabled
in-, im-, il-, ir-	not	illiterate
re-	again	return
un-	not	unpredictable
anti-	against	antibacterial
fore-	before	forefront
mis-	wrongly	misunderstand
non-	not	nonsense
over-	more than normal	overabundance
pre-	before	preheat
super-	above	superman

Suffixes

A **suffix** is a letter or group of letters added at the end of a word to form another word. The word created from the root and suffix is either a different tense of the same root (*help* + *ed* = *helped*) or a new word (*help* + *ful* = *helpful*). When written alone, suffixes are preceded by a dash to indicate that the root word comes before.

Some of the most common suffixes are the following:

Suffix	Meaning	Example
-ed	makes a verb past tense	washed
-ing	makes a verb a present participle verb	washing
-ly	to make characteristic of	lovely
-s, -es	to make more than one	chairs, boxes
-able	can be done	deplorable
-al	having characteristics of	comical
-est	comparative	greatest
-ful	full of	wonderful
-ism	belief in	communism
-less	without	faithless
-ment	action or process	accomplishment
-ness	state of	happiness
-ize, -ise	to render, to make	sterilize, advertise
-cede, -ceed, -sede	go	concede, proceed, supersede

Here are some helpful tips:

- When adding a suffix that starts with a vowel (for example, -*ed*) to a one-syllable root whose vowel has a short sound and ends in a consonant (for example, *stun*), the final consonant of the root (*n*) gets doubled.

  stun + ed = stun*n*ed

- Exception: If the past tense verb ends in *x* such as *box*, the *x* does not get doubled.

  box + ed = boxed

- If adding a suffix that starts with a vowel (-*er*) to a multi-syllable word ending in a consonant (*begin*), the consonant (*n*) is doubled.

  begin + er = begin*n*er

- If a short vowel is followed by two or more consonants in a word such as *i+t+c+h = itch,* the last consonant should not be doubled.

  itch + ed = itched

- If adding a suffix that starts with a vowel (-*ing*) to a word ending in *e* (for example, *name*), that word's final *e* is generally (but not always) dropped.

  name + ing = naming
  exception: manage + able = manag*e*able

- If adding a suffix that starts with a consonant (-*ness*) to a word ending in *e* (*complete*), the *e* generally (but not always) remains.

  complete + ness = completeness
  exception: judge + ment = judgment

- There is great diversity on handling words that end in *y*. For words ending in a vowel + *y*, nothing changes in the original word.

  play + ed = played

- For words ending in a consonant + *y*, the *y* id changed to i when adding any suffix except for -*ing*.

  marry + ed = married
  marry + ing = marrying

Conventions of Standard English

Sentence Structure and Formation

<u>Sentence Structure</u>
Simple sentence: composed of one independent clause

> Many people watch hummingbirds.

> Note that it has one subject and one verb; however, a simple sentence can have a compound subject and/or a compound verb.

> Adults and children often enjoy watching and photographing hummingbirds.

Compound sentence: composed of two independent clauses

> The wind knocked down lots of trees, but no trees in my yard were affected.

Complex sentence: composed of one independent clause and one dependent clause

> Although the wind knocked down lots of trees, no trees in my yard were affected.

<u>Sentence Fluency</u>
Learning and utilizing the mechanics of structure will encourage effective, professional results, and adding some creativity will elevate one's writing to a higher level.

First, the basic elements of sentences will be reviewed.

A **sentence** is a set of words that make up a grammatical unit. The words must have certain elements and be spoken or written in a specific order to constitute a complete sentence that makes sense.

> 1. A sentence must have a **subject** (a noun or noun phrase). The subject tells whom or what the sentence is addressing (i.e. what it is about).

> 2. A sentence must have an **action** or **state of being** (*a* verb). To reiterate: A verb forms the main part of the predicate of a sentence. This means that it explains what the noun is doing.

> 3. A sentence must convey a complete thought.

When examining writing, readers should be mindful of grammar, structure, spelling, and patterns. Sentences can come in varying sizes and shapes, so the point of grammatical correctness is not to stamp out creativity or diversity in writing. Rather, grammatical correctness ensures that writing will be enjoyable and clear. One of the most common methods successful test takers employ to catch errors is to mouth the words as they read them. Many typos are fixed automatically by the brain, but mouthing the words often circumvents this instinct and helps one read what's actually on the page. Often, grammar errors are caught not by memorization of grammar rules but by the training of one's mind to know whether something *sounds* right or not.

<u>Types of Sentences</u>

There isn't an overabundance of absolutes in grammar, but here is one: every sentence in the English language falls into one of four categories.

Declarative: a simple statement that ends with a period

The price of milk per gallon is the same as the price of gasoline.

Imperative: a command, instruction, or request that ends with a period

Buy milk when you stop to fill up your car with gas.

Interrogative: a question that ends with a question mark

Will you buy the milk?

Exclamatory: a statement or command that expresses emotions like anger, urgency, or surprise and ends with an exclamation mark

Buy the milk now!

Declarative sentences are the most common type, probably because they are comprised of the most general content, without any of the bells and whistles that the other three types contain. They are, simply, declarations or statements of any degree of seriousness, importance, or information.

Imperative sentences often seem to be missing a subject. The subject is there, though; it is just not visible or audible because it is *implied*. For example:

Buy the milk when you fill up your car with gas.

In this sentence, *you* is the implied subject, the one to whom the command is issued. This is sometimes called *the understood you* because it is understood that *you* is the subject of the sentence.

Interrogative sentences—those that ask questions—are defined as such from the idea of the word **interrogation**, the action of questions being asked of suspects by investigators. Although that is serious business, interrogative sentences apply to all kinds of questions.

To exclaim is at the root of **exclamatory** sentences. These are made with strong emotions behind them. The only technical difference between a declarative or imperative sentence and an exclamatory one is the exclamation mark at the end. The example declarative and imperative sentences can both become an exclamatory one simply by putting an exclamation mark at the end of the sentences.

The price of milk per gallon is the same as the price of gasoline!

Buy milk when you stop to fill up your car with gas!

After all, someone might be really excited by the price of gas or milk, or they could be mad at the person that will be buying the milk! However, as stated before, exclamation marks in abundance defeat their own purpose! After a while, they begin to cause fatigue! When used only for their intended purpose, they can have their expected and desired effect.

Transitions

Transitions are the glue use to make organized thoughts adhere to one another. Transitions are the glue that helps put ideas together seamlessly, within sentences and paragraphs, between them, and (in longer documents) even between sections. Transitions may be single words, sentences, or whole paragraphs (as in the prior example). Transitions help readers to digest and understand what to feel about what has gone on and clue readers in on what is going on, what will be, and how they might react to all these factors. Transitions are like good clues left at a crime scene.

Parallel Structure in a Sentence

Parallel structure, also known as **parallelism**, refers to using the same grammatical form within a sentence. This is important in lists and for other components of sentences.

> Incorrect: At the recital, the boys and girls were dancing, singing, and played musical instruments.

> Correct: At the recital, the boys and girls were dancing, singing, and playing musical instruments.

Notice that in the first example, *played* is not in the same verb tense as the other verbs nor is it compatible with the helping verb *were*. To test for parallel structure in lists, try reading each item as if it were the only item in the list.

> The boys and girls were dancing.

> The boys and girls were singing.

> The boys and girls were played musical instruments.

Suddenly, the error in the sentence becomes very clear. Here's another example:

Incorrect: After the accident, I informed the police *that Mrs. Holmes backed* into my car, *that Mrs. Holmes got out* of her car to look at the damage, and *she was driving* off without leaving a note.

Correct: After the accident, I informed the police *that Mrs. Holmes backed* into my car, *that Mrs. Holmes got out* of her car to look at the damage, and *that Mrs. Holmes drove off* without leaving a note.

Correct: After the accident, I informed the police that Mrs. Holmes *backed* into my car, *got out* of her car to look at the damage, and *drove off* without leaving a note.

Note that there are two ways to fix the nonparallel structure of the first sentence. The key to parallelism is consistent structure.

Modifier Placement

Modifiers are words or phrases (often adjectives or nouns) that add detail to, explain, or limit the meaning of other parts of a sentence. Look at the following example:

> A big pine tree is in the yard.

In the sentence, the words *big* (an adjective) and *pine* (a noun) modify *tree* (the head noun).

All related parts of a sentence must be placed together correctly. *Misplaced* and *dangling modifiers* are common writing mistakes. In fact, they're so common that many people are accustomed to seeing them and can decipher an incorrect sentence without much difficulty.

Misplaced Modifiers

Since *modifiers* refer to something else in the sentence (*big* and *pine* refer to *tree* in the example above), they need to be placed close to what they modify. If a modifier is so far away that the reader isn't sure what it's describing, it becomes a *misplaced modifier*. For example:

> Seat belts almost saved 5,000 lives in 2009.

It's likely that the writer means that the total number of lives saved by seat belts in 2009 is close to 5,000. However, due to the misplaced modifier (*almost*), the sentence actually says there are 5,000 examples when seat belts *almost saved lives*. In this case, the position of the modifier is actually the difference between life and death (at least in the meaning of the sentence). A clearer way to write the sentence is:

> Seat belts saved almost 5,000 lives in 2009.

Now that the modifier is close to the 5,000 lives it references, the sentence's meaning is clearer.

Another common example of a misplaced modifier occurs when the writer uses the modifier to begin a sentence. For example:

> Having saved 5,000 lives in 2009, Senator Wilson praised the seat belt legislation.

It seems unlikely that Senator Wilson saved 5,000 lives on her own, but that's what the writer is saying in this sentence. To correct this error, the writer should move the modifier closer to the intended object it modifies. Here are two possible solutions:

> Having saved 5,000 lives in 2009, the seat belt legislation was praised by Senator Wilson.

> Senator Wilson praised the seat belt legislation, which saved 5,000 lives in 2009.

When choosing a solution for a misplaced modifier, look for an option that places the modifier close to the object or idea it describes.

Dangling Modifiers

A modifier must have a target word or phrase that it's modifying. Without this, it's a *dangling modifier*. Dangling modifiers are usually found at the beginning of sentences:

> After passing the new law, there is sure to be an improvement in highway safety.

This sentence doesn't say anything about who is passing the law. Therefore, "After passing the new law" is a dangling modifier because it doesn't modify anything in the sentence. To correct this type of error, determine what the writer intended the modifier to point to:

> After passing the new law, legislators are sure to see an improvement in highway safety.

"After passing the new law" now points to *legislators*, which makes the sentence clearer and eliminates the dangling modifier.

Agreement

In English writing, certain words connect to other words. People often learn these connections (or *agreements*) as young children and use the correct combinations without a second thought. However, the questions on the test dealing with agreement probably aren't simple ones.

Subject-Verb Agreement
Which of the following sentences is correct?

> A large crowd of protesters was on hand.

> A large crowd of protesters were on hand.

Many people would say the second sentence is correct, but they'd be wrong. However, they probably wouldn't be alone. Most people just look at two words: *protesters were*. Together they make sense. They sound right. The problem is that the verb *were* doesn't refer to the word *protesters*. Here, the word *protesters* is part of a prepositional phrase that clarifies the actual subject of the sentence (*crowd*). Take the phrase "of protesters" away and re-examine the sentences:

> A large crowd was on hand.

> A large crowd were on hand.

Without the prepositional phrase to separate the subject and verb, the answer is obvious. The first sentence is correct. On the test, look for confusing prepositional phrases when answering questions about subject-verb agreement. Take the phrase away, and then recheck the sentence.

Noun Agreement
Nouns that refer to other nouns must also match in number. Take the following example:

> John and Emily both served as an intern for Senator Wilson.

Two people are involved in this sentence: John and Emily. Therefore, the word *intern* should be plural to match. Here is how the sentence should read:

> John and Emily both served as interns for Senator Wilson.

Shift in Noun-Pronoun Agreement
Pronouns are used to replace nouns so sentences don't have a lot of unnecessary repetition. This repetition can make a sentence seem awkward as in the following example:

> Seat belts are important because seat belts save lives, but seat belts can't do so unless seat belts are used.

Replacing some of the nouns (*seat belts*) with a pronoun (*they*) improves the flow of the sentence:

> Seat belts are important because they save lives, but they can't do so unless they are used.

A pronoun should agree in number (singular or plural) with the noun that precedes it. Another common writing error is the shift in *noun-pronoun agreement*. Here's an example:

> When people are getting in a car, he should always remember to buckle his seatbelt.

The first half of the sentence talks about a plural (*people*), while the second half refers to a singular person (*he* and *his*). These don't agree, so the sentence should be rewritten as:

> When people are getting in a car, they should always remember to buckle their seatbelt.

Fragments and Run-Ons

A *sentence fragment* is a failed attempt to create a complete sentence because it's missing a required noun or verb. Fragments don't function properly because there isn't enough information to understand the writer's intended meaning. For example:

> Seat belt use corresponds to a lower rate of hospital visits, reducing strain on an already overburdened healthcare system. Insurance claims as well.

Look at the last sentence: *Insurance claims as well.* What does this mean? This is a fragment because it has a noun but no verb, and it leaves the reader guessing what the writer means about insurance claims. Many readers can probably infer what the writer means, but this distracts them from the flow of the writer's argument. Choosing a suitable replacement for a sentence fragment may be one of the questions on the test. The fragment is probably related to the surrounding content, so look at the overall point the writer is trying to make and choose the answer that best fits that idea.

Remember that sometimes a fragment can *look* like a complete sentence or have all the nouns and verbs it needs to make sense. Consider the following two examples:

> Seat belt use corresponds to a lower rate of hospital visits.

> Although seat belt use corresponds to a lower rate of hospital visits.

Both examples above have nouns and verbs, but only the first sentence is correct. The second sentence is a fragment, even though it's actually longer. The key is the writer's use of the word *although*. Starting a sentence with *although* turns that part into a *subordinate clause* (more on that next). Keep in mind that one doesn't have to remember that it's called a subordinate clause on the test. Just be able to recognize that the words form an incomplete thought and identify the problem as a sentence fragment.

A *run-on sentence* is, in some ways, the opposite of a fragment. It contains two or more sentences that have been improperly forced together into one. An example of a run-on sentence looks something like this:

> Seat belt use corresponds to a lower rate of hospital visits it also leads to fewer insurance claims.

Here, there are two separate ideas in one sentence. It's difficult for the reader to follow the writer's thinking because there is no transition from one idea to the next. On the test, choose the best way to correct the run-on sentence.

Here are two possibilities for the sentence above:

> Seat belt use corresponds to a lower rate of hospital visits. It also leads to fewer insurance claims.

> Seat belt use corresponds to a lower rate of hospital visits, but it also leads to fewer insurance claims.

Both solutions are grammatically correct, so which one is the best choice? That depends on the point that the writer is trying to make. Always read the surrounding text to determine what the writer wants to demonstrate, and choose the option that best supports that thought.

Punctuation

<u>Ellipses</u>

An **ellipsis** (. . .) consists of three handy little dots that can speak volumes on behalf of irrelevant material. Writers use them in place of words, lines, phrases, list content, or paragraphs that might just as easily have been omitted from a passage of writing. This can be done to save space or to focus only on the specifically relevant material.

> Exercise is good for some unexpected reasons. Watkins writes, "Exercise has many benefits such as . . . reducing cancer risk."

In the example above, the ellipsis takes the place of the other benefits of exercise that are more expected.

The ellipsis may also be used to show a pause in sentence flow.

> "I'm wondering . . . how this could happen," Dylan said in a soft voice.

<u>Commas</u>

A **comma** (,) is the punctuation mark that signifies a pause—breath—between parts of a sentence. It denotes a break of flow. As with so many aspects of writing structure, authors will benefit by reading their writing aloud or mouthing the words. This can be particularly helpful if one is uncertain about whether the comma is needed.

In a complex sentence—one that contains a **subordinate (dependent)** clause or clauses—the use of a comma is dictated by where the subordinate clause is located. If the subordinate clause is located before the main clause, a comma is needed between the two clauses.

> I will not pay for the steak, *because I don't have that much money.*

Generally, if the subordinate clause is placed after the main clause, no punctuation is needed. I did well on my exam because I studied two hours the night before. Notice how the last clause is dependent because it requires the earlier independent clauses to make sense.

Use a comma on both sides of an interrupting phrase.

> I will pay for the ice cream, chocolate and vanilla, and then will eat it all myself.

The words forming the phrase in italics are nonessential (extra) information. To determine if a phrase is nonessential, try reading the sentence without the phrase and see if it's still coherent.

A comma is not necessary in this next sentence because no interruption—nonessential or extra information—has occurred. Read sentences aloud when uncertain.

I will pay for his chocolate and vanilla ice cream and then will eat it all myself.

If the nonessential phrase comes at the beginning of a sentence, a comma should only go at the end of the phrase. If the phrase comes at the end of a sentence, a comma should only go at the beginning of the phrase.

Other types of interruptions include the following:

- interjections: Oh no, I am not going.
- abbreviations: Barry Potter, M.D., specializes in heart disorders.
- direct addresses: Yes, Claudia, I am tired and going to bed.
- parenthetical phrases: His wife, lovely as she was, was not helpful.
- transitional phrases: Also, it is not possible.

The second comma in the following sentence is called an Oxford comma.

I will pay for ice cream, syrup, and pop.

It is a comma used after the second-to-last item in a series of three or more items. It comes before the word *or* or *and*. Not everyone uses the Oxford comma; it is optional, but many believe it is needed. The comma functions as a tool to reduce confusion in writing. So, if omitting the Oxford comma would cause confusion, then it's best to include it.

Commas are used in math to mark the place of thousands in numerals, breaking them up so they are easier to read. Other uses for commas are in dates (*March 19, 2016*), letter greetings (*Dear Sally,*), and in between cities and states (*Louisville, KY*).

Semicolons

The **semicolon** (;) might be described as a heavy-handed comma. Take a look at these two examples:

I will pay for the ice cream, but I will not pay for the steak.
I will pay for the ice cream; I will not pay for the steak.

What's the difference? The first example has a comma and a conjunction separating the two independent clauses. The second example does not have a conjunction, but there are two independent clauses in the sentence, so something more than a comma is required. In this case, a semicolon is used.

Two independent clauses can only be joined in a sentence by either a comma and conjunction or a semicolon. If one of those tools is not used, the sentence will be a run-on. Remember that while the clauses are independent, they need to be closely related in order to be contained in one sentence.

Another use for the semicolon is to separate items in a list when the items themselves require commas.

The family lived in Phoenix, Arizona; Oklahoma City, Oklahoma; and Raleigh, North Carolina.

Colons

Colons (:) have many miscellaneous functions. Colons can be used to proceed further information or a list. In these cases, a colon should only follow an independent clause.

Humans take in sensory information through five basic senses: sight, hearing, smell, touch, and taste.

The meal includes the following components:

- Caesar salad
- spaghetti
- garlic bread
- cake

The family got what they needed: a reliable vehicle.

While a comma is more common, a colon can also proceed a formal quotation.

> He said to the crowd: "Let's begin!"

The colon is used after the greeting in a formal letter.

> Dear Sir:
> To Whom It May Concern:

In the writing of time, the colon separates the minutes from the hour (*4:45 p.m.*). The colon can also be used to indicate a ratio between two numbers (*50:1*).

Hyphens
The **hyphen** (-) is a little hash mark that can be used to join words to show that they are linked.

Hyphenate two words that work together as a single adjective (a compound adjective).

> honey-covered biscuits

Some words always require hyphens, even if not serving as an adjective.

> merry-go-round

Hyphens always go after certain prefixes like *anti-* & *all-*.

Hyphens should also be used when the absence of the hyphen would cause a strange vowel combination (*semi-engineer*) or confusion. For example, *re-collect* should be used to describe something being gathered twice rather than being written as *recollect*, which means to remember.

Parentheses and Dashes
Parentheses are half-round brackets that look like this: ( ). They set off a word, phrase, or sentence that is an afterthought, explanation, or side note relevant to the surrounding text but not essential. A pair of commas is often used to set off this sort of information, but parentheses are generally used for information that would not fit well within a sentence or that the writer deems not important enough to be structurally part of the sentence.

> The picture of the heart (see above) shows the major parts you should memorize.
> Mount Everest is one of three mountains in the world that are over 28,000 feet high (K2 and Kanchenjunga are the other two).

See how the sentences above are complete without the parenthetical statements? In the first example, *see above* would not have fit well within the flow of the sentence. The second parenthetical statement could have been a separate sentence, but the writer deemed the information not pertinent to the topic.

The **dash** (—) is a mark longer than a hyphen used as a punctuation mark in sentences and to set apart a relevant thought. Even after plucking out the line separated by the dash marks, the sentence will be intact and make sense.

> Looking out the airplane window at the landmarks—Lake Clarke, Thompson Community College, and the bridge—she couldn't help but feel excited to be home.

The dashes use is similar to that of parentheses or a pair of commas. So, what's the difference? Many believe that using dashes makes the clause within them stand out while using parentheses is subtler. It's advised to not use dashes when commas could be used instead.

Quotation Marks

Here are some instances where **quotation marks** should be used:

- Dialogue for characters in narratives. When characters speak, the first word should always be capitalized and the punctuation goes inside the quotes. For example:

   > Janie said, "The tree fell on my car during the hurricane."

- Around titles of songs, short stories, essays, and chapter in books
- To emphasize a certain word
- To refer to a word as the word itself

Apostrophes

This punctuation mark, the apostrophe ('), is a versatile little mark. It has a few different functions:

- Quotes: Apostrophes are used when a second quote is needed within a quote.

   > In my letter to my friend, I wrote, "The girl had to get a new purse, and guess what Mary did? She said, 'I'd like to go with you to the store.' I knew Mary would buy it for her."

- Contractions: Another use for an apostrophe in the quote above is a contraction. *I'd* is used for *I would.*

- Possession: An apostrophe followed by the letter *s* shows possession (*Mary's* purse). If the possessive word is plural, the apostrophe generally just follows the word.

   > The trees' leaves are all over the ground.

Usage

<u>Homophones</u>

Homophones are two or more words that have no particular relationship to one another except their identical pronunciations. Homophones make spelling English words fun and challenging. Examples include:

Common Homophones
affect, effect
allot, a lot
barbecue, barbeque
bite, byte
brake, break
capital, capitol
cash, cache
cell, sell
colonel, kernel
do, due, dew
dual, duel
eminent, imminent
flew, flu, flue
gauge, gage
holy, wholly
it's, its
knew, new
libel, liable
principal, principle
their, there, they're
to, too, two
yoke, yolk

<u>Word Confusion</u>

That/Which

The pronouns *that* and *which* are both used to refer to animals, objects, ideas, and events—but they are not interchangeable. The rule is to use the word *that* in essential clauses and phrases that are help convey the meaning of the sentence. Use the word *which* in nonessential (less important) clauses. Typically, *which* clauses are enclosed in commas.

The morning <u>that I fell asleep in class</u> caused me a lot of trouble.

This morning's coffee, <u>which had too much creamer</u>, woke me up.

31

Who/Whom

We use the pronouns *who* and *whom* to refer to people. We always use *who* when it is the subject of the sentence or clause. We never use *whom* as the subject; it is always the object of a verb or preposition.

> <u>Who</u> hit the baseball for the home run? (subject)

> The baseball fell into the glove of <u>whom</u>? (object of the preposition *of*)

> The umpire called <u>whom</u> "out"? (object of the verb *called*)

To/Too/Two

> to: a preposition or infinitive (*to walk, to run, walk to the store, run to the tree*)
> too: means also, as well, or very (*She likes cookies, too.; I ate too much.*)
> two: a number (*I have two cookies. She walked to the store two times.*)

There/Their/They're

> there: an adjective, adverb, or pronoun used to start a sentence or indicate place (*There are four vintage cars over there.*)
> their: a possessive pronoun used to indicate belonging (*Their car is the blue and white one.*)
> they're: a contraction of the words "they are" (*They're going to enter the vintage car show.*)

Your/You're

> your: a possessive pronoun (*Your artwork is terrific.*)
> you're: a contraction of the words "you are" (*You're a terrific artist.*)

Its/It's

> its: a possessive pronoun (*The elephant had its trunk in the water.*)
> it's: a contraction of the words "it is" (*It's an impressive animal.*)

Affect/Effect

> affect: as a verb means "to influence" (*How will the earthquake affect your home?*); as a noun means "emotion or mood" (*Her affect was somber.*)
> effect: as a verb means "to bring about" (*She will effect a change through philanthropy.*); as a noun means "a result of" (*The effect of the earthquake was devastating.*)

> Other mix-ups: Other pairs of words cause mix-ups but are not necessarily homonyms. Here are a few of those:

Bring/Take

> bring: when the action is coming toward (*Bring me the money.*)
> take: when the action is going away from (*Take her the money.*)

Can/May

> can: means "able to" (*The child can ride a bike.*)
> may: asks permission (*The child asked if he may ride his bike.*)

Than/Then

> than: a conjunction used for comparison (*I like tacos better than pizza.*)
> then: an adverb telling when something happened (*I ate and then slept.*)

Disinterested/Uninterested
> disinterested: used to mean "neutral" (*The jury remains disinterested during the trial.*)
> uninterested: used to mean "bored" (*I was uninterested during the lecture.*)

Percent/Percentage
> percent: used when there is a number involved (*Five percent of us like tacos.*)
> percentage: used when there is no number (*That is a low percentage.*)

Fewer/Less
> fewer: used for things you can count (*He has fewer playing cards.*)
> less: used for things you cannot count, as well as time (*He has less talent. You have less than a minute.*)

Farther/Further
> farther: used when discussing distance (*His paper airplane flew farther than mine.*)
> further: used to mean "more" (*He needed further information.*)

Lend/Loan
> lend: a verb used for borrowing (*Lend me your lawn mower. He will lend it to me.*)
> loan: a noun used for something borrowed (*She applied for a student loan.*)

Note
Some people have problems with these:

- regardless/irregardless
- a lot/alot

Irregardless and *alot* are always incorrect. Don't use them.

Practice Questions

Aircraft Engineers

(1) The knowledge of an aircraft engineer is acquired through years of education and the attainment of special licenses. Ideally, an individual will begin his or her preparation for the profession in high school by taking chemistry, physics, trigonometry, and calculus courses. Such (2) curricula will aid in the pursuit of a bachelor's degree in aircraft engineering, which requires several physical and life sciences, mathematics, and design courses.

There are many areas of expertise included under the general title of "aircraft engineer." Aircraft engineers design, build, and (3) test manned and unmanned aircraft, and aerial vehicles, missiles, spacecraft, and national defense systems. They also research, design, and construct (4) sites, such as airports, and equipment, such as launching pads, that facilitate air travel.

Aircraft planning engineers use planning software to coordinate the materials, plant, equipment, and labor needed to build aircraft and manage large construction projects, such as building airports. Aircraft structural design engineers design new airframe structures, modify existing structures, and configure mechanical, routing and electrical, and avionics systems. (5) Aircraft systems engineers focuses on the various systems (hydraulics, thermal, fuel, communications, emergency power, fire suppression, and the like) that must work in coordination for an aircraft to fly successfully and safely. Aircraft performance engineers apply engineering principles and best practices to designing and developing aircraft and systems that operate as safely, efficiently, and effectively as possible.

Aircraft engineers must be able to apply technical and mechanical knowledge–coupled with scientific theories and principles–to solve problems related to the applied and industrial sciences, which includes designing innovative devices, applications, tools, and workflow procedures. In addition to having a hard-science education, aircraft engineers must be able to communicate their critical thinking clearly in writing and verbally. They are often project/team leads, and must possess strong leadership skills. To instill structure, they must be able to listen carefully to team members and be open to new ways of solving technical problems. They must understand (6) risk management and cost management, task management and quality management, and be able to move and negotiate among different parties and points of view.

(7) Some of universities provide internship or apprentice opportunities for the students enrolled in aircraft engineer programs. A bachelor's degree in aircraft engineering is commonly accompanied by a master's degree in advanced engineering or business administration. Such advanced degrees enable an individual to position himself or herself for executive, faculty, and/or research opportunities. (8) These advanced offices oftentimes require a Professional Engineering (PE) license which can be obtained through additional college courses, professional experience, and acceptable scores on the Fundamentals of Engineering (FE) and Professional Engineering (PE) standardized assessments.

(9) Aircraft engineers are employed primarily in the areas of analysis and design, research and development, manufacturing, and the federal government. (10) Once the job begins, aircraft

engineers use their critical thinking and creativity, their business skills, and their aptitude for problem solving. This level of (11) expertise (12) allows aircraft engineers to apply mathematical equations and scientific processes to aeronautical and aerospace issues or inventions. As aircraft engineers may design, construct, and test flying vessels such as airplanes, space shuttles, and missile weapons, they are compensated with generous salaries. In fact, in May 2014, the lowest 10 percent of all American aircraft engineers earned less than $60,110 while the highest paid 10 percent of all American aircraft engineers earned $155,240. (13) In May 2015, the United States Bureau of Labor Statistics (BLS) reported that the median annual salary of aircraft engineers was $107, 830. (14) Accordingly, (15) employment opportunities for aircraft engineers are projected to decrease by 2 percent by 2024. This decrease may be the result of a decline in the manufacturing industry. Nevertheless, aircraft engineers who know how to utilize modeling and simulation programs, fluid dynamic software, and robotic engineering tools are projected to remain the most employable.

1. Which statement serves to support the claim in the underlined sentence?
   a. Aircraft engineers are compensated with generous salaries.
   b. Such advanced degrees enable an individual to position himself or herself for executive, faculty, or research opportunities.
   c. Ideally, an individual will begin his or her preparation for the profession in high school by taking chemistry, physics, trigonometry, and calculus.
   d. Aircraft engineers who know how to utilize modeling and simulation programs, fluid dynamic software, and robotic engineering tools will be the most employable.

2. Which choice is the closest in meaning to the underlined word?
   a. NO CHANGE
   b. A curricula
   c. Curriculas
   d. Curriculum vitae

3. Which of the following would be the best choice for the underlined text?
   a. NO CHANGE
   b. test manned and unmanned aircraft and aerial vehicles, missiles, spacecraft, and national defense systems
   c. test manned and unmanned aircraft and aerial vehicles, missiles, spacecraft and national defense systems
   d. test manned and unmanned aircraft and manned and unmanned aerial vehicles, missiles, spacecraft, and national defense systems

4. Which choice is the closest in meaning to the underlined word?
   a. Places
   b. Settings
   c. Areas
   d. Spots

5. Which of the following would be the best choice for the underlined text?
    a. NO CHANGE
    b. Aircraft system engineers focus
    c. Aircraft systems engineers' focus
    d. Aircraft systems engineers focus

6. Which of the following would be the best choice for the underlined text?
    a. NO CHANGE
    b. risk management, and cost management, task management, and quality management, and be able to move and negotiate
    c. risk, cost, task, and quality management, and be able to move and negotiate
    d. risk management, cost management, task management, and quality management; and they must be able to move and negotiate

7. Which of the following would be the best choice for the underlined text?
    a. NO CHANGE
    b. Some of universities provided internship or apprentice opportunities
    c. Some of universities provide internship or apprenticeship opportunities
    d. Some universities provide internship or apprenticeship opportunities

8. Which of the following would be the best choice for the underlined sentence?
    a. NO CHANGE
    b. These advanced positions oftentimes require acceptable scores on the Fundamentals of Engineering (FE) and Professional Engineering (PE) standardized assessments in order to achieve a Professional Engineering (PE) license. Additional college courses and professional experience help.
    c. These advanced offices oftentimes require acceptable scores on the Fundamentals of Engineering (FE) and Professional Engineering (PE) standardized assessments to gain the Professional Engineering (PE) license which can be obtained through additional college courses, professional experience.
    d. These advanced positions oftentimes require a Professional Engineering (PE) license, which is obtained by acceptable scores on the Fundamentals of Engineering (FE) and Professional Engineering (PE) standardized assessments. Further education and professional experience can help prepare for the assessments.

9. In the fifth paragraph, which of the following claims is supported?
    a. This line of work requires critical thinking, business skills, problem solving, and creativity.
    b. Aircraft engineers are compensated with generous salaries.
    c. The knowledge of an aircraft engineer is acquired through years of education.
    d. Those who work hard are rewarded accordingly.

10. Which word should begin the underlined sentence?
    a. NO CHANGE
    b. Therefore,
    c. However,
    d. Furthermore,

11. What is the meaning of the underlined word "expertise" in this passage?
    a. Care
    b. Skill
    c. Work
    d. Composition

12. Which of the following would be the best choice for the underlined word?
    a. NO CHANGE
    b. Inhibits
    c. Requires
    d. Should

13. Which of the following would be the best choice for the underlined text?
    a. NO CHANGE
    b. May of 2015, the United States Bureau of Labor Statistics (BLS) reported that the median annual salary of aircraft engineers was $107, 830.
    c. In May of 2015 the United States Bureau of Labor Statistics (BLS) reported that the median annual salary of aircraft engineers was $107, 830.
    d. In May, 2015, the United States Bureau of Labor Statistics (BLS) reported that the median annual salary of aircraft engineers was $107, 830.

14. Which of the following would be the best choice for the underlined text?
    a. NO CHANGE
    b. Similarly,
    c. In other words,
    d. Conversely,

15. Which of the following would be the best choice for the underlined text?
    a. NO CHANGE
    b. Employment opportunities for aircraft engineers will be projected to decrease by 2 percent in 2024.
    c. Employment opportunities for aircraft engineers is projected to decrease by 2 percent in 2024.
    d. Employment opportunities for aircraft engineers were projected to decrease by 2 percent in 2024.

Attacks of September 11

(16) On September 11, 2001, a group of terrorists hijacked four American airplanes. The terrorists crashed the planes into the World Trade Center in New York City, the Pentagon in Washington D.C., and a field in Pennsylvania. Nearly three thousand people died during the attacks, which propelled the United States into a "War on Terror."

About the Terrorists

Terrorists commonly use fear and violence to achieve political goals. The nineteen terrorists who orchestrated and implemented the attacks of September 11 were militants associated with al-Qaeda, an Islamic extremist group founded by Osama bin

Laden, Abdullah Azzam, and others in the late 1980s. (17) <u>Bin Laden orchestrated the attacks as a response to what he felt was American injustice against Islam, and hatred toward Muslims.</u> In his words, "Terrorism against America deserves to be praised."

Islam is the religion of Muslims, who live mainly in South and Southwest Asia and Sub-Saharan Africa. (18) <u>The majority of Muslims practices Islam peacefully</u>. However, fractures in Islam have led to the growth of Islamic extremists who strictly oppose Western influences. They seek to institute stringent Islamic law and destroy those who (19) <u>violate</u> Islamic code.

In November 2002, bin Laden provided the explicit motives for the 9/11 terror attacks. According to this list, (20) <u>America's support </u>of Israel, military presence in Saudi Arabia, and other anti-Muslim actions were the causes.

The Timeline of the Attacks

The morning of September 11 began like any other for most Americans. Then, at 8:45 a.m., a Boeing 767 plane crashed into the north tower of the World Trade Center in New York City. Hundreds were instantly killed. Others were trapped on higher floors. (21) <u>The crash was initially thought to be</u> a freak accident. When a second plane flew directly into the south tower eighteen minutes later, it was (22) <u>determined that America</u> was under attack.

At 9:45 a.m., a third plane slammed into the Pentagon, America's military headquarters in Washington D.C. The jet fuel of this plane caused a major fire and partial building collapse that resulted in nearly two hundred deaths. By 10:00 a.m., the south tower of the World Trade Center collapsed. Thirty minutes later, the north tower followed (23) <u>suit</u>.

While this was happening, a fourth plane that departed from New Jersey, United Flight 93, was hijacked. The passengers learned of the attacks that occurred in New York and Washington D.C. and realized that (24) <u>they faced the same fate as the other planes that crashed</u>. The passengers were determined to overpower the terrorists in an effort to prevent the deaths of additional innocent American citizens. Although the passengers were successful in (25) <u>diverging</u> the plane, it crashed in a western Pennsylvania field and killed everyone on board. The plane's final target remains uncertain, but many believe that United Flight 93 was heading for the White House.

Heroes and Rescuers

Close to three thousand people died in the World Trade Center attacks. This figure includes 343 New York City firefighters and paramedics, twenty-three New York City police officers, and thirty-seven Port Authority officers. (26) <u>Nevertheless</u>, thousands of men and women in service worked valiantly to evacuate the buildings, save trapped workers, extinguish infernos, uncover victims trapped in fallen rubble, and tend to nearly ten thousand injured individuals.

About three hundred rescue dogs played a major role (27) <u>in the after-attack salvages</u>. Working twelve-hour shifts, the dogs scoured the rubble and alerted paramedics when they found signs of life. While doing so, the dogs served as a source of comfort and therapy for the rescue teams.

Initial Impacts on America

The attacks of September 11, 2001 resulted in the immediate suspension of all air travel. No flights could take off from or land on American soil. American airports and airspace closed to all national and international flights. Therefore, over five hundred flights had to turn back or be redirected to other countries. Canada alone received 226 flights and thousands of stranded passengers. Needless to say, (28) <u>as canceled flights are rescheduled, air travel became backed up</u> and chaotic for quite some time.

At the time of the attacks, George W. Bush was the president of the United States. President Bush announced that, "We will make no distinction between the terrorists who committed these acts and those who harbor them." The rate of hate crimes against American Muslims spiked, despite President Bush's call for the country to treat them with respect.

Additionally, relief funds were quickly arranged. The funds were used to support families of the victims, orphaned children, and those with major injuries. In this way, the tragic event brought the citizens together through acts of service toward those directly impacted by the attack.

Long-Term Effects of the Attacks

Over the past fifteen years, the attacks of September 11 have transformed the United States' government, travel safety protocols, and international relations. Anti-terrorism legislation became a priority for many countries as law enforcement and intelligence agencies teamed up to find and defeat alleged terrorists.

Present George W. Bush announced a War on Terror. He (29) <u>desired</u> to bring bin Laden and al-Qaeda to justice and to prevent future terrorist networks from gaining strength. The War in Afghanistan began in October of 2001 when the United States and British forces bombed al-Qaeda camps. (30) <u>The Taliban, a group of fundamentalist Muslims who protected Osama bin Laden, was overthrown on December 9, 2001. However, the war continued in order to defeat insurgency campaigns in neighboring countries.</u> Ten years later, the United State Navy SEALS killed Osama bin Laden in Pakistan. During 2014, the United States declared the end of its involvement in the War on Terror in Afghanistan.

Museums and memorials have since been erected to honor and remember the thousands of people who died during the September 11 attacks, including the brave rescue workers who gave their lives in the effort to help others.

16. How does the structure of the text help readers better understand the topic?
    a. By stating that anti-terrorism legislation was a priority for many countries, the text helps the reader determine which laws were made and how they changed everyday life in the country.
    b. By placing the events in the order in which they occurred, the text helps readers to better understand how the day unfolded.
    c. By using descriptive language, the text helps the readers picture detailed images of the events that occurred on September 11, 2001.
    d. None of the above.

17. Which of the following would be the best choice for the underlined sentence?
    a. NO CHANGE
    b. Bin Laden orchestrated the attacks as a response to what he felt was American injustice against Islam and hatred toward Muslims.
    c. Bin Laden orchestrated the attacks, as a response to what he felt was American injustice against Islam and hatred toward Muslims.
    d. Bin Laden orchestrated the attacks as responding to what he felt was American injustice against Islam and hatred toward Muslims.

18. Which of the following would be the best choice for the underlined text?
    a. NO CHANGE
    b. The majorities of Muslims practice Islam peacefully.
    c. The majorities of Muslims practices Islam peacefully.
    d. The majority of Muslims practice Islam peacefully.

19. Which choice is the closest in meaning to the underlined word?
    a. Respect
    b. Defile
    c. Deny
    d. Obey

20. Which of the following would be the best choice for the underlined text?
    a. NO CHANGE
    b. Americas' support
    c. America supports
    d. Americas' supports

21. Which of the following would NOT be an appropriate replacement for the underlined portion of the sentence?
    a. The first crash was thought to be
    b. The initial crash was thought to be
    c. The thought was that the crash initially was
    d. The initial thought was that the crash was

22. Which of the following would be the best choice for the underlined text?
    a. determined how America
    b. determined which America
    c. determined America
    d. determined why America

23. Which choice is the closest in meaning to the underlined word?
    a. NO CHANGE
    b. suite
    c. en suite
    d. in suite

24. Which of the following would be the best choice for the underlined text?
    a. NO CHANGE
    b. they faced the same fate as the other planes who crashed
    c. they faced the same fate as the other planes which crashed
    d. they faced the same fate as passengers on the other planes that crashed

25. Which choice is the closest in meaning to the underlined word?
    a. NO CHANGE
    b. Diverting
    c. Converging
    d. Distracting

26. Which choice is the closest substitute for the underlined word?
    a. Regardless
    b. In addition
    c. Furthermore
    d. Moreover

27. Which of the following would be the best choice for the underlined text?
    a. NO CHANGE
    b. in the savage after-attacks
    c. to salvage the after-attacks
    d. after the attack salvages

28. Which of the following would be the best choice for the underlined text?
    a. NO CHANGE
    b. as canceled flights were rescheduled, air travel became backed up
    c. as canceled flights are rescheduled, air travel becomes backed up
    d. as canceled flights were rescheduled, air travel becomes backed up

29. Which of the following would be the best choice for the underlined word?
    a. NO CHANGE
    b. Perceived
    c. Intended
    d. Assimilated

30. Which of the following would be the best choice for the underlined text?
   a. NO CHANGE
   b. The Taliban was overthrown on December 9, 2001. They were a group of fundamentalist Muslims who protected Osama bin Laden. However, the war continued in order to defeat insurgency campaigns in neighboring countries.
   c. The Taliban, a group of fundamentalist Muslims who protected Osama bin Laden, on December 9, 2001 was overthrown. However, the war continued in order to defeat insurgency campaigns in neighboring countries.
   d. Osama bin Laden's fundamentalist Muslims who protected him were called the Taliban and overthrown on December 9, 2001. Yet the war continued in order to defeat the insurgency campaigns in neighboring countries.

Fred Hampton

Fred Hampton desired to see lasting social change for African American people acquired through nonviolent means and community recognition. (31) As a result, he became an African American activist during the American Civil Rights Movement and led the Chicago chapter of the Black Panther Party (BPP).

Hampton's Education

Hampton was born and raised in Maywood of Chicago, Illinois in 1948. (32) Gifted academically and a natural athlete, he became a stellar baseball player in high school. After graduating from Proviso East High School in 1966, he later went on to study law at Triton Junior College.

While studying at Triton, Hampton joined and became a leader of the National Association for the Advancement of Colored People (NAACP). (33) As a result of his leadership, the NAACP gained more than five hundred members. Hampton worked relentlessly to acquire recreational facilities in the neighborhood and improve the educational resources provided to the impoverished black community of Maywood.

The Black Panthers

The Black Panther Party was another activist group that formed around the same time as the NAACP. Hampton was quickly attracted to the Black Panther's approach to the fight for equal rights for African Americans. (34) Hampton eventually joined the chapter and relocated to downtown Chicago to be closer to its headquarters.

His (35) charismatic personality, organizational abilities, sheer determination, and rhetorical skills enabled him to quickly rise through the chapter's ranks. (36) Hampton soon became the leader of the Chicago chapter of the BPP where he organized rallies, taught political education classes, and established a free medical clinic. He also took part in the community police supervision project and played an instrumental role in establishing the BPP breakfast program for impoverished African American children.

Hampton's greatest achievement as the leader of the BPP (37) may be his fight against street gang violence in Chicago. In 1969, Hampton held a press conference where he made the gangs agree to a nonaggression pact known as the Rainbow Coalition. As a result of the pact, a (38) <u>multiracial</u> alliance between blacks, Puerto Ricans, and poor youth was developed.

Assassination

As the Black Panther Party's popularity and influence grew, the Federal Bureau of Investigation (FBI) placed the group under (39) <u>constant</u> surveillance. In an attempt to (40) <u>neutralize</u> the party, the (41) <u>FBI launched several harassment campaigns</u> against the BPP, raided its headquarters in Chicago three times, and arrested over one hundred of the group's members. (42) <u>Hampton was shot and killed during such a raid that occurred on the morning of December 4, 1969.</u>

In 1976, seven years after the event, it was revealed that William O'Neal, Hampton's trusted bodyguard, was an undercover FBI agent. (43) <u>O'Neal provided the FBI with detailed floor plans of the BPP's headquarters, identifying the exact location of Hampton's bed.</u> It was because of these floor plans that the police were able to target and kill Hampton.

The (44) <u>assassination of Hampton</u> fueled outrage amongst the African American community. It was not until years after the assassination that the police admitted wrongdoing. The Chicago City Council now (45) <u>commemorates</u> December 4 as Fred Hampton Day.

31. Which of the following would be the best choice for the underlined text?
    a. NO CHANGE
    b. As a result he became an African American activist
    c. As a result: he became an African American activist
    d. As a result of, he became an African American activist

32. What word could be used in place of the underlined description?
    a. Vacuous
    b. Energetic
    c. Intelligent
    d. Athletic

33. Which of the following statements, if true, would further validate the selected sentence?
    a. Several of these new members went on to earn scholarships.
    b. With this increase in numbers, Hampton was awarded a medal for his contribution to the NAACP.
    c. Many of these new members would go on to hold high positions in the organization, often accrediting Hampton for his encouragement and guidance.
    d. The NAACP has been growing steadily every year.

34. How else could this sentence be re-structured while maintaining the context of the fourth paragraph?
    a. NO CHANGE
    b. Eventually, Hampton joined the chapter and relocated to downtown Chicago to be closer to its headquarters.
    c. Nevertheless, Hampton joined the chapter and relocated to downtown Chicago to be closer to its headquarters.
    d. Hampton then joined the chapter and relocated to downtown Chicago to be closer to its headquarters

35. What word is synonymous with the underlined description?
    a. Egotistical
    b. Obnoxious
    c. Chauvinistic
    d. Charming

36. Which of the following would be the best choice for the underlined sentence?
    a. NO CHANGE
    b. As the leader of the BPP, Hampton: organized rallies, taught political education classes, and established a free medical clinic.
    c. As the leader of the BPP, Hampton; organized rallies, taught political education classes, and established a free medical clinic.
    d. As the leader of the BPP, Hampton—organized rallies, taught political education classes, and established a medical free clinic.

37. Which is the grammatically correct alternative to the underlined word?
    a. might
    b. could
    c. can
    d. ought to

38. Which choice should NOT be substituted for the underlined word (multiracial)?
    a. Interracial
    b. Multinational
    c. Racially mixed
    d. Biracial

39. Which choice is the closest in meaning to the underlined word?
    a. conspicuous
    b. continuous
    c. consistent
    d. conditional

40. Which choice is the closest in meaning to the underlined word?
    a. NO CHANGE
    b. Accommodate
    c. Assuage
    d. Praise

41. How would the author likely describe the FBI during the events of the passage?
   a. Corrupt
   b. Confused
   c. Well-intended
   d. Prejudiced

42. Which of the following would be the best choice for the underlined text?
   a. NO CHANGE
   b. Hampton was shot, and killed, during such a raid that occurred on the morning of December 4, 1969.
   c. Hampton was shot and killed during just such a raid, that occurred on the morning of December 4, 1969.
   d. Hampton was shot and killed during just such a raid, which occurred on the morning of December 1969.

43. Which of the following would be the best choice for the underlined sentence?
   a. NO CHANGE
   b. O'Neal provided the FBI with detailed floor plans of the BPP's headquarters, which identified the exact location of Hampton's bed.
   c. O'Neal provided the FBI with detailed floor plans and Hampton's bed.
   d. O'Neal identified the exact location of Hampton's bed that provided the FBI with detailed floor plans of the BPP's headquarters.

44. The author develops the idea that Frank Hampton should not have been killed at the hands of the police. Which could best be used to support that claim?
   a. The manner in which the police raided the BPP headquarters.
   b. The eventual admission from the police that they were wrong in killing Hampton.
   c. The description of previous police raids that resulted in the arrest of hundreds BPP members.
   d. ALL OF THE ABOVE.

45. Which word could be used in place of the underlined word?
   a. disregards
   b. memorializes
   c. communicates
   d. denies

Here Comes the Flood!

A flood occurs when an area of land that is normally dry becomes submerged (46) amid water. Floods have affected Earth since the beginning of time and are caused by many different factors. (47) Flooding can occur slowly or within seconds and can submerge small regions or extend over vast areas of land. The impact on society and the environment can be harmful or helpful.

What Causes Flood?

Floods may be caused by natural (48) phenomenon, induced by the activities of humans and other animals, or be the consequence of the failure of an infrastructure. Areas located near bodies of water are prone to flooding, as are low-lying regions.

Global warming is the product of air pollution that prevents the sun's radiation from being emitted back into space. Instead, the radiation is trapped in Earth and results in global warming. The warming of the Earth has brought about climate changes. Inevitably, floods have been occurring with increasing regularity. Some claim that the increased temperatures on Earth may cause the icebergs to melt. They fear that the melting of icebergs will cause the (49) oceans levels to rise and flood coastal regions.

Most commonly, flooding is the outcome of excessive rain. The ground is not able to absorb all the water produced by a sudden heavy rainfall or rainfall that occurs over a prolonged period of time. Such rainfall may induce the water in rivers and other bodies of water to overflow. The excess water can cause dams to break, which can result in flooding of the surrounding riverbanks or coastal regions.

Flash flooding can occur without warning and without rainfall. (50) Flash floods may occur when a river is blocked: by a glacier, avalanche, landslide, logjam, a beaver's obstruction, construction, or a dam. Water builds behind such a blockage. Eventually, the mass and force of the built-up water become so extreme that they force the obstruction to break. Thus, enormous amounts of water rush out toward the surrounding areas.

Areal or urban flooding transpires because the land has become hardened. The hardening of land may result from urbanization or drought. Either way, the hardened land prevents water from seeping into the ground. Instead, the water resides on top of the land.

Finally, flooding may develop after severe hurricanes, tsunamis, or tropical cyclones. Local defenses and infrastructures are no matches for the tidal surges and waves caused by these natural phenomena. Such events are bound to result in the flooding of nearby coastal regions or estuaries.

(51) A Flood's After-Effects

Flooding can result in severe devastation of nearby areas. Flash floods and tsunamis can induce sweeping waters that travel at (52) destructive speeds. Fast-moving water has the power to demolish all obstacles in its path such as homes, trees, bridges, and buildings. Animals, plants, and humans may all lose their lives during a flood.

Floods can also cause pollution and infection. Sewage may seep from drains or septic tanks and contaminate drinking water or surrounding lands. Similarly, toxins, fuels, debris from annihilated buildings, and other hazardous materials can leave water unusable for consumption. (53) As the water begins to drain, mold may begin to grow. As a result, residents of flooded areas may be left without power, drinkable water, or be exposed to toxins and other diseases.

(54) Although often associated with devastation, not all flooding results in adverse circumstances. For millions of years, peoples have inhabited floodplains of rivers. (55) Examples include the Mississippi Valley of the United States, the Nile River in Egypt, and the Tigris River of the Middle East. The flooding of such rivers (56) caused nutrient-rich silts to be deposited on the floodplains. Thus, after the floods recede, an extremely

fertile soil is left behind. This soil is conducive to the agriculture of bountiful crops and has sustained the diets of humans for millennium.

Proactive Measures Against Flooding

Technologies now allow scientists to predict where and when flooding is likely to occur. Such technologies can also be used (57) <u>to project</u> the severity of an anticipated flood. In this way, local inhabitants can be warned and take preventative measures such as boarding up their homes, gathering necessary provisions, and moving themselves and possessions to higher grounds.

The (58) <u>picturesque</u> views of coastal regions and rivers have long enticed people to build near such locations. Due to the costs associated with the repairs needed after the flooding of such residencies, many governments now require inhabitants of flood-prone areas to purchase flood insurance and build flood-resistant structures. Pictures of all items within a building or home should be taken so that proper reimbursement for losses can be made in the event that a flood does occur.

Staying Safe During a Flood

If a forecasted flood does develop, then people should retreat to higher ground such as a mountain, attic, or roof. Flooded waters may be contaminated, contain hidden debris, or travel at high speeds. (59) <u>Therefore,</u> people should not attempt to walk or drive through a flooded area. To prevent electrocution, electrical outlets and downed power lines must be avoided.

The Flood Dries Up

(60) <u>Regardless</u> of the type or cause of a flood, floods can result in detrimental alterations to nearby lands and serious injuries to nearby inhabitants. By understanding flood cycles, civilizations can learn to take advantage of flood seasons. By taking the proper precautionary measures, people can stay safe when floods occur. Thus, proper knowledge can lead to safety and prosperity during such an adverse natural phenomenon.

46. Which of the following would be the best choice for the underlined text?
    a. NO CHANGE
    b. in
    c. under
    d. by

47. Which revision will maintain the original meaning while also making the sentence more concise?
    a. NO CHANGE
    b. Flooding can either be slow or occur within seconds. It doesn't take long to submerge small regions or extend vast areas of land.
    c. Flooding occurs slowly or rapidly submerging vast areas of land.
    d. Vast areas of land can be flooded slowly or within seconds.

48. Which choice is the correct substitution for the underlined word?
   a. NO CHANGE
   b. Phenomenone
   c. Phenomenal
   d. Phenomena

49. Which of the following would be the best choice for the underlined text?
   a. NO CHANGE
   b. Ocean levels
   c. Ocean's levels
   d. Levels of the oceans

50. Which of the following would be the best choice for the underlined text?
   a. NO CHANGE
   b. Flash floods may occur when a river is blocked by a: glacier, avalanche, landslide, logjam, beaver's obstruction, construction, or dam.
   c. Flash floods may occur when a river is blocked by a glacier, by an avalanche, by a landslide, by a logjam, by a beaver's obstruction, by a construction, or by a dam.
   d. Flash floods may occur when a river is blocked by: a glacier, an avalanche, a landslide, a logjam, a beaver's obstruction, a construction, or a dam.

51. One of the headings in this essay is entitled "A Floods After-Effects." How should this heading be rewritten?
   a. A Flood's After-Effect
   b. A Flood's After-Effects
   c. A Floods After-Affect
   d. A Flood's After-Affects

52. Which word would be the LEAST accurate substitute for the underlined word?
   a. Raging
   b. Ruinous
   c. Ravenous
   d. Ravaging

53. Which choice best maintains the pattern of the first sentence of the paragraph?
   a. NO CHANGE
   b. As the rain subsides, mold may begin to grow.
   c. Mold grows as the water may begin to drain.
   d. The water will begin to drain and mold will begin to grow.

54. Which of the following would be the best choice for the underlined text?
   a. NO CHANGE
   b. Although often associated with devastation not all flooding results
   c. Although often associated with devastation. Not all flooding results
   d. Even often associated with devastation, not all flooding results

55. The author is considering deleting this sentence from the tenth paragraph. Should the sentence be kept or deleted?

    a. Kept, because it provides examples of floodplains that have been successfully inhabited by civilizations.

    b. Kept, because it provides an example of how floods can be beneficial.

    c. Deleted, because it blurs the paragraph's focus on the benefits of floods.

    d. Deleted, because it distracts from the overall meaning of the paragraph.

56. Which of the following would be the best choice for the underlined text?

    a. NO CHANGE

    b. cause

    c. causing

    d. causes

57. Which of the following would be the best choice for the underlined text?

    a. NO CHANGE

    b. projecting

    c. project

    d. projected

58. Which term could best replace the underlined word?

    a. colorful

    b. drab

    c. scenic

    d. candid

59. Which choice is the closest in meaning to the underlined word?

    a. Meanwhile

    b. In addition

    c. However

    d. Thus

60. What is the author's intent in the final paragraph?

    a. To explain that all bad occurrences eventually come to an end.

    b. To summarize the key points in the passage.

    c. To explain that, with time, all flooded lands will eventually dry.

    d. To relay a final key point about floods.

Dog Breeds

While all dogs (61) descend through gray wolves, it's easy to notice that dog breeds come in a variety of shapes and sizes. With such a (62) drastic range of traits, appearances and body types dogs are one of the most variable and adaptable species on the planet. (63) But why so many differences. The answer is that humans have actually played a major role in altering the biology of dogs. (64) This was done through a process called selective breeding.

(65) Selective breeding which is also called artificial selection is the processes in which animals with desired traits are bred in order to produce offspring that share the same traits. In natural selection, (66) animals must adapt to their environments increase their chances of survival. Over time, certain traits develop in animals that enable them to thrive in these environments. Those

animals with more of these traits, or better versions of these traits, gain an (67) <u>advantage over others of their species.</u> Therefore, the animal's chances to mate are increased and these useful (68) <u>genes are passed into their offspring.</u> With dog breeding, humans select traits that are desired and encourage more of these desired traits in other dogs by breeding dogs that already have them.

The reason for different breeds of dogs is that there were specific needs that humans wanted to fill with their animals. For example, scent hounds are known for their extraordinary ability to track game through scent. These breeds are also known for their endurance in seeking deer and other prey. Therefore, early hunters took dogs that displayed these abilities and bred them to encourage these traits. Later, these generations took on characteristics that aided these desired traits. (69) <u>For example, Bloodhounds</u> have broad snouts and droopy ears that fall to the ground when they smell. These physical qualities not only define the look of the Bloodhound, but also contribute to their amazing tracking ability. The broad snout is able to define and hold onto scents longer than many other breeds. The long floppy hears serve to collect and hold the scents the earth holds so that the smells are clearer and able to be distinguished.

Police dogs, sometimes referred to as K9s, are selectively bred for (70) <u>a variety of traits which make them invaluable aids</u> to police and other law enforcement personnel. Intelligent, strong, aggressive, disease resistant, and easily trained breeds such as the German shepherd are favored to provide protection, fulfill ground-based and air-based tracking duties, search for drugs and explosives, and perform rescue operation services. The Belgian Malinois breed is known for a tireless work ethic and their highly efficient sense of smell makes them (71) <u>proficient at locating drugs, IEDs, and human remains</u>. Beagles are used worldwide in airports and other venues to locate bombs and drugs, while English Cocker Spaniels have been taught to be especially good at detecting the scent of money. Doberman pinschers and rottweilers specialize most often as protection and attack dogs; they can be taught to attack and detain individuals (72) <u>targeted</u> by law enforcement officials following a method known as Bark and Hold. These dogs have all been selectively bred with the idea of producing, preserving, heightening—and sometimes removing—physical, mental, and skills-based traits.

(73) <u>There is a downside, however, to the selective breeding of dogs.</u> Breeders can, over generations, create physical disabilities in dog breeds, (74) <u>some of that are directly related to</u> the features and physical characteristics that were initially desired. Engineering the shortened snout that makes a pug's wrinkly face adorable to so many people has resulted in a dog that often suffers from breathing problems because its nasal cavity has been (75) <u>squashed</u>. In addition, selectively bred dogs are at risk having disease from other breeds added to their lineage, genes of undesirable traits can be handed down to offspring, and, over time, genetic diversity will be diminished. The benefits and the consequences of selective breeding have led to much debate over whether selective breeding is safe on an ethical level. We know we can do it, but should we do it?

61. Which of the following would be the best choice for the underlined text?
    a. NO CHANGE
    b. descend by gray wolves
    c. descend from gray wolves
    d. descended through gray wolves

62. Which of the following would be the best choice for the underlined text?
    a. NO CHANGE
    b. drastic range of traits, appearances, and body types
    c. drastic range of traits and appearances and body types
    d. drastic range of traits, appearances, as well as body types

63. Which of the following would be the best choice for the underlined sentence?
    a. NO CHANGE
    b. But are there so many differences?
    c. But why so many differences are there.
    d. But why so many differences?

64. Which of the following would be the best choice for the underlined sentence?
    a. NO CHANGE
    b. This was done, through a process called selective breeding.
    c. This was done, through a process, called selective breeding.
    d. This was done through selective breeding, a process.

65. Which of the following would be the best choice for the underlined text?
    a. NO CHANGE
    b. Selective breeding, which is also called artificial selection is the processes
    c. Selective breeding which is also called, artificial selection, is the processes
    d. Selective breeding, which is also called artificial selection, is the processes

66. Which of the following would be the best choice for the underlined text?
    a. NO CHANGE
    b. animals must adapt to their environments to increase their chances of survival.
    c. animals must adapt to their environments, increase their chances of survival.
    d. animals must adapt to their environments, increasing their chances of survival.

67. Which of the following would be the best choice for the underlined text?
    a. NO CHANGE
    b. advantage over others, of their species.
    c. advantages over others of their species.
    d. advantage over others.

68. Which of the following would be the best choice for the underlined text?
    a. NO CHANGE
    b. genes are passed onto their offspring.
    c. genes are passed on to their offspring.
    d. genes are passed within their offspring.

69. Which of the following would be the best choice for the underlined text?
    a. NO CHANGE
    b. For example, Bloodhounds,
    c. For example Bloodhounds
    d. For example, bloodhounds

70. Which of the following would be the best choice for the underlined text?
    a. NO CHANGE
    b. a variety of traits who make them invaluable aids
    c. a variety of traits, which make them invaluable aids
    d. a variety of traits, that make them invaluable aids

71. Which word or words does "locating" apply to?
    a. proficient
    b. drugs
    c. drugs, IEDs,
    d. drugs, IEDs, and human remains

72. Which choice is the closest in meaning to the underlined word?
    a. NO CHANGE
    b. Isolated
    c. Prosecuted
    d. Marked

73. Which of the following would be the best choice for the underlined text?
    a. NO CHANGE
    b. There is a downside however to the selective breeding of dogs.
    c. There is a downside, however to the selective breeding of dogs.
    d. There is a downside however to, the selective breeding of dogs.

74. Which of the following would be the best choice for the underlined text?
    a. NO CHANGE
    b. some of whom are directly related to
    c. some of them are directly related to
    d. some of which are directly related to

75. Which choice is the closest in meaning to the underlined word?
    a. quashed
    b. smashed
    c. foreshortened
    d. flattened

Answer Explanations

1. C: Any time a writer wants to validate a claim, he or she ought to provide factual information that proves or supports that claim. The phrase "will begin his or her preparation for the profession in high school" supports the claim that aircraft engineers undergo years of education. For this reason, Choice *C* is the correct response. However, completing such courses in high school does not guarantee that aircraft engineers will earn generous salaries (Choice *A*), become employed in executive positions (Choice *B*), or stay employed (Choice *D*).

2. A: "Curricula" is the plural form of "curriculum" and is defined as all the courses of study offered by an educational institute. Choice *B* is incorrect because it puts an article defining a single thing ("a") before a plural; it would be like saying, "A apples are tasty." Choice *C* is incorrect because the word "curriculas" does not exist—"curricula" is already plural, so there is no need to add an "s" to the end of the word. Choice *D*, "curriculum vitae," refers to a short resume of a person's career and therefore is not appropriate here.

3. B: As written, the underlined passage is ambiguous. Do the words "manned and unmanned" modify just aircraft, or both aircraft and aerial vehicles? Choice *B* clarifies that it modifies aircraft and aerial vehicles, and then lays out a list of the remaining items, each one separated from the one after it by a comma. In Choice *C*, a comma should follow "spacecraft" and the "and" should be deleted. The repetition of "manned and unmanned," makes Choice *D* unwieldy compared with the correct answer, Choice *B*.

4. B: Choice *B*, "settings" is closest to "sites" because a site is a place where an event is held or a thing is located. Choices *A* ("post"), *B* ("areas") and *D* ("spots") are more casual and less precise than "settings."

5. D: Choice *D* is correct because the engineers' title is as it should be and the verb form agrees with the plural subject. Choice *B* is incorrect because the passage is about *systems* engineers, not *system* engineers. By making "engineers" possessive (engineers'), Choice *C* changes the subject of the sentence from the engineers to their focus, and then the second part of the sentence does not fit.

6. D: The underlined passage is awkward because it groups the four management categories (risk, cost, task, quality) into two conjunctive phrases that are not themselves united by another conjunction. Choice *B* separates each of the categories, but misplaces the two "and" conjunction. By deleting "management" after "risk," "cost," and "task" Choice *C* becomes problematic: are "risk," "cost," and "task" all supposed to modify "management" as "quality" does? Or does the writer really mean just risk, as opposed to risk management (they are two different things), just cost, instead of cost management? And what does that mean for "task"? Choice *D* may seem wordier than the other options, but it is unambiguous. To deal with the wordiness aspect, the semicolon creates two main clauses.

7. D: The word *of* is not required here. *Apprenticeship* is also more appropriate in this context than *apprentice opportunities*. The word *apprentice* describes an individual in an apprenticeship, not an apprenticeship itself. Both of these changes are needed, making Choice *D* the correct answer.

8. D: The selected sentence is a run-on sentence, and its information is presented in a confusing way. The sentence does need revision, so Choice *A* is wrong. The main objective of the selected section of the passage is to communicate that many positions require a PE license, which is gained by scoring well on the FE and PE assessments. This must be the primary focus of the revision. It is necessary to break the sentence into two, to avoid a run-on sentence. Choice *B* fixes the run-on aspect, but the sentence is indirect and awkward in construction. It takes too long to establish the importance of the PE license. Choice *C* is wrong for the same reason and it is a run-on sentence. Choice *D* is correct because it breaks the section into coherent sentences and emphasizes the main point the author is trying to communicate: the PE license is required for some higher positions, it's obtained by scoring well on the two standardized assessments, and college and experience can be used to prepare for the assessments in order to gain the certification.

9. B: The fifth paragraph discusses reports made by the United States Bureau of Labor Statistics (BLS) in regard to the median, upper 10 percent, and lower 10 percent of annual salaries of aircraft engineers in 2015. Therefore, this paragraph is used to support the claim that aircraft engineers are compensated with generous salaries (Choice *B*). The paragraph has nothing to do with an aircraft engineer's skill set (Choice *A*), education (Choice *C*), or incentive program (Choice *D*).

10. A: Choice *A* is the correct response because this statement's intent is to give examples as to how aircraft engineers apply mathematical equations and scientific processes toward aeronautical and aerospace issues and/or inventions. The answer is not "therefore" (Choice *B*) or "furthermore" (Choice *D*) because no relationship of causality is being made between ideas. Two items are neither being compared nor contrasted, so "however" (Choice *C*) is also not the correct answer.

11. B: Choice *B* is correct because "skill" means the ability to do the given task well. Choice *C* is incorrect because "work" does not necessarily mean skilled work. Choice *A* is incorrect because the word "care" doesn't fit into the context of the passage, and Choice *D*, "composition," is incorrect because nothing in this statement points to the way in which something is structured.

12. C: The word *allows* is inappropriate because it does not stress what those in the position of aircraft engineers actually need to be able to do. The word *requires* is the only alternative that fits because it actually describes necessary skills of the job.

13. A: No change is required. The comma is properly placed after the introductory phrase "In May of 2015." Choice *B* is missing the word "in." Choice *C* does not separate the introductory phrase from the rest of the sentence. Choice *D* places an unnecessary comma prior to 2015.

14. D: *Accordingly* is incorrect because the previous statement is not a cause for the sentence in question. The word "conversely" best demonstrates the opposite sentiments in this passage. Choice *B* is incorrect because it denotes agreement with the previous statement. Choice C is incorrect because the sentiment is not restated but opposed.

15. A: Choice *A* is the correct answer because the projections are taking place in the present, even though they are making reference to a future date.

16. B: The passage contains clearly labeled subheadings. These subheadings inform the reader what will be addressed in upcoming paragraphs. Choice *A* is incorrect because the anti-terrorism laws of other countries are not addressed in the passage. The text is written in an informative manner; overly descriptive language is not utilized. Therefore, Choice *C* is incorrect. Choice *D* is incorrect because, as mentioned, the structure of the text does help in the manner described in Choice *B*.

17. B: No comma is needed in this sentence. Both the original sentence and Choice *C* use incorrect comma placements. Choice *D* uses an incorrect verb tense ("responding").

18. D: "Majority" is singular and "Muslims" is plural. If "majority" were not modified by a plural word, the correct verb would be "practices" ("The majority practices Islam peacefully.") But because the modifier is plural, the correct verb choice is "practice," as in Choice D. Choices B and C are incorrect because only one majority is being considered.

19. B: The term "violate" implies a lack of respect or compliance. "Defile" means to degrade or show no respect. Therefore, Choice B is the correct answer. Choice A is incorrect because "respect" is the opposite of violate. To "deny" is to refuse, so Choice C is not the correct answer because the weight of the word "deny" is not as heavy as the word "violate." To "obey" is to follow orders, so Choice D is not the answer.

20. A: The phrase is correct as written. In this case, "America" means the United States, a single entity, not the plural Americas (North and South together). Choices B and D are incorrect because *Americas'* is the plural possessive form. Choice C is incorrect because it indicates a singular America but shows no possessive.

21. C: All the choices except Choice C go with the flow of the original underlined portion of the sentence and communicate the same idea. Choice C, however, is subtly different; by shifting "initial" to after the word "crash," it communicates that the thought was that there was a shift in the crash from being a freak accident at its onset to something different partway through it.

22. C: Choice A is incorrect because the second plane proved the attacks were not an accident; the manner of attack, "how," was not in question. Choice B is incorrect because no one at the time thought some other America, such as South America or Central America was being attacked; it was the United States of America. Choice D is incorrect because nothing in the passage indicates why America should be attacked. Choice C is correct because even though it lacks the word "that," its meaning is identical to the underlined passage.

23. A: The word "suit" is appropriate here because it means "to follow the example of, or do as another has done." Choices B, C, and D are incorrect for their use of "suite," which does not mean the same thing as "suit."

24. D: Choice D is the most accurate way of expressing the idea behind the underlined phrase. It aligns the fate of passengers with the fate of other passengers, rather than aligning the fates of passengers with the fates of planes, as the underlined phrase does. Choice B is incorrect because of the pronoun "who" used to modify the plane. Choice C is incorrect because it still aligns the fate of passengers with the fate of planes.

25. B: Although "diverging" means to separate from the main route and go in a different direction, it is used awkwardly and unconventionally in this sentence. A thing can diverge, as in the Robert Frost poem "Two roads diverged in a yellow wood." But an object cannot be diverged, as in the phrase "the passengers diverged the plane." Therefore, Choice A is not the answer. Choice B is the correct answer because it means what the passengers did caused a change in the plane's direction. "Converging" (Choice C) is incorrect because it means that the plane met another in a central location. Although the passengers may have distracted the terrorists, they did not distract the plane. Therefore, Choice D is incorrect.

26. A: Choice A, "regardless" is the closest substitute for "nevertheless." Choice B, "in addition," Choice C, "furthermore," and Choice D, "moreover," do make sense, but they do not convey the meaning "in spite of everything" that "nevertheless" does.

27. A: The underlined passage is correct as written, since the dogs were called in after the attacks on salvage missions. Choice *B* confuses the word "savage" with "salvage" and suggests that there were two phases of attacks (attacks and after-attacks). Choice *C* implies that the dogs salvaged after-attacks, not victims. Choice *D* does not make sense.

28. B: Choice *A* is incorrect because the present tense "are" should be the past tense "were." Choice *C* is incorrect because the essay is in past tense; changing to present tense is confusing. In Choice *D*, "becomes" should be in past tense. Choice *B* is correct because the tenses are consistent with each other and with the tense of the entire essay.

29. C: "Desired" communicates wishing or direct motive, so the goal here is to pick a term that communicates a similar meaning, if not better. Choices *B* and *D* have irrelevant meanings and wouldn't serve the sentence at all. However, "intended" means planned or meant to. "Intended" is a far better choice than "desired," because it communicates goals and strategy more than simply saying that Bush desired to do something.

30. A: While Choice *B* isn't necessarily wrong, it lacks the direct nature that the original sentence has. Also breaking up the sentences like this makes the text confusing; the connection between the Taliban's defeat and ongoing war is now separated by a second, unnecessary sentence. Choice *C* corrects this problem but the fluidity of the sentence is marred because of the awkward construction of the first sentence. Choice *D* begins well, but lacks the use of "was" before "overthrown," which discombobulates the sentence. While "yet" provides an adequate transition for the next sentence, the term "however" is more appropriate. Thus, the original structure of the two sentences is correct, making Choice *A*, NO CHANGE, the correct answer.

31. A: The comma after *result* is necessary for the sentence structure, making it an imperative component. The original sentence is correct, making Choice *A* correct. Choice *B* is incorrect because it lacks the crucial comma. Choice *C* is incorrect because a colon is unnecessary, and Choice *D* is incorrect because the addition of the word "of" is both unnecessary and incorrect when applied to the rest of the sentence.

32. C: To be gifted is to be talented. "Academically" refers to education. Therefore, Fred Hampton was intellectually talented, or intelligent (Choice *C*). Choice *B* is incorrect because it refers to a level of energy or activity. Choice *A* is incorrect because "vacuous" means empty-minded, the opposite of academically gifted. Choice *D* is incorrect because it refers to physical abilities.

33. C: The goal for this question is to select a sentence that not only affirms, or backs up, the selected statement, but could also appear after it and flows with the rest of the piece. Choice *A* is irrelevant to the sentence; just because new members earned scholarships doesn't necessarily mean that this was a testament to Hampton's leadership or that this actually benefitted the NAACP. Choice *B* is very compelling. If Hampton got an award for the increase in numbers, this could bolster the idea that he was the direct cause of the rise in numbers and that he was of great value to the organization. However, it does not say directly that he was the cause of the increase and that this was extremely beneficial to the NAACP. Choice *C* is a much better choice than Choice *B*. Choice *C* has the new members directly crediting Hampton's leadership for their success; the fact that such new members went on to hold high positions is also testament to Hampton's leadership. Thus, Choice *C* is correct. Choice *D* does nothing for the underlined section.

34. B: Choice *B* moves the word "eventually" to the beginning of the sentence. By using the term as an introductory word, continuity from one sentence to another is created. Meanwhile, the syntax is not lost. Choice *A* is incorrect because the sentence requires a proper transition. Choice *C* is incorrect because the sentence does not contain surprising or contrasting information, as is indicated by the introductory word "nevertheless." Choice *D* is incorrect because the term "then" implies that Hampton's relocation to the BPP's headquarters in Chicago occurred shortly or immediately after leading the NAACP.

35. D: An individual with a charismatic personality is charming and appealing to others. Therefore, Choice *D* is the correct answer. Choice *A* is incorrect because someone with an egotistical personality is conceited or self-serving. Choice *B* is incorrect because "obnoxious" is the opposite of charismatic. Choice *C* is incorrect because someone with a chauvinistic personality is prejudiced toward their own purpose, gender, or other group.

36. A: No change is needed. The list of events accomplished by Hampton is short enough that each item in the list can be separated by a comma. Choice *B* is incorrect. Although a colon can be used to introduce a list of items, it is not a conventional choice for separating items within a series. Semicolons are used to separate at least three items in a series that have an internal comma. Semicolons can also be used to separate clauses in a sentence that contain internal commas intended for clarification purposes. Neither of the two latter uses of semicolons is required in the example sentence. Therefore, Choice *C* is incorrect. Choice *D* is incorrect because a dash is not a conventional choice for punctuating items in a series.

37. A: The grammatically correct alternative to "may" is "might" (Choice *A*). Choice *B* ("could") is a close second choice. Choice *C* ("can") is not as precise as "might," and Choice *D* ("should") implies there might be some disagreement over what Fred Hampton's greatest achievement was.

38. D: Choices *A* ("interracial"), *B* ("multinational") and *C* ("racially mixed") are all serviceable substitutes for "multiracial." At first glance, Choice *D* ("biracial") seems to fit well in the sentence. But, looking more closely, it would be correct only if the "poor youth" consisted solely of blacks and Puerto Ricans. The passage does not indicate that this is the situation, so it would be best to avoid this choice.

39. C: Choice *A*, "conspicuous" is precisely what the FBI would not want its surveillance to be. Choice *B*, "consistent," is a desirable trait of surveillance, but it is not as exact as Choice *C*, "continuous." Choice *D*, "conditional," has no particular association with the word "surveillance."

40. A: The term "neutralize" means to counteract or render ineffective. "Accommodate" means to be helpful or lend aid, which is the opposite of "neutralize." Therefore, Choice *B* is wrong. "Assuage" means to ease, and "praise" means to express warm feeling, so they are in no way close to the needed context. "Neutralize" is the best option, making Choice *A*, NO CHANGE, the correct answer.

41. D: From the context of the passage, it is clear that the author does not think highly of the FBI's investigation of Hampton and the Black Panthers. Choices *B* and *C* can be easily eliminated. "Well-intended" is positive, which is not a characteristic the author would probably attribute to the FBI in the passage. Nor would the author think the FBI was "confused"; the author represents them as deliberate in their methods. Choice *A*, "corrupt," is very compelling; the author would likely agree with this, but Choice *D*, "prejudiced" is better. The FBI may not have been corrupt but there certainly seemed to have been a particular dislike or distrust of the Black Panthers. Thus, Choice *D*, "prejudiced," is correct.

42. D: By using the word "such," the author signals that the raid in the underlined sentence refers to those in in the previous sentence. To be grammatically correct and completely clear, however, the phrase "just such" is needed. Choice *B* does not incorporate "just," and so it is incorrect. Choice *C* is correct in the use pf "just such," but the comma after "raid" should not be there. Choice *D* is correct; it uses "which" instead of "that" and a comma before "which."

43. B: The order of the original sentence suggests that the floor plans that were provided to the FBI by O'Neal enabled the FBI to identify the exact location of Hampton's bed. This syntax is maintained in Choice *B*. Therefore, Choice *B* is correct, which makes Choice *A* incorrect. Choice *C* is incorrect because the sentence's word order conveys the meaning that O'Neal provided the FBI with Hampton's bed as well as the floor plans. Choice *D* is incorrect because it implies that it was the bed that provided the FBI with the headquarters' floor plans.

44. D: Claims can be supported with evidence or supporting details found within the text. Choice *D* is correct because Choices *A*, *B*, and *C* are all either directly stated or alluded to within the passage.

45. B: "Commemorates" means to honor, celebrate, or memorialize a person or event. Therefore, Choice *B* is correct. Choice *A* is incorrect because "disregards" is the opposite of "commemorates." Choice *C* is incorrect because to communicate means to converse or to speak. Choice *D* is incorrect because to "deny" means to reject, negate, refuse, or rebuff.

46. C: This question deals with selecting the most appropriate preposition. "Submerged" means to place or plunge under water, or to cover with water or another liquid. Choice *C*, "under" is the correct answer. The underlined word "amid" (Choice *A*) means "in the midst of," which does not necessarily mean underneath. Choice *B* ("in") and Choice *D* ("by") are not technically accurate.

47. D: The sentence should maintain the original meaning while being more concise, or shorter. Choice *B* can be eliminated because it splits the original sentence into two distinct sentences, and the second of the two sentences is incorrectly constructed. Choice *C* is very intriguing but there is a jumble of verbs in it. The phrase "Flooding occurs slowly or rapidly submerging" makes the sentence awkward and difficult to understand without the use of a comma after "rapidly," making it a poor construction. Choice *D* is certainly more concise and it is correctly phrased; it communicates the meaning message that flooding can overtake great lengths of land either slowly or very fast. The use of "Vast areas of land" implies that smaller regions or small areas can flood just as well. Thus, Choice *D* is a good revision that maintains the meaning of the original sentence while being concise and more direct.

48. D: The underlined word ("phenomenon") is the singular form of the plural noun "phenomena." Several causes of flooding are listed, and so the plural form (Choice *D*) is correct. The word in Choice *B* ("phenomenone") does not exist, and the word in Choice *C* ("phenomenal") is an adjective meaning "very remarkable or extraordinary"; since it is not a noun, it is incorrect.

49. B: In this sentence, the word "ocean" does not require an "s" after it to make it plural because "ocean levels" is plural. Therefore, Choices *A* and *C* are incorrect. Because the passage is referring to multiple ocean levels (if not all ocean levels), "ocean" does not require an apostrophe because that would indicate that only one ocean is the focus, which is not the case. Choice *D* does not fit well into the sentence and, once again, "ocean" has an "s" after it. This leaves Choice *B*, which correctly completes the sentence and maintains the intended meaning.

50. B: The underlined passage contains two errors that make it awkward. The first is a misplaced colon, and the second is an uneven treatment of articles. Using a colon is advisable when listing more than three or four items, but this sentence would flow more naturally if the colon followed either the second "by" or "by a." When listing many items, a single article at the top of the list, preceding the colon, serves to cover all the items ("a" followed by items that do not have an article, as in the correct choice, *B*). Choice *D* is grammatically correct, but tedious to work through.

51. B: Although "affect" and "effect" sound the same, they have different meanings. "Affect" is used as a verb. It is defined as the influence of a person, place, or event on another. "Effect" is used as a noun. It is defined as the result of an event. Therefore, the latter ought to be used in the heading. For this reason, Choices *C* and *D* are incorrect. Because the effect is a result of the flood, a possessive apostrophe is needed for the singular noun "flood." For this reason, Choice *A* is incorrect and Choice *B* is correct.

52. C: Choice *C*, "ravenous," means "extremely hungry, voracious," so it is the least accurate way to describe destructive waters. In a poetic sense, it might work, but the passage is about fact, not poetry. The fast-moving waters could more accurately be described as "ruinous" (Choice *B*) or "ravaging" (Choice *D*), because both describe destruction. "Raging" (Choice *A*) is a poor choice because it denotes violent anger, which is emotional rather than scientific.

53. B: Choice *B* is the best answer because it most closely maintains the sentence pattern of the first sentence of the paragraph, even though the content of Choice *B* is different from the original. Choices *A* and *C* are incorrect. Choice *C* is incorrect because it does not maintain the sentence pattern of the first sentence of the paragraph. Instead, Choice *C* makes the verb "grow" no longer conditional ("may grow"). Choice *D* is incorrect because it switches to the future tense.

54. A: Choice *C* can be eliminated because "although often associated with devastation" is a sentence fragment. Choice *B* is incorrect because a comma is needed after "devastation" in the sentence. Choice *D* is also incorrect because the phrase "even often" is nonsensical in this sentence. "Although," in this context, is meant to show contradiction with the idea that floods are associated with devastation. Therefore, none of these choices would be suitable revisions, so Choice *A* is the correct answer.

55. A: Ideas and claims are best expressed and supported in a text through examples, evidence, and descriptions. Choice *A* is correct because it provides examples of rivers that support the tenth paragraph's claim that "not all flooding results in adverse circumstances." Choice *B* is incorrect because the sentence does not explain how floods are beneficial. Therefore, Choices *C* and *D* are incorrect.

56. D: In the sentence, "caused" is an incorrect tense, making Choice *A* wrong. Choice *B* is incorrect because this used as a noun; "cause" in verb form is needed. Choices *C* and *D* are very compelling. "Causing" (Choice *C*) is a verb and it is in the present continuous tense, which appears to agree with the verb flooding, but it is incorrectly used. This leaves Choice *D*, "causes," which does fit because it is in the indefinite present tense. Fitting each choice into the sentence and reading it also reveal that Choice *D*, "causes," correctly completes the sentence.

57. A: To project means to anticipate or forecast. This word goes very well with the sentence because it describes how new technology is trying to estimate flood activity in order to prevent damage and save lives. "Project" in this case needs to be assisted by "to" in order to function in the sentence. Therefore, Choice *A* is correct. Choices *B* and *D* are in the incorrect tenses. Choice *C* is also wrong because it lacks the word "to."

58. C: "Picturesque" is an adjective used for an attractive, scenic, or otherwise striking image. Thus, Choice *C* is correct. Choice *A* is incorrect because although a picturesque view can be colorful, the word "colorful" does not encompass the full meaning of the word "picturesque." Choice *B* is incorrect because "drab" is the opposite of "picturesque." Choice *D* is incorrect because "candid" is defined as being frank, open, truthful, or honest.

59. D: "Therefore" is an adverb that means "for that reason." Choice *D*, "thus," is a synonym of "therefore" and so it is the correct answer. "Meanwhile" (Choice *A*) is also an adverb, meaning "during the intervening time," which does not mean the same as "for that reason." Idiomatically, "in addition" (Choice *B*) means "also," or "as well as," neither of which is appropriate in this context. Choice *C* ("however"), is used here as a conjunction to indicate "nevertheless," which is not synonymous with "therefore."

60. B: Choice *B* is the correct answer because the final paragraph summarizes key points from each subsection of the text. Choice *A* is incorrect because the last paragraph does not just mention adverse effects of floods. For example, the paragraph states "By understanding flood cycles, civilizations can learn to take advantage of flood seasons." Choice *C* is incorrect; although the subheading mentions the drying of floods, the phenomenon is not mentioned in the paragraph. Finally, Choice *D* is incorrect because no new information is presented in the last paragraph of the passage.

61. C: Choice *C* correctly uses the word *from* in describing the fact that dogs are related to wolves. The word *through* is incorrectly used here, so Choices *A* is incorrect. Choice *B* makes no sense. Choice *D* unnecessarily changes the verb tense in addition to incorrectly using *through*.

62. B: Choice *B* is correct because the Oxford comma is applied, clearly separating the specific terms. Choice *A* lacks this clarity, making it not the *best* answer choice. Choice *C* is correct but too wordy because commas can be easily applied. Choice *D* doesn't flow with the sentence's structure.

63. D: Choice *D* correctly uses the question mark, fixing the sentence's main issue. Thus, Choice *A* is incorrect because questions do not end with periods. Choice *B*, although correctly written, changes the meaning of the original sentence. Choice *C* is incorrect because it completely changes the direction of the sentence, disrupts the flow of the paragraph, and lacks the crucial question mark.

64. A: Choice *A* is correct because there are no errors in the sentence. Choices *B* and *C* both have extraneous commas, disrupting the flow of the sentence. Choice *D* unnecessarily rearranges the sentence.

65. D: Choice *D* is correct because the commas serve to clearly distinguish that artificial selection is just another term for selective breeding before the sentence continues. The structure is preserved, and the sentence can flow with more clarity. Choice *A* is incorrect because the sentence needs commas to avoid being a run-on sentence. Choice *B* is close but still lacks the required comma after *selection*, so this is also incorrect. Choice *C* is incorrect because the comma to set off the aside should be placed after *breeding* instead of after *called*.

66. B: Choice *B* is correct because the sentence is talking about a continuing process. Therefore, the best modification is simply to add the word *to* in front of *increase*. Choice *A* is incorrect because this modifier is missing. Choice *C* is incorrect because, with the additional comma, the present tense of *increase* is inappropriate. Choice *D* makes more sense, but the tense is still not the best to use.

67. A: The sentence has no errors, so Choice *A* is correct. Choice *B* is incorrect because it adds an unnecessary comma. Choice *C* is incorrect because *advantage* should not be plural in this sentence unless the singular article *an* is removed. Choice *D* is very tempting. Although this would make the sentence more concise, it leaves out critical information, which is incorrect.

68. C: Choice *C* correctly uses *on to*, describing the way genes are passed down generationally. The use of *into* is inappropriate for this context, which makes Choice *A* incorrect. Choice *B* is close, but *onto* refers to something being placed on a surface. Choice *D* doesn't make logical sense.

69. D: Choice *D* is correct, since only proper names should be capitalized. Because the name of a dog breed is not a proper name, Choice *A* is incorrect. In terms of punctuation, only one comma after *example* is needed, so Choices *B* and *C* are incorrect.

70. C: The underlined passage is incorrect; "which" is not preceded by a comma to separate the dependent clause from the main one. Choice *B* is incorrect because the pronoun "who" should be either "which" or "that." Choice *D* is incorrect because a comma precedes "that"; it would be correct to use "that" without the comma.

71. D: "Locating" is a gerund, which is a noun that is based on a verb and ends in "ing." "Proficient" modifies "locating," so Choice *A* is incorrect. Choices *B* and *C* are also incorrect because the dogs are proficient at locating all three items on the list: they locate drugs, they locate IEDs, and they locate human remains. If not, there would be gerunds before "IEDs" and "human remains," for example, "locating drugs, identifying IEDS, and unearthing human remains." Choice *D* is the correct answer.

72. A: The underlined word is completely appropriate, so the correct answer is Choice *A*. Choice *B* is incorrect because it is implied by "Bark and Hold" that the dogs isolate the targeted individuals so that law enforcement officials can approach them. Choice *C* is incorrect because at this early stage in detention, no one is prosecuting the individuals. Choice *D* is closest to the underlined word, but it is not the best choice possible because the reader is not told the specific way in which individuals are targeted. In other words, are they physically marked, identified by scent, or perhaps target through voice command?

73. A: No change to the underlined passage is necessary. Choice *B* is incorrect because the adverb "however" should be set off by commas: "There is a downside, however, to the selective breeding of dogs." Choices *C* and *D* are incorrect because the comma placement interrupts the structure of the main clause.

74. D: The underlined passage is incorrect because the pronoun "that" does not agree with the noun "disabilities." The same is true for Choices *B* and *C*, "whom" and "them," respectively. Choice *D*, "which," is the pronoun that agrees with "disabilities."

75. D: Choice *D*, "flattened," is the best substitute for "squashed." Choice *A*, "quashed" means "to set aside or annul, or to put down forcibly." Choice *B*, "smashed," suggests force was used, but pugs' squashed noses have been bred into them over the years. Choice *C*, "foreshortened," describes a technique used to visually represent an object as having less depth than it does.

ACT Mathematics Test

What to Expect

The Math test contains 60 multiple-choice questions and lasts 60 minutes. Unlike the English and Reading sections, which each contain four answers options, the math questions all have five choices. Certain calculators are permitted, but the questions are all designed to be answerable without the use of a calculator.

Tips

- Use your calculator strategically. Some questions are actually solved faster with reasoning or freehand work. Test takers often rely excessively on their calculators and can get bogged down or miss obvious elements of the question. When a calculator is used, consider substituting numbers for variables to solve equations and test your answer.

- Double-check your work. Any extra time in the section can be used performing the reverse operations or plugging your answer into the problem to ensure it is correct.

- Backsolve when you're stuck. If you can't figure out the answer, try using the provided choices and working backward, selecting the one that works. This strategy may not always work and is time-consuming, but it can be helpful with those questions that you cannot figure out.

- Carefully consider all diagrams and figures. Word problems, data interpretation, and geometry questions, in particular, often include important graphics with valuable information. Examine them carefully.

- Consider the reasonableness of your response in the context of the problem. Careless mistakes are often made when test takers are rushing. By evaluating if your response is reasonable, some of these mistakes can be avoided.

Number and Quantity

Structure of the Number System

The mathematical number system is made up of two general types of numbers: real and complex. **Real numbers** are those that are used in normal settings, while **complex numbers** are those composed of both a real number and an imaginary one. Imaginary numbers are the result of taking the square root of -1, and $\sqrt{-1} = i$.

The real number system is often explained using a Venn diagram similar to the one below. After a number has been labeled as a real number, further classification occurs when considering the other groups in this diagram. If a number is a never-ending, non-repeating decimal, it falls in the irrational category. Otherwise, it is rational. More information on these types of numbers is provided in the previous section. Furthermore, if a number does not have a fractional part, it is classified as an integer, such as -2, 75, or zero. Whole numbers are an even smaller group that only includes positive integers and zero. The last group of natural numbers is made up of only positive integers, such as 2, 56, or 12.

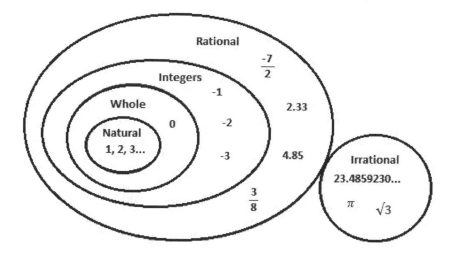

Real numbers can be compared and ordered using the number line. If a number falls to the left on the real number line, it is less than a number on the right. For example, $-2 < 5$ because -2 falls to the left of zero, and 5 falls to the right. Numbers to the left of zero are negative while those to the right are positive.

Complex numbers are made up of the sum of a real number and an imaginary number. Some examples of complex numbers include $6 + 2i$, $5 - 7i$, and $-3 + 12i$. Adding and subtracting complex numbers is similar to collecting like terms. The real numbers are added together, and the imaginary numbers are added together. For example, if the problem asks to simplify the expression $6 + 2i - 3 + 7i$, the 6 and (-3) are combined to make 3, and the $2i$ and $7i$ combine to make $9i$. Multiplying and dividing complex numbers is similar to working with exponents. One rule to remember when multiplying is that $i \times i = -1$. For example, if a problem asks to simplify the expression $4i(3 + 7i)$, the $4i$ should be distributed throughout the 3 and the $7i$. This leaves the final expression $12i - 28$. The 28 is negative because $i \times i$ results in a negative number. The last type of operation to consider with complex numbers is the conjugate. The **conjugate** of a complex number is a technique used to change the complex number into a real number. For example, the conjugate of $4 - 3i$ is $4 + 3i$. Multiplying $(4 - 3i)(4 + 3i)$ results in $16 + 12i - 12i + 9$, which has a final answer of $16 + 9 = 25$.

The order of operations—PEMDAS—simplifies longer expressions with real or imaginary numbers. Each operation is listed in the order of how they should be completed in a problem containing more than one operation. Parenthesis can also mean grouping symbols, such as brackets and absolute value. Then, exponents are calculated. Multiplication and division should be completed from left to right, and addition and subtraction should be completed from left to right.

Simplification of another type of expression occurs when radicals are involved. Root is another word for radical. For example, the following expression is a radical that can be simplified: $\sqrt{24x^2}$. First, the number must be factored out to the highest perfect square. Any perfect square can be taken out of a radical. Twenty-four can be factored into 4 and 6, and 4 can be taken out of the radical. $\sqrt{4} = 2$ can be taken out, and 6 stays underneath. If $x > 0$, x can be taken out of the radical because it is a perfect square. The simplified radical is $2x\sqrt{6}$. An approximation can be found using a calculator.

There are also properties of numbers that are true for certain operations. The **commutative** property allows the order of the terms in an expression to change while keeping the same final answer. Both addition and multiplication can be completed in any order and still obtain the same result. However, order does matter in subtraction and division. The **associative** property allows any terms to be "associated" by parenthesis and retain the same final answer. For example, $(4 + 3) + 5 = 4 + (3 + 5)$. Both addition and multiplication are associative; however, subtraction and division do not hold this property. The **distributive** property states that $a(b + c) = ab + ac$. It is a property that involves both addition and multiplication, and the a is distributed onto each term inside the parentheses.

Rational and Irrational Numbers

All real numbers can be separated into two groups: rational and irrational numbers. **Rational numbers** are any numbers that can be written as a fraction, such as $\frac{1}{3}, \frac{7}{4}$, and -25. Alternatively, **irrational numbers** are those that cannot be written as a fraction, such as numbers with never-ending, non-repeating decimal values. Many irrational numbers result from taking roots, such as $\sqrt{2}$ or $\sqrt{3}$. An irrational number may be written as:

$$34.5684952\ldots$$

The ellipsis (…) represents the line of numbers after the decimal that does not repeat and is never-ending.

When rational and irrational numbers interact, there are different types of number outcomes. For example, when adding or multiplying two rational numbers, the result is a rational number. No matter what two fractions are added or multiplied together, the result can always be written as a fraction. The following expression shows two rational numbers multiplied together:

$$\frac{3}{8} \times \frac{4}{7} = \frac{12}{56}$$

The product of these two fractions is another fraction that can be simplified to $\frac{3}{14}$.

As another interaction, rational numbers added to irrational numbers will always result in irrational numbers. No part of any fraction can be added to a never-ending, non-repeating decimal to make a rational number. The same result is true when multiplying a rational and irrational number. Taking a fractional part of a never-ending, non-repeating decimal will always result in another never-ending, non-repeating decimal. An example of the product of rational and irrational numbers is shown in the following expression: $2 \times \sqrt{7}$.

The last type of interaction concerns two irrational numbers, where the sum or product may be rational or irrational depending on the numbers being used. The following expression shows a rational sum from two irrational numbers:

$$\sqrt{3} + (6 - \sqrt{3}) = 6$$

The product of two irrational numbers can be rational or irrational. A rational result can be seen in the following expression:

$$\sqrt{2} \times \sqrt{8} = \sqrt{2 \times 8} = \sqrt{16} = 4$$

An irrational result can be seen in the following:

$$\sqrt{3} \times \sqrt{2} = \sqrt{6}$$

Integers

An integer is any number that does not have a fractional part. This includes all positive and negative **whole numbers** and zero. Fractions and decimals—which aren't whole numbers—aren't integers.

Prime Numbers

A **prime** number cannot be divided except by 1 and itself. A prime number has no other factors, which means that no other combination of whole numbers can be multiplied to reach that number. For example, the set of prime numbers between 1 and 27 is {2, 3, 5, 7, 11, 13, 17, 19, 23}.

The number 7 is a prime number because its only factors are 1 and 7. In contrast, 12 isn't a prime number, as it can be divided by other numbers like 2, 3, 4, and 6. Because they are composed of multiple factors, numbers like 12 are called **composite** numbers. All numbers greater than 1 that aren't prime numbers are composite numbers.

Even and Odd Numbers

An integer is **even** if one of its factors is 2, while those integers without a factor of 2 are **odd**. No numbers except for integers can have either of these labels. For example, 2, 40, -16, and 108 are all even numbers, while -1, 13, 59, and 77 are all odd numbers since they are integers that cannot be divided by 2 without a remainder. Numbers like 0.4, $\frac{5}{9}$, π, and $\sqrt{7}$ are neither odd nor even because they are not integers.

Order of Rational Numbers

A common question type on the ACT asks test takers to order rational numbers from least to greatest or greatest to least. The numbers will come in a variety of formats, including decimals, percentages, roots, fractions, and whole numbers. These questions test for knowledge of different types of numbers and the ability to determine their respective values.

Whether the question asks to order the numbers from greatest to least or least to greatest, the crux of the question is the same—convert the numbers into a common format. Generally, it's easiest to write the numbers as whole numbers and decimals so they can be placed on a number line. The following examples illustrate this strategy:

1. Order the following rational numbers from greatest to least:

$$\sqrt{36}, 0.65, 78\%, \frac{3}{4}, 7, 90\%, \frac{5}{2}$$

Of the seven numbers, the whole number (7) and decimal (0.65) are already in an accessible form, so test takers should concentrate on the other five.

First, the square root of 36 equals 6. (If the test asks for the root of a non-perfect root, determine which two whole numbers the root lies between.) Next, the percentages should be converted to decimals. A percentage means "per hundred," so this conversion requires moving the decimal point two places to the left, leaving 0.78 and 0.9. Lastly, the fractions are evaluated: $\frac{3}{4} = \frac{75}{100} = 0.75; \frac{5}{2} = 2\frac{1}{2} = 2.5$

Now, the only step left is to list the numbers in the requested order:

$$7, \sqrt{36}, \frac{5}{2}, 90\%, 78\%, \frac{3}{4}, 0.65$$

2. Order the following rational numbers from least to greatest:

$$2.5, \sqrt{9}, -10.5, 0.853, 175\%, \sqrt{4}, \frac{4}{5}$$

$$\sqrt{9} = 3$$

$$175\% = 1.75$$

$$\sqrt{4} = 2$$

$$\frac{4}{5} = 0.8$$

From least to greatest, the answer is: $-10.5, \frac{4}{5}, 0.853, 175\%, \sqrt{4}, 2.5, \sqrt{9}$

Basic Addition, Subtraction, Multiplication, and Division

Gaining more of something is related to addition, while taking something away relates to subtraction. Vocabulary words such as *total, more, less, left,* and *remain* are common when working with these problems. The $+$ sign means *plus.* This shows that addition is happening. The $-$ sign means *minus.* This shows that subtraction is happening. The symbols will be important when you write out equations.

Addition
Addition can also be defined in equation form. For example, $4 + 5 = 9$ shows that $4 + 5$ is the same as 9. Therefore, $9 = 9$, and "four plus five equals nine." When two quantities are being added together, the result is called the **sum**. Therefore, the sum of 4 and 5 is 9. The numbers being added, such as 4 and 5, are known as the **addends.**

Subtraction
Subtraction can also be in equation form. For example, $9 - 5 = 4$ shows that $9 - 5$ is the same as 4 and that "9 minus 5 is 4." The result of subtraction is known as a **difference.** The difference of $9 - 5$ is 4. 4 represents the amount that is left once the subtraction is done. The order in which subtraction is completed does matter. For example, $9 - 5$ and $5 - 9$ do not result in the same answer. $5 - 9$ results in a negative number. So, subtraction does not adhere to the commutative or associative property. The order in which subtraction is completed is important.

Multiplication
Multiplication is when we add equal amounts. The answer to a multiplication problem is called a **product**. Products stand for the total number of items within different groups. The symbol for multiplication is $\times$ or $\cdot$. We say 2×3 or $2 \cdot 3$ means "2 times 3."

As an example, there are three sets of four apples. The goal is to know how many apples there are in total. Three sets of four apples gives $4 + 4 + 4 = 12$. Also, three times four apples gives $3 \times 4 = 12$. Therefore, for any whole numbers a and b, where a is not equal to zero, $a \times b = b + b + \cdots b$, where b is added a times. Also, $a \times b$ can be thought of as the number of units in a rectangular block consisting of a rows and b columns.

For example, 3 × 7 is equal to the number of squares in the following rectangle:

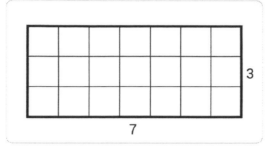

The answer is 21, and there are 21 squares in the rectangle.

When any number is multiplied by one (for example, 8 × 1 = 8), the value of original number does not change. Therefore, 1 is the **multiplicative identity**. For any whole number a, $1 \times a = a$. Also, any number multiplied by zero results in zero. Therefore, for any whole number a, $0 \times a = 0$.

Another method of multiplication can be done with the use of an **area model**. An area model is a rectangle that is divided into rows and columns that match up to the number of place values within each number. For example, $29 \times 65 = 25 + 4$ and $66 = 60 + 5$. The products of those 4 numbers are found within the rectangle and then summed up to get the answer. The entire process is:

$$(60 \times 25) + (5 \times 25) + (60 \times 4) + (5 \times 4) = 1,500 + 240 + 125 + 20 = 1,885.$$

Here is the actual area model:

	25	4
60	60x25 1,500	60x4 240
5	5x25 125	5x4 20

$$
\begin{array}{r}
1,500 \\
240 \\
125 \\
+\quad 20 \\
\hline
1,885
\end{array}
$$

Division

Division is based on dividing a given number into parts. The simplest problem involves dividing a number into equal parts. For example, if a pack of 20 pencils is to be divided among 10 children, you would have to divide 20 by 10. In this example, each child would receive 2 pencils.

The symbol for division is ÷ or /. The equation above is written as $20 \div 10 = 2$, or $20 / 10 = 2$. This means "20 divided by 10 is equal to 2." Division can be explained as the following: for any whole numbers a and b, where b is not equal to zero, $a \div b = c$ if—and only if—$a = b \times c$. This means, division can be thought of as a multiplication problem with a missing part. For instance, calculating $20 \div 10$ is the same as asking the following: "If there are 20 items in total with 10 in each group, how many are in each group?" Therefore, 20 is equal to ten times what value? This question is the same as asking, "If there are 20 items in total with 2 in each group, how many groups are there?" The answer to each question is 2.

In a division problem, a is known as the **dividend,** b is the **divisor**, and c is the **quotient**. Zero cannot be divided into parts. Therefore, for any nonzero whole number a, $0 \div a = 0$. Also, division by zero is undefined. Dividing an amount into zero parts is not possible.

More difficult division problems involve dividing a number into equal parts, but having some left over. An example is dividing a pack of 20 pencils among 8 friends so that each friend receives the same number of pencils. In this setting, each friend receives 2 pencils, but there are 4 pencils leftover. 20 is the dividend, 8 is the divisor, 2 is the quotient, and 4 is known as the **remainder**. Within this type of division problem, for whole numbers a, b, c, and d, $a \div b = c$ with a remainder of d. This is true if and only if $a = (b \times c) + d$. When calculating $a \div b$, if there is no remainder, a is said to be *divisible* by b. **Even numbers** are all divisible by the number 2. **Odd numbers** are not divisible by 2. An odd number of items cannot be paired up into groups of 2 without having one item leftover.

Dividing a number by a single digit or two digits can be turned into repeated subtraction problems. An area model can be used throughout the problem that represents multiples of the divisor. For example, the answer to $8580 \div 55$ can be found by subtracting 55 from 8580 one at a time and counting the total number of subtractions necessary. However, a simpler process involves using larger multiples of 55. First, $100 \times 55 = 5,500$ is subtracted from 8,580, and 3,080 is leftover. Next, $50 \times 55 = 2,750$ is subtracted from 3,080 to obtain 380. $5 \times 55 = 275$ is subtracted from 330 to obtain 55, and finally, $1 \times 55 = 55$ is subtracted from 55 to obtain zero. Therefore, there is no remainder, and the answer is $100 + 50 + 5 + 1 = 156$. Here is a picture of the area model and the repeated subtraction process:

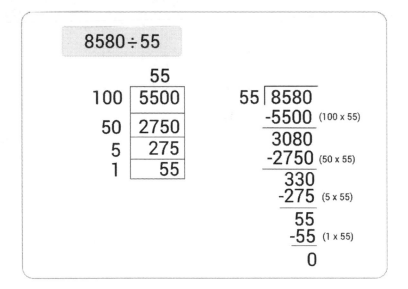

If you want to check the answer of a division problem, multiply the answer by the divisor. This will help you check to see if the dividend is obtained. If there is a remainder, the same process is done, but the remainder is added on at the end to try to match the dividend. In the previous example, $156 \times 64 =$

9984 would be the checking procedure. Dividing decimals involves the same repeated subtraction process. The only difference would be that the subtractions would involve numbers that include values in the decimal places. Lining up decimal places is crucial in this type of problem.

Order of Operations

When reviewing calculations consisting of more than one operation, the order in which the operations are performed affects the resulting answer. Consider $5 \times 2 + 7$. Performing multiplication then addition results in an answer of 17 because $(5 \times 2 = 10; 10 + 7 = 17)$. However, if the problem is written $5 \times (2 + 7)$, the order of operations dictates that the operation inside the parenthesis must be performed first. The resulting answer is 45 because $(2 + 7 = 9$, then $5 \times 9 = 45)$.

The order in which operations should be performed is remembered using the acronym PEMDAS. PEMDAS stands for parenthesis, exponents, multiplication/division, addition/subtraction. Multiplication and division are performed in the same step, working from left to right with whichever comes first. Addition and subtraction are performed in the same step, working from left to right with whichever comes first.

Consider the following example: $8 \div 4 + 8(7 - 7)$. Performing the operation inside the parenthesis produces $8 \div 4 + 8(0)$ or $8 \div 4 + 8 \times 0$. There are no exponents, so multiplication and division are performed next from left to right resulting in: $2 + 8 \times 0$, then $2 + 0$. Finally, addition and subtraction are performed to obtain an answer of 2. Now consider the following example: $6 \times 3 + 3^2 - 6$. Parenthesis are not applicable. Exponents are evaluated first, which brings us to $6 \times 3 + 9 - 6$. Then multiplication/division forms $18 + 9 - 6$. At last, addition/subtraction leads to the final answer of 21.

Properties of Operations

Properties of operations exist that make calculations easier and solve problems for missing values. The following table summarizes commonly used properties of real numbers.

Property	Addition	Multiplication
Commutative	$a + b = b + a$	$a \times b = b \times a$
Associative	$(a + b) + c = a + (b + c)$	$(a \times b) \times c = a \times (bc)$
Identity	$a + 0 = a; 0 + a = a$	$a \times 1 = a; 1 \times a = a$
Inverse	$a + (-a) = 0$	$a \times \dfrac{1}{a} = 1; a \neq 0$
Distributive	$a(b + c) = ab + ac$	

The **cumulative property of addition** states that the order in which numbers are added does not change the sum. Similarly, the **commutative property of multiplication** states that the order in which numbers are multiplied does not change the product. The **associative property** of addition and multiplication state that the grouping of numbers being added or multiplied does not change the sum or product, respectively. The commutative and associative properties are useful for performing calculations. For example, $(47 + 25) + 3$ is equivalent to $(47 + 3) + 25$, which is easier to calculate.

The **identity property of addition** states that adding zero to any number does not change its value. The **identity property of multiplication** states that multiplying a number by 1 does not chan[ge]. [The] **inverse property of addition** states that the sum of a number and its opposite equals ze[ro]. [They] are numbers that are the same with different signs (ex. 5 and -5; $-\frac{1}{2}$ and $\frac{1}{2}$). The **inverse** [property of] **multiplication** states that the product of a number (other than 0) and its reciprocal equ[als].

numbers have numerators and denominators that are inverted (ex. $\frac{2}{5}$ and $\frac{5}{2}$). Inverse properties are useful for canceling quantities to find missing values (see algebra content). For example, $a + 7 = 12$ is solved by adding the inverse of 7(-7) to both sides in order to isolate a.

The **distributive property** states that multiplying a sum (or difference) by a number produces the same result as multiplying each value in the sum (or difference) by the number and adding (or subtracting) the products. Consider the following scenario: You are buying three tickets for a baseball game. Each ticket costs $18. You are also charged a fee of $2 per ticket for purchasing the tickets online. The cost is calculated: $3 \times 18 + 3 \times 2$. Using the distributive property, the cost can also be calculated $3(18 + 2)$.

Adding and Subtracting Positive and Negative Numbers

Some problems require adding positive and negative numbers or subtracting positive and negative numbers. Adding a negative number to a positive one can be thought of a reducing or subtracting from the positive number, and the result should be less than the original positive number. For example, adding 8 and -3 is the same is subtracting 3 from 8; the result is 5. This can be visualized by imagining that the positive number (8) represents 8 apples that a student has in her basket. The negative number (-3) indicates the number of apples she is in debt or owes to her friend. In order to pay off her debt and "settle the score," she essentially is in possession of three fewer apples than in her basket (8 − 3 = 5), so she actually has five apples that are hers to keep. Should the negative addend be of higher magnitude than the positive addend (for example -9 + 3), the result will be negative, but "less negative" or closer to zero than the large negative number. This is because adding a positive value, even if relatively smaller, to a negative value, reduces the magnitude of the negative in the total. Considering the apple example again, if the girl owed 9 apples to her friend (-9) but she picked 3 (+3) off a tree and gave them to her friend, she now would only owe him six apples (-6), which reduced her debt burden (her negative number of apples) by three.

Subtracting positive and negative numbers works the same way with one key distinction: subtracting a negative number from a negative number yields a "less negative" or more positive result because again, this can be considered as removing or alleviating some debt. For example, if the student with the apples owed 5 apples to her friend, she essentially has -5 applies. If her mom gives that friend 10 apples on behalf of the girl, she now has removed the need to pay back the 5 apples and surpassed neutral (no net apples owed) and now her friend owes *her* five apples (+5). Stated mathematically -5 + -10 = +5.

When subtracting integers and negative rational numbers, one has to change the problem to adding the opposite and then apply the rules of addition.

- Subtracting two positive numbers is the same as adding one positive and one negative number.
  - For example, $4.9 − 7.1$ is the same as $4.9 + (−7.1)$. The solution is -2.2 since the absolute value of -7.1 is greater than 4.9. Another example is $8.5 − 6.4$ which is the same as $8.5 + (−6.4)$. The solution is 2.1 since the absolute value of 8.5 is greater than 6.4.
- Subtracting a positive number from a negative number results in negative value.
  - For example, $(−12) − 7$ is the same as $(−12) + (−7)$ with a solution of -19.
- Subtracting a negative number from a positive number results in a positive value.
  - For example, $12 − (−7)$ is the same as $12 + 7$ with a solution of 19.

- For multiplication and division of integers and rational numbers, if both numbers are positive or both numbers are negative, the result is a positive value.
  - For example, $(-1.7) \times (-4)$ has a solution of 6.8 since both numbers are negative values.
- If one number is positive and another number is negative, the result is a negative value.
  - For example, $(-15) \div 5$ has a solution of -3 since there is one negative number.

Adding one positive and one negative number requires taking the absolute values and finding the difference between them. Then, the sign of the number that has the higher absolute value for the final solution is used.

Operations with Fractions, Decimals, and Percentages

<u>Fractions</u>
A **fraction** is a part of something that is whole. Items such as apples can be cut into parts to help visualize fractions. If an apple is cut into 2 equal parts, each part represents ½ of the apple. If each half is then cut into two parts, the apple now is cut into quarters. Each piece now represents ¼ of the apple. In this example, each part is equal because they all have the same size. Geometric shapes, such as circles and squares, can also be utilized to help visualize the idea of fractions. For example, a circle can be drawn on the board and divided into 6 equal parts:

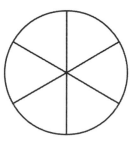

Shading can be used to represent parts of the circle that can be translated into fractions. The top of the fraction, the **numerator,** can represent how many segments are shaded. The bottom of the fraction, the **denominator,** can represent the number of segments that the circle is broken into. A pie is a good analogy to use in this example. If one piece of the circle is shaded, or one piece of pie is cut out, $^1/_6$ of the object is being referred to. An apple, a pie, or a circle can be utilized in order to compare simple fractions. For example, showing that ½ is larger than ¼ and that ¼ is smaller than $^1/_3$ can be accomplished through shading. A **unit fraction** is a fraction in which the numerator is 1, and the denominator is a positive whole number. It represents one part of a whole—one piece of pie.

Imagine that an apple pie has been baked for a holiday party, and the full pie has eight slices. After the party, there are five slices left. How could the amount of the pie that remains be expressed as a fraction? The numerator is 5 since there are 5 pieces left, and the denominator is 8 since there were eight total slices in the whole pie. Thus, expressed as a fraction, the leftover pie totals $\frac{5}{8}$ of the original amount.

Fractions come in three different varieties: proper fractions, improper fractions, and mixed numbers. **Proper fractions** have a numerator less than the denominator, such as $\frac{3}{8}$, but **improper fractions** have a numerator greater than the denominator, such as $\frac{15}{8}$. **Mixed numbers** combine a whole number with a proper fraction, such as $3\frac{1}{2}$. Any mixed number can be written as an improper fraction by multiplying the integer by the denominator, adding the product to the value of the numerator, and dividing the sum by the original denominator. For example, $3\frac{1}{2} = \frac{3 \times 2 + 1}{2} = \frac{7}{2}$. Whole numbers can also be converted into fractions by placing the whole number as the numerator and making the denominator 1. For example, $3 = \frac{3}{1}$.

The bar in a fraction represents division. Therefore $^6/_5$ is the same as $6 \div 5$. In order to rewrite it as a mixed number, division is performed to obtain $6 \div 5 = 1\ R1$. The remainder is then converted into fraction form. The actual remainder becomes the numerator of a fraction, and the divisor becomes the denominator. Therefore $1\ R1$ is written as $1\frac{1}{5}$, a mixed number. A mixed number can also decompose into the addition of a whole number and a fraction. For example,

$$1\frac{1}{5} = 1 + \frac{1}{5} \text{ and } 4\frac{5}{6} = 4 + \frac{1}{6} + \frac{1}{6} + \frac{1}{6} + \frac{1}{6} + \frac{1}{6}$$

Every fraction can be built from a combination of unit fractions.

One of the most fundamental concepts of fractions is their ability to be manipulated by multiplication or division. This is possible since $\frac{n}{n} = 1$ for any non-zero integer. As a result, multiplying or dividing by $\frac{n}{n}$ will not alter the original fraction since any number multiplied or divided by 1 doesn't change the value of that number. Fractions of the same value are known as equivalent fractions. For example, $\frac{2}{8}, \frac{25}{100}$, and $\frac{40}{160}$ are equivalent, as they are all equal $\frac{1}{4}$.

Like fractions, or **equivalent fractions**, are the terms used to describe these fractions that are made up of different numbers but represent the same quantity. For example, the given fractions are $^4/_8$ and $^3/_6$. If a pie was cut into 8 pieces and 4 pieces were removed, half of the pie would remain. Also, if a pie was split into 6 pieces and 3 pieces were eaten, half of the pie would also remain. Therefore, both of the fractions represent half of a pie. These two fractions are referred to as like fractions. **Unlike fractions** are fractions that are different and do not represent equal quantities. When working with fractions in mathematical expressions, like fractions should be simplified. Both $^4/_8$ and $^3/_6$ can be simplified into $^1/_2$.

Comparing fractions can be completed through the use of a number line. For example, if $^3/_5$ and $^6/_{10}$ need to be compared, each fraction should be plotted on a number line. To plot $^3/_5$, the area from 0 to 1 should be broken into 5 equal segments, and the fraction represents 3 of them. To plot $^6/_{10}$, the area from 0 to 1 should be broken into 10 equal segments and the fraction represents 6 of them.

It can be seen that $\frac{3}{5} = \frac{6}{10}$

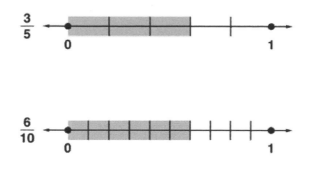

Like fractions are plotted at the same point on a number line. Unit fractions can also be used to compare fractions. For example, if it is known that

$$\frac{4}{5} > \frac{1}{2}$$

and

$$\frac{1}{2} > \frac{4}{10}$$

then it is also known that

$$\frac{4}{5} > \frac{4}{10}$$

Also, converting improper fractions to mixed numbers can be helpful in comparing fractions because the whole number portion of the number is more visible.

Adding and subtracting mixed numbers and fractions can be completed by decomposing fractions into a sum of whole numbers and unit fractions. For example, the given problem is

$$5\frac{3}{7} + 2\frac{1}{7}$$

Decomposing into

$$5 + \frac{1}{7} + \frac{1}{7} + \frac{1}{7} + 2 + \frac{1}{7}$$

This shows that the whole numbers can be added separately from the unit fractions. The answer is:

$$5 + 2 + \frac{1}{7} + \frac{1}{7} + \frac{1}{7} + \frac{1}{7} = 7 + \frac{4}{7} = 7\frac{4}{7}$$

Although many equivalent fractions exist, they are easier to compare and interpret when reduced or simplified. The numerator and denominator of a simple fraction will have no factors in common other than 1. When reducing or simplifying fractions, divide the numerator and denominator by the greatest common factor. A simple strategy is to divide the numerator and denominator by low numbers, like 2, 3, or 5 until arriving at a simple fraction, but the same thing could be achieved by determining the greatest common factor for both the numerator and denominator and dividing each by it. Using the first method is preferable when both the numerator and denominator are even, end in 5, or are obviously a multiple of another number. However, if no numbers seem to work, it will be necessary to factor the numerator and denominator to find the GCF. Let's look at examples:

1) Simplify the fraction $\frac{6}{8}$:

Dividing the numerator and denominator by 2 results in $\frac{3}{4}$, which is a simple fraction.

2) Simplify the fraction $\frac{12}{36}$:

Dividing the numerator and denominator by 2 leaves $\frac{6}{18}$. This isn't a simple fraction, as both the numerator and denominator have factors in common. Diving each by 3 results in $\frac{2}{6}$, but this can be further simplified by dividing by 2 to get $\frac{1}{3}$. This is the simplest fraction, as the numerator is 1. In cases like this, multiple division operations can be avoided by determining the greatest common factor (12, in this case) between the numerator and denominator.

3) Simplify the fraction $\frac{18}{54}$ by dividing by the greatest common factor:

First, determine the factors for the numerator and denominator. The factors of 18 are 1, 2, 3, 6, 9, and 18. The factors of 54 are 1, 2, 3, 6, 9, 18, 27, and 54. Thus, the greatest common factor is 18. Dividing $\frac{18}{54}$ by 18 leaves $\frac{1}{3}$, which is the simplest fraction. This method takes slightly more work, but it definitively arrives at the simplest fraction.

Adding and Subtracting Fractions
Adding and subtracting fractions that have the same denominators involves adding or subtracting the numerators. The denominator will stay the same. Therefore, the decomposition process can be made simpler, and the fractions do not have to be broken into unit fractions.

For example, the given problem is:

$$4\frac{7}{8} - 2\frac{6}{8}$$

The answer is found by adding the answers to both

$$4 - 2 \text{ and } \frac{7}{8} - \frac{6}{8}$$

$$2 + \frac{1}{8} = 2\frac{1}{8}$$

A common mistake would be to add the denominators so that $\frac{1}{4} + \frac{1}{4} = \frac{1}{8}$ or to add numerators and denominators so that $\frac{1}{4} + \frac{1}{4} = \frac{2}{8}$. However, conceptually, it is known that two quarters make a half, so neither one of these are correct.

If two fractions have different denominators, equivalent fractions must be used to add or subtract them. The fractions must be converted into fractions that have common denominators. A **least common denominator** or the product of the two denominators can be used as the common denominator. For example, in the problem $\frac{5}{6} + \frac{2}{3}$, either 6, which is the least common denominator, or 18, which is the product of the denominators, can be used. In order to use 6, $\frac{2}{3}$ must be converted to sixths. A number line can be used to show the equivalent fraction is $\frac{4}{6}$. What happens is that $\frac{2}{3}$ is multiplied by a fractional form of 1 to obtain a denominator of 6. Hence, $\frac{2}{3} \times \frac{2}{2} = \frac{4}{6}$. Therefore, the problem is now $\frac{5}{6} + \frac{4}{6} = \frac{9}{6}$, which can be simplified into $\frac{3}{2}$. In order to use 18, both fractions must be converted into having 18 as their denominator. $\frac{5}{6}$ would have to be multiplied by $\frac{3}{3}$, and $\frac{2}{3}$ would need to be multiplied by $\frac{6}{6}$. The addition problem would be $\frac{15}{18} + \frac{12}{18} = \frac{27}{18}$, which reduces into $\frac{3}{2}$.

It is always possible to find a common denominator by multiplying the denominators. However, when the denominators are large numbers, this method is unwieldy, especially if the answer must be provided in its simplest form. Thus, it's beneficial to find the **least common denominator** of the fractions—the least common denominator is incidentally also the **least common multiple**.

Once equivalent fractions have been found with common denominators, simply add or subtract the numerators to arrive at the answer:

1) $\frac{1}{2} + \frac{3}{4} = \frac{2}{4} + \frac{3}{4} = \frac{5}{4}$

2) $\frac{3}{12} + \frac{11}{20} = \frac{15}{60} + \frac{33}{60} = \frac{48}{60} = \frac{4}{5}$

3) $\frac{7}{9} - \frac{4}{15} = \frac{35}{45} - \frac{12}{45} = \frac{23}{45}$

4) $\frac{5}{6} - \frac{7}{18} = \frac{15}{18} - \frac{7}{18} = \frac{8}{18} = \frac{4}{9}$

Multiplying and Dividing Fractions
Of the four basic operations that can be performed on fractions, the one which involves the least amount of work is multiplication. To multiply two fractions, simply multiply the numerators, multiply the denominators, and place the products as a fraction. Whole numbers and mixed numbers can also be expressed as a fraction, as described above, to multiply with a fraction.

Because multiplication is commutative, multiplying a fraction by a whole number is the same as multiplying a whole number by a fraction. The problem involves adding a fraction a specific number of times. The problem $3 \times \frac{1}{4}$ can be translated into adding the unit fraction three times: $\frac{1}{4} + \frac{1}{4} + \frac{1}{4} = \frac{3}{4}$. In the problem $4 \times \frac{2}{5}$, the fraction can be decomposed into $\frac{1}{5} + \frac{1}{5}$ and then added four times to obtain $\frac{8}{5}$. Also, both of these answers can be found by just multiplying the whole number by the numerator of the fraction being multiplied.

The whole numbers can be written in fraction form as:

$$\frac{3}{1} \times \frac{1}{4} = \frac{3}{4}$$

$$\frac{4}{1} \times \frac{2}{5} = \frac{8}{5}$$

Multiplying a fraction times a fraction involves multiplying the numerators together separately and the denominators together separately. For example,

$$\frac{3}{8} \times \frac{2}{3} = \frac{3 \times 2}{8 \times 3} = \frac{6}{24}$$

This can then be reduced to $^1/_4$.

Dividing a fraction by a fraction is actually a multiplication problem. It involves flipping the divisor and then multiplying normally. For example,

$$\frac{22}{5} \div \frac{1}{2} = \frac{22}{5} \times \frac{2}{1} = \frac{44}{5}$$

The same procedure can be implemented for division problems involving fractions and whole numbers. The whole number can be rewritten as a fraction over a denominator of 1, and then division can be completed.

A common denominator approach can also be used in dividing fractions. Considering the same problem, $\frac{22}{5} \div \frac{1}{2}$, a common denominator between the two fractions is 10. $\frac{22}{5}$ would be rewritten as $\frac{22}{5} \times \frac{2}{2} = \frac{44}{10}$, and $\frac{1}{2}$ would be rewritten as $\frac{1}{2} \times \frac{5}{5} = \frac{5}{10}$. Dividing both numbers straight across results in:

$$\frac{44}{10} \div \frac{5}{10} = \frac{^{44}/_5}{^{10}/_{10}} = \frac{^{44}/_5}{1} = {}^{44}/_5$$

Many real-world problems will involve the use of fractions. Key words include actual fraction values, such as *half, quarter, third, fourth*, etc. The best approach to solving word problems involving fractions is to draw a picture or diagram that represents the scenario being discussed, while deciding which type of operation is necessary in order to solve the problem. A phrase such as "one fourth of 60 pounds of coal" creates a scenario in which multiplication should be used, and the mathematical form of the phrase is $\frac{1}{4} \times 60$.

Decimals

The **decimal system** is a way of writing out numbers that uses ten different numerals: 0, 1, 2, 3, 4, 5, 6, 7, 8, and 9. This is also called a "base ten" or "base 10" system. Other bases are also used. For example, computers work with a base of 2. This means they only use the numerals 0 and 1.

The **decimal place** denotes how far to the right of the decimal point a numeral is. The first digit to the right of the decimal point is in the **tenths'** place. The next is the **hundredths'** place. The third is the **thousandths'** place.

So, 3.142 has a 1 in the tenths place, a 4 in the hundredths place, and a 2 in the thousandths place.

The **decimal point** is a period used to separate the **ones'** place from the **tenths'** place when writing out a number as a decimal.

A **decimal number** is a number written out with a decimal point instead of as a fraction, for example, 1.25 instead of $\frac{5}{4}$. Depending on the situation, it may be easier to work with fractions, while other times, it may be easier to work with decimal numbers.

A decimal number is **terminating** if it stops at some point. It is called **repeating** if it never stops but repeats a pattern over and over. It is important to note that every rational number can be written as a terminating decimal or as a repeating decimal.

Addition with Decimals
To add decimal numbers, each number in columns needs to be lined up by the decimal point. For each number being added, the zeros to the right of the last number need to be filled in so that each of the numbers has the same number of places to the right of the decimal. Then, the columns can be added together. Here is an example of 2.45 + 1.3 + 8.891 written in column form:

$$
\begin{array}{r}
2.450 \\
1.300 \\
+\ 8.891 \\
\hline
\end{array}
$$

Zeros have been added in the columns so that each number has the same number of places to the right of the decimal.

Added together, the correct answer is 12.641:

$$
\begin{array}{r}
2.450 \\
1.300 \\
+\ 8.891 \\
\hline
12.641
\end{array}
$$

Subtraction with Decimals
Subtracting decimal numbers is the same process as adding decimals. Here is 7.89 – 4.235 written in column form:

$$
\begin{array}{r}
7.890 \\
-\ 4.235 \\
\hline
3.655
\end{array}
$$

A zero has been added in the column so that each number has the same number of places to the right of the decimal.

Multiplication with Decimals
Decimals can be multiplied as if there were no decimal points in the problem. For example, 0.5 x 1.25 can be rewritten and multiplied as 5 x 125, which equals 625.

The final answer will have the same number of decimal places as the total number of decimal places in the problem. The first number has one decimal place, and the second number has two decimal places. Therefore, the final answer will contain three decimal places:

$$0.5 \times 1.25 = 0.625$$

Division with Decimals
Dividing a decimal by a whole number entails using long division first by ignoring the decimal point. Then, the decimal point is moved the number of places given in the problem.

For example, 6.8 ÷ 4 can be rewritten as 68 ÷ 4, which is 17. There is one non-zero integer to the right of the decimal point, so the final solution would have one decimal place to the right of the solution. In this case, the solution is 1.7.

Dividing a decimal by another decimal requires changing the divisor to a whole number by moving its decimal point. The decimal place of the dividend should be moved by the same number of places as the divisor. Then, the problem is the same as dividing a decimal by a whole number.

For example, 5.72 ÷ 1.1 has a divisor with one decimal point in the denominator. The expression can be rewritten as 57.2 ÷ 11 by moving each number one decimal place to the right to eliminate the decimal. The long division can be completed as 572 ÷ 11 with a result of 52. Since there is one non-zero integer to the right of the decimal point in the problem, the final solution is 5.2.

In another example, 8 ÷ 0.16 has a divisor with two decimal points in the denominator. The expression can be rewritten as 800 ÷ 16 by moving each number two decimal places to the right to eliminate the decimal in the divisor. The long division can be completed with a result of 50.

Percentages

Think of percentages as fractions with a denominator of 100. In fact, **percentage** means "per hundred." Problems often require converting numbers from percentages, fractions, and decimals.

The basic percent equation is the following:

$$\frac{is}{of} = \frac{\%}{100}$$

The placement of numbers in the equation depends on what the question asks.

Example 1
Find 40% of 80.

Basically, the problem is asking, "What is 40% of 80?" The 40% is the percent, and 80 is the number to find the percent "of." The equation is:

$$\frac{x}{80} = \frac{40}{100}$$

Solving the equation by cross-multiplication, the problem becomes 100x = 80(40). Solving for x gives the answer: x = 32.

Example 2
What percent of 90 is 20?

The 20 fills in the "is" portion, while 90 fills in the "of." The question asks for the percent, so that will be x, the unknown. The following equation is set up:

$$\frac{20}{90} = \frac{x}{100}$$

Cross-multiplying yields the equation 90x = 20(100). Solving for x gives the answer of 22.2%.

Example 3
30% of what number is 30?

The following equation uses the clues and numbers in the problem:

$$\frac{30}{x} = \frac{30}{100}$$

Cross-multiplying results in the equation 30(100) = 30x. Solving for x gives the answer x = 100.

Conversions
Decimals and Percentages
Since a percentage is based on "per hundred," decimals and percentages can be converted by multiplying or dividing by 100. Practically speaking, this always involves moving the decimal point two places to the right or left, depending on the conversion. To convert a percentage to a decimal, move the decimal point two places to the left and remove the % sign. To convert a decimal to a percentage, move the decimal point two places to the right and add a "%" sign. Here are some examples:

65% = 0.65
0.33 = 33%
0.215 = 21.5%
99.99% = 0.9999
500% = 5.00
7.55 = 755%

Fractions and Percentages
Remember that a percentage is a number per one hundred. So a percentage can be converted to a fraction by making the number in the percentage the numerator and putting 100 as the denominator:

$$43\% = \frac{43}{100}$$

$$97\% = \frac{97}{100}$$

Note that the percent symbol (%) kind of looks like a 0, a 1, and another 0. So think of a percentage like 54% as 54 over 100.

To convert a fraction to a percent, follow the same logic. If the fraction happens to have 100 in the denominator, you're in luck. Just take the numerator and add a percent symbol:

$$\frac{28}{100} = 28\%$$

Otherwise, divide the numerator by the denominator to get a decimal:

$$\frac{9}{12} = 0.75$$

Then convert the decimal to a percentage:

$$0.75 = 75\%$$

Another option is to make the denominator equal to 100. Be sure to multiply the numerator by the same number as the denominator. For example:

$$\frac{3}{20} \times \frac{5}{5} = \frac{15}{100}$$

$$\frac{15}{100} = 15\%$$

Changing Fractions to Decimals

To change a fraction into a decimal, divide the denominator into the numerator until there are no remainders. There may be repeating decimals, so rounding is often acceptable. A straight line above the repeating portion denotes that the decimal repeats.

Example: Express 4/5 as a decimal.

Set up the division problem.

$$5\overline{)4}$$

5 does not go into 4, so place the decimal and add a zero.

$$5\overline{)4\,.\,0}$$

5 goes into 40 eight times. There is no remainder.

$$\begin{array}{r} 0\,.\,8 \\ 5\overline{)4\,.\,0} \\ -\ 4\,.\,0 \\ \hline 0 \end{array}$$

The solution is 0.8.

Example: Express 33 1/3 as a decimal.

Since the whole portion of the number is known, set it aside to calculate the decimal from the fraction portion.

Set up the division problem.

$$3\overline{)1}$$

3 does not go into 1, so place the decimal and add zeros. 3 goes into 10 three times.

$$\begin{array}{r} 0\,.\,3 \\ 3\overline{)1\,.\,0} \end{array}$$

This will repeat with a remainder of 1.

$$
\begin{array}{r}
0.333 \\
3\overline{)1.000} \\
-9 \\
\hline
10 \\
-9 \\
\hline
10
\end{array}
$$

So, we will place a line over the 3 to denote the repetition. The solution is written $0.\overline{3}$.

Changing Decimals to Fractions
To change decimals to fractions, place the decimal portion of the number—the numerator—over the respective place value—the denominator—then reduce, if possible.

Example: Express 0.25 as a fraction.

This is read as twenty-five hundredths, so put 25 over 100. Then reduce to find the solution.

$$
\frac{25}{100} = \frac{1}{4}
$$

Example: Express 0.455 as a fraction

This is read as four hundred fifty-five thousandths, so put 455 over 1000. Then reduce to find the solution.

$$
\frac{455}{1000} = \frac{91}{200}
$$

There are two types of problems that commonly involve percentages. The first is to calculate some percentage of a given quantity, where you convert the percentage to a decimal, and multiply the quantity by that decimal. Secondly, you are given a quantity and told it is a fixed percent of an unknown quantity. In this case, convert to a decimal, then divide the given quantity by that decimal.

Example: What is 30% of 760?

Convert the percent into a useable number. "Of" means to multiply.

$$
30\% = 0.30
$$

Set up the problem based on the givens, and solve.

$$
0.30 \times 760 = 228
$$

Example: 8.4 is 20% of what number?

Convert the percent into a useable number.

$$
20\% = 0.20
$$

The given number is a percent of the answer needed, so divide the given number by this decimal rather than multiplying it.

$$\frac{8.4}{0.20} = 42$$

Factorization

Factors are the numbers multiplied to achieve a product. Thus, every product in a multiplication equation has, at minimum, two factors. Of course, some products will have more than two factors. For the sake of most discussions, assume that factors are positive integers.

To find a number's factors, start with 1 and the number itself. Then divide the number by 2, 3, 4, and so on, seeing if any divisors can divide the number without a remainder, keeping a list of those that do. Stop upon reaching either the number itself or another factor.

Let's find the factors of 45. Start with 1 and 45. Then try to divide 45 by 2, which fails. Now divide 45 by 3. The answer is 15, so 3 and 15 are now factors. Dividing by 4 doesn't work, and dividing by 5 leaves 9. Lastly, dividing 45 by 6, 7, and 8 all don't work. The next integer to try is 9, but this is already known to be a factor, so the factorization is complete. The factors of 45 are 1, 3, 5, 9, 15 and 45.

Prime Factorization

Prime factorization involves an additional step after breaking a number down to its factors: breaking down the factors until they are all prime numbers. A **prime number** is any number that can only be divided by 1 and itself. The prime numbers between 1 and 20 are 2, 3, 5, 7, 11, 13, 17, and 19. As a simple test, numbers that are even or end in 5 are not prime, though there are other numbers that are not prime, but are odd and do not end in 5. For example, 21 is odd and divisible by 1, 3, 7, and 21, so it is not prime.

Let's break 129 down into its prime factors. First, the factors are 3 and 43. Both 3 and 43 are prime numbers, so we're done. But if 43 was not a prime number, then it would also need to be factorized until all of the factors are expressed as prime numbers.

Common Factor

A **common factor** is a factor shared by two numbers. Let's take 45 and 30 and find the common factors:

The factors of 45 are: 1, 3, 5, 9, 15, and 45.
The factors of 30 are: 1, 2, 3, 5, 6, 10, 15, and 30.
Thus, the common factors are 1, 3, 5, and 15.

Greatest Common Factor

The **greatest common factor** is the largest number among the shared, common factors. From the factors of 45 and 30, the common factors are 3, 5, and 15. Therefore, 15 is the greatest common factor, as it's the largest number.

Least Common Multiple

The **least common multiple** is the smallest number that's a multiple of two numbers. Let's try to find the least common multiple of 4 and 9. The multiples of 4 are 4, 8, 12, 16, 20, 24, 28, 32, 36, and so on. For 9, the multiples are 9, 18, 27, 36, 45, 54, etc. Thus, the least common multiple of 4 and 9 is 36 because this is the lowest number where 4 and 9 share multiples.

If two numbers share no factors besides 1 in common, then their least common multiple will be simply their product. If two numbers have common factors, then their least common multiple will be their product divided by their greatest common factor. This can be visualized by the formula $LCM = \frac{x \times y}{GCF}$, where x and y are some integers and LCM and GCF are their least common multiple and greatest common factor, respectively.

Exponents

An **exponent** is an operation used as shorthand for a number multiplied or divided by itself for a defined number of times.

$$3^7 = 3 \times 3 \times 3 \times 3 \times 3 \times 3 \times 3$$

In this example, the 3 is called the **base** and the 7 is called the **exponent**. The exponent is typically expressed as a superscript number near the upper right side of the base but can also be identified as the number following a caret symbol (^). This operation is verbally expressed as "3 to the 7th power" or "3 raised to the power of 7." Common exponents are 2 and 3. A base raised to the power of 2 is referred to as having been "squared," while a base raised to the power of 3 is referred to as having been "cubed."

Several special rules apply to exponents. First, the **Zero Power Rule** finds that any number raised to the zero power equals 1. For example, 100^0, 2^0, $(-3)^0$ and 0^0 all equal 1 because the bases are raised to the zero power.

Second, exponents can be negative. With negative exponents, the equation is expressed as a fraction, as in the following example:

$$3^{-7} = \frac{1}{3^7} = \frac{1}{3 \times 3 \times 3 \times 3 \times 3 \times 3 \times 3}$$

Third, the **Power Rule** concerns exponents being raised by another exponent. When this occurs, the exponents are multiplied by each other:

$$(x^2)^3 = x^6 = (x^3)^2$$

Fourth, when multiplying two exponents with the same base, the **Product Rule** requires that the base remains the same and the exponents are added. For example, $a^x \times a^y = a^{x+y}$. Since addition and multiplication are commutative, the two terms being multiplied can be in any order.

$$x^3 x^5 = x^{3+5} = x^8 = x^{5+3} = x^5 x^3$$

Fifth, when dividing two exponents with the same base, the **Quotient Rule** requires that the base remains the same, but the exponents are subtracted. So, $a^x \div a^y = a^{x-y}$. Since subtraction and division are not commutative, the two terms must remain in order.

$$x^5 x^{-3} = x^{5-3} = x^2 = x^5 \div x^3 = \frac{x^5}{x^3}$$

Additionally, 1 raised to any power is still equal to 1, and any number raised to the power of 1 is equal to itself. In other words, $a^1 = a$ and $14^1 = 14$.

Exponents play an important role in scientific notation to present extremely large or small numbers as follows: $a \times 10^b$. To write the number in scientific notation, the decimal is moved until there is only one digit on the left side of the decimal point, indicating that the number *a* has a value between 1 and 10. The number of times the decimal moves indicates the exponent to which 10 is raised, here represented by *b*. If the decimal moves to the left, then *b* is positive, but if the decimal moves to the right, then *b* is negative. The following examples demonstrate these concepts:

$$3,050 = 3.05 \times 10^3$$

$$-777 = -7.77 \times 10^2$$

$$0.000123 = 1.23 \times 10^{-4}$$

$$-0.0525 = -5.25 \times 10^{-2}$$

Roots

The **square root** symbol is expressed as $\sqrt{}$ and is commonly known as the radical. Taking the root of a number is the inverse operation of multiplying that number by itself some number of times. For example, squaring the number 7 is equal to 7 × 7, or 49. Finding the square root is the opposite of finding an exponent, as the operation seeks a number that when multiplied by itself, equals the number in the square root symbol.

For example, $\sqrt{36}$ = 6 because 6 multiplied by 6 equals 36. Note, the square root of 36 is also -6 since -6 × -6 = 36. This can be indicated using a **plus/minus** symbol like this: ±6. However, square roots are often just expressed as a positive number for simplicity, with it being understood that the true value can be either positive or negative.

Perfect squares are numbers with whole number square roots. The list of perfect squares begins with 0, 1, 4, 9, 16, 25, 36, 49, 64, 81, and 100.

Determining the square root of imperfect squares requires a calculator to reach an exact figure. It's possible, however, to approximate the answer by finding the two perfect squares that the number fits between. For example, the square root of 40 is between 6 and 7 since the squares of those numbers are 36 and 49, respectively.

Square roots are the most common root operation. If the radical doesn't have a number to the upper left of the symbol $\sqrt{}$, then it's a **square root**. Sometimes a radical includes a number in the upper left, like $\sqrt[3]{27}$, as in the other common root type—the **cube root**. Complicated roots, like the cube root, often require a calculator.

Estimation

Estimation is finding a value that is close to a solution, but is not the exact answer. For example, if there are values in the thousands to be multiplied, then each value can be estimated to the nearest thousand and the calculation performed. This value provides an approximate solution that can be determined very quickly.

Rounding is the process of either bumping a number up or down, based on a specified place value. First, the place value is specified. Then, the digit to its right is looked at. For example, if rounding to the nearest hundreds place, the digit in the tens place is used. If it is a 0, 1, 2, 3, or 4, the digit being rounded to is left alone. If it is a 5, 6, 7, 8 or 9, the digit being rounded to is increased by one. All other digits before the decimal point are then changed to zeros, and the digits in decimal places are dropped. If a decimal place is being rounded to, all subsequent digits are just dropped. For example, if 845,231.45 was to be rounded to the nearest thousands place, the answer would be 845,000. The 5 would remain the same due to the 2 in the hundreds place. Also, if 4.567 was to be rounded to the nearest tenths place, the answer would be 4.6. The 5 increased to 6 due to the 6 in the hundredths place, and the rest of the decimal is dropped.

Sometimes when performing operations such as multiplying numbers, the result can be estimated by rounding. For example, to estimate the value of 11.2×2.01, each number can be rounded to the nearest integer. This will yield a result of 22.

Rounding numbers helps with estimation because it changes the given number to a simpler, although less accurate, number than the exact given number. Rounding allows for easier calculations, which estimate the results of using the exact given number. The accuracy of the estimate and ease of use depends on the place value to which the number is rounded. Rounding numbers consists of:

- determining what place value the number is being rounded to
- examining the digit to the right of the desired place value to decide whether to round up or keep the digit, and
- replacing all digits to the right of the desired place value with zeros.

To round 746,311 to the nearest ten thousand, the digit in the ten thousands place should be located first. In this case, this digit is 4 (746,311). Then, the digit to its right is examined. If this digit is 5 or greater, the number will be rounded up by increasing the digit in the desired place by one. If the digit to the right of the place value being rounded is 4 or less, the number will be kept the same. For the given example, the digit being examined is a 6, which means that the number will be rounded up by increasing the digit to the left by one. Therefore, the digit 4 is changed to a 5. Finally, to write the rounded number, any digits to the left of the place value being rounded remain the same and any to its right are replaced with zeros. For the given example, rounding 746,311 to the nearest ten thousand will produce 750,000. To round 746,311 to the nearest hundred, the digit to the right of the three in the hundreds place is examined to determine whether to round up or keep the same number. In this case, that digit is a 1, so the number will be kept the same and any digits to its right will be replaced with zeros. The resulting rounded number is 746,300.

Rounding place values to the right of the decimal follows the same procedure, but digits being replaced by zeros can simply be dropped. To round 3.752891 to the nearest thousandth, the desired place value is located (3.752891) and the digit to the right is examined. In this case, the digit 8 indicates that the number will be rounded up, and the 2 in the thousandths place will increase to a 3. Rounding up and replacing the digits to the right of the thousandths place produces 3.753000 which is equivalent to 3.753. Therefore, the zeros are not necessary and the rounded number should be written as 3.753.

When rounding up, if the digit to be increased is a 9, the digit to its left is increased by 1 and the digit in the desired place value is changed to a zero. For example, the number 1,598 rounded to the nearest ten is 1,600. Another example shows the number 43.72961 rounded to the nearest thousandth is 43.730 or 43.73.

Vectors

A **vector** can be thought of as an abstract list of numbers or as giving a location in a space. For example, the coordinates (x, y) for points in the Cartesian plane are vectors. Each entry in a vector can be referred to by its location in the list: first, second, third, and so on. The total length of the list is the

85

dimension of the vector. A vector is often denoted as such by putting an arrow on top of it, e.g. $\vec{v} = (v_1, v_2, v_3)$.

Adding Vectors Graphically and Algebraically

There are two basic operations for vectors. First, two vectors can be added together. Let:

$$\vec{v} = (v_1, v_2, v_3)$$

$$\vec{w} = (w_1, w_2, w_3)$$

The the sum of the two vectors is defined to be:

$$\vec{v} + \vec{w} = (v_1 + w_1, v_2 + w_2, v_3 + w_3)$$

Subtraction of vectors can be defined similarly.

Vector addition can be visualized in the following manner. First, each vector can be visualized as an arrow. Then, the base of one arrow is placed at the tip of the other arrow. The tip of this first arrow now hits some point in space, and there will be an arrow from the origin to this point. This new arrow corresponds to the new vector. In subtraction, the direction of the arrow being subtracted is reversed.

For example, if adding together the vectors (-2, 3) and (4, 1), the new vector will be (-2 + 4, 3 + 1), or (2, 4). Graphically, this may be pictured in the following manner:

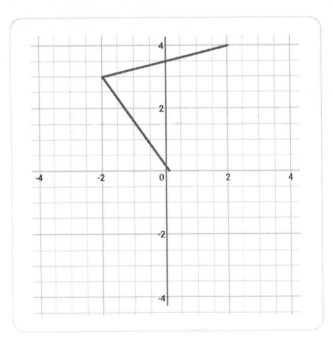

Performing Scalar Multiplications

The second basic operation for vectors is called **scalar multiplication**. Scalar multiplication is multiplying any vector by any real number, which is denoted here as a scalar. Let $\vec{v} = (v_1, v_2, v_3)$, and let a be an arbitrary real number. Then the scalar multiple $a\vec{v} = (av_1, av_2, av_3)$. Graphically, this corresponds to changing the length of the arrow corresponding to the vector by a factor, or scale, of a. That is why the real number is called a **scalar** in this instance.

As an example, let $\vec{v} = (2, -1, 1)$. Then $3\vec{v} = (3 \cdot 2, 3(-1), 3 \cdot 1) = (6, -3, 3)$.

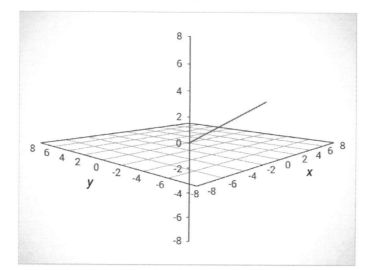

Note that scalar multiplication is **distributive** over vector addition, meaning that $a(\vec{v} + \vec{w}) = a\vec{v} + a\vec{w}$.

Determinants

A **matrix** is a rectangular arrangement of numbers in rows and columns. The **determinant** of a matrix is a special value that can be calculated for any square matrix.

Using the *square 2 x 2 matrix* $\begin{bmatrix} a & b \\ c & d \end{bmatrix}$, the determinant is $ad - bc$.

For example, the determinant of the matrix $\begin{bmatrix} -5 & 1 \\ 3 & 4 \end{bmatrix}$ is *-5(4) – 1(3) = -20 – 3 = -23.*

Using a *3 x 3 matrix* $\begin{bmatrix} a & b & c \\ d & e & f \\ g & h & i \end{bmatrix}$, the determinant is $a(ei - fh) - b(di - fg) + c(dh - eg)$.

For example, the determinant of the matrix $\begin{bmatrix} 2 & 0 & 1 \\ -1 & 3 & 2 \\ 2 & -2 & -1 \end{bmatrix}$ is

$$2(3(-1) - 2(-2)) - 0(-1(-1) - 2(2)) + 1(-1(-2) - 3(2))$$

$$= 2(-3 + 4) - 0(1 - 4) + 1(2 - 6)$$

$$= 2(1) - 0(-3) + 1(-4)$$

$$= 2 - 0 - 4 = -2$$

The pattern continues for larger square matrices.

Algebra

Algebraic Expressions and Equations

An **algebraic expression** is a statement about an unknown quantity expressed in mathematical symbols. A **variable** is used to represent the unknown quantity, usually denoted by a letter. An equation is a statement in which two expressions (at least one containing a variable) are equal to each other. An algebraic expression can be thought of as a mathematical phrase and an equation can be thought of as a mathematical sentence.

Algebraic expressions and equations both contain numbers, variables, and mathematical operations. The following are examples of algebraic expressions: $5x + 3$, $7xy - 8(x^2 + y)$, and $\sqrt{a^2 + b^2}$. An expression can be simplified or evaluated for given values of variables. The following are examples of equations: $2x + 3 = 7$, $a^2 + b^2 = c^2$, and $2x + 5 = 3x - 2$. An equation contains two sides separated by an equal sign. Equations can be solved to determine the value(s) of the variable for which the statement is true.

Parts of Expressions

Algebraic expressions consist of variables, numbers, and operations. A **term** of an expression is any combination of numbers and/or variables, and terms are separated by addition and subtraction. For example, the expression $5x^2 - 3xy + 4 - 2$ consists of 4 terms: $5x^2$, -3xy, 4y, and -2. Note that each term includes its given sign (+ or −). The **variable** part of a term is a letter that represents an unknown quantity. The **coefficient** of a term is the number by which the variable is multiplied. For the term 4y, the variable is y and the coefficient is 4. Terms are identified by the power (or exponent) of its variable.

A number without a variable is referred to as a **constant**. If the variable is to the first power (x^1 or simply x), it is referred to as a linear term. A term with a variable to the second power (x^2) is quadratic and a term to the third power (x^3) is cubic. Consider the expression $x^3 + 3x - 1$. The constant is -1. The linear term is 3x. There is no quadratic term. The cubic term is x^3.

An algebraic expression can also be classified by how many terms exist in the expression. Any like terms should be combined before classifying. A **monomial** is an expression consisting of only one term. Examples of monomials are: 17, 2x, and $-5ab^2$. A **binomial** is an expression consisting of two terms separated by addition or subtraction. Examples include $2x - 4$ and $-3y^2 + 2y$. A **trinomial** consists of 3 terms. For example, $5x^2 - 2x + 1$ is a trinomial.

Adding and Subtracting Linear Algebraic Expressions

An algebraic expression is simplified by combining like terms. As mentioned, term is a number, variable, or product of a number, and variables separated by addition and subtraction. For the algebraic expression $3x^2 - 4x + 5 - 5x^2 + x - 3$, the terms are $3x^2$, -4x, 5, $-5x^2$, x, and -3. Like terms have the same variables raised to the same powers (exponents). The like terms for the previous example are $3x^2$ and $-5x^2$, -4x and x, 5 and -3. To combine like terms, the coefficients (numerical factor of the term including sign) are added and the variables and their powers are kept the same. Note that if a coefficient is not written, it is an implied coefficient of 1 ($x = 1x$). The previous example will simplify to $-2x^2 - 3x + 2$.

When adding or subtracting algebraic expressions, each expression is written in parenthesis. The negative sign is distributed when necessary, and like terms are combined. Consider the following: add $2a + 5b - 2$ to $a - 2b + 8c - 4$. The sum is set as follows:

$$(a - 2b + 8c - 4) + (2a + 5b - 2)$$

In front of each set of parentheses is an implied positive one, which, when distributed, does not change any of the terms. Therefore, the parentheses are dropped and like terms are combined:

$$a - 2b + 8c - 4 + 2a + 5b - 2$$

$$3a + 3b + 8c - 6$$

Consider the following problem: Subtract $2a + 5b - 2$ from $a - 2b + 8c - 4$. The difference is set as follows:

$$(a - 2b + 8c - 4) - (2a + 5b - 2)$$

The implied one in front of the first set of parentheses will not change those four terms. However, distributing the implied -1 in front of the second set of parentheses will change the sign of each of those three terms:

$$a - 2b + 8c - 4 - 2a - 5b + 2$$

Combining like terms yields the simplified expression: $-a - 7b + 8c - 2$.

Distributive Property
The distributive property states that multiplying a sum (or difference) by a number produces the same result as multiplying each value in the sum (or difference) by the number and adding (or subtracting) the products. Using mathematical symbols, the distributive property states $a(b + c) = ab + ac$. The expression $4(3 + 2)$ is simplified using the order of operations. Simplifying inside the parenthesis first produces 4×5, which equals 20. The expression $4(3 + 2)$ can also be simplified using the distributive property:

$$4(3 + 2)$$

$$4 \times 3 + 4 \times 2$$

$$12 + 8 = 20$$

Consider the following example: $4(3x - 2)$. The expression cannot be simplified inside the parenthesis because $3x$ and -2 are not like terms, and therefore cannot be combined. However, the expression can be simplified by using the distributive property and multiplying each term inside of the parenthesis by the term outside of the parenthesis: $12x - 8$. The resulting equivalent expression contains no like terms, so it cannot be further simplified.

Consider the expression $(3x + 2y + 1) - (5x - 3) + 2(3y + 4)$. Again, there are no like terms, but the distributive property is used to simplify the expression. Note there is an implied one in front of the first set of parentheses and an implied -1 in front of the second set of parentheses.

Distributing the one, -1, and 2 produces:

$$1(3x) + 1(2y) + 1(1) - 1(5x) - 1(-3) + 2(3y) + 2(4)$$

$$3x + 2y + 1 - 5x + 3 + 6y + 8$$

This expression contains like terms that are combined to produce the simplified expression $-2x + 8y + 12$.

Algebraic expressions are tested to be equivalent by choosing values for the variables and evaluating both expressions (see 2.A.4). For example, $4(3x - 2)$ and $12x - 8$ are tested by substituting 3 for the variable x and calculating to determine if equivalent values result.

Evaluating Expressions for Given Values

An algebraic expression is a statement written in mathematical symbols, typically including one or more unknown values represented by variables. For example, the expression $2x + 3$ states that an unknown number (x) is multiplied by 2 and added to 3. If given a value for the unknown number, or variable, the value of the expression is determined. For example, if the value of the variable x is 4, the value of the expression 4 is multiplied by 2, and 3 is added. This results in a value of 11 for the expression.

When given an algebraic expression and values for the variable(s), the expression is evaluated to determine its numerical value. To evaluate the expression, the given values for the variables are substituted (or replaced) and the expression is simplified using the order of operations. Parenthesis should be used when substituting. Consider the following: Evaluate $a - 2b + ab$ for $a = 3$ and $b = -1$. To evaluate, any variable a is replaced with 3 and any variable b with -1, producing (3)-2(-1)+(3)(-1). Next, the order of operations is used to calculate the value of the expression, which is 2.

Verbal Statements and Algebraic Expressions

As mentioned, an algebraic expression is a statement about unknown quantities expressed in mathematical symbols. The statement *five times a number added to forty* is expressed as $5x + 40$. An equation is a statement in which two expressions (with at least one containing a variable) are equal to one another. The statement *five times a number added to forty is equal to ten* is expressed as $5x + 40 = 10$.

Real world scenarios can also be expressed mathematically. Suppose a job pays its employees $300 per week and $40 for each sale made. The weekly pay is represented by the expression $40x + 300$ where x is the number of sales made during the week.

Consider the following scenario: Bob had $20 and Tom had $4. After selling 4 ice cream cones to Bob, Tom has as much money as Bob. The cost of an ice cream cone is an unknown quantity and can be represented by a variable (x). The amount of money Bob has after his purchase is four times the cost of an ice cream cone subtracted from his original $20 → $20 - 4x$. The amount of money Tom has after his sale is four times the cost of an ice cream cone added to his original $4 → $4x + 4$. After the sale, the amount of money that Bob and Tom have are equal → $20 - 4x = 4x + 4$. Solving for x yields $x = 2$.

Use of Formulas

Formulas are mathematical expressions that define the value of one quantity, given the value of one or more different quantities. Formulas look like equations because they contain variables, numbers, operators, and an equal sign. All formulas are equations but not all equations are formulas. A formula must have more than one variable. For example, $2x + 7 = y$ is an equation and a formula (it relates the unknown quantities x and y). However, $2x + 7 = 3$ is an equation but not a formula (it only expresses the value of the unknown quantity x).

Formulas are typically written with one variable alone (or isolated) on one side of the equal sign. This variable can be thought of as the *subject* in that the formula is stating the value of the *subject* in terms of the relationship between the other variables. Consider the distance formula: $distance = rate \times time$ or $d = rt$. The value of the subject variable d (distance) is the product of the variable r and t (rate and time). Given the rate and time, the distance traveled can easily be determined by substituting the values into the formula and evaluating.

The formula $P = 2l + 2w$ expresses how to calculate the perimeter of a rectangle (P) given its length (l) and width (w). To find the perimeter of a rectangle with a length of 3ft and a width of 2ft, these values are substituted into the formula for l and w: $P = 2(3ft) + 2(2ft)$. Following the order of operations, the perimeter is determined to be 10ft. When working with formulas such as these, including units is an important step.

Given a formula expressed in terms of one variable, the formula can be manipulated to express the relationship in terms of any other variable. In other words, the formula can be rearranged to change which variable is the **subject.** To solve for a variable of interest by manipulating a formula, the equation may be solved as if all other variables were numbers. The same steps for solving are followed, leaving operations in terms of the variables instead of calculating numerical values. For the formula $P = 2l + 2w$, the perimeter is the subject expressed in terms of the length and width. To write a formula to calculate the width of a rectangle, given its length and perimeter, the previous formula relating the three variables is solved for the variable w. If P and l were numerical values, this is a two-step linear equation solved by subtraction and division. To solve the equation $P = 2l + 2w$ for w, $2l$ is first subtracted from both sides: $P - 2l = 2w$. Then both sides are divided by 2: $\frac{P-2l}{2} = w$.

Word Problems

Word problems can appear daunting, but prepared test takers shouldn't let the verbiage psyche them out. No matter the scenario or specifics, the key to answering them is to translate the words into a math problem. It is critical to keep in mind what the question is asking and what operations could lead to that answer. The following word problems highlight the most commonly tested question types.

Working with Money
Walter's Coffee Shop sells a variety of drinks and breakfast treats.

Price List	
Hot Coffee	$2.00
Slow Drip Iced Coffee	$3.00
Latte	$4.00
Muffins	$2.00
Crepe	$4.00
Egg Sandwich	$5.00

Costs	
Hot Coffee	$0.25
Slow Drip Iced Coffee	$0.75
Latte	$1.00
Muffins	$1.00
Crepe	$2.00
Egg Sandwich	$3.00

Walter's utilities, rent, and labor costs him $500 per day. Today, Walter sold 200 hot coffees, 100 slow drip iced coffees, 50 lattes, 75 muffins, 45 crepes, and 60 egg sandwiches. What was Walter's total profit today?

To accurately answer this type of question, the first step is to determine the total cost of making his drinks and treats, then determine how much revenue he earned from selling those products. After arriving at these two totals, the profit is measured by deducting the total cost from the total revenue.

Walter's costs for today:

200 hot coffees	× $0.25	= $50
100 slow drip iced coffees	× $0.75	= $75
50 lattes	× $1.00	= $50
75 muffins	× $1.00	= $75
45 crepes	× $2.00	= $90
60 egg sandwiches	× $3.00	= $180
Utilities, Rent, and Labor		= $500
Total costs		= $1,020

Walter's revenue for today:

200 hot coffees	× $2.00	= $400
100 slow drip iced coffees	× $3.00	= $300
50 lattes	× $4.00	= $200
75 muffins	× $2.00	= $150
45 crepes	× $4.00	= $180
60 egg sandwiches	× $5.00	= $300
Total revenue		= $1,530

Walter's $Profit = Revenue - Costs = \$1,530 - \$1,020 = \$510$

This strategy can be applied to other question types. For example, calculating salary after deductions, balancing a checkbook, and calculating a dinner bill are common word problems similar to business planning. In all cases, the most important step is remembering to use the correct operations. When a balance is increased, addition is used. When a balance is decreased, the problem requires subtraction. Common sense and organization are one's greatest assets when answering word problems.

Unit Rate
Unit rate word problems ask test takers to calculate the rate or quantity of something in a different value. For example, a problem might say that a car drove a certain number of miles in a certain number of minutes and then ask how many miles per hour the car was traveling. These questions involve solving proportions. Consider the following examples:

1. Alexandra made $96 during the first 3 hours of her shift as a temporary worker at a law office. She will continue to earn money at this rate until she finishes in 5 more hours. How much does Alexandra make per hour? How much money will Alexandra have made at the end of the day?

This problem can be solved in two ways. The first is to set up a proportion, as the rate of pay is constant. The second is to determine her hourly rate, multiply the 5 hours by that rate, and then adding the $96.

To set up a proportion, the money already earned (numerator) is placed over the hours already worked (denominator) on one side of an equation. The other side has x over 8 hours (the total hours worked in the day). It looks like this: $\frac{96}{3} = \frac{x}{8}$. Now, cross-multiply yields $768 = 3x$. To get x, the 768 is divided by 3, which leaves $x = 256$. Alternatively, as x is the numerator of one of the proportions, multiplying by its denominator will reduce the solution by one step. Thus, Alexandra will make $256 at the end of the day. To calculate her hourly rate, the total is divided by 8, giving $32 per hour.

Alternatively, it is possible to figure out the hourly rate by dividing $96 by 3 hours to get $32 per hour. Now her total pay can be figured by multiplying $32 per hour by 8 hours, which comes out to $256.

2. Jonathan is reading a novel. So far, he has read 215 of the 335 total pages. It takes Jonathan 25 minutes to read 10 pages, and the rate is constant. How long does it take Jonathan to read one page? How much longer will it take him to finish the novel? Express the answer in time.

To calculate how long it takes Jonathan to read one page, 25 minutes is divided by 10 pages to determine the page per minute rate. Thus, it takes 2.5 minutes to read one page.

Jonathan must read 120 more pages to complete the novel. (This is calculated by subtracting the pages already read from the total.) Now, his rate per page is multiplied by the number of pages. Thus, $120 \times 2.5 = 300$. Expressed in time, 300 minutes is equal to 5 hours.

3. At a hotel, $\frac{4}{5}$ of the 120 rooms are booked for Saturday. On Sunday, $\frac{3}{4}$ of the rooms are booked. On which day are more of the rooms booked, and by how many more?

The first step is to calculate the number of rooms booked for each day. This is done by multiplying the fraction of the rooms booked by the total number of rooms.

Saturday: $\frac{4}{5} \times 120 = \frac{4}{5} \times \frac{120}{1} = \frac{480}{5} = 96$ rooms

Sunday: $\frac{3}{4} \times 120 = \frac{3}{4} \times \frac{120}{1} = \frac{360}{4} = 90$ rooms

Thus, more rooms were booked on Saturday by 6 rooms.

4. In a veterinary hospital, the veterinarian-to-pet ratio is 1:9. The ratio is always constant. If there are 45 pets in the hospital, how many veterinarians are currently in the veterinary hospital?

A proportion is set up to solve for the number of veterinarians: $\frac{1}{9} = \frac{x}{45}$

Cross-multiplying results in $9x = 45$, which works out to 5 veterinarians.

Alternatively, as there are always 9 times as many pets as veterinarians, is it possible to divide the number of pets (45) by 9. This also arrives at the correct answer of 5 veterinarians.

5. At a general practice law firm, 30% of the lawyers work solely on tort cases. If 9 lawyers work solely on tort cases, how many lawyers work at the firm?

The first step is to solve for the total number of lawyers working at the firm, which will be represented here with x. The problem states that 9 lawyers work solely on torts cases, and they make up 30% of the total lawyers at the firm. Thus, 30% multiplied by the total, x, will equal 9. Written as equation, this is: $30\% \times x = 9$.

It's easier to deal with the equation after converting the percentage to a decimal, leaving $0.3x = 9$. Thus, $x = \frac{9}{0.3} = 30$ lawyers working at the firm.

6. Xavier was hospitalized with pneumonia. He was originally given 35mg of antibiotics. Later, after his condition continued to worsen, Xavier's dosage was increased to 60mg. What was the percent increase of the antibiotics? Round the percentage to the nearest tenth.

An increase or decrease in percentage can be calculated by dividing the difference in amounts by the original amount and multiplying by 100. Written as an equation, the formula is:

$$\frac{new\ quantity\ -\ old\ quantity}{old\ quantity} \times 100$$

Here, the question states that the dosage was increased from 35mg to 60mg, so these values are plugged into the formula to find the percentage increase.

$$\frac{60 - 35}{35} \times 100 = \frac{25}{35} \times 100 = .7142 \times 100 = 71.4\%$$

Linear Expressions or Equations in One Variable

Linear expressions and equations are concise mathematical statements that can be written to model a variety of scenarios. Questions found pertaining to this topic will contain one variable only. A variable is an unknown quantity, usually denoted by a letter (*x, n, p,* etc.). In the case of linear expressions and equations, the power of the variable (its exponent) is 1. A variable without a visible exponent is raised to the first power.

Writing Linear Expressions and Equations
A linear expression is a statement about an unknown quantity expressed in mathematical symbols. The statement "five times a number added to forty" can be expressed as $5x + 40$. A linear equation is a statement in which two expressions (at least one containing a variable) are equal to each other. The statement "five times a number added to forty is equal to ten" can be expressed as $5x + 40 = 10$. Real-world scenarios can also be expressed mathematically. Consider the following:

> Bob had $20 and Tom had $4. After selling 4 ice cream cones to Bob, Tom has as much money as Bob.

The cost of an ice cream cone is an unknown quantity and can be represented by a variable. The amount of money Bob has after his purchase is four times the cost of an ice cream cone subtracted from his original $20. The amount of money Tom has after his sale is four times the cost of an ice cream cone added to his original $4. This can be expressed as: $20 - 4x = 4x + 4$, where *x* represents the cost of an ice cream cone.

When expressing a verbal or written statement mathematically, it is key to understand words or phrases that can be represented with symbols. The following are examples:

Symbol	Phrase
$+$	added to, increased by, sum of, more than
$-$	decreased by, difference between, less than, take away
x	multiplied by, 3 (4, 5 . . .) times as large, product of
$\div$	divided by, quotient of, half (third, etc.) of
$=$	is, the same as, results in, as much as
$x, t, n, etc.$	a number, unknown quantity, value of

Solving Linear Equations

When asked to solve a linear equation, one must determine a numerical value for the unknown variable. Given a linear equation involving addition, subtraction, multiplication, and division, isolation of the variable is done by working backward. Addition and subtraction are inverse operations, as are multiplication and division; therefore, they can be used to cancel each other out.

The first steps to solving linear equations are to distribute if necessary and combine any like terms that are on the same side of the equation. Sides of an equation are separated by an $=$ sign. Next, the equation should be manipulated to get the variable on one side. Whatever is done to one side of an equation, must be done to the other side to remain equal. Then, the variable should be isolated by using inverse operations to undo the order of operations backward. Undo addition and subtraction, then undo multiplication and division. For example:

Solve $4(t - 2) + 2t - 4 = 2(9 - 2t)$

Distribute: $4t - 8 + 2t - 4 = 18 - 4t$

Combine like terms: $6t - 12 = 18 - 4t$

Add 4t to each side to move the variable: $10t - 12 = 18$

Add 12 to each side to isolate the variable: $10t = 30$

Divide each side by 10 to isolate the variable: $t = 3$

The answer can be checked by substituting the value for the variable into the original equation and ensuring both sides calculate to be equal.

Linear Inequalities in One Variable

Linear inequalities and linear equations are both comparisons of two algebraic expressions. However, unlike equations in which the expressions are equal to each other, linear inequalities compare expressions that are unequal. Linear equations typically have one value for the variable that makes the statement true. Linear inequalities generally have an infinite number of values that make the statement true. Exceptions to these last two statements are covered later on.

Writing Linear Inequalities

Linear inequalities are a concise mathematical way to express the relationship between unequal values. More specifically, they describe in what way the values are unequal. A value could be greater than ($>$); less than ($<$); greater than or equal to ($\geq$); or less than or equal to ($\leq$) another value. The statement "five times a number added to forty is more than sixty-five" can be expressed as $5x + 40 > 65$. Common words and phrases that express inequalities are:

Symbol	Phrase
$<$	is under, is below, smaller than, beneath
$>$	is above, is over, bigger than, exceeds
$\leq$	no more than, at most, maximum
$\geq$	no less than, at least, minimum

Solving Linear Inequalities

When solving a linear inequality, the solution is the set of all numbers that makes the statement true. The inequality $x + 2 \geq 6$ has a solution set of 4 and every number greater than 4 (4.0001, 5, 12, 107, etc.). Adding 2 to 4 or any number greater than 4 would result in a value that is greater than or equal to 6. Therefore, $x \geq 4$ would be the solution set.

Solution sets for linear inequalities often will be displayed using a number line. If a value is included in the set ($\geq$ or $\leq$), there is a shaded dot placed on that value and an arrow extending in the direction of the solutions. For a variable $>$ or $\geq$ a number, the arrow would point right on the number line (the direction where the numbers increase); and if a variable is $<$ or $\leq$ a number, the arrow would point left (where the numbers decrease). If the value is not included in the set ($>$ or $<$), an open circle on that value would be used with an arrow in the appropriate direction.

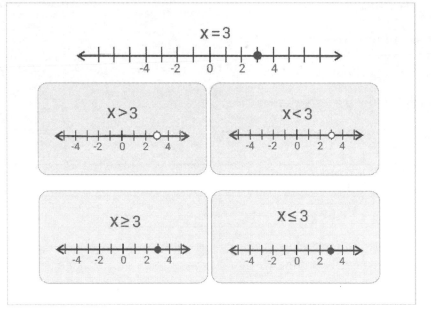

Students may be asked to write a linear inequality given a graph of its solution set. To do so, they should identify whether the value is included (shaded dot or open circle) and the direction in which the arrow is pointing.

In order to algebraically solve a linear inequality, the same steps should be followed as in solving a linear equation (see section on *Solving Linear Equations*). The inequality symbol stays the same for all operations EXCEPT when dividing by a negative number. If dividing by a negative number while solving an inequality, the relationship reverses (the sign flips). Dividing by a positive does not change the relationship, so the sign stays the same. In other words, $>$ switches to $<$ and vice versa. An example is shown below.

Solve $-2(x + 4) \leq 22$

Distribute: $-2x - 8 \leq 22$

Add 8 to both sides: $-2x \leq 30$

Divide both sides by -2: $x \geq 15$

Quadratic Equations

A **quadratic equation** is an equation in the form $ax^2 + bx + c = 0$. There are several methods to solve such equations. The easiest method will depend on the quadratic equation in question.

It sometimes is possible to solve quadratic equations by manually *factoring* them. This means rewriting them in the form $(x + A)(x + B) = 0$. If this is done, then they can be solved by remembering that when $ab = 0$, either a or b must be equal to zero. Therefore, to have $(x + A)(x + B) = 0$, $(x + A) = 0$ or $(x + B) = 0$ is needed. These equations have the solutions $x = -A$ and $x = -B$, respectively.

In order to factor a quadratic equation, note that $(x + A)(x + B) = x^2 + (A + B)x + AB$. So, if an equation is in the form $x^2 + bx + c$, two numbers, A and B, need to be found that will add up to give us b, and multiply together to give us c.

As an example, consider solving the equation $-3x^2 + 6x + 9 = 0$. Start by dividing both sides by -3, leaving $x^2 - 2x - 3 = 0$. Now, notice that $1 - 3 = -2$, and also that $(1)(-3) = -3$. This means the equation can be factored into $(x + 1)(x - 3) = 0$. Now, solve $(x + 1) = 0$ and $(x - 3) = 0$ to get $x = -1$ and $x = 3$ as the solutions.

It is useful when trying to factor to remember these three things:

$$x^2 + 2xy + y^2 = (x + y)^2$$

$$x^2 - 2xy + y^2 = (x - y)^2$$

and $x^2 - y^2 = (x + y)(x - y)$.

However, factoring by hand is often hard to do. If there are no obvious ways to factor the quadratic equation, solutions can still be found by using the *quadratic formula*.

The quadratic formula is:

$$x = \frac{-b \pm \sqrt{b^2 - 4ac}}{2a}$$

This method will always work, although it sometimes can take longer than factoring by hand, if the factors are easy to guess. Using the standard form $ax^2 + bx + c = 0$, plug the values of a, b, and c from the equation into the formula and solve for x. There will either be two answers, one answer, or no real answer. No real answer comes when the value of the discriminant, the number under the square root, is a negative number. Since there are no real numbers that square to get a negative, the answer will be no real roots.

Here is an example of solving a quadratic equation using the quadratic formula. Suppose the equation to solve is $-2x^2 + 3x + 1 = 0$. There is no obvious way to factor this, so the quadratic formula is used, with $a = -2, b = 3, c = 1$. After substituting these values into the quadratic formula, it yields this:

$$x = \frac{-3 \pm \sqrt{3^2 - 4(-2)(1)}}{2(-2)}$$

This can be simplified to obtain:

$$\frac{3 \pm \sqrt{9 + 8}}{4}$$

or

$$\frac{3 \pm \sqrt{17}}{4}$$

Challenges can be encountered when asked to find a quadratic equation with specific roots. Given roots A and B, a quadratic function can be constructed with those roots by taking $(x - A)(x - B)$. So, in constructing a quadratic equation with roots $x = -2, 3$, it would result in:

$$(x + 2)(x - 3) = x^2 - x - 6$$

Multiplying this by a constant also could be done without changing the roots.

Rewriting Expressions

Algebraic expressions are made up of numbers, variables, and combinations of the two, using mathematical operations. Expressions can be rewritten based on their factors. For example, the expression $6x + 4$ can be rewritten as $2(3x + 2)$ because 2 is a factor of both $6x$ and 4. More complex expressions can also be rewritten based on their factors. The expression $x^4 - 16$ can be rewritten as $(x^2 - 4)(x^2 + 4)$. This is a different type of factoring, where a difference of squares is factored into a sum and difference of the same two terms. With some expressions, the factoring process is simple and only leads to a different way to represent the expression. With others, factoring and rewriting the expression leads to more information about the given problem.

In the following quadratic equation, factoring the binomial leads to finding the zeros of the function:

$$x^2 - 5x + 6 = y$$

This equations factors into $(x - 3)(x - 2) = y$, where 2 and 3 are found to be the zeros of the function when y is set equal to zero. The zeros of any function are the x-values where the graph of the function on the coordinate plane crosses the x-axis.

Factoring an equation is a simple way to rewrite the equation and find the zeros, but factoring is not possible for every quadratic. Completing the square is one way to find zeros when factoring is not an option. The following equation cannot be factored: $x^2 + 10x - 9 = 0$. The first step in this method is to move the constant to the right side of the equation, making it $x^2 + 10x = 9$. Then, the coefficient of x is divided by 2 and squared. This number is then added to both sides of the equation, to make the equation still true. For this example, $\left(\frac{10}{2}\right)^2 = 25$ is added to both sides of the equation to obtain:

$$x^2 + 10x + 25 = 9 + 25$$

This expression simplifies to $x^2 + 10x + 25 = 34$, which can then be factored into $(x + 5)^2 = 34$. Solving for x then involves taking the square root of both sides and subtracting 5.

This leads to two zeros of the function:

$$x = \pm\sqrt{34} - 5$$

Depending on the type of answer the question seeks, a calculator may be used to find exact numbers.

Given a **quadratic equation in standard form**— $ax^2 + bx + c = 0$—the sign of a tells whether the function has a minimum value or a maximum value. If $a > 0$, the graph opens up and has a minimum value. If $a < 0$, the graph opens down and has a maximum value. Depending on the way the quadratic equation is written, multiplication may need to occur before a max/min value is determined.

Exponential expressions can also be rewritten, just as quadratic equations. Properties of exponents must be understood. Multiplying two exponential expressions with the same base involves adding the exponents:

$$a^m a^n = a^{m+n}$$

Dividing two exponential expressions with the same base involves subtracting the exponents:

$$\frac{a^m}{a^n} = a^{m-n}$$

Raising an exponential expression to another exponent includes multiplying the exponents:

$$(a^m)^n = a^{mn}$$

The zero power always gives a value of 1: $a^0 = 1$. Raising either a product or a fraction to a power involves distributing that power:

$$(ab)^m = a^m b^m \text{ and } \left(\frac{a}{b}\right)^m = \frac{a^m}{b^m}$$

Finally, raising a number to a negative exponent is equivalent to the reciprocal including the positive exponent:

$$a^{-m} = \frac{1}{a^m}$$

Polynomials

An expression of the form ax^n, where n is a non-negative integer, is called a **monomial** because it contains one term. A sum of monomials is called a **polynomial**. For example, $-4x^3 + x$ is a polynomial, while $5x^7$ is a monomial. A function equal to a polynomial is called a **polynomial function**.

The monomials in a polynomial are also called the **terms** of the polynomial.

The constants that precede the variables are called **coefficients.**

The highest value of the exponent of x in a polynomial is called the **degree** of the polynomial. So, $-4x^3 + x$ has a degree of 3, while $-2x^5 + x^3 + 4x + 1$ has a degree of 5. When multiplying polynomials, the degree of the result will be the sum of the degrees of the two polynomials being multiplied.

Addition and subtraction operations can be performed on polynomials with like terms. **Like terms** refers to terms that have the same variable and exponent. The two following polynomials can be added together by collecting like terms:

$$(x^2 + 3x - 4) + (4x^2 - 7x + 8)$$

The x^2 terms can be added as $x^2 + 4x^2 = 5x^2$. The x terms can be added as $3x + -7x = -4x$, and the constants can be added as $-4 + 8 = 4$. The following expression is the result of the addition:

$$5x^2 - 4x + 4$$

When subtracting polynomials, the same steps are followed, only subtracting like terms together.

Multiplication of polynomials can also be performed. Given the two polynomials, $(y^3 - 4)$ and $(x^2 + 8x - 7)$, each term in the first polynomial must be multiplied by each term in the second polynomial. The steps to multiply each term in the given example are as follows:

$$(y^3 \times x^2) + (y^3 \times 8x) + (y^3 \times -7) + (-4 \times x^2) + (-4 \times 8x) + (-4 \times -7)$$

Simplifying each multiplied part, yields:

$$x^2y^3 + 8xy^3 - 7y^3 - 4x^2 - 32x + 28$$

None of the terms can be combined because there are no like terms in the final expression. Any polynomials can be multiplied by each other by following the same set of steps, then collecting like terms at the end.

FOIL Method

FOIL is a technique for generating polynomials through the multiplication of binomials. A **polynomial** is an expression of multiple variables (for example, x, y, z) in at least three terms involving only the four basic operations and exponents. FOIL is an acronym for First, Outer, Inner, and Last. "First" represents the multiplication of the terms appearing first in the binomials. "Outer" means multiplying the outermost terms. "Inner" means multiplying the terms inside. "Last" means multiplying the last terms of each binomial.

After completing FOIL and solving the operations, **like terms** are combined. To identify like terms, test takers should look for terms with the same variable and the same exponent. For example, in $4x^2 - x^2 + 15x + 2x^2 - 8$, the $4x^2$, $-x^2$, and $2x^2$ are all like terms because they have the variable (x) and exponent (2). Thus, after combining the like terms, the polynomial has been simplified to $5x^2 + 15x - 8$.

The purpose of FOIL is to simplify an equation involving multiple variables and operations. Although it sounds complicated, working through some examples will provide some clarity:

1. Simplify $(x + 10)(x + 4) =$

$$\underset{\text{First}}{(x \times x)} + \underset{\text{Outer}}{(x \times 4)} + \underset{\text{Inner}}{(10 \times x)} + \underset{\text{Last}}{(10 \times 4)}$$

After multiplying these binomials, it's time to solve the operations and combine like terms. Thus, the expression becomes: $2x^2 + 4x + 10x + 40 = 2x^2 + 14x + 40$.

2. Simplify $2x(4x^3 - 7y^2 + 3x^2 + 4)$

Here, a monomial ($2x$) is multiplied into a polynomial ($4x^3 - 7y^2 + 3x^2 + 4$). Using the distributive property, the monomial gets multiplied by each term in the polynomial. This becomes $2x(4x^3) - 2x(7y^2) + 2x(3x^2) + 2x(4)$.

Now, each monomial is simplified, starting with the coefficients:

$$(2 \times 4)(x \times x^3) - (2 \times 7)(x \times y^2) + (2 \times 3)(x \times x^2) + (2 \times 4)(x)$$

When multiplying powers with the same base, their exponents are added. Remember, a variable with no listed exponent has an exponent of 1, and exponents of distinct variables cannot be combined. This produces the answer:

$$8x^{1+3} - 14xy^2 + 6x^{1+2} + 8x = 8x^4 - 14xy^2 + 6x^3 + 8x$$

3. Simplify $(8x^{10}y^2z^4) \div (4x^2y^4z^7)$

The first step is to divide the coefficients of the first two polynomials: $8 \div 4 = 2$. The second step is to divide exponents with the same variable, which requires subtracting the exponents. This results in:

$$2(x^{10-2}y^{2-4}z^{4-7}) = 2x^8y^{-2}z^{-3}$$

However, the most simplified answer should include only positive exponents. Thus, $y^{-2}z^{-3}$ needs to be converted into fractions, respectively $\frac{1}{y^2}$ and $\frac{1}{z^3}$. Since the $2x^8$ has a positive exponent, it is placed in the numerator, and $\frac{1}{y^2}$ and $\frac{1}{z^3}$ are combined into the denominator, leaving $\frac{2x^8}{y^2z^3}$ as the final answer.

Zeros of Polynomials

Finding the **zeros of polynomial functions** is the same process as finding the solutions of polynomial equations. These are the points at which the graph of the function crosses the x-axis. As stated previously, factors can be used to find the zeros of a polynomial function. The degree of the function shows the number of possible zeros. If the highest exponent on the independent variable is 4, then the degree is 4, and the number of possible zeros is 4. If there are complex solutions, the number of roots is less than the degree.

Given the function $y = x^2 + 7x + 6$, y can be set equal to zero, and the polynomial can be factored. The equation turns into $0 = (x + 1)(x + 6)$, where $x = -1$ and $x = -6$ are the zeros. Since this is a quadratic equation, the shape of the graph will be a parabola. Knowing that zeros represent the points where the parabola crosses the x-axis, the maximum or minimum point is the only other piece needed to sketch a rough graph of the function. By looking at the function in standard form, the coefficient of x is positive; therefore, the parabola opens up. Using the zeros and the minimum, the following rough sketch of the graph can be constructed:

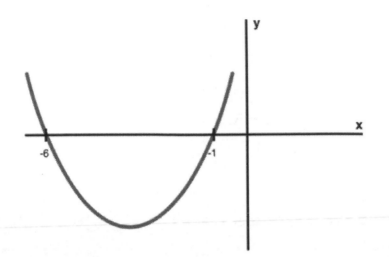

Rational Expressions and Equations

A **rational expression** is a fraction where the numerator and denominator are both polynomials. Some examples of rational expressions include the following: $\frac{4x^3y^5}{3z^4}$, $\frac{4x^3+3x}{x^2}$, and $\frac{x^2+7x+10}{x+2}$. Since these refer to expressions and not equations, they can be simplified but not solved. Using the rules in the previous *Exponents* and *Roots* sections, some rational expressions with monomials can be simplified. Other rational expressions such as the last example, $\frac{x^2+7x+10}{x+2}$, require more steps to be simplified. First, the polynomial on top can be factored from $x^2 + 7x + 10$ into $(x + 5)(x + 2)$. Then the common factors can be canceled and the expression can be simplified to $(x + 5)$.

The following problem is an example of using rational expressions:

Reggie wants to lay sod in his rectangular backyard. The length of the yard is given by the expression $4x + 2$ and the width is unknown. The area of the yard is $20x + 10$. Reggie needs to find the width of the yard. Knowing that the area of a rectangle is length multiplied by width, an expression can be written to find the width: $\frac{20x+10}{4x+2}$, area divided by length. Simplifying this expression by factoring out 10 on the top and 2 on the bottom leads to this expression:

$$\frac{10(2x + 1)}{2(2x + 1)}$$

Canceling out the $2x + 1$ results in $\frac{10}{2} = 5$. The width of the yard is found to be 5 by simplifying the rational expression.

A **rational equation** can be as simple as an equation with a ratio of polynomials, $\frac{p(x)}{q(x)}$, set equal to a value, where $p(x)$ and $q(x)$ are both polynomials. A rational equation has an equal sign, which is different from expressions. This leads to solutions, or numbers that make the equation true.

It is possible to solve rational equations by trying to get all of the x terms out of the denominator and then isolating them on one side of the equation. For example, to solve the equation $\frac{3x+2}{2x+3} = 4$, both sides get multiplied by $(2x + 3)$. This will cancel on the left side to yield:

$$3x + 2 = 4(2x + 3)$$

Then:

$$3x + 2 = 8x + 12$$

Now, subtract $8x$ from both sides, which yields $-5x + 2 = 12$. Subtracting 2 from both sides results in $-5x = 10$. Finally, both sides get divided by -5 to obtain $x = -2$.

Sometimes, when solving rational equations, it can be easier to try to simplify the rational expression by factoring the numerator and denominator first, then cancelling out common factors. For example, to solve $\frac{2x^2-8x+6}{x^2-3x+2} = 1$, the first step is to factor:

$$2x^2 - 8x + 6$$

$$2(x^2 - 4x + 3)$$

$$2(x - 1)(x - 3)$$

Then, factor $x^2 - 3x + 2$ into $(x - 1)(x - 2)$. This turns the original equation into:

$$\frac{2(x - 1)(x - 3)}{(x - 1)(x - 2)} = 1$$

The common factor of $(x - 1)$ can be canceled, leaving $\frac{2(x-3)}{x-1} = 1$. Now the same method used in the previous example can be followed. Multiplying both sides by $x - 1$ and performing the multiplication on the left yields $2x - 6 = x - 1$, which can be simplified to $x = 5$.

Matrices

As mentioned, **matrices** can be used to represent linear equations, solve systems of equations, and manipulate data to simulate change. Matrices consist of numerical entries in both rows and columns. The following matrix A is a 3×4 matrix because it has three rows and four columns:

$$A = \begin{bmatrix} 3 & 2 & -5 & 3 \\ 3 & 6 & 2 & -5 \\ -1 & 3 & 7 & 0 \end{bmatrix}$$

Matrices can be added or subtracted only if they have the same dimensions. For example, the following matrices can be added by adding corresponding matrix entries:

$$\begin{bmatrix} 3 & 4 \\ 2 & 6 \end{bmatrix} + \begin{bmatrix} -1 & 4 \\ 4 & 2 \end{bmatrix} = \begin{bmatrix} 2 & 8 \\ 6 & -4 \end{bmatrix}$$

Multiplication can also be used to manipulate matrices. *Scalar multiplication* involves multiplying a matrix by a constant. Each matrix entry needs to be multiplied times the constant. The following example shows a 3 × 2 matrix being multiplied by the constant 6:

$$6 \times \begin{bmatrix} 3 & 4 \\ 2 & -6 \\ 1 & 0 \end{bmatrix} = \begin{bmatrix} 18 & 24 \\ 12 & -36 \\ 6 & 0 \end{bmatrix}$$

Matrix multiplication of two matrices involves finding multiple dot products. The **dot product** of a row and column is the sum of the products of each corresponding row and column entry. In the following example, a 2 × 2 matrix is multiplied by a 2 × 2 matrix. The dot product of the first row and column is $(2 \times 1) + (1 \times 2) = (2) + (2) = 4$.

$$\begin{bmatrix} 2 & 1 \\ 3 & 5 \end{bmatrix} \times \begin{bmatrix} 1 & 4 \\ 2 & 0 \end{bmatrix} = \begin{bmatrix} 4 & 8 \\ 13 & 12 \end{bmatrix}$$

The same process is followed to find the other three values in the solution matrix. Matrices can only be multiplied if the number of columns in the first matrix equals the number of rows in the second matrix. The previous example is also an example of square matrix multiplication because they are both square matrices. A **square matrix** has the same number of rows and columns. For square matrices, the order in which they are multiplied does matter. Therefore, matrix multiplication does not satisfy the commutative property. It does, however, satisfy the associative and distributive properties.

Another transformation of matrices can be found by using the **identity matrix**—also referred to as the "I" matrix. The identity matrix is similar to the number one in normal multiplication. The identity matrix is a square matrix with ones in the diagonal spots and zeros everywhere else. The identity matrix is also the result of multiplying a matrix by its inverse. This process is similar to multiplying a number by its reciprocal.

The **zero matrix** is also a matrix acting as an additive identity. The zero matrix consists of zeros in every entry. It does not change the values of a matrix when using addition.

Given a system of linear equations, a matrix can be used to represent the entire system. Operations can then be performed on the matrix to solve the system. The following system offers an example:

$$x + y + z = 4$$

$$y + 3z = -2$$

$$2x + y - 2z = 12$$

There are three variables and three equations. The coefficients in the equations can be used to form a 3 x 3 matrix:

$$\begin{bmatrix} 1 & 1 & 1 \\ 0 & 1 & 3 \\ 2 & 1 & -2 \end{bmatrix}$$

The number of rows equals the number of equations, and the number of columns equals the number of variables. The numbers on the right side of the equations can be turned into a 3 x 1 matrix. That matrix is shown here:

$$\begin{bmatrix} 4 \\ -2 \\ 12 \end{bmatrix}$$

It can also be referred to as a *vector*. The variables are represented in a matrix of their own:

$$\begin{bmatrix} x \\ y \\ z \end{bmatrix}$$

The system can be represented by the following matrix equation:

$$\begin{bmatrix} 1 & 1 & 1 \\ 0 & 1 & 3 \\ 2 & 1 & -2 \end{bmatrix} \begin{bmatrix} x \\ y \\ z \end{bmatrix} = \begin{bmatrix} 4 \\ -2 \\ 12 \end{bmatrix}$$

Simply, this is written as $AX = B$. By using the inverse of a matrix, the solution can be found: $X = A^{-1}B$. Once the inverse of A is found using operations, it is then multiplied by B to find the solution to the system: $x = 12, y = -8,$ and $z = 2$.

The determinant of a 2 x 2 matrix is the following:

$$|A| = \begin{vmatrix} a & b \\ c & d \end{vmatrix} = ad - bc$$

It is a number related to the size of the matrix. The absolute value of the determinant of matrix A is equal to the area of a parallelogram with vertices $(0, 0)$, $(a. b)$, (c, d), and $(a + b, c + d)$.

Systems of Equations

A **system of equations** is a group of equations that have the same variables or unknowns. These equations can be linear, but they are not always so. Finding a solution to a system of equations means finding the values of the variables that satisfy each equation. For a linear system of two equations and two variables, there could be a single solution, no solution, or infinitely many solutions.

A single solution occurs when there is one value for *x* and *y* that satisfies the system. This would be shown on the graph where the lines cross at exactly one point. When there is no solution, the lines are parallel and do not ever cross. With infinitely many solutions, the equations may look different, but they are the same line. One equation will be a multiple of the other, and on the graph, they lie on top of each other.

The **process of elimination** can be used to solve a system of equations. For example, the following equations make up a system: $x + 3y = 10$ and $2x - 5y = 9$. Immediately adding these equations does not eliminate a variable, but it is possible to change the first equation by multiplying the whole equation by -2. This changes the first equation to $-2x - 6y = -20$. The equations can be then added to obtain $-11y = -11$. Solving for y yields $y = 1$. To find the rest of the solution, 1 can be substituted in for y in either original equation to find the value of $x = 7$. The solution to the system is (7, 1) because it makes both equations true, and it is the point in which the lines intersect. If the system is **dependent**—having infinitely many solutions—then both variables will cancel out when the elimination method is used, resulting in an equation that is true for many values of x and y. Since the system is dependent, both equations can be simplified to the same equation or line.

A system can also be solved using **substitution.** This involves solving one equation for a variable and then plugging that solved equation into the other equation in the system. This equation can be solved for one variable, which can then be plugged in to either original equation and solved for the other variable. For example, $x - y = -2$ and $3x + 2y = 9$ can be solved using substitution. The first equation can be solved for x, where $x = -2 + y$. Then it can be plugged into the other equation: $3(-2 + y) + 2y = 9$. Solving for y yields $-6 + 3y + 2y = 9$, where $y = 3$. If $y = 3$, then $x = 1$. This solution can be checked by plugging in these values for the variables in each equation to see if it makes a true statement.

Finally, a solution to a system of equations can be found graphically. The solution to a linear system is the point or points where the lines cross. The values of x and y represent the coordinates (x, y) where the lines intersect. Using the same system of equation as above, they can be solved for y to put them in slope-intercept form, $y = mx + b$. These equations become $y = x + 2$ and $y = -\frac{3}{2}x + 4.5$. This system with the solution is shown below:

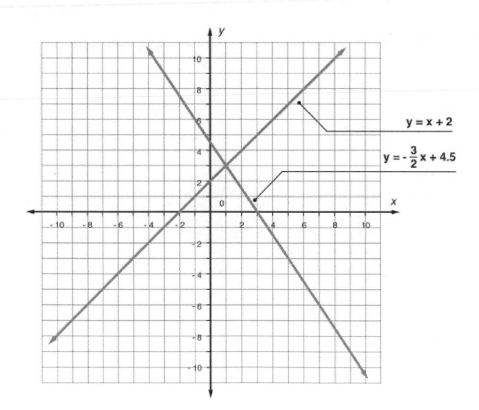

A system of equations may also be made up of a linear and a quadratic equation. These systems may have one solution, two solutions, or no solutions. The graph of these systems involves one straight line and one parabola. Algebraically, these systems can be solved by solving the linear equation for one variable and plugging that answer in to the quadratic equation. If possible, the equation can then be solved to find part of the answer. The graphing method is commonly used for these types of systems. On a graph, these two lines can be found to intersect at one point, at two points across the parabola, or at no points.

Finding solutions to systems of equations is essentially finding what values of the variables make both equations true. It is finding the input value that yields the same output value in both equations. For functions $g(x)$ and $f(x)$, the equation $g(x) = f(x)$ means the output values are being set equal to each other. Solving for the value of x means finding the x-coordinate that gives the same output in both functions. For example, $f(x) = x + 2$ and $g(x) = -3x + 10$ is a system of equations. Setting $f(x) = g(x)$ yields the equation $x + 2 = -3x + 10$. Solving for x, gives the x-coordinate $x = 2$ where the two lines cross. This value can also be found by using a table or a graph. On a table, both equations can be given the same inputs, and the outputs can be recorded to find the point(s) where the lines cross. Any method of solving finds the same solution, but some methods are more appropriate for some systems of equations than others.

Systems of **linear inequalities** are like systems of equations, but the solutions are different. Since inequalities have infinitely many solutions, their systems also have infinitely many solutions. Finding the solutions of inequalities involves graphs. A system of two equations and two inequalities is linear; thus, the lines can be graphed using slope-intercept form. If the inequality has an equals sign, the line is solid. If the inequality only has a greater than or less than symbol, the line on the graph is dotted. Dashed lines indicate that points lying on the line are not included in the solution. After the lines are graphed, a region is shaded on one side of the line. This side is found by determining if a point—known as a **test point**—lying on one side of the line produces a true inequality. If it does, that side of the graph is shaded. If the point produces a false inequality, the line is shaded on the opposite side from the point. The graph of a system of inequalities involves shading the intersection of the two shaded regions.

Functions

Functions

A **function** is defined as a relationship between inputs and outputs where there is only one output value for a given input. As an example, the following function is in function notation: $f(x) = 3x - 4$. The $f(x)$ represents the output value for an input of x. If $x = 2$, the equation becomes:

$$f(2) = 3(2) - 4$$

$$6 - 4 = 2$$

The input of 2 yields an output of 2, forming the ordered pair $(2, 2)$. The following set of ordered pairs corresponds to the given function: $(2, 2), (0, -4), (-2, -10)$. The set of all possible inputs of a function is its **domain**, and all possible outputs is called the **range**. By definition, each member of the domain is paired with only one member of the range.

Functions can also be defined recursively. In this form, they are not defined explicitly in terms of variables. Instead, they are defined using previously-evaluated function outputs, starting with either $f(0)$ or $f(1)$. An example of a recursively-defined function is:

$$f(1) = 2$$

$$f(n) = 2f(n-1) + 2n$$

$$n > 1$$

The domain of this function is the set of all integers.

A function $f(x)$ is a mathematical object which takes one number, x, as an input and gives a number in return. The input is called the **independent variable**. If the variable is set equal to the output, as in $y = f(x)$, then this is called the **dependent variable**. To indicate the dependent value a function, y, gives for a specific independent variable, x, the notation y = $f(x)$ is used.

The **domain** of a function is the set of values that the independent variable is allowed to take. Unless otherwise specified, the domain is any value for which the function is well defined. The **range** of the function is the set of possible outputs for the function.

In many cases, a function can be defined by giving an equation. For instance, $f(x) = x^2$ indicates that given a value for x, the output of f is found by squaring x.

Not all equations in x and y can be written in the form $y = f(x)$. An equation can be written in such a form if it satisfies the **vertical line test**: no vertical line meets the graph of the equation at more than a single point. In this case, y is said to be a *function of x*. If a vertical line meets the graph in two places, then this equation cannot be written in the form $y = f(x)$.

The graph of a function $f(x)$ is the graph of the equation $y = f(x)$. Thus, it is the set of all pairs (x, y) where $y = f(x)$. In other words, it is all pairs $(x, f(x))$. The x-intercepts are called the **zeros** of the function. The y-intercept is given by $f(0)$.

If, for a given function f, the only way to get $f(a) = f(b)$ is for $a = b$, then f is *one-to-one*. Often, even if a function is not one-to-one on its entire domain, it is one-to-one by considering a restricted portion of the domain.

A function $f(x) = k$ for some number k is called a **constant function**. The graph of a constant function is a horizontal line.

The function $f(x) = x$ is called the **identity function**. The graph of the identity function is the diagonal line pointing to the upper right at 45 degrees, $y = x$.

A function is called **monotone** if it is either always increasing or always decreasing. For example, the functions $f(x) = 3x$ and $f(x) = -x^5$ are monotone.

An **even function** looks the same when flipped over the y-axis: $f(x) = f(-x)$. The following image shows a graphic representation of an even function.

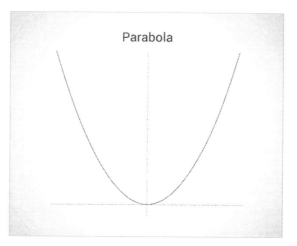

Parabola

An **odd function** looks the same when flipped over the y-axis and then flipped over the x-axis: $f(x) = -f(-x)$. The following image shows an example of an odd function.

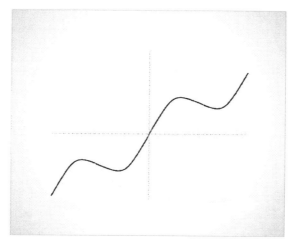

Domain and Range

The domain and range of a function can be found visually by its plot on the coordinate plane. In the function $f(x) = x^2 - 3$, for example, the domain is all real numbers because the parabola stretches as far left and as far right as it can go, with no restrictions. This means that any input value from the real number system will yield an answer in the real number system. For the range, the inequality $y \geq -3$ would be used to describe the possible output values because the parabola has a minimum at $y = -3$. This means there will not be any real output values less than -3 because -3 is the lowest value it reaches on the y-axis.

These same answers for domain and range can be found by observing a table. The table below shows that from input values $x = -1$ to $x = 1$, the output results in a minimum of -3. On each side of $x = 0$, the numbers increase, showing that the range is all real numbers greater than or equal to -3.

x (domain/input)	y (range/output)
-2	1
-1	-2
0	-3
-1	-2
2	1

Function Behavior

Different types of functions behave in different ways. A function is defined to be increasing over a subset of its domain if for all $x_1 \geq x_2$ in that interval, $f(x_1) \geq f(x_2)$. Also, a function is decreasing over an interval if for all $x_1 \geq x_2$ in that interval, $f(x_1) \leq f(x_2)$. A point in which a function changes from increasing to decreasing can also be labeled as the **maximum value** of a function if it is the largest point the graph reaches on the y-axis. A point in which a function changes from decreasing to increasing can be labeled as the minimum value of a function if it is the smallest point the graph reaches on the y-axis. Maximum values are also known as **extreme values**. The graph of a continuous function does not have any breaks or jumps in the graph. This description is not true of all functions. A radical function, for example, $f(x) = \sqrt{x}$, has a restriction for the domain and range because there are no real negative inputs or outputs for this function. The domain can be stated as $x \geq 0$, and the range is $y \geq 0$.

Logarithmic and exponential functions also have different behavior than other functions. These two types of functions are inverses of each other. The **inverse** of a function can be found by switching the place of x and y, and solving for y. When this is done for the exponential equation, $y = 2^x$, the function $y = \log_2 x$ is found. The general form of a **logarithmic function** is $y = \log_b x$, which says b raised to the y power equals x.

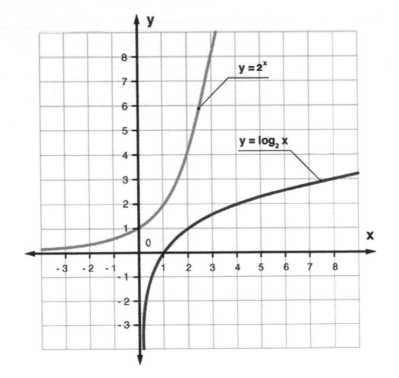

The thick black line on the graph above represents the logarithmic function $y = \log_2 x$. This curve passes through the point $(1, 0)$, just as all log functions do, because any value $b^0 = 1$. The graph of this logarithmic function starts very close to zero but does not touch the y-axis. The output value will never be zero by the definition of logarithms. The thinner gray line seen above represents the exponential function $y = 2^x$. The behavior of this function is opposite the logarithmic function because the graph of an inverse function is the graph of the original function flipped over the line $y = x$. The curve passes through the point $(0, 1)$ because any number raised to the zero power is one. This curve also gets very close to the x-axis but never touches it because an exponential expression never has an output of zero. The x-axis on this graph is called a horizontal asymptote. An **asymptote** is a line that represents a boundary for a function. It shows a value that the function will get close to, but never reach.

Functions can also be described as being even, odd, or neither. If $f(-x) = f(x)$, the function is even. For example, the function $f(x) = x^2 - 2$ is even. Plugging in $x = 2$ yields an output of $y = 2$. After changing the input to $x = -2$, the output is still $y = 2$. The output is the same for opposite inputs. Another way to observe an even function is by the symmetry of the graph. If the graph is symmetrical about the axis, then the function is even. If the graph is symmetric about the origin, then the function is odd. Algebraically, if $f(-x) = -f(x)$, the function is odd.

Also, a function can be described as **periodic** if it repeats itself in regular intervals. Common periodic functions are trigonometric functions. For example, $y = \sin x$ is a periodic function with period 2π because it repeats itself every 2π units along the x-axis.

Linear Functions

A function is called **linear** if it can take the form of the equation $f(x) = ax + b$, or $y = ax + b$, for any two numbers a and b. A linear equation forms a straight line when graphed on the coordinate plane. An example of a linear function is shown below on the graph.

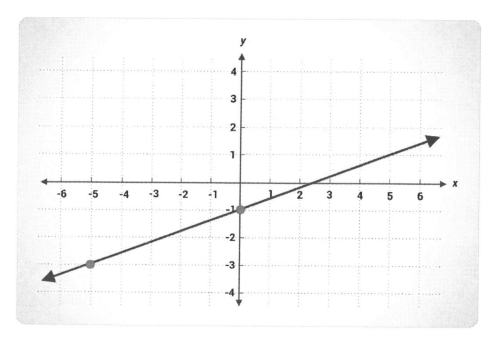

This is a graph of the following function:

$$y = \frac{2}{5}x - 1$$

A table of values that satisfies this function is shown below.

x	y
-5	-3
0	-1
5	1
10	3

These points can be found on the graph using the form (x,y).

To graph relations and functions, the Cartesian plane is used. This means to think of the plane as being given a grid of squares, with one direction being the *x*-axis and the other direction the *y*-axis. Generally, the independent variable is placed along the horizontal axis, and the dependent variable is placed along the vertical axis. Any point on the plane can be specified by saying how far to go along the *x*-axis and how far along the *y*-axis with a pair of numbers (x, y). Specific values for these pairs can be given names such as $C = (-1, 3)$. Negative values mean to move left or down; positive values mean to move right or up. The point where the axes cross one another is called the **origin.** The origin has coordinates $(0, 0)$ and is usually called *O* when given a specific label. An illustration of the Cartesian plane, along with graphs of $(2, 1)$ and $(-1, -1)$, are below.

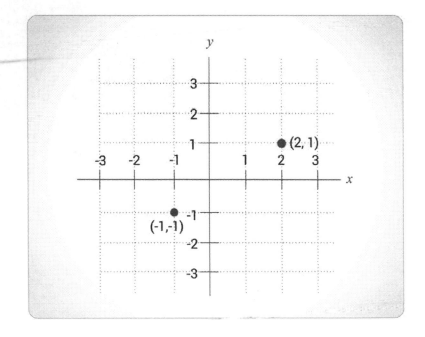

Relations also can be graphed by marking each point whose coordinates satisfy the relation. If the relation is a function, then there is only one value of *y* for any given value of *x*. This leads to the **vertical**

line test: if a relation is graphed, then the relation is a function if any possible vertical line drawn anywhere along the graph would only touch the graph of the relation in no more than one place. Conversely, when graphing a function, then any possible vertical line drawn will not touch the graph of the function at any point or will touch the function at just one point. This test is made from the definition of a function, where each x-value must be mapped to one and only one y-value.

When graphing a linear function, note that the ratio of the change of the y coordinate to the change in the x coordinate is constant between any two points on the resulting line, no matter which two points are chosen. In other words, in a pair of points on a line, (x_1, y_1) and (x_2, y_2), with $x_1 \neq x_2$ so that the two points are distinct, then the ratio $\frac{y_2 - y_1}{x_2 - x_1}$ will be the same, regardless of which particular pair of points are chosen. This ratio, $\frac{y_2 - y_1}{x_2 - x_1}$, is called the *slope* of the line and is frequently denoted with the letter m. If slope m is positive, then the line goes upward when moving to the right, while if slope m is negative, then the line goes downward when moving to the right. If the slope is 0, then the line is called horizontal, and the y coordinate is constant along the entire line. In lines where the x coordinate is constant along the entire line, y is not actually a function of x. For such lines, the slope is not defined. These lines are called vertical lines.

Linear functions may take forms other than $y = ax + b$. The most common forms of linear equations are explained below:

1. Standard Form: $Ax + By = C$, in which the slope is given by $m = \frac{-A}{B}$, and the y-intercept is given by $\frac{C}{B}$.

2. Slope-Intercept Form: $y = mx + b$, where the slope is m and the y intercept is b.

3. Point-Slope Form: $y - y_1 = m(x - x_1)$, where the slope is m and (x_1, y_1) is any point on the chosen line.

4. Two-Point Form: $\frac{y - y_1}{x - x_1} = \frac{y_2 - y_1}{x_2 - x_1}$, where (x_1, y_1) and (x_2, y_2) are any two distinct points on the chosen line. Note that the slope is given by $m = \frac{y_2 - y_1}{x_2 - x_1}$.

5. Intercept Form: $\frac{x}{x_1} + \frac{y}{y_1} = 1$, in which x_1 is the x-intercept and y_1 is the y-intercept.

These five ways to write linear equations are all useful in different circumstances. Depending on the given information, it may be easier to write one of the forms over another.

If $y = mx$, y is directly proportional to x. In this case, changing x by a factor changes y by that same factor. If $y = \frac{m}{x}$, y is inversely proportional to x. For example, if x is increased by a factor of 3, then y will be decreased by the same factor, 3.

The **midpoint** between two points, (x_1, y_1) and (x_2, y_2), is given by taking the average of the x coordinates and the average of the y coordinates:

$$\left(\frac{x_1 + x_2}{2}, \frac{y_1 + y_2}{2} \right)$$

The **distance** between two points, (x_1, y_1) and (x_2, y_2), is given by the **Pythagorean formula:**

$$\sqrt{(x_2 - x_1)^2 + (y_2 - y_1)^2}$$

To find the perpendicular distance between a line $Ax + By = C$ and a point (x_1, y_1) not on the line, we need to use the formula

$$\frac{|Ax_1 + By_1 + C|}{\sqrt{A^2 + B^2}}$$

Quadratic Functions

A polynomial of degree 2 is called **quadratic.** Every quadratic function can be written in the form $ax^2 + bx + c$. The graph of a quadratic function, $y = ax^2 + bx + c$, is called a **parabola.** Parabolas are vaguely U-shaped.

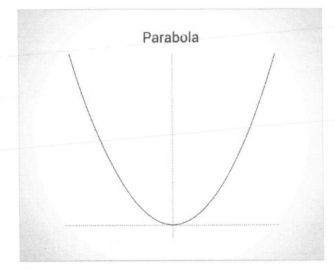

Parabola

Whether the parabola opens upward or downward depends on the sign of a. If a is positive, then the parabola will open upward. If a is negative, then the parabola will open downward. The value of a will also affect how wide the parabola is. If the absolute value of a is large, then the parabola will be fairly skinny. If the absolute value of a is small, then the parabola will be quite wide.

Changes to the value of b affect the parabola in different ways, depending on the sign of a. For positive values of a, increasing b will move the parabola to the left, and decreasing b will move the parabola to the right. On the other hand, if a is negative, the effects will be the opposite: increasing b will move the parabola to the right, while decreasing b will move the parabola to the left.

Changes to the value of c move the parabola vertically. The larger that c is, the higher the parabola gets. This does not depend on the value of a.

The quantity $D = b^2 - 4ac$ is called the **discriminant** of the parabola. When the discriminant is positive, then the parabola has two real zeros, or x intercepts. However, if the discriminant is negative, then there are no real zeros, and the parabola will not cross the x-axis. The highest or lowest point of the parabola is called the **vertex.** If the discriminant is zero, then the parabola's highest or lowest point is on the x-axis, and it will have a single real zero. The x-coordinate of the vertex can be found using the equation $x = -\frac{b}{2a}$. Plug this x-value into the equation and find the y-coordinate.

A quadratic equation is often used to model the path of an object thrown into the air. The x-value can represent the time in the air, while the y-value can represent the height of the object. In this case, the maximum height of the object would be the y-value found when the x-value is $-\frac{b}{2a}$.

Quadratic equations can be used to model real-world area problems. For example, a farmer may have a rectangular field that he needs to sow with seed. The field has length $x + 8$ and width $2x$. The formula for area should be used: $A = lw$. Therefore:

$$A = (x + 8) \times 2x = 2x^2 + 16x$$

The possible values for the length and width can be shown in a table, with input x and output A. If the equation was graphed, the possible area values can be seen on the y-axis for given x-values.

Exponential Functions

An **exponential function** is a function of the form $f(x) = b^x$, where b is a positive real number other than 1. In such a function, b is called the **base**.

The **domain** of an exponential function is all real numbers, and the **range** is all positive real numbers. There will always be a horizontal asymptote of $y = 0$ on one side. If b is greater than 1, then the graph will be increasing when moving to the right. If b is less than 1, then the graph will be decreasing when moving to the right. Exponential functions are one-to-one. The basic exponential function graph will go through the point (0, 1).

The following example demonstartes this more clearly:

Solve $5^{x+1} = 25$.

The first step is to get the x out of the exponent by rewriting the equation $5^{x+1} = 5^2$ so that both sides have a base of 5. Since the bases are the same, the exponents must be equal to each other. This leaves $x + 1 = 2$ or $x = 1$. To check the answer, the x-value of 1 can be substituted back into the original equation.

Exponential growth and decay can be found in real-world situations. For example, if a piece of notebook paper is folded 25 times, the thickness of the paper can be found. To model this situation, a table can be used. The initial point is one-fold, which yields a thickness of 2 papers. For the second fold, the thickness is 4. Since the thickness doubles each time, the table below shows the thickness for the next few folds. Notice the thickness changes by the same factor each time. Since this change for a constant interval of folds is a factor of 2, the function is exponential. The equation for this is $y = 2^x$. For twenty-five folds, the thickness would be 33,554,432 papers.

x (folds)	y (paper thickness)
0	1
1	2
2	4
3	8
4	16
5	32

One exponential formula that is commonly used is the **interest formula**: $A = Pe^{rt}$. In this formula, interest is compounded continuously. A is the value of the investment after the time, t, in years. P is the initial amount of the investment, r is the interest rate, and e is the constant equal to approximately 2.718. Given an initial amount of $200 and a time of 3 years, if interest is compounded continuously at a rate of 6%, the total investment value can be found by plugging each value into the formula. The invested value at the end is $239.44. In more complex problems, the final investment may be given, and the rate may be the unknown. In this case, the formula becomes $239.44 = 200e^{r3}$. Solving for r requires isolating the exponential expression on one side by dividing by 200, yielding the equation $1.20 = e^{r3}$. Taking the natural log of both sides results in $\ln(1.2) = r3$. Using a calculator to evaluate the logarithmic expression, $r = 0.06 = 6\%$.

When working with logarithms and exponential expressions, it is important to remember the relationship between the two. In general, the logarithmic form is $y = log_b x$ for an exponential form $b^y = x$. Logarithms and exponential functions are inverses of each other.

Logarithmic Functions

A **logarithmic function** is an inverse for an exponential function. The inverse of the base b exponential function is written as $log_b(x)$, and is called the **base b logarithm**. The domain of a logarithm is all positive real numbers. It has the properties that $log_b(b^x) = x$. For positive real values of x, $b^{log_b(x)} = x$.

When there is no chance of confusion, the parentheses are sometimes skipped for logarithmic functions: $log_b(x)$ may be written as $log_b x$. For the special number e, the base e logarithm is called the **natural logarithm** and is written as $\ln x$. Logarithms are one-to-one.

When working with logarithmic functions, it is important to remember the following properties. Each one can be derived from the definition of the logarithm as the inverse to an exponential function:

- $log_b 1 = 0$
- $log_b b = 1$
- $log_b b^p = p$
- $log_b MN = log_b M + log_b N$
- $log_b \frac{M}{N} = log_b M - log_b N$
- $log_b M^p = p \, log_b M$

When solving equations involving exponentials and logarithms, the following fact should be used:

If f is a one-to-one function, $a = b$ is equivalent to $f(a) = f(b)$.

Using this, together with the fact that logarithms and exponentials are inverses, allows for manipulations of the equations to isolate the variable as is demonstrated in the following example:

Solve $4 = \ln(x - 4)$.

Using the definition of a logarithm, the equation can be changed to $e^4 = e^{\ln(x-4)}$. The functions on the right side cancel with a result of $e^4 = x - 4$. This then gives $x = 4 + e^4$.

Rational Functions

A rational function is similar to an equation, but it includes two variables. In general, a rational function is in the form: $f(x) = \frac{p(x)}{q(x)}$, where $p(x)$ and $q(x)$ are polynomials. Rational functions are defined everywhere except where the denominator is equal to zero. When the denominator is equal to zero, this indicates either a hole in the graph or an asymptote. An asymptote can be either vertical, horizontal, or slant. A hole occurs when both the numerator and denominator are equal to 0 for a given value of x. A rational function can have at most one vertical asymptote and one horizontal or slant asymptote. An asymptote is a line such that the distance between the curve and the line tends toward 0, but never reaches it, as the line heads toward infinity. Examples of these types of functions are shown below. The first graph shows a rational function with a vertical asymptote at x = 0. This can be found by setting the denominator equal to 0. In this case it is just x = 0.

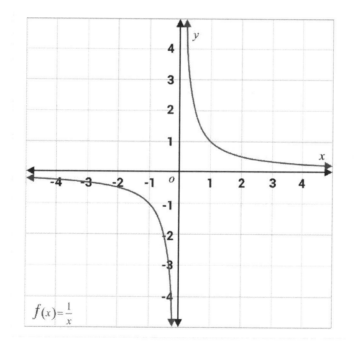

$f(x) = \frac{1}{x}$

The second graph shows a rational function with a vertical asymptote at x = -.5. Again this can be found by just setting the denominator equal to 0. So, $2x^2 + x = 0, 2x + 1 = 0, 2x = -1, x = -.5$. This graph also has a hole in the graph at $x = 0$. This is because both the numerator and denominator are equal to 0 when $x = 0$.

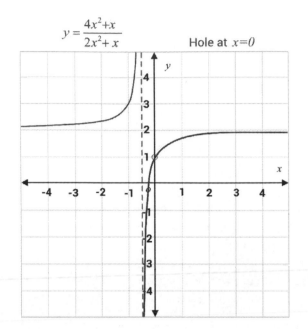

$$y = \frac{4x^2 + x}{2x^2 + x}$$

Hole at $x=0$

Piecewise Functions

A piecewise-defined function also has a different appearance on the graph. In the following function, there are three equations defined over different intervals. It is a function because there is only one y-value for each x-value, passing the Vertical Line Test. The domain is all real numbers less than or equal to 6. The range is all real numbers greater than zero. From left to right, the graph decreases to zero, then increases to almost 4, and then jumps to 6.

From input values greater than 2, the input decreases just below 8 to 4, and then stops.

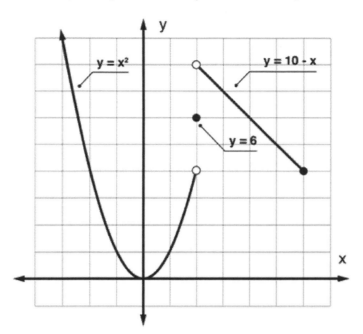

Trigonometric Functions

Trigonometric functions are built out of two basic functions, the **sine** and **cosine**, written as $\sin \theta$ and $\cos \theta$, respectively. Note that similar to logarithms, it is customary to drop the parentheses as long as the result is not confusing.

Sine and cosine are defined using the **unit circle**. If θ is the angle going counterclockwise around the origin from the x-axis, then the point on the unit circle in that direction will have the coordinates $(\cos \theta, \sin \theta)$.

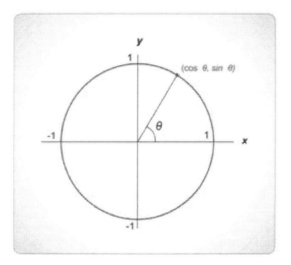

Since the angle returns to the start every 2π radians (or 360 degrees), the graph of these functions is **periodic**, with period 2π. This means that the graph repeats itself as one moves along the x-axis because $\sin \theta = \sin(\theta + 2\pi)$. Cosine works similarly.

From the unit circle definition, the sine function starts at 0 when $\theta = 0$. It grows to 1 as θ grows to $\pi/2$, and then back to 0 at $\theta = \pi$. Then it decreases to -1 as θ grows to $3\pi/2$, and goes back up to 0 at $\theta = 2\pi$.

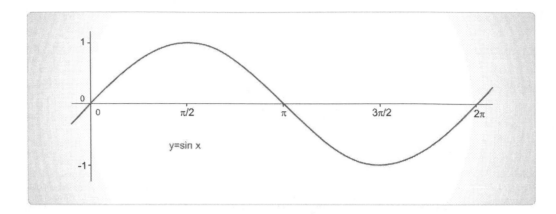

The graph of the cosine is similar. The cosine graph will start at 1, decreasing to 0 at $\pi/2$ and continuing to decrease to -1 at $\theta = \pi$. Then, it grows to 0 as θ grows to $3\pi/2$ and back up to 1 at $\theta = 2\pi$.

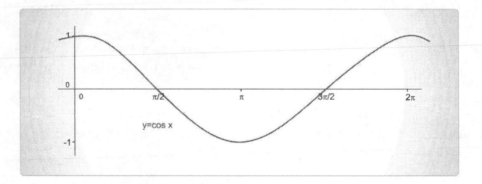

Another trigonometric function that is frequently used, is the **tangent** function. This is defined as the following equation: $\tan \theta = \frac{\sin \theta}{\cos \theta}$.

The tangent function is a period of π rather than 2π because the sine and cosine functions have the same absolute values after a change in the angle of π, but they flip their signs. Since the tangent is a ratio of the two functions, the changes in signs cancel.

The tangent function will be zero when sine is zero, and it will have a vertical asymptote whenever cosine is zero. The following graph shows the tangent function:

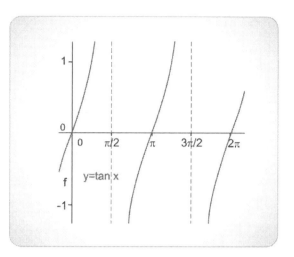

Three other trigonometric functions are sometimes useful. These are the **reciprocal** trigonometric functions, so named because they are just the reciprocals of sine, cosine, and tangent. They are the **cosecant**, defined as $\csc\theta = \frac{1}{\sin\theta}$, the **secant**, $\sec\theta = \frac{1}{\cos\theta}$, and the **cotangent**, $\cot\theta = \frac{1}{\tan\theta}$. Note that from the definition of tangent, $\cot\theta = \frac{\cos\theta}{\sin\theta}$.

In addition, there are three identities that relate the trigonometric functions to one another:

- $\cos\theta = \sin(\frac{\pi}{2} - \theta)$
- $\csc\theta = \sec\left(\frac{\pi}{2} - \theta\right)$
- $\cot\theta = \tan(\frac{\pi}{2} - \theta)$

Here is a list of commonly-needed values for trigonometric functions, given in radians, for the first quadrant:

Table for trigonometric functions

$\sin 0 = 0$	$\cos 0 = 1$	$\tan 0 = 0$
$\sin\dfrac{\pi}{6} = \dfrac{1}{2}$	$\cos\dfrac{\pi}{6} = \dfrac{\sqrt{3}}{2}$	$\tan\dfrac{\pi}{6} = \dfrac{\sqrt{3}}{3}$
$\sin\dfrac{\pi}{4} = \dfrac{\sqrt{2}}{2}$	$\cos\dfrac{\pi}{4} = \dfrac{\sqrt{2}}{2}$	$\tan\dfrac{\pi}{4} = 1$
$\sin\dfrac{\pi}{3} = \dfrac{\sqrt{3}}{2}$	$\cos\dfrac{\pi}{3} = \dfrac{1}{2}$	$\tan\dfrac{\pi}{3} = \sqrt{3}$
$\sin\dfrac{\pi}{2} = 1$	$\cos\dfrac{\pi}{2} = 0$	$\tan\dfrac{\pi}{2} = undefined$
$\csc 0 = undefined$	$\sec 0 = 1$	$\cot 0 = undefined$
$\csc\dfrac{\pi}{6} = 2$	$\sec\dfrac{\pi}{6} = \dfrac{2\sqrt{3}}{3}$	$\cot\dfrac{\pi}{6} = \sqrt{3}$
$\csc\dfrac{\pi}{4} = \sqrt{2}$	$\sec\dfrac{\pi}{4} = \sqrt{2}$	$\cot\dfrac{\pi}{4} = 1$
$\csc\dfrac{\pi}{3} = \dfrac{2\sqrt{3}}{3}$	$\sec\dfrac{\pi}{3} = 2$	$\cot\dfrac{\pi}{3} = \dfrac{\sqrt{3}}{3}$
$\csc\dfrac{\pi}{2} = 1$	$\sec\dfrac{\pi}{2} = undefined$	$\cot\dfrac{\pi}{2} = 0$

To find the trigonometric values in other quadrants, complementary angles can be used. The **complementary angle** is the smallest angle between the x-axis and the given angle.

Once the complementary angle is known, the following rule is used:

For an angle θ with complementary angle x, the absolute value of a trigonometric function evaluated at θ is the same as the absolute value when evaluated at x.

The correct sign for sine and cosine is determined by the x and y coordinates on the unit circle.

- Sine will be positive in quadrants I and II and negative in quadrants III and IV.
- Cosine will be positive in quadrants I and IV, and negative in II and III.
- Tangent will be positive in I and III, and negative in II and IV.

The signs of the reciprocal functions will be the same as the sign of the function of which they are the reciprocal. For example:

Find $\sin \frac{3\pi}{4}$.

The complementary angle must be found first. This angle is in the II quadrant, and the angle between it and the x-axis is $\frac{\pi}{4}$. Now, $\sin \frac{\pi}{4} = \frac{\sqrt{2}}{2}$. Since this is in the II quadrant, sine takes on positive values (the y coordinate is positive in the II quadrant). Therefore, $\sin \frac{3\pi}{4} = \frac{\sqrt{2}}{2}$.

In addition to the six trigonometric functions defined above, there are inverses for these functions. However, since the trigonometric functions are not one-to-one, one can only construct inverses for them on a restricted domain.

Usually, the domain chosen will be $[0, \pi)$ for cosine and $(-\frac{\pi}{2}, \frac{\pi}{2}]$ for sine. The inverse for tangent can use either of these domains. The inverse functions for the trigonometric functions are also called **arc functions.** In addition to being written with a -1 as the exponent to denote that the function is an inverse, they will sometimes be written with an "a" or "arc" in front of the function name, so $\cos^{-1} \theta = a\cos \theta = \arccos \theta$.

When solving equations that involve trigonometric functions, there are often multiple solutions. For example, $2 \sin \theta = \sqrt{2}$ can be simplified to $\sin \theta = \frac{\sqrt{2}}{2}$. This has solutions $\theta = \frac{\pi}{4}, \frac{3\pi}{4}$, but in addition, because of the periodicity, any integer multiple of 2π can also be added to these solutions to find another solution.

The full set of solutions is $\theta = \frac{\pi}{4} + 2\pi k, \frac{3\pi}{4} + 2\pi k$ for all integer values of k. It is very important to remember to find all possible solutions when dealing with equations that involve trigonometric functions.

The name *trigonometric* comes from the fact that these functions play an important role in the geometry of triangles, particularly right triangles. Consider the right triangle shown in this figure:

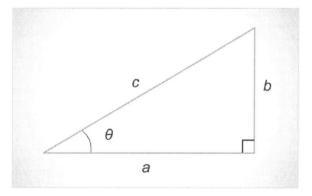

The following hold true:

- $c \sin \theta = b$.
- $c \cos \theta = a$.
- $\tan \theta = \frac{b}{a}$.

123

- $b \csc \theta = c.$
- $a \sec \theta = c.$
- $\cot \theta = \dfrac{a}{b}.$

It is important to remember that the angles of a triangle must add up to π radians (180 degrees).

Radical Functions

A radical function is any function involving a root. For instance, $y = \sqrt[n]{x}$ is a radical function with index n. If n is odd, the function represents an odd root, and its domain and range are both all real numbers. This is because the odd root of any real number is a real number. Radical functions, for example, $f(x) = \sqrt{x}$, have a restriction for the domain and range because there are no real negative inputs or outputs for this function. The domain can be stated as $x \geq 0$, and the range is $y \geq 0$.

Building a Function

Functions can be built out of the context of a situation. For example, the relationship between the money paid for a gym membership and the months that someone has been a member can be described through a function. If the one-time membership fee is $40 and the monthly fee is $30, then the function can be written $f(x) = 30x + 40$. The x-value represents the number of months the person has been part of the gym, while the output is the total money paid for the membership. The table below shows this relationship. It is a representation of the function because the initial cost is $40 and the cost increases each month by $30.

x (months)	y (money paid to gym)
0	40
1	70
2	100
3	130

Functions can also be built from existing functions. For example, a given function $f(x)$ can be transformed by adding a constant, multiplying by a constant, or changing the input value by a constant. The new function $g(x) = f(x) + k$ represents a vertical shift of the original function. In $f(x) = 3x - 2$, a vertical shift 4 units up would be:

$$g(x) = 3x - 2 + 4 = 3x + 2$$

Multiplying the function times a constant k represents a vertical stretch, based on whether the constant is greater than or less than 1. The function

$$g(x) = kf(x) = 4(3x - 2) = 12x - 8$$

represents a stretch. Changing the input x by a constant forms the function:

$$g(x) = f(x + k) = 3(x + 4) - 2 = 3x + 12 - 2 = 3x + 10$$

and this represents a horizontal shift to the left 4 units. If $(x - 4)$ was plugged into the function, it would represent a vertical shift.

A composition function can also be formed by plugging one function into another. In function notation, this is written:

$$(f \circ g)(x) = f(g(x))$$

For two functions $f(x) = x^2$ and $g(x) = x - 3$, the composition function becomes:

$$f(g(x)) = (x - 3)^2$$

$$x^2 - 6x + 9$$

The composition of functions can also be used to verify if two functions are inverses of each other. Given the two functions $f(x) = 2x + 5$ and $g(x) = \frac{x-5}{2}$, the composition function can be found $(f \circ g)(x)$. Solving this equation yields:

$$f(g(x)) = 2\left(\frac{x-5}{2}\right) + 5$$

$$x - 5 + 5 = x$$

It also is true that $g(f(x)) = x$. Since the composition of these two functions gives a simplified answer of x, this verifies that $f(x)$ and $g(x)$ are inverse functions. The domain of $f(g(x))$ is the set of all x-values in the domain of $g(x)$ such that $g(x)$ is in the domain of $f(x)$. Basically, both $f(g(x))$ and $g(x)$ have to be defined.

To build an inverse of a function, $f(x)$ needs to be replaced with y, and the x and y values need to be switched. Then, the equation can be solved for y. For example, given the equation $y = e^{2x}$, the inverse can be found by rewriting the equation $x = e^{2y}$. The natural logarithm of both sides is taken down, and the exponent is brought down to form the equation:

$$\ln(x) = \ln(e)\, 2y$$

$\ln(e)$=1, which yields the equation $\ln(x) = 2y$. Dividing both sides by 2 yields the inverse equation

$$\frac{\ln(x)}{2} = y = f^{-1}(x)$$

The domain of an inverse function is the range of the original function, and the range of an inverse function is the domain of the original function. Therefore, an ordered pair (x, y) on either a graph or a table corresponding to $f(x)$ means that the ordered pair (y, x) exists on the graph of $f^{-1}(x)$. Basically, if $f(x) = y$, then $f^{-1}(y) = x$. For a function to have an inverse, it must be one-to-one. That means it must pass the **Horizontal Line Test**, and if any horizontal line passes through the graph of the function twice, a function is not one-to-one. The domain of a function that is not one-to-one can be restricted to an interval in which the function is one-to-one, to be able to define an inverse function.

Functions can also be formed from combinations of existing functions.

Given $f(x)$ and $g(x)$, the following can be built:

$$f + g$$

$$f - g$$

$$fg$$

$$\frac{f}{g}$$

The domains of $f + g, f - g,$ and fg are the intersection of the domains of f and g. The domain of $\frac{f}{g}$ is the same set, excluding those values that make $g(x) = 0$.

For example, if:

$$f(x) = 2x + 3$$

$$g(x) = x + 1$$

then

$$\frac{f}{g} = \frac{2x + 3}{x + 1}$$

Its domain is all real numbers except -1.

Comparing Functions

As mentioned, three common functions used to model different relationships between quantities are linear, quadratic, and exponential functions. **Linear functions** are the simplest of the three, and the independent variable x has an exponent of 1. Written in the most common form, $y = mx + b$, the coefficient of x tells how fast the function grows at a constant rate, and the b-value tells the starting point. A **quadratic** function has an exponent of 2 on the independent variable x. Standard form for this type of function is $y = ax^2 + bx + c$, and the graph is a parabola. These type functions grow at a changing rate. An **exponential** function has an independent variable in the exponent $y = ab^x$. The graph of these types of functions is described as **growth** or **decay**, based on whether the base, b, is greater than or less than 1. These functions are different from quadratic functions because the base stays constant. A common base is base e.

The following three functions model a linear, quadratic, and exponential function respectively: $y = 2x$, $y = x^2$, and $y = 2^x$. Their graphs are shown below. The first graph, modeling the linear function, shows that the growth is constant over each interval. With a horizontal change of 1, the vertical change is 2. It models a constant positive growth. The second graph shows the quadratic function, which is a curve that is symmetric across the y-axis. The growth is not constant, but the change is mirrored over the axis. The last graph models the exponential function, where the horizontal change of 1 yields a vertical change that increases more and more. The exponential graph gets very close to the x-axis, but never touches it, meaning there is an asymptote there. The y-value can never be zero because the base of 2 can never be raised to an input value that yields an output of zero.

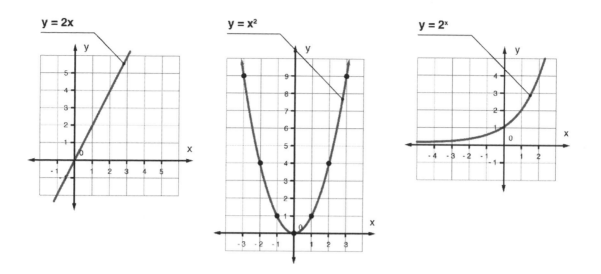

The three tables below show specific values for three types of functions. The third column in each table shows the change in the y-values for each interval. The first table shows a constant change of 2 for each equal interval, which matches the slope in the equation $y = 2x$. The second table shows an increasing change, but it also has a pattern. The increase is changing by 2 more each time, so the change is quadratic. The third table shows the change as factors of the base, 2. It shows a continuing pattern of factors of the base.

y = 2x				y = x²				y = 2ˣ		
x	y	Δy		x	y	Δy		x	y	Δy
1	2			1	1			1	2	
2	4	2		2	4	3		2	4	2
3	6	2		3	9	5		3	8	4
4	8	2		4	16	7		4	16	8
5	10	2		5	25	9		5	32	16

Given a table of values, the type of function can be determined by observing the change in y over equal intervals. For example, the tables below model two functions. The changes in interval for the x-values is 1 for both tables. For the first table, the y-values increase by 5 for each interval. Since the change is constant, the situation can be described as a linear function. The equation would be $y = 5x + 3$. For the second table, the change for y is 5, 20, 100, and 500, respectively. The increases are multiples of 5, meaning the situation can be modeled by an exponential function. The equation $y = 5^x + 3$ models this situation.

x	y
0	3
1	8
2	13
3	18
4	23

x	y
0	3
1	8
2	28
3	128
4	628

Evaluating Functions

To evaluate functions, plug in the given value everywhere the variable appears in the expression for the function. For example, find $g(-2)$ where $g(x) = 2x^2 - \frac{4}{x}$. To complete the problem, plug in -2 in the following way:

$$g(-2) = 2(-2)^2 - \frac{4}{-2}$$

$$2 \times 4 + 2$$

$$8 + 2 = 10$$

Geometry

Shapes and Solids

A **polygon** is a closed geometric figure in a plane (flat surface) consisting of at least 3 sides formed by line segments. These are often defined as two-dimensional shapes. Common two-dimensional shapes include circles, triangles, squares, rectangles, pentagons, and hexagons. Note that a circle is a two-dimensional shape without sides.

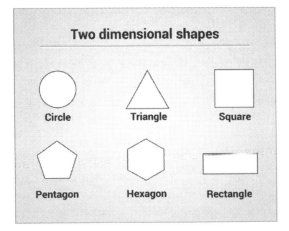

Polygons can be either convex or concave. A polygon that has interior angles all measuring less than 180° is convex. A concave polygon has one or more interior angles measuring greater than 180°. Examples are shown below.

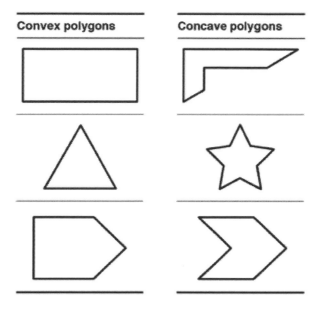

Polygons can be classified by the number of sides (also equal to the number of angles) they have. The following are the names of polygons with a given number of sides or angles:

# of sides	3	4	5	6	7	8	9	10
Name of polygon	Triangle	Quadrilateral	Pentagon	Hexagon	Septagon (or heptagon)	Octagon	Nonagon	Decagon

Equiangular polygons are polygons in which the measure of every interior angle is the same. The sides of equilateral polygons are always the same length. If a polygon is both equiangular and equilateral, the polygon is defined as a regular polygon.

Triangles can be further classified by their sides and angles. A triangle with its largest angle measuring 90° is a right triangle. A triangle with the largest angle less than 90° is an acute triangle. A triangle with the largest angle greater than 90° is an obtuse triangle. Below is an example of a right triangle.

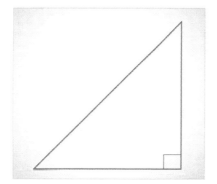

A triangle consisting of two equal sides and two equal angles is an isosceles triangle. A triangle with three equal sides and three equal angles is an equilateral triangle. A triangle with no equal sides or angles is a scalene triangle.

Isosceles triangle:

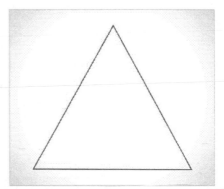

Equilateral triangle:

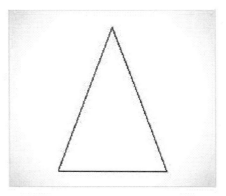

Scalene triangle:

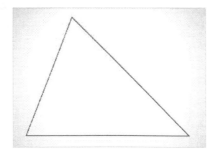

Quadrilaterals can be further classified according to their sides and angles. A quadrilateral with exactly one pair of parallel sides is called a trapezoid. A quadrilateral that shows both pairs of opposite sides parallel is a parallelogram. Parallelograms include rhombuses, rectangles, and squares. A rhombus has four equal sides. A rectangle has four equal angles (90° each). A square has four 90° angles and four equal sides. Therefore, a square is both a rhombus and a rectangle.

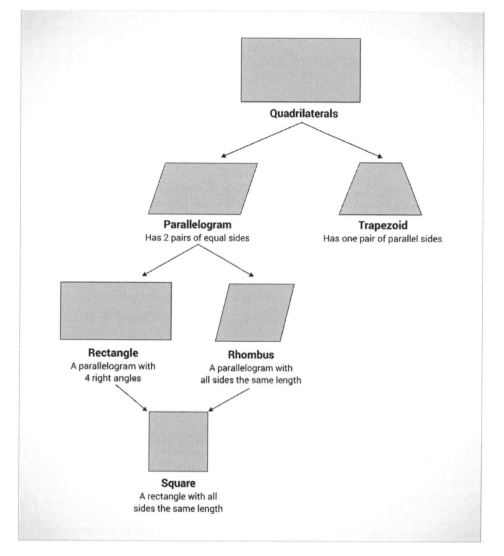

Angles and Diagonals

Diagonals are lines (excluding sides) that connect two vertices within a polygon. **Mutually bisecting diagonals** intersect at their midpoints. Parallelograms, rectangles, squares, and rhombuses have mutually bisecting diagonals. However, trapezoids don't have such lines. **Perpendicular diagonals** occur when they form four right triangles at their point of intersection. Squares and rhombuses have perpendicular diagonals, but trapezoids, rectangles, and parallelograms do not. Finally, **perpendicular bisecting diagonals** (also known as **perpendicular bisectors**) form four right triangles at their point of intersection, but this intersection is also the midpoint of the two lines. Both rhombuses and squares have perpendicular bisecting angles, but trapezoids, rectangles, and parallelograms do not. Knowing these definitions can help tremendously in problems that involve both angles and diagonals.

<u>Polygons with More than Four Sides</u>

A **pentagon** is a five-sided figure. A six-sided shape is a **hexagon**. A seven-sided figure is classified as a **heptagon**, and an eight-sided figure is called an **octagon**. An important characteristic is whether a polygon is regular or irregular. If it's **regular,** the side lengths and angle measurements are all equal. An **irregular** polygon has unequal side lengths and angle measurements. Mathematical problems involving polygons with more than four sides usually involve side length and angle measurements. The sum of all internal angles in a polygon equals $180(n - 2)$ degrees, where n is the number of sides. Therefore, the total of all internal angles in a pentagon is 540 degrees because there are five sides so $180(5 - 2) = 540$ degrees. Unfortunately, area formulas don't exist for polygons with more than four sides. However, their shapes can be split up into triangles, and the formula for area of a triangle can be applied and totaled to obtain the area for the entire figure.

<u>Solids</u>

A solid is a three-dimensional figure that encloses a part of space. Common three-dimensional shapes include spheres, prisms, cubes, pyramids, cylinders, and cones.

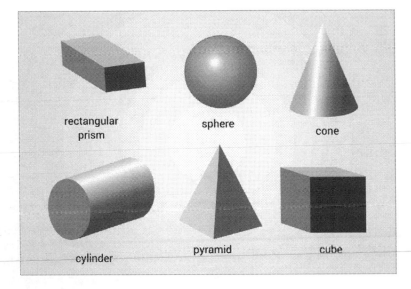

Solids consisting of all flat surfaces that are polygons are called polyhedrons. The two-dimensional surfaces that make up a polyhedron are called faces. Types of polyhedrons include prisms and pyramids. A prism consists of two parallel faces that are congruent (or the same shape and same size), and lateral faces going around (which are parallelograms). A prism is further classified by the shape of its base, as shown below:

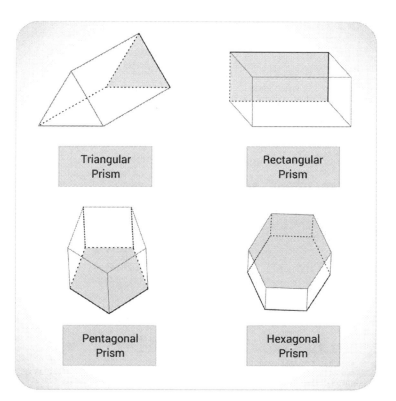

A pyramid consists of lateral faces (triangles) that meet at a common point called the vertex and one other face that is a polygon, called the base. A pyramid can be further classified by the shape of its base, as shown below.

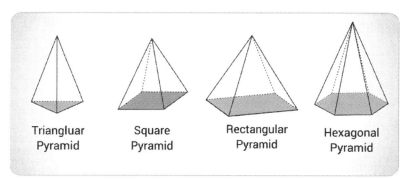

A tetrahedron is another name for a triangular pyramid. All the faces of a tetrahedron are triangles.

Solids that are not polyhedrons include spheres, cylinders, and cones. A sphere is the set of all points a given distance from a given center point. A sphere is commonly thought of as a three-dimensional circle. A cylinder consists of two parallel, congruent (same size) circles and a lateral curved surface. A cone consists of a circle as its base and a lateral curved surface that narrows to a point called the vertex.

Similar polygons are the same shape but different sizes. More specifically, their corresponding angle measures are congruent (or equal) and the length of their sides is proportional. For example, all sides of one polygon may be double the length of the sides of another. Likewise, similar solids are the same shape but different sizes. Any corresponding faces or bases of similar solids are the same polygons that are proportional by a consistent value.

Congruence and Similarity

Sometimes, two figures are similar, meaning they have the same basic shape and the same interior angles, but they have different dimensions. If the ratio of two corresponding sides is known, then that ratio, or scale factor, holds true for all of the dimensions of the new figure.

Likewise, triangles are similar if they have the same angle measurements, and their sides are proportional to one another. Triangles are **congruent** if the angles of the triangles are equal in measurement and the sides of the triangles are equal in measurement.

There are five ways to show that triangles are congruent:

1. SSS (Side-Side-Side Postulate) – when all three corresponding sides are equal in length, then the two triangles are congruent.

2. SAS (Side-Angle-Side Postulate) – if a pair of corresponding sides and the angle in between those two sides are equal, then the two triangles are congruent.

3. ASA (Angle-Side-Angle Postulate) – if a pair of corresponding angles are equal and the side lengths within those angles are equal, then the two triangles are equal.

4. AAS (Angle-Angle-Side Postulate) – when a pair of corresponding angles for two triangles and a non-included side are equal, then the two triangles are congruent.

5. HL (Hypotenuse-Leg Theorem) – if two right triangles have the same hypotenuse length, and one of the other sides in each triangle are of the same length, then the two triangles are congruent.

If two triangles are discovered to be similar or congruent, this information can assist in determining unknown parts of triangles, such as missing angles and sides.

The example below involves the question of congruent triangles. The first step is to examine whether the triangles are congruent. If the triangles are congruent, then the measure of a missing angle can be found.

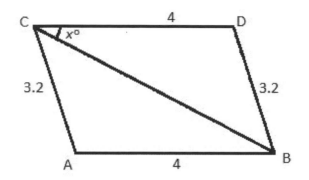

The above diagram provides values for angle measurements and side lengths in triangles *CAB* and *CDB*. Note that side *CA* is 3.2 and side *DB* is 3.2. Side *CD* is 4 and side *AB* is 4. Furthermore, line *CB* is congruent to itself by the reflexive property. Therefore, the two triangles are congruent by SSS (Side-Side-Side). Because the two triangles are congruent, all of the corresponding parts of the triangles are also congruent. Therefore, angle *x* is congruent to the inside of the angle for which a measurement is not provided in triangle *CAB*. Thus, 115º + 32º = 147º. A triangle's angles sum to 180º, therefore, 180º – 147º = 33º. Angle *x* = 33º, because the two triangles are reversed.

Transformations of a Plane
Given a figure drawn on a plane, many changes can be made to that figure, including rotation, translation, and reflection. **Rotations** turn the figure about a point, **translations** slide the figure, and **reflections** flip the figure over a specified line. When performing these transformations, the original figure is called the **pre-image**, and the figure after transformation is called the **image**.

More specifically, **translation** means that all points in the figure are moved in the same direction by the same distance. In other words, the figure is slid in some fixed direction. Of course, while the entire figure is slid by the same distance, this does not change any of the measurements of the figures involved. The result will have the same distances and angles as the original figure.

In terms of Cartesian coordinates, a translation means a shift of each of the original points (x, y) by a fixed amount in the *x* and *y* directions, to become $(x + a, y + b)$.

Another procedure that can be performed is called **reflection**. To do this, a line in the plane is specified, called the **line of reflection**. Then, take each point and flip it over the line so that it is the same distance from the line but on the opposite side of it. This does not change any of the distances or angles involved, but it does reverse the order in which everything appears.

To reflect something over the *x*-axis, the points (x, y) are sent to $(x, -y)$. To reflect something over the *y*-axis, the points (x, y) are sent to the points $(-x, y)$. Flipping over other lines is not something easy to express in Cartesian coordinates. However, by drawing the figure and the line of reflection, the distance to the line and the original points can be used to find the reflected figure.

Example: Reflect this triangle with vertices (-1, 0), (2, 1), and (2, 0) over the *y*-axis. The pre-image is shown below.

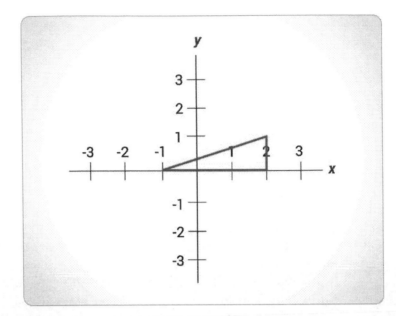

To do this, flip the *x* values of the points involved to the negatives of themselves, while keeping the *y* values the same. The image is shown here.

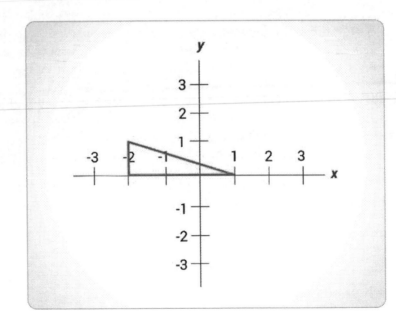

The new vertices will be (1, 0), (-2, 1), and (-2, 0).

Another procedure that does not change the distances and angles in a figure is **rotation**. In this procedure, pick a center point, then rotate every vertex along a circle around that point by the same angle. This procedure is also not easy to express in Cartesian coordinates, and this is not a requirement on this test. However, as with reflections, it's helpful to draw the figures and see what the result of the rotation would look like. This transformation can be performed using a compass and protractor.

Each one of these transformations can be performed on the coordinate plane without changes to the original dimensions or angles.

If two figures in the plane involve the same distances and angles, they are called **congruent figures**. In other words, two figures are congruent when they go from one form to another through reflection, rotation, and translation, or a combination of these.

Remember that rotation and translation will give back a new figure that is identical to the original figure, but reflection will give back a mirror image of it.

To recognize that a figure has undergone a rotation, check to see that the figure has not been changed into a mirror image, but that its orientation has changed (that is, whether the parts of the figure now form different angles with the x and y axes).

To recognize that a figure has undergone a translation, check to see that the figure has not been changed into a mirror image, and that the orientation remains the same.

To recognize that a figure has undergone a reflection, check to see that the new figure is a mirror image of the old figure.

Keep in mind that sometimes a combination of translations, reflections, and rotations may be performed on a figure.

Dilation
A **dilation** is a transformation that preserves angles, but not distances. This can be thought of as stretching or shrinking a figure. If a dilation makes figures larger, it is called an **enlargement**. If a dilation makes figures smaller, it is called a **reduction**. The easiest example is to dilate around the origin. In this case, multiply the x and y coordinates by a **scale factor**, k, sending points (x, y) to (kx, ky).

As an example, draw a dilation of the following triangle, whose vertices will be the points (-1, 0), (1, 0), and (1, 1).

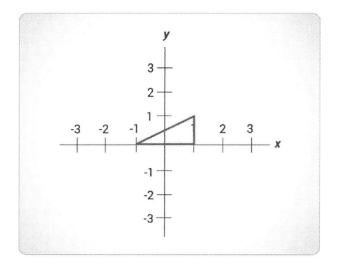

For this problem, dilate by a scale factor of 2, so the new vertices will be (-2, 0), (2, 0), and (2, 2).

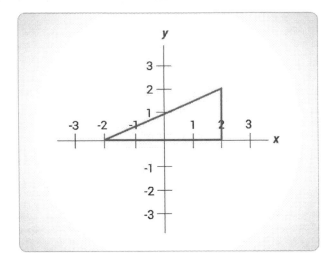

Note that after a dilation, the distances between the vertices of the figure will have changed, but the angles remain the same. The two figures that are obtained by dilation, along with possibly translation, rotation, and reflection, are all *similar* to one another. Another way to think of this is that similar figures have the same number of vertices and edges, and their angles are all the same. Similar figures have the same basic shape but are different in size.

Surface Area and Volume

Surface area and volume are two- and three-dimensional measurements. Surface area measures the total surface space of an object, like the six sides of a cube. Questions about surface area will ask how much of something is needed to cover a three-dimensional object, like wrapping a present. **Volume** is the measurement of how much space an object occupies, like how much space is in the cube. Volume questions will ask how much of something is needed to completely fill the object. The most common surface area and volume questions deal with spheres, cubes, and rectangular prisms.

The formula for a cube's surface area is $SA = 6 \times s^2$, where s is the length of a side. A cube has 6 equal sides, so the formula expresses the area of all the sides. Volume is simply measured by taking the cube of the length, so the formula is $V = s^3$.

The surface area formula for a rectangular prism or a general box is $SA = 2(lw + lh + wh)$, where l is the length, h is the height, and w is the width. The volume formula is $V = l \times w \times h$, which is the cube's volume formula adjusted for the unequal lengths of a box's sides.

The formula for a sphere's surface area is $SA = 4\pi r^2$, where r is the sphere's radius. The surface area formula is the area for a circle multiplied by four. To measure volume, the formula is $V = \frac{4}{3}\pi r^3$.

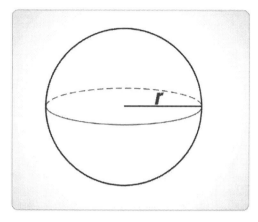

A **rectangular pyramid** is a figure with a rectangular base and four triangular sides that meet at a single vertex. If the rectangle has sides of lengths x and y, then the volume will be given by $V = \frac{1}{3}xyh$.

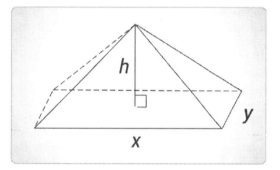

To find the surface area, the dimensions of each triangle must be known. However, these dimensions can differ depending on the problem in question. Therefore, there is no general formula for calculating total surface area.

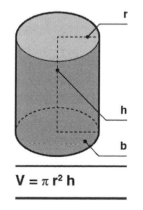

$$V = \pi r^2 h$$

The formula to find the volume of a cylinder is $\pi r^2 h$. This formula contains the formula for the area of a circle (πr^2) because the base of a cylinder is a circle. To calculate the volume of a cylinder, the slices of circles needed to build the entire height of the cylinder are added together. For example, if the radius is 5 feet and the height of the cylinder is 10 feet, the cylinder's volume is calculated by using the following equation: $\pi 5^2 \times 10$. Substituting 3.14 for π, the volume is 785.4 ft³.

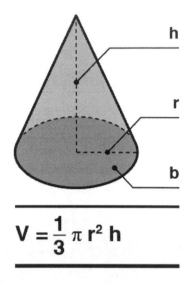

$$V = \frac{1}{3}\,\pi\,r^2\,h$$

The formula used to calculate the volume of a cone is $\frac{1}{3}\pi r^2 h$. Essentially, the area of the base of the cone is multiplied by the cone's height. In a real-life example where the radius of a cone is 2 meters and the height of a cone is 5 meters, the volume of the cone is calculated by utilizing the formula $\frac{1}{3}\pi 2^2 \times 5 = 21$. After substituting 3.14 for π, the volume is 785.4 ft³.

Solving for Missing Values in Shapes

Perimeter is the distance measurement around something. It can be thought of as the length of the boundary, like a fence. In contrast, area is the space occupied by a defined enclosure, like a field enclosed by a fence.

The perimeter of a square is measured by adding together all of the sides. Since a square has four equal sides, its perimeter can be calculated by multiplying the length of one side by 4. Thus, the formula is $P = 4 \times s$, where s equals one side. The area of a square is calculated by squaring the length of one side, which is expressed as the formula $A = s^2$.

Like a square, a rectangle's perimeter is measured by adding together all of the sides. But as the sides are unequal, the formula is different. A rectangle has equal values for its lengths (long sides) and equal values for its widths (short sides), so the perimeter formula for a rectangle is $P = l + l + w + w = 2l + 2w$, where l equals length and w equals width. The area is found by multiplying the length by the width, so the formula is $A = l \times w$.

A triangle's perimeter is measured by adding together the three sides, so the formula is $P = a + b + c$, where $a, b,$ and c are the values of the three sides. The area is calculated by multiplying the length of the base times the height times ½, so the formula is $A = \frac{1}{2} \times b \times h = \frac{bh}{2}$. The base is the bottom of the triangle, and the height is the distance from the base to the peak. If a problem asks one to calculate the area of a triangle, it will provide the base and height.

A circle's perimeter—also known as its **circumference**—is measured by multiplying the **diameter** (the straight line measured from one side, through the center, to the direct opposite side of the circle) by π, so the formula is $\pi \times d$. This is sometimes expressed by the formula $C = 2 \times \pi \times r$, where r is the **radius** of the circle. These formulas are equivalent, as the radius equals half of the diameter. The area of a circle is calculated with the formula $A = \pi \times r^2$. The test will indicate either to leave the answer with π attached or to calculate to the nearest decimal place, which means multiplying by 3.14 for π.

The perimeter of a parallelogram is measured by adding the lengths and widths together. Thus, the formula is the same as for a rectangle, $P = l + l + w + w = 2l + 2w$. However, the area formula differs from the rectangle. For a parallelogram, the area is calculated by multiplying the length by the height: $A = h \times l$

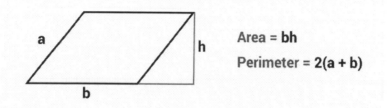

Area = bh

Perimeter = 2(a + b)

The perimeter of a trapezoid is calculated by adding the two unequal bases and two equal sides, so the formula is $P = a + b_1 + c + b_2$. Although unlikely to be a test question, the formula for the area of a trapezoid is $A = \frac{b_1 + b_2}{2} \times h$, where h equals height, and b_1 and b_2 equal the bases.

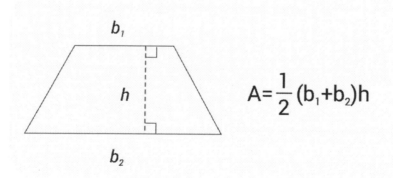

$$A = \frac{1}{2}(b_1 + b_2)h$$

Using formulas such as perimeter and area for different shapes, it's possible to solve for missing side lengths.

Consider the following problem:

The total perimeter of a rectangular garden is 36 m. If the length of each side is 12 m, what is the width?

The formula for the perimeter of a rectangle is P=2L+2W, where P is the perimeter, L is the length, and W is the width. The first step is to substitute all of the data into the formula:

$$36 = 2(12) + 2W$$

Simplify by multiplying 2x12:

$$36 = 24 + 2W$$

Simplifying this further by subtracting 24 on each side, which gives:

$$36-24 = 24-24+2W$$

$$12 = 2W$$

Divide by 2:

$$6 = W$$

The width is 6 m. Remember to test this answer by substituting this value into the original formula:

$$36 = 2(12) + 2(6)$$

More complicated situations can arise where missing side lengths can be calculated by using concepts of similarity and proportional relationships. Suppose that Lara is 5 feet tall and is standing 30 feet from the base of a light pole, and her shadow is 6 feet long. How high is the light on the pole? To figure this out, it helps to make a sketch of the situation:

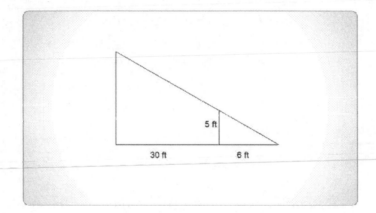

The light pole is the left side of the triangle. Lara is the 5-foot vertical line. Test takers should notice that there are two right triangles here, and that they have all the same angles as one another. Therefore, they form similar triangles. So, the ratio of proportionality between them must be found.

The bases of these triangles are known. The small triangle, formed by Lara and her shadow, has a base of 6 feet. The large triangle, formed by the light pole along with the line from the base of the pole out to the end of Lara's shadow is $30 + 6 = 36$ feet long. So, the ratio of the big triangle to the little triangle is $\frac{36}{6} = 6$. The height of the little triangle is 5 feet. Therefore, the height of the big triangle will be $6 \cdot 5 = 30$ feet, meaning that the light is 30 feet up the pole.

Composite Shapes
The perimeter of an irregular polygon is found by adding the lengths of all of the sides. In cases where all of the sides are given, this will be very straightforward, as it will simply involve finding the sum of the provided lengths. Other times, a side length may be missing and must be determined before the perimeter can be calculated.

Consider the example below:

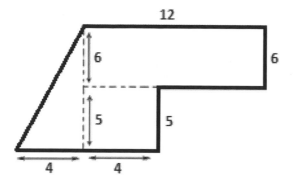

All of the side lengths are provided except for the angled side on the left. Test takers should notice that this is the hypotenuse of a right triangle. The other two sides of the triangle are provided (the base is 4 and the height is 6 + 5 = 11). The Pythagorean Theorem can be used to find the length of the hypotenuse, remembering that $a^2 + b^2 = c^2$.

Substituting the side values provided yields $(4)^2 + (11)^2 = c^2$.

Therefore, $c = \sqrt{16 + 121} = 11.7$

Finally, the perimeter can be found by adding this new side length with the other provided lengths to get the total length around the figure: 4+4+5+8+6+12+11.7=50.7. Although units are not provided in this figure, remember that reporting units with a measurement is important.

The area of irregular polygons is found by decomposing, or breaking apart, the figure into smaller shapes. When the area of the smaller shapes is determined, the area of the smaller shapes will produce the area of the original figure when added together. Consider the earlier example:

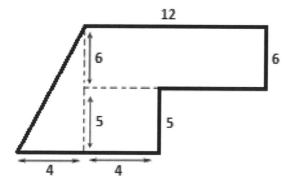

The irregular polygon is decomposed into two rectangles and a triangle. The area of the large rectangles ($A = l \times w \rightarrow A = 12 \times 6$) is 72 square units. The area of the small rectangle is 20 square units ($A = 4 \times 5$). The area of the triangle ($A = \frac{1}{2} \times b \times h \rightarrow A = \frac{1}{2} \times 4 \times 11$) is 22 square units. The sum of the areas of these figures produces the total area of the original polygon: $A = 72 + 20 + 22 \rightarrow A = 114$ square units.

Here's another example:

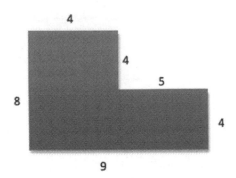

This irregular polygon is decomposed into two rectangles. The area of the large rectangle ($A = l \times w \to A = 8 \times 4$) is 32 square units. The area of the small rectangle is 20 square units ($A = 4 \times 5$). The sum of the areas of these figures produces the total area of the original polygon: $A = 32 + 20 \to A = 52$ square units.

The Pythagorean Theorem and Right Triangles

<u>Trigonometric Functions</u>
From the unit circle, the trigonometric ratios were found for the special right triangle with a hypotenuse of 1.

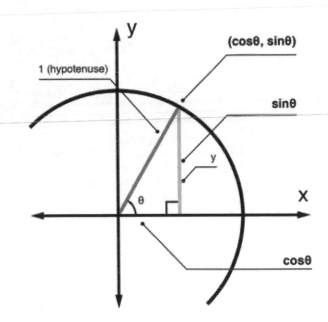

From this triangle, the following Pythagorean identities are formed: $\sin^2 \theta + \cos^2 \theta = 1$, $\tan^2 \theta + 1 = \sec^2 \theta$, and $1 + \cot^2 \theta = \csc^2 \theta$. The second two identities are formed by manipulating the first identity. Since identities are statements that are true for any value of the variable, then they may be used to manipulate equations. For example, a problem may ask for simplification of the expression $\cos^2 x + \cos^2 x \tan^2 x$.

Using the fact that $\tan(x) = \frac{\sin x}{\cos x}$, $\frac{\sin^2 x}{\cos^2 x}$ can then be substituted in for $\tan^2 x$, making the expression:

$$\cos^2 x + \cos^2 x \frac{\sin^2 x}{\cos^2 x}$$

Then the two $\cos^2 x$ terms on top and bottom cancel each other out, simplifying the expression to $\cos^2 x + \sin^2 x$. By the first Pythagorean identity stated above, the expression can be turned into $\cos^2 x + \sin^2 x = 1$.

Another set of trigonometric identities are the double-angle formulas:

$$\sin 2\alpha = 2 \sin \alpha \ \cos \alpha$$

$$\cos 2\alpha = \begin{cases} \cos^2\alpha - \sin^2\alpha \\ 2 \cos^2\alpha - 1 \\ 1 - 2 \sin^2\alpha \end{cases}$$

Using these formulas, the following identity can be proved: $\sin 2x = \frac{2 \tan x}{1 + \tan^2 x}$. By using one of the Pythagorean identities, the denominator can be rewritten as $1 + \tan^2 x = \sec^2 x$. By knowing the reciprocals of the trigonometric identities, the secant term can be rewritten to form the equation $\sin 2x = \frac{2 \tan x}{1} * \cos^2 x$. Replacing $\tan(x)$, the equation becomes $\sin 2x = \frac{2 \sin x}{\cos x} * \cos^2 x$, where the $\cos x$ can cancel out. The new equation is $\sin 2x = 2 \sin x * \cos x$. This final equation is one of the double-angle formulas.

Other trigonometric identities such as half-angle formulas, sum and difference formulas, and difference of angles formulas can be used to prove and rewrite trigonometric equations. Depending on the given equation or expression, the correct identities need to be chosen to write equivalent statements.

The graph of sine is equal to the graph of cosine, shifted $\frac{\pi}{2}$ units. Therefore, the function $y = \sin x$ is equal to $y = \cos(\frac{\pi}{2} - x)$. Within functions, adding a constant to the independent variable shifts the graph either left or right. By shifting the cosine graph, the curve lies on top of the sine function. By transforming the function, the two equations give the same output for any given input.

Complementary Angles
Angles that add up to 90 degrees are **complementary**. Within a right triangle, two complementary angles exist because the third angle is always 90 degrees. In this scenario, the **sine** of one of the complementary angles is equal to the **cosine** of the other angle. The opposite is also true. This relationship exists because sine and cosine will be calculated as the ratios of the same side lengths.

The Pythagorean Theorem
The Pythagorean theorem is an important result in geometry. It states that for right triangles, the sum of the squares of the two shorter sides will be equal to the square of the longest side (also called the **hypotenuse**). The longest side will always be the side opposite to the 90° angle. If this side is called c, and the other two sides are a and b, then the Pythagorean theorem states that $c^2 = a^2 + b^2$.

Since lengths are always positive, this also can be written as:

$$c = \sqrt{a^2 + b^2}.$$

A diagram to show the parts of a triangle using the Pythagorean theorem is below.

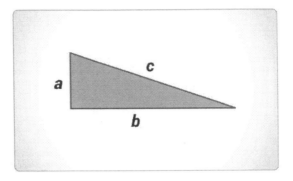

As an example of the theorem, suppose that Shirley has a rectangular field that is 5 feet wide and 12 feet long, and she wants to split it in half using a fence that goes from one corner to the opposite corner. How long will this fence need to be? To figure this out, note that this makes the field into two right triangles, whose hypotenuse will be the fence dividing it in half. Therefore, the fence length will be given by $\sqrt{5^2 + 12^2} = \sqrt{169} = 13$ feet long.

Translating Between a Geometric Description and an Equation for a Conic Section

<u>Equation of a Circle</u>
A **circle** can be defined as the set of all points that are the same distance (known as the **radius**, r) from a single point C (known as the center of the circle). The center has coordinates (h, k), and any point on the circle can be labelled with coordinates (x, y).

As shown below, a **right triangle** is formed with these two points:

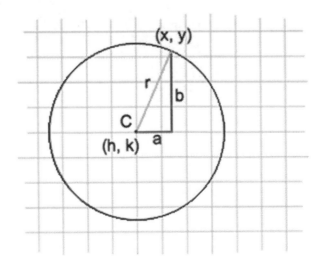

The **Pythagorean theorem** states that:

$$a^2 + b^2 = r^2$$

However, a can be replaced by $|x - h|$ and b can be replaced by $|y - k|$ by using the **distance formula** which is:

$$d = \sqrt{(x_2 - x_1)^2 + (y_2 - y_1)^2}$$

That substitution results in:

$$(x - h)^2 + (y - k)^2 = r^2$$

This is the formula for finding the equation of any circle with a center (h, k) and a radius r. Note that sometimes c is used instead of r.

Finding the Center and Radius
Circles aren't always given in the form of the circle equation where the center and radius can be seen so easily. Oftentimes, they're given in the more general format of:

$$ax^2 + by^2 + cx + dy + e = 0$$

This can be converted to the center-radius form using the algebra technique of completing the square in both variables. First, the constant term is moved over to the other side of the equals sign, and then the x and y variable terms are grouped together. Then the equation is divided through by a and, because this is the equation of a circle, $a = b$. At this point, the x -term coefficient is divided by 2, squared, and then added to both sides of the equation. This value is grouped with the x terms. The same steps then need to be completed with the y-term coefficient. The trinomial in both x and y can now be factored into a square of a binomial, which gives both:

$$(x - h)^2 \text{ and}$$

$$(y - k)^2$$

Parabola Equations
A **parabola** is defined as a specific type of curve such that any point on it is the same distance from a fixed point (called the **foci**) and a fixed straight line (called the **directrix**). A parabola is the shape formed from the intersection of a cone with a plane that's parallel to its side. Every parabola has an **axis of symmetry**, and its **vertex** (h, k) is the point at which the axis of symmetry intersects the curve. If the parabola has an axis of symmetry parallel to the y-axis, the focus is the point $(h, k + f)$ and the directrix is the line $y = k - f$. For example, a parabola may have a vertex at the origin, focus $(0, f)$, and directrix $y = -f$. The equation of this parabola can be derived by using both the focus and the directrix. The distance from any coordinate on the curve to the focus is the same as the distance to the directrix, and the Pythagorean theorem can be used to find the length of d. The triangle has sides with length $|x|$ and $|y - f|$ and therefore:

$$d = \sqrt{x^2 + (y - f)^2}$$

By definition, the **vertex** is halfway between the focus and the directrix and $d = y + f$. Setting these two equations equal to one another, squaring each side, simplifying, and solving for y gives the equation of a parabola with the focus f and the vertex being the origin:

$$y = \frac{1}{4f}x^2$$

If the vertex (h, k) is not the origin, a similar process can be completed to derive the equation $(x - h)^2 = 4f(y - k)$ for a parabola with focus f.

Ellipse and Hyperbola Equations

An **ellipse** is the set of all points for which the sum of the distances from two fixed points (known as the *foci*) is constant. A **hyperbola** is the set of all points for which the difference between the distances from two fixed points (also known as the *foci*) is constant. The **distance formula** can be used to derive the formulas of both an ellipse and a hyperbola, given the coordinates of the foci. Consider an ellipse where its major axis is horizontal (i.e., it's longer along the x-axis) and its foci are the coordinates $(-c, 0)$ and $(c, 0)$. The distance from any point (x, y) to $(-c, 0)$ is

$$d_1 = \sqrt{(x + c)^2 + y^2}$$

and the distance from the same point (x, y) to $(c, 0)$ is:

$$d_1 = \sqrt{(x - c)^2 + y^2}$$

Using the definition of an ellipse, it's true that the sum of the distances from the vertex a to each foci is equal to $d_1 + d_2$. Therefore:

$$d_1 + d_2 = (a + c) + (a - c) = 2a$$

and

$$\sqrt{(x + c)^2 + y^2} + \sqrt{(x - c)^2 + y^2} = 2a$$

After a series of algebraic steps, this equation can be simplified to $\frac{x^2}{a^2} + \frac{y^2}{b^2} = 1$, which is the equation of an ellipse with a horizontal major axis. In this case, $a > b$. When the ellipse has a vertical major axis, similar techniques result in $\frac{x^2}{b^2} + \frac{y^2}{a^2} = 1$, and $a > b$.

The equation of a hyperbola can be derived in a similar fashion. Consider a hyperbola with a horizontal major axis and its foci are also the coordinates $(-c, 0)$ and $(c, 0)$. Again, the distance from any point (x, y) to $(-c, 0)$ is

$$d_1 = \sqrt{(x + c)^2 + y^2}$$

and the distance from the same point (x, y) to $(c, 0)$ is:

$$d_1 = \sqrt{(x - c)^2 + y^2}$$

Using the definition of a hyperbola, it's true that the difference of the distances from the vertex a to each foci is equal to $d_1 - d_2$. Therefore:

$$d_1 - d_2 = (c + a) - (c - a) = 2a$$

This means that:

$$\sqrt{(x + c)^2 + y^2} - \sqrt{(x - c)^2 + y^2} = 2a$$

After a series of algebraic steps, this equation can be simplified to:

$$\frac{x^2}{a^2} - \frac{y^2}{b^2} = 1$$

This is the equation of a hyperbola with a horizontal major axis. In this case, $a > b$. Similar techniques result in the equation $\frac{x^2}{b} - \frac{y^2}{a^2} = 1$, where $a > b$, when the hyperbola has a vertical major axis.

Using Coordinate Geometry to Algebraically Prove Simple Geometric Theorems

<u>Proving Theorems with Coordinates</u>
Many important formulas and equations exist in geometry that use coordinates. The distance between two points (x_1, y_1) and (x_2, y_2) is:

$$d = \sqrt{(x_2 - x_1)^2 + (y_2 - y_1)^2}.$$

The slope of the line containing the same two points is:

$$m = \frac{y_2 - y_1}{x_2 - x_1}$$

Also, the midpoint of the line segment with endpoints (x_1, y_1) and (x_2, y_2) is:

$$M = \left(\frac{x_1 + x_2}{2}, \frac{y_1 + y_2}{2}\right)$$

The equations of a circle, parabola, ellipse, and hyperbola can also be used to prove theorems algebraically. Knowing when to use which formula or equation is extremely important, and knowing which formula applies to which property of a given geometric shape is an integral part of the process. In some cases, there are a number of ways to prove a theorem; however, only one way is required.

<u>Solving Problems with Parallel and Perpendicular Lines</u>
Two lines can be parallel, perpendicular, or neither. If two lines are **parallel**, they have the same slope. This is proven using the idea of similar triangles. Consider the following diagram with two parallel lines, L1 and L2:

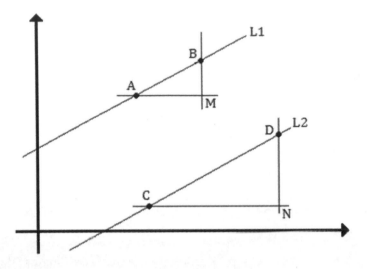

A and B are points on L1, and C and D are points on L2. Right triangles are formed with vertex M and N where lines BM and DN are parallel to the y-axis and AM and CN are parallel to the x-axis. Because all three sets of lines are parallel, the triangles are similar. Therefore:

$$\frac{BM}{DN} = \frac{MA}{NC}$$

This shows that the rise/run is equal for lines L1 and L2. Hence, their slopes are equal.

Secondly, if two lines are **perpendicular**, the product of their slopes equals -1. This means that their slopes are negative reciprocals of each other. Consider two perpendicular lines, l and n:

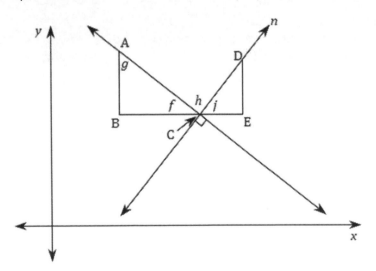

Right triangles ABC and CDE are formed so that lines BC and CE are parallel to the x-axis, and AB and DE are parallel to the y-axis. Because line BE is a straight line, angles $f + h + i = 180\ degrees$. However, angle h is a right angle, so $f + j = 90\ degrees$. By construction, $f + g = 90$, which means that $g = j$. Therefore, because angles $B = E$ and $g = j$, the triangles are similar and:

$$\frac{AB}{BC} = \frac{CE}{DE}$$

Because slope is equal to rise/run, the slope of line l is $-\frac{AB}{BC}$ and the slope of line n is $\frac{DE}{CE}$.

Multiplying the slopes together gives:

$$-\frac{AB}{BC} \cdot \frac{DE}{CE} = -\frac{CE}{DE} \cdot \frac{DE}{CE} = -1$$

This proves that the product of the slopes of two perpendicular lines equals -1. Both parallel and perpendicular lines can be integral in many geometric proofs, so knowing and understanding their properties is crucial for problem-solving.

Formulas for Ratios

If a line segment with endpoints (x_1, y_1) and (x_2, y_2) is partitioned into two equal parts, the formula for **midpoint** is used. Recall this formula is:

$$M = \left(\frac{x_1 + x_2}{2}, \frac{y_1 + y_2}{2} \right)$$

The ratio of line segments is 1:1. However, if the ratio needs to be anything other than 1:1, a different formula must be used. Consider a ratio that is $a : b$. This means the desired point that partitions the line segment is $\frac{a}{a+b}$ of the way from (x_1, y_1) to (x_2, y_2). The actual formula for the coordinate is:

$$\left(\frac{bx_1 + ax_2}{a + b}, \frac{by_1 + ay_2}{a + b} \right)$$

Computing Side Length, Perimeter, and Area

The side lengths of each shape can be found by plugging the endpoints into the distance formula between two ordered pairs (x_1, y_1) and (x_2, y_2).

As a reminder, this is the **distance formula**:

$$d = \sqrt{(x_2 - x_1)^2 + (y_2 - y_1)^2}$$

The distance formula is derived from the Pythagorean theorem. Once the side lengths are found, they can be added together to obtain the perimeter of the given polygon. Simplifications can be made for specific shapes such as squares and equilateral triangles. For example, one side length can be multiplied by 4 to obtain the perimeter of a square. Also, one side length can be multiplied by 3 to obtain the perimeter of an equilateral triangle. A similar technique can be used to calculate areas. For polygons, both side length and height can be found by using the same distance formula. Areas of triangles and quadrilaterals are straightforward through the use of $A = \frac{1}{2}bh$ or $A = bh$, depending on the shape.

To find the area of other polygons, their shapes can be partitioned into rectangles and triangles. The areas of these simpler shapes can be calculated and then added together to find the total area of the polygon.

Statistics and Probability

Center and Spread of Distributions

Descriptive statistics are utilized to gain an understanding of properties of a data set. This entails examining the center, spread, and shape of the sample data.

Center

The **center** of the sample set can be represented by its mean, median or mode. The **mean** is the average of the data set. It is calculated by adding the data values together and dividing this sum by the sample size (the number of data points). The **median** is the value of the data point in the middle when the sample is arranged in numerical order. If the sample has an even number of data points, the mean of the two middle values is the median. The **mode** is the value which appears most often in a data set. It is possible to have multiple modes (if different values repeat equally as often) or no mode (if no value repeats).

Spread

Methods for determining the **spread** of the sample include calculating the range and standard deviation for the data. The *range* is calculated by subtracting the lowest value from the highest value in the set. The **standard deviation** of the sample can be calculated using the formula:

$$\sigma = \sqrt{\frac{\Sigma(x - \bar{x})^2}{n - 1}}$$

$\bar{x}$ = sample mean
n = sample size

Shape

The **shape** of the sample when displayed as a histogram or frequency distribution plot helps to determine if the sample is normally distributed (bell-shaped curve), symmetrical, or displays skewness (lack of symmetry), or kurtosis. **Kurtosis** is a measure of whether the data are heavy-tailed (high number of outliers) or light-tailed (low number of outliers).

Data Collection Methods

Statistical inference, based in probability theory, makes calculated assumptions about an entire population based on data from a sample set from that population.

Population Parameters

A population is the entire set of people or things of interest. For example, if researchers wanted to determine the number of hours of sleep per night for college females in the U.S, the population would consist of *every* college female in the country. A **sample** is a subset of the population that may be used for the study. A sample might consist of 100 students per school from 20 different colleges in the country. From the results of the survey, a sample statistic can be calculated. A **sample statistic** is a numerical characteristic of the sample data including mean and variance. A sample statistic can be used to estimate a corresponding **population parameter**, which is a numerical characteristic of the entire population.

Confidence Intervals

A population parameter estimated using a sample statistic may be very accurate or relatively inaccurate based on errors in sampling. A **confidence interval** indicates a range of values likely to include the true population parameter. A given confidence interval such as 95% means that the true population parameter will occur within the interval for 95% of samples.

Measurement Error

The accuracy of a population parameter based on a sample statistic may also be affected by measurement error. **Measurement error** can be divided into random error and systematic error. An example of **random error** for the previous scenario would be a student reporting 8 hours of sleep when she actually sleeps 7 hours per night. **Systematic errors** are those attributed to the measurement system. If the sleep survey gave response options of 2,4,6,8, or 10 hours. This would lead to systematic measurement error because certain values could not be accurately reported.

Evaluating Reports and Determining the Appropriateness of Data Collection Methods

The presentation of statistics can be manipulated to produce a desired outcome. For example, in the statement "four out of five dentists recommend our toothpaste", critical readers should wonder: *who are the five dentists?* While the wording is similar, this statement is very different from "four out of every five dentists recommend our toothpaste." The context of the numerical values allows one to decipher the meaning, intent, and significance of the survey or study.

When analyzing a report, the researchers who conducted the study and their intent must be considered. Was it performed by a neutral party or by a person or group with a vested interest? The sampling method and the data collection method should also be evaluated. Was it a true random sample of the population or was one subgroup over- or underrepresented? Lastly, the measurement system used to obtain the data should be assessed. Was the system accurate and precise or was it a flawed system?

Understanding and Modeling Relationships in Bivariate Data

In an experiment, variables are the key to analyzing data, especially when data is in a graph or table. Variables can represent anything, including objects, conditions, events, and amounts of time.

Covariance is a general term referring to how two variables move in relation to each other. Take for example an employee that gets paid by the hour. For them, hours worked and total pay have a positive covariance. As hours worked increases, so does pay.

Constant variables remain unchanged by the scientist across all trials. Because they are held constant for all groups in an experiment, they aren't being measured in the experiment, and they are usually ignored. Constants can either be controlled by the scientist directly like the nutrition, water, and sunlight given to plants, or they can be selected by the scientist specifically for an experiment like using a certain animal species or choosing to investigate only people of a certain age group.

Independent variables are also controlled by the scientist, but they are the same only for each group or trial in the experiment. Each group might be composed of students that all have the same color of car or each trial may be run on different soda brands. The independent variable of an experiment is what is being indirectly tested because it causes change in the dependent variables.

Dependent variables experience change caused by the independent variable and are what is being measured or observed. For example, college acceptance rates could be a dependent variable of an experiment that sorted a large sample of high school students by an independent variable such as test scores. In this experiment, the scientist groups the high school students by the independent variable (test scores) to see how it affects the dependent variable (their college acceptance rates).

Note that most variables can be held constant in one experiment but independent or dependent in another. For example, when testing how well a fertilizer aids plant growth, its amount of sunlight should be held constant for each group of plants, but if the experiment is being done to determine the proper amount of sunlight a plant should have, the amount of sunlight is an independent variable because it is necessarily changed for each group of plants.

Correlation

An **X-Y diagram**, also known as a scatter diagram, visually displays the relationship between two variables. The independent variable is placed on the **x-axis**, or horizontal axis, and the dependent variable is placed on the **y-axis**, or vertical axis.

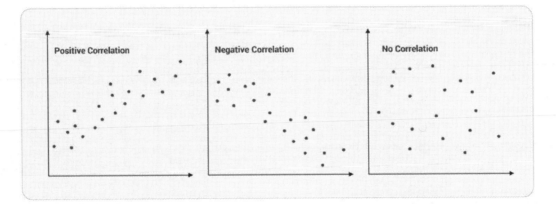

As shown in the figures above, an X-Y diagram may result in positive, negative, or no correlation between the two variables. So, in the first scatter plot as the Y factor increases the X factor increases as well. The opposite is true as well: as the X factor increases the Y factor also increases. Thus, there is a positive correlation because one factor appears to positively affect the other factor.

Correlation Coefficient

The **correlation coefficient** (r) measures the association between two variables. Its value is between -1 and 1, where -1 represents a perfect negative linear relationship, 0 represents no relationship, and 1 represents a perfect positive linear relationship. A **negative linear relationship** means that as x values increase, y values decrease. A **positive linear relationship** means that as x values increase, y values increase. The formula for computing the correlation coefficient is:

$$r = \frac{n(\sum xy) - (\sum x)(\sum y)}{\sqrt{n(\sum x^2) - (\sum x)^2}\sqrt{n(\sum y^2) - (\sum y)^2}}$$

n is the number of data points.

Both Microsoft Excel® and a graphing calculator can evaluate this easily once the data points are entered. A correlation greater than 0.8 or less than -0.8 is classified as "strong" while a correlation between -0.5 and 0.5 is classified as "weak."

Calculating Probabilities, Including Related Sample Spaces

Probability, represented by variable *p,* always has a value from 0 to 1. The total probability for all the possible outcomes (sample space) should equal 1.

Sample Spaces

Probabilities are based on observations of events. The probability of an event occurring is equal to the ratio of the number of favorable outcomes over the total number of possible outcomes. The total number of possible outcomes is found by constructing the sample space. The sum of probabilities of all possible distinct outcomes is equal to 1. A simple example of a sample space involves a deck of cards. They contain 52 distinct cards, and therefore the sample space contains each individual card. To find the probability of selecting a queen on one draw from the deck, the ratio would be equal to $\frac{4}{52} = \frac{1}{13}$, which equals 4 possible queens over the total number of possibilities in the sample space.

Verifying Independent Events

Two events aren't always independent. For examples, females with glasses and brown hair aren't independent characteristics. There definitely can be overlap because females with brown hair can wear glasses. Also, two events that exist at the same time don't have to have a relationship. For example, even if all females in a given sample are wearing glasses, the characteristics aren't related. In this case, the probability of a brunette wearing glasses is equal to the probability of a female being a brunette multiplied by the probability of a female wearing glasses. This mathematical test of $P(A \cap B) = P(A)P(B)$ verifies that two events are independent.

Simple and Compound Events

A **simple event** consists of only one outcome. The most popular simple event is flipping a coin, which results in either heads or tails. A **compound event** results in more than one outcome and consists of more than one simple event. An example of a compound event is flipping a coin while tossing a die. The result is either heads or tails on the coin and a number from one to six on the die. The probability of a simple event is calculated by dividing the number of possible outcomes by the total number of outcomes. Therefore, the probability of obtaining heads on a coin is $^1/_2$, and the probability of rolling a 6 on a die is $^1/_6$. The probability of compound events is calculated using the basic idea of the probability of simple events. If the two events are independent, the probability of one outcome is equal to the product of the probabilities of each simple event. For example, the probability of obtaining heads on a coin and rolling a 6 is equal to:

$$^1/_2 \times {}^1/_6 = {}^1/_{12}$$

The probability of either A or B occurring is equal to the sum of the probabilities minus the probability that both A and B will occur. Therefore, the probability of obtaining either heads on a coin or rolling a 6 on a die is

$$^1/_2 + {}^1/_6 - {}^1/_{12} = {}^7/_{12}$$

The two events aren't mutually exclusive because they can happen at the same time. If two events are mutually exclusive, and the probability of both events occurring at the same time is zero, the probability of event A or B occurring equals the sum of both probabilities. An example of calculating the probability of two mutually exclusive events is determining the probability of pulling a king or a queen from a deck of cards. The two events cannot occur at the same time.

Integrating Essential Skills

Using Ratios, Rates, Proportions, and Scale Drawings to Solve Single- and Multistep Problems

Ratios, rates, proportions, and scale drawings are used when comparing two quantities. Questions on this material will include expressing relationships in simplest terms and solving for missing quantities.

Ratios

A ratio is a comparison of two quantities that represent separate groups. For example, if a recipe calls for 2 eggs for every 3 cups of milk, it can be expressed as a ratio. Ratios can be written three ways: (1) with the word "to"; (2) using a colon; or (3) as a fraction. For the previous example, the ratio of eggs to cups of milk can be written as: 2 to 3, 2:3, or $\frac{2}{3}$. When writing ratios, the order is important. The ratio of eggs to cups of milk is not the same as the ratio of cups of milk to eggs, 3:2.

In simplest form, both quantities of a ratio should be written as integers. These should also be reduced just as a fraction would be. For example, 5:10 would reduce to 1:2. Given a ratio where one or both quantities are expressed as a decimal or fraction, both should be multiplied by the same number to produce integers. To write the ratio $\frac{1}{3}$ to 2 in simplest form, both quantities should be multiplied by 3. The resulting ratio is 1 to 6.

When a problem involving ratios gives a comparison between two groups, then: (1) a total should be provided and a part should be requested; or (2) a part should be provided and a total should be requested. Consider the following:

> The ratio of boys to girls in the 11th grade is 5:4. If there is a total of 270 11th grade students, how many are girls?

To solve this, the total number of "ratio pieces" first needs to be determined. The total number of 11th grade students is divided into 9 pieces. The ratio of boys to total students is 5:9; and the ratio of girls to total students is 4:9. Knowing the total number of students, the number of girls can be determined by setting up a proportion:

$$\frac{4}{9} = \frac{x}{270}$$

Solving the proportion, it shows that there are 120 11th grade girls.

Rates

A rate is a ratio comparing two quantities expressed in different units. A unit rate is one in which the second is one unit. Rates often include the word *per*. Examples include miles per hour, beats per minute, and price per pound. The word *per* can be represented with a / symbol or abbreviated with the letter "p" and the units abbreviated. For example, miles per hour would be written mi/h. Given a rate that is not in simplest form (second quantity is not one unit), both quantities should be divided by the value of the second quantity. Suppose a patient had 99 heartbeats in 1½ minutes. To determine the heart rate, 1½ should divide both quantities. The result is 66 bpm.

Scale Drawings

Scale drawings are used in designs to model the actual measurements of a real-world object. For example, the blueprint of a house might indicate that it is drawn at a scale of 3 inches to 8 feet. Given one value and asked to determine the width of the house, a proportion should be set up to solve the problem. Given the scale of 3in:8ft and a blueprint width of 1 ft (12 in.), to find the actual width of the building, the proportion $\frac{3}{8} = \frac{12}{x}$ should be used. This results in an actual width of 32 ft.

Proportions

A proportion is a statement consisting of two equal ratios. Proportions will typically give three of four quantities and require solving for the missing value. The key to solving proportions is to set them up properly. Here's a sample problem:

If 7 gallons of gas costs $14.70, how many gallons can you get for $20?

The information should be written as equal ratios with a variable representing the missing quantity:

$$\left(\frac{gallons}{cost} = \frac{gallons}{cost} \right) : \frac{7}{14.70} = \frac{x}{20}$$

To solve, cross multiply (multiply the numerator of the first ratio by the denominator of the second and vice versa) is used and the products are set equal to each other. Cross-multiplying results in:

$$(7)(20) = (14.7)(x)$$

Solving the equation for x, it can be determined that 9.5 gallons of gas can be purchased for $20.

For direct proportions, as one quantity increases, the other quantity also increases. For indirect proportions (also referred to as indirect variations, inverse proportions, or inverse variations), as one quantity increases, the other decreases. Direct proportions can be written:

$$\frac{y_1}{x_1} = \frac{y_2}{x_2}$$

Conversely, indirect proportions are written:

$$y_1 x_1 = y_2 x_2$$

Here's a sample problem:

It takes 3 carpenters 10 days to build the frame of a house. How long should it take 5 carpenters to build the same frame?

In this scenario, as one quantity increases (number of carpenters), the other decreases (number of days building); therefore, this is an inverse proportion. To solve, the products of the two variables (in this scenario, the total work performed) are set equal to each other ($y_1 x_1 = y_2 x_2$). Using y to represent carpenters and x to represent days, the resulting equation is: $(3)(10) = (5)(x2)$. Solving for x_2, it is determined that it should take 5 carpenters 6 days to build the frame of the house.

Solving Single- and Multistep Problems Involving Percentages

The word percent means "per hundred." When dealing with percentages, it may be helpful to think of the number as a value in hundredths. For example, 15% can be expressed as "fifteen hundredths" and written as $\frac{15}{100}$ or .15.

Percent Problems

Material on percentages can include questions such as: What is 15% of 25? What percent of 45 is 3? Five is $\frac{1}{2}$% of what number? To solve these problems, the information should be rewritten as an equation where the following helpful steps are completed: (1) "what" is represented by a variable (x); (2) "is" is represented by an = sign; and (3) "of" is represented by multiplication. Any values expressed as a percent should be written as a decimal; and if the question is asking for a percent, the answer should be converted accordingly. Here are three sample problems based on the information above:

What is 15% of 25?	What percent of 45 is 3?	Five is $\frac{1}{2}$% of what number?
$x = .15 \times 25$	$x \times 45 = 3$	$5 = .005 \times x$
$x = 3.75$	$x = 0.0\overline{6}$	$x = 1,000$
	$x = 6.\overline{6}\%$	

Percent Increase/Decrease

Problems dealing with percentages may involve an original value, a change in that value, and a percentage change. A problem will provide two pieces of information and ask to find the third. To do so, this formula is used:

$$\frac{change}{original\ value} \times 100 = percent\ change$$

Here's a sample problem:

> Attendance at a baseball stadium has dropped 16% from last year. Last year's average attendance was 40,000. What is this year's average attendance?

Using the formula and information, the change is unknown (x), the original value is 40,000, and the percent change is 16%. The formula can be written as:

$$\frac{x}{40,000} \times 100 = 16$$

When solving for x, it is determined the change was 6,400. The problem asked for this year's average attendance, so to calculate, the change (6,400) is subtracted from last year's attendance (40,000) to determine this year's average attendance is 33,600.

Percent More Than/Less Than

Percentage problems may give a value and what percent that given value is more than or less than an original unknown value. Here's a sample problem:

> A store advertises that all its merchandise has been reduced by 25%. The new price of a pair of shoes is $60. What was the original price?

This problem can be solved by writing a proportion. Two ratios should be written comparing the cost and the percent of the original cost. The new cost is 75% of the original cost (100% - 25%); and the original cost is 100% of the original cost. The unknown original cost can be represented by x. The proportion would be set up as: $\frac{60}{75} = \frac{x}{100}$. Solving the proportion, it is determined the original cost was $80.

Solving Single- and Multistep Problems Involving Measurement Quantities, Units, and Unit Conversion

Unit conversions apply to many real-world scenarios, including cooking, measurement, construction, and currency. Problems on this material can be solved similarly to those involving unit rates. Given the conversion rate, it can be written as a fraction (ratio) and multiplied by a quantity in one unit to convert it to the corresponding unit. For example, someone might want to know how many minutes are in 3½ hours. The conversion rate of 60 minutes to 1 hour can be written as:

$$\frac{60 \ min}{1 \ h}$$

Multiplying the quantity by the conversion rate results in:

$$3\frac{1}{2}h \times \frac{60 \ min}{1 \ h} = 210 \ min$$

The "h" unit is canceled. To convert a quantity in minutes to hours, the fraction for the conversion rate would be flipped (to cancel the "min" unit). To convert 195 minutes to hours, the equation $195 \ min \times \frac{1h}{60min}$ would be used. The result is $\frac{195h}{60}$, which reduces to $3\frac{1}{4}$ hours.

Converting units may require more than one multiplication. The key is to set up the conversion rates so that units cancel out each other and the desired unit is left. Suppose someone wants to convert 3.25 yards to inches, given that 1yd = 3ft and 12in = 1ft. To calculate, the equation use:

$$3.25yd \ \times \frac{3ft}{1yd} \times \frac{12in}{1ft}$$

The "yd" and "ft" units will cancel, resulting in 117 inches.

Area, Surface Area, and Volume

The area of a two-dimensional figure refers to the number of square units needed to cover the interior region of the figure. This concept is similar to wallpaper covering the flat surface of a wall. For example, if a rectangle has an area of 21 square centimeters (written $21cm^2$), it will take 21 squares, each with sides one centimeter in length, to cover the interior region of the rectangle. Note that area is measured in square units such as: square feet or ft^2; square yards or yd^2; square miles or mi^2.

The surface area of a three-dimensional figure refers to the number of square units needed to cover the entire surface of the figure. This concept is similar to using wrapping paper to completely cover the outside of a box. For example, if a triangular pyramid has a surface area of 17 square inches (written $17in^2$), it will take 17 squares, each with sides one inch in length, to cover the entire surface of the pyramid. Surface area is also measured in square units.

Many three-dimensional figures (solid figures) can be represented by nets consisting of rectangles and triangles. The surface area of such solids can be determined by adding the areas of each of its faces and bases. Finding the surface area using this method requires calculating the areas of rectangles and triangles. To find the area (A) of a rectangle, the length (l) is multiplied by the width (w) $\rightarrow A = l \times w$. The area of a rectangle with a length of 8cm and a width of 4cm is calculated:

$$A = (8cm) \times (4cm) \rightarrow A = 32cm^2.$$

To calculate the area (A) of a triangle, the product of $\frac{1}{2}$, the base (b), and the height (h) is found:

$$\rightarrow A = \frac{1}{2} \times b \times h$$

Note that the height of a triangle is measured from the base to the vertex opposite of it forming a right angle with the base. The area of a triangle with a base of 11cm and a height of 6cm is calculated:

$$A = \frac{1}{2} \times (11cm) \times (6cm) \rightarrow A = 33cm^2.$$

Consider the following triangular prism, which is represented by a net consisting of two triangles and three rectangles.

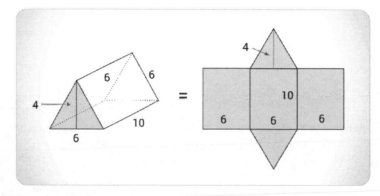

The surface area of the prism can be determined by adding the areas of each of its faces and bases. The surface area (SA) = area of triangle + area of triangle + area of rectangle + area of rectangle + area of rectangle.

$$SA = \left(\frac{1}{2} \times b \times h\right) + \left(\frac{1}{2} \times b \times h\right) + (l \times w) + (l \times w) + (l \times w)$$

$$SA = \left(\frac{1}{2} \times 6 \times 4\right) + \left(\frac{1}{2} \times 6 \times 4\right) + (6 \times 10) + (6 \times 10) + (6 \times 10)$$

$$SA = (12) + (12) + (60) + (60) + (60)$$

$$SA = 204 \; square \; units$$

Effects of Changes to Dimensions on Area and Volume

Similar polygons are figures that are the same shape but different sizes. Likewise, similar solids are different sizes but are the same shape. In both cases, corresponding angles in the same positions for both figures are congruent (equal), and corresponding sides are proportional in length. For example, the triangles below are similar. The following pairs of corresponding angles are congruent: $\angle A$ and $\angle D$; $\angle B$ and $\angle E$; $\angle C$ and $\angle F$. The corresponding sides are proportional:

$$\frac{AB}{DE} = \frac{6}{3} = 2$$

$$\frac{BC}{EF} = \frac{9}{4.5} = 2$$

$$\frac{CA}{FD} = \frac{10}{5} = 2$$

In other words, triangle *ABC* is the same shape but twice as large as triangle *DEF*.

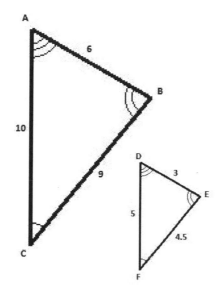

An example of similar triangular pyramids is shown below.

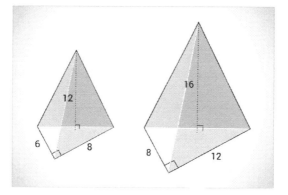

Given the nature of two- and three-dimensional measurements, changing dimensions by a given scale (multiplier) does not change the area of volume by the same scale. Consider a rectangle with a length of 5 centimeters and a width of 4 centimeters. The area of the rectangle is $20cm^2$. Doubling the dimensions of the rectangle (multiplying by a scale factor of 2) to 10 centimeters and 8 centimeters *does not* double the area to $40cm^2$. Area is a two-dimensional measurement (measured in square units). Therefore, the dimensions are multiplied by a scale that is squared (raised to the second power) to determine the scale of the corresponding areas. For the previous example, the length and width are multiplied by 2. Therefore, the area is multiplied by 2^2, or 4. The area of a 5cm × 4cm rectangle is $20cm^2$. The area of a 10cm × 8cm rectangle is $80cm^2$.

Volume is a three-dimensional measurement, which is measured in cubic units. Therefore, the scale between dimensions of similar solids is cubed (raised to the third power) to determine the scale between their volumes. Consider similar right rectangular prisms: one with a length of 8 inches, a width of 24 inches, and a height of 16 inches; the second with a length of 4 inches, a width of 12 inches, and a height of 8 inches. The first prism, multiplied by a scalar of $\frac{1}{2}$, produces the measurement of the second prism. The volume of the first prism, multiplied by $(\frac{1}{2})^3$, which equals $\frac{1}{8}$, produces the volume of the second prism. The volume of the first prism is 8in × 24in × 16in which equals $3,072in^3$. The volume of the second prism is 4in × 12in × 8in which equals $384in^3$ ($3,072in^3 \times \frac{1}{8} = 384in^3$).

The rules for squaring the scalar for area and cubing the scalar for volume only hold true for similar figures. In other words, if only one dimension is changed (changing the width of a rectangle but not the length) or dimensions are changed at different rates (the length of a prism is doubled and its height is tripled) the figures are not similar (same shape). Therefore, the rules above do not apply.

Average, Median, and Measures of Central Tendency

Suppose that X is a set of data points $(x_1, x_2, x_3, \dots x_n)$ and some description of the general properties of this data need to be found.

The first property that can be defined for this set of data is the **mean**. To find the mean, add up all the data points, then divide by the total number of data points. This can be expressed using **summation notation** as:

$$\bar{X} = \frac{x_1 + x_2 + x_3 + \cdots + x_n}{n} = \frac{1}{n}\sum_{i=1}^{n} x_i$$

For example, suppose that in a class of 10 students, the scores on a test were 50, 60, 65, 65, 75, 80, 85, 85, 90, 100. Therefore, the average test score will be $\frac{1}{10}(50 + 60 + 65 + 65 + 75 + 80 + 85 + 85 + 90 + 100) = 75.5$.

The mean is a useful number if the distribution of data is normal (more on this later), which roughly means that the frequency of different outcomes has a single peak and is roughly equally distributed on both sides of that peak. However, it is less useful in some cases where the data might be split or where there are some **outliers**. Outliers are data points that are far from the rest of the data. For example, suppose there are 90 employees and 10 executives at a company. The executives make $1000 per hour, and the employees make $10 per hour. Therefore, the average pay rate will be

$$\frac{1000 \cdot 10 + 10 \cdot 90}{100} = 109$$

OR $109 per hour. In this case, this average is not very descriptive.

Another useful measurement is the **median**. In a data set X consisting of data points $x_1, x_2, x_3, \ldots x_n$, the median is the point in the middle. The middle refers to the point where half the data comes before it and half comes after, when the data is recorded in numerical order. If n is odd, then the median is:

$$x_{\frac{n+1}{2}}$$

If n is even, it is defined as:

$$\frac{1}{2}\left(x_{\frac{n}{2}} + x_{\frac{n}{2}+1}\right)$$

It is the mean of the two data points closest to the middle of the data points. In the previous example of test scores, the two middle points are 75 and 80. Since there is no single point, the average of these two scores needs to be found. The average is:

$$\frac{75 + 80}{2} = 77.5$$

The median is generally a good value to use if there are a few outliers in the data. It prevents those outliers from affecting the "middle" value as much as when using the mean.

Since an outlier is a data point that is far from most of the other data points in a data set, this means an outlier also is any point that is far from the median of the data set. The outliers can have a substantial effect on the mean of a data set, but usually do not change the median or mode, or do not change them by a large quantity. For example, consider the data set (3, 5, 6, 6, 6, 8). This has a median of 6 and a mode of 6, with a mean of $\frac{34}{6} \approx 5.67$. Now, suppose a new data point of 1000 is added so that the data set is now (3, 5, 6, 6, 6, 8, 1000). This does not change the median or mode, which are both still 6. However, the average is now $\frac{1034}{7}$, which is approximately 147.7. In this case, the median and mode will be better descriptions for most of the data points.

The reason for outliers in a given data set is a complicated problem. It is sometimes the result of an error by the experimenter, but often they are perfectly valid data points that must be taken into consideration.

One additional measure to define for X is the **mode**. This is the data point that appears more frequently. If two or more data points all tie for the most frequent appearance, then each of them is considered a mode. In the case of the test scores, where the numbers were 50, 60, 65, 65, 75, 80, 85, 85, 90, 100, there are two modes: 65 and 85.

The **first quartile** of a set of data X refers to the largest value from the first ¼ of the data points. In practice, there are sometimes slightly different definitions that can be used, such as the median of the first half of the data points (excluding the median itself if there are an odd number of data points). The term also has a slightly different use: when it is said that a data point lies in the first quartile, it means it is less than or equal to the median of the first half of the data points. Conversely, if it lies *at* the first quartile, then it is equal to the first quartile.

When it is said that a data point lies in the **second quartile**, it means it is between the first quartile and the median.

The **third quartile** refers to data that lies between ½ and ¾ of the way through the data set. Again, there are various methods for defining this precisely, but the simplest way is to include all of the data that lie between the median and the median of the top half of the data.

Data that lies in the **fourth quartile** refers to all of the data above the third quartile.

Percentiles may be defined in a similar manner to quartiles. Generally, this is defined in the following manner:

If a data point lies *in* the n-th percentile, this means it lies in the range of the first *n*% of the data.

If a data point lies *at* the *n*-th percentile, then it means that *n*% of the data lies below this data point.

Given a data set X consisting of data points $(x_1, x_2, x_3, \ldots x_n)$, the **variance of X** is defined to be:

$$\frac{\sum_{i=1}^{n}(x_i - \bar{X})^2}{n}$$

This means that the variance of X is the average of the squares of the differences between each data point and the mean of X. In the formula, $\bar{X}$ is the mean of the values in the data set, and x_i represents each individual value in the data set. The sigma notation indicates that the sum should be found with n being the number of values to add together. $i = 1$ means that the values should begin with the first value.

Given a data set X consisting of data points $(x_1, x_2, x_3, \ldots x_n)$, the **standard deviation of X** is defined to be

$$s_x = \sqrt{\frac{\sum_{i=1}^{n}(x_i - \bar{X})^2}{n}}$$

In other words, the standard deviation is the square root of the variance.

Both the variance and the standard deviation are measures of how much the data tend to be spread out. When the standard deviation is low, the data points are mostly clustered around the mean. When the standard deviation is high, this generally indicates that the data are quite spread out, or else that there are a few substantial outliers.

As a simple example, compute the standard deviation for the data set (1, 3, 3, 5). First, compute the mean, which will be:

$$\frac{1 + 3 + 3 + 5}{4} = \frac{12}{4} = 3$$

Now, find the variance of X with the formula:

$$\sum_{i=1}^{4}(x_i - \bar{X})^2 = (1-3)^2 + (3-3)^2 + (5-3)^2 = -2^2 + 0^2 + 0^2 + 2^2 = 8$$

Therefore, the variance is

$$\frac{8}{4} = 2$$

Taking the square root, the standard deviation will be $\sqrt{2}$.

Note that the standard deviation only depends upon the mean, not upon the median or mode(s). Generally, if there are multiple modes that are far apart from one another, the standard deviation will be high. A high standard deviation does not always mean there are multiple modes, however.

Representing Numbers in Various Ways

Concrete Models
Concrete objects are used to develop a tangible understanding of operations of rational numbers. Tools such as tiles, blocks, beads, and hundred charts are used to model problems. For example, a hundred chart (10×10) and beads can be used to model multiplication. If multiplying 5 by 4, beads are placed across 5 rows and down 4 columns producing a product of 20. Similarly, tiles can be used to model division by splitting the total into equal groups. If dividing 12 by 4, 12 tiles are placed one at a time into 4 groups. The result is 4 groups of 3. This is also an effective method for visualizing the concept of remainders.

Representations of objects can be used to expand on the concrete models of operations. Pictures, dots, and tallies can help model these concepts. Utilizing concrete models and representations creates a foundation upon which to build an abstract understanding of the operations.

Rational Numbers on a Number Line
A number line typically consists of integers (...3, 2, 1, 0, -1, -2, -3...), and is used to visually represent the value of a rational number. Each rational number has a distinct position on the line determined by comparing its value with the displayed values on the line. For example, if plotting -1.5 on the number line below, it is necessary to recognize that the value of -1.5 is .5 less than -1 and .5 greater than -2. Therefore, -1.5 is plotted halfway between -1 and -2.

Number lines can also be useful for visualizing sums and differences of rational numbers. Adding a value indicates moving to the right (values increase to the right), and subtracting a value indicates moving to the left (numbers decrease to the left). For example, $-3 - 2$ is displayed by starting at -3 and moving to the left 5 spaces, if the number line is in increments of 1. This will result in an answer of -5.

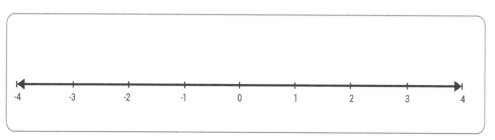

Rectangular Arrays and Area Models

Rectangular arrays include an arrangement of rows and columns that correspond to the factors and display product totals.

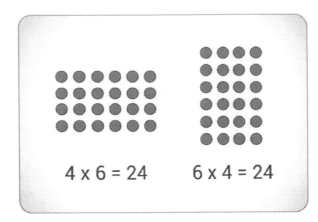

$$4 \times 6 = 24 \qquad 6 \times 4 = 24$$

An area model is a rectangle that is divided into rows and columns that match up to the number of place values within each number. For example, $29 \times 65 = 25 + 4$ and $66 = 60 + 5$. The products of those 4 numbers are found within the rectangle and then summed up to get the answer. The entire process is: $(60 \times 25) + (5 \times 25) + (60 \times 4) + (5 \times 4) = 1,500 + 240 + 125 + 20 = 1,885$.

Here is the actual area model:

	25	**4**
60	60x25 1,500	60x4 240
5	5x25 125	5x4 20

$$
\begin{array}{r}
1,500 \\
240 \\
125 \\
+ \quad 20 \\
\hline
1,885
\end{array}
$$

Practice Questions

1. At the beginning of the day, Xavier has 20 apples. At lunch, he meets his sister Emma and gives her half of his apples. After lunch, he stops by his neighbor Jim's house and gives him 6 of his apples. He then uses ¾ of his remaining apples to make an apple pie for dessert at dinner. At the end of the day, how many apples does Xavier have left?

    a. 4
    b. 6
    c. 2
    d. 1
    e. 3

2. Find the determinant of the matrix $\begin{bmatrix} -4 & 2 \\ 3 & -1 \end{bmatrix}$.

    a. -10
    b. -2
    c. 0
    d. 2
    e. -1

3. After a 20% discount, Frank purchased a new refrigerator for $850. How much did he save from the original price?

    a. $170
    b. $212.50
    c. $105.75
    d. $200
    e. $187.50

4. If the volume of a sphere is 288π cubic meters, what are the radius and surface area of the same sphere?

    a. Radius is 6 meters and surface area is 144π square meters
    b. Radius is 36 meters and surface area is 144π square meters
    c. Radius is 6 meters and surface area is 12π square meters
    d. Radius is 36 meters and surface area is 12π square meters
    e. Radius 12 meters and surface area 144π square meters

5. What is the solution to the following problem in decimal form?
$$\frac{3}{5} \times \frac{7}{10} \div \frac{1}{2}$$

    a. 0.042
    b. 84%
    c. 0.84
    d. 0.42
    e. 42%

6. If $\sqrt{1 + x} = 4$, what is x?

    a. 10

    b. 15

    c. 20

    d. 25

    e. 36

7. Karen gets paid a weekly salary and a commission for every sale that she makes. The table below shows the number of sales and her pay for different weeks.

Sales	2	7	4	8
Pay	$380	$580	$460	$620

Which of the following equations represents Karen's weekly pay?

    a. $y = 90x + 200$

    b. $y = 90x - 200$

    c. $y = 40x + 300$

    d. $y = 40x - 300$

8. Dwayne has received the following scores on his math tests: 78, 92, 83, and 97. What score must Dwayne get on his next math test to have an overall average of at least 90?

    a. 89

    b. 98

    c. 95

    d. 94

    e. 100

9. What is the domain for the function $y = \sqrt{x}$?

    a. All real numbers

    b. $x \geq 0$

    c. $x > 0$

    d. $y \geq 0$

    e. $x < 0$

10. Which of the following augmented matrices represents the system of equations below?

$$2x - 3y + z = -5$$
$$4x - y - 2z = -7$$
$$-x + 2z = -1$$

a. $\begin{bmatrix} 2 & -3 & 1 & 5 \\ 4 & -1 & 0 & -7 \\ -1 & 0 & 2 & 1 \end{bmatrix}$

b. $\begin{bmatrix} 2 & 4 & -1 \\ -3 & -1 & 0 \\ 1 & -2 & 2 \\ -5 & -7 & -1 \end{bmatrix}$

c. $\begin{bmatrix} 2 & 4 & -1 & -5 \\ -3 & -1 & 0 & -7 \\ 2 & -2 & 2 & -1 \end{bmatrix}$

d. $\begin{bmatrix} 2 & -3 & 1 \\ 4 & -1 & -2 \\ -1 & 0 & 2 \end{bmatrix}$

e. $\begin{bmatrix} 2 & -3 & 1 & -5 \\ 4 & -1 & -2 & -7 \\ -1 & 0 & 2 & -1 \end{bmatrix}$

11. What are the zeros of the function: $f(x) = x^3 + 4x^2 + 4x$?
   a. -2
   b. 0, -2
   c. 2
   d. 0, 2
   e. 0

12. If $g(x) = x^3 - 3x^2 - 2x + 6$ and $f(x) = 2$, then what is $g(f(x))$?
   a. -26
   b. 6
   c. $2x^3 - 6x^2 - 4x + 12$
   d. -2
   e. $2x^2 - 6$

13. What is the solution to the following system of equations?

$$x^2 - 2x + y = 8$$
$$x - y = -2$$

   a. $(-2, 3)$
   b. There is no solution.
   c. $(-2, 0) \, (1, 3)$
   d. $(-2, 0) \, (3, 5)$
   e. $(2, 0) \, (-1, 3)$

14. Which of the following is the result after simplifying the expression: $(7n + 3n^3 + 3) + (8n + 5n^3 + 2n^4)$?

    a. $9n^4 + 15n - 2$
    b. $2n^4 + 5n^3 + 15n - 2$
    c. $9n^4 + 8n^3 + 15n$
    d. $2n^4 + 8n^3 + 15n + 3$
    e. $2n^4 + 5n^3 + 15n - 3$

15. What is the product of the following expression?
$$(4x - 8)(5x^2 + x + 6)$$

    a. $20x^3 - 36x^2 + 16x - 48$
    b. $6x^3 - 41x^2 + 12x + 15$
    c. $204 + 11x^2 - 37x - 12$
    d. $2x^3 - 11x^2 - 32x + 20$
    e. $20x^3 - 40x^2 + 24x - 48$

16. How could the following equation be factored to find the zeros?
$$y = x^3 - 3x^2 - 4x$$

    a. $0 = x^2(x - 4), x = 0, 4$
    b. $0 = 3x(x + 1)(x + 4), x = 0, -1, -4$
    c. $0 = x(x + 1)(x + 6), x = 0, -1, -6$
    d. $0 = 3x(x + 1)(x - 4), x = 0, 1, -4$
    e. $0 = x(x + 1)(x - 4), x = 0, -1, 4$

17. What is the probability of randomly picking the winner and runner-up from a race of 4 horses and distinguishing which is the winner?

    a. $\dfrac{1}{4}$
    b. $\dfrac{1}{2}$
    c. $\dfrac{1}{16}$
    d. $\dfrac{1}{12}$
    e. $\dfrac{1}{64}$

18. Which of the following is the solution for the given equation?
$$\frac{x^2 + x - 30}{x - 5} = 11$$

    a. $x = -6$
    b. All real numbers.
    c. $x = 16$
    d. $x = 5$
    e. There is no solution.

19. Mom's car drove 72 miles in 90 minutes. How fast did she drive in feet per second?
    a. 0.8 feet per second
    b. 48.9 feet per second
    c. 0.009 feet per second
    d. 70.4 feet per second
    e. 21.3 feet per second

20. If $\frac{5}{2} \div \frac{1}{3} = n$, then n is between:
    a. 5 and 7
    b. 7 and 9
    c. 9 and 11
    d. 3 and 5
    e. 11 and 13

21.

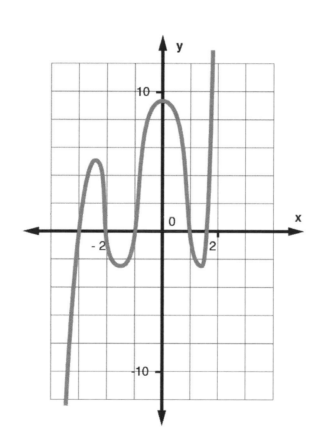

Which of the following functions represents the graph above?
    a. $y = x^5 + 3.5x^4 - 2.5x^2 + 1.5x + 9$
    b. $y = x^5 - 3.5x^4 + 2.5x^2 - 1.5x - 9$
    c. $y = 5x^4 - 2.5x^2 + 1.5x + 9$
    d. $y = -5x^4 - 2.5x^2 + 1.5x + 9$
    e. $y = 5x^4 + 3.5x^2 - 1.5x - 9$

22. If Sarah reads at an average rate of 21 pages in four nights, how long will it take her to read 140 pages?
   a. 6 nights
   b. 26 nights
   c. 8 nights
   d. 27 nights
   e. 21 nights

23. The phone bill is calculated each month using the equation $c = 50g + 75$. The cost of the phone bill per month is represented by c, and g represents the gigabytes of data used that month. Identify and interpret the slope of this equation.
   a. 75 dollars per day
   b. 75 gigabytes per day
   c. 50 dollars per day
   d. 50 dollars per gigabyte
   e. The slope cannot be determined

24. What is the function that forms an equivalent graph to $y = \cos(x)$?
   a. $y = \tan(x)$
   b. $y = \csc(x)$
   c. $y = \sin\left(x + \frac{\pi}{2}\right)$
   d. $y = \sin\left(x - \frac{\pi}{2}\right)$
   e. $y = \tan\left(x + \frac{\pi}{2}\right)$

25. Which equation best represents the scatterplot below?

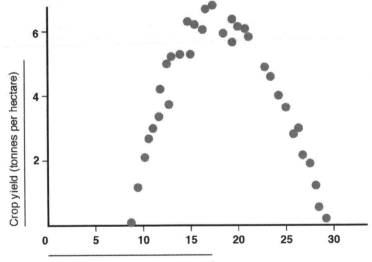

a. $y = 3x - 4$
b. $y = 2x^2 + 7x - 9$
c. $y = (3)(4^x)$
d. $y = -\frac{1}{14}x^2 + 2x - 8$
e. c. $y = -(2)(3^x)$

172

$$G = .035O + .26$$

26. The linear regression model above is based on an analysis of the price of a gallon of gas (G) at 15 gas stations compared to the price of a barrel of oil (O) at the time. Based on this model, which of the following statements are true?

    I. There is a negative correlation between G and O.

    II. When oil is $55 per barrel then gas is approximately $2.19 per gallon.

    III. The slope of the line indicates that as O increases by 1, G increases by .035.

    IV. If the price of oil increases by $8 per barrel then the price of gas will increase by approximately $0.18 per gallon.

  a. I and II

  b. II only

  c. II and III

  d. I and III

  e. II, III, and IV

27. The width of a rectangular house is 22 feet. What is the perimeter of this house if it has the same area as a house that is 33 feet wide and 50 feet long?

  a. 184 feet

  b. 200 feet

  c. 192 feet

  d. 206 feet

  e. 194 feet

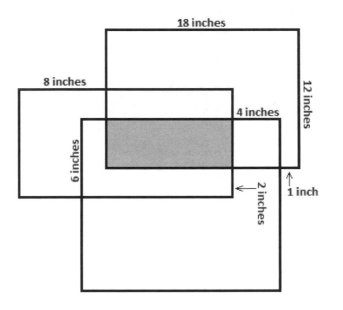

28. In the figure above, what is the area of the shaded region?

  a. 48 sq. inches

  b. 52 sq. inches

  c. 44 sq. inches

  d. 56 sq. inches

  e. 46 sq. inches

29. If $3x = 6y = -2z = 24$, then what does $4xy + z$ equal?
   a. 116
   b. 130
   c. 84
   d. 108
   e. 98

30. If $n = 2^2$, and $m = n^2$, then m^n equals?
   a. 2^{12}
   b. 2^{10}
   c. 2^{18}
   d. 2^{16}
   e. 2^{20}

31. What are the y-intercept(s) for $y = x^2 + 3x - 4$?
   a. $y = 1$
   b. $y = -4$
   c. $y = 3$
   d. $y = 4$
   e. $y = -3$

32. What is the simplified quotient of the following expression?
$$\frac{5x^3}{3x^2y} \div \frac{25}{3y^9}$$

   a. $\dfrac{125x}{9y^{10}}$

   b. $\dfrac{x}{5y^8}$

   c. $\dfrac{5}{xy^8}$

   d. $\dfrac{xy^8}{5}$

   e. $\dfrac{xy^2}{5x}$

33. What's the midpoint of a line segment with endpoints $(-1, 2)$ and $(3, -6)$?
   a. $(1, 2)$
   b. $(1, 0)$
   c. $(-1, 2)$
   d. $(1, -2)$
   e. $(1, 4)$

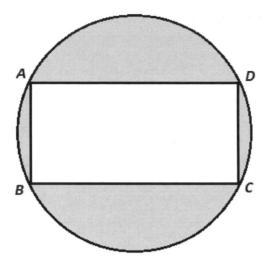

34. Rectangle *ABCD* is inscribed in the circle above. The length of side *AB* is 9 inches and the length of side *BC* is 12 inches. What is the area of the shaded region?
    a. 64.4 sq. in.
    b. 68.6 sq. in.
    c. 62.8 sq. in.
    d. 61.3 sq. in.
    e. 64.6 sq. in.

35. A six-sided die is rolled. What is the probability that the roll is 1 or 2?
    a. $\frac{1}{6}$

    b. $\frac{1}{4}$

    c. $\frac{1}{3}$

    d. $\frac{1}{2}$

    e. $\frac{1}{36}$

36. A line passes through the origin and through the point (-3, 4). What is the slope of the line?
    a. $-\frac{4}{3}$

    b. $-\frac{3}{4}$

    c. $\frac{4}{3}$

    d. $\frac{3}{4}$

    e. $\frac{1}{3}$

37. What type of function is modeled by the values in the following table?

x	$f(x)$
1	2
2	4
3	8
4	16
5	32

    a. Linear
    b. Exponential
    c. Quadratic
    d. Cubic
    e. Logarithmic

38. An investment of $2,000 is made into an account with an annual interest rate of 5%, compounded continuously. What is the total value of the investment after eight years?
    a. $4,707
    b. $3,000
    c. $2,983.65
    d. $10,919.63
    e. $1,977.61

39. A ball is drawn at random from a ball pit containing 8 red balls, 7 yellow balls, 6 green balls, and 5 purple balls. What's the probability that the ball drawn is yellow?
    a. $^1/_{26}$

    b. $^{19}/_{26}$

    c. $^{14}/_{26}$

    d. 1

    e. $^7/_{26}$

40. Two cards are drawn from a shuffled deck of 52 cards. What's the probability that both cards are Kings if the first card isn't replaced after it's drawn and is a King?
    a. $^1/_{169}$
    b. $^1/_{221}$
    c. $^1/_{13}$
    d. $^4/_{13}$
    e. $^1/_{104}$

41. What's the probability of rolling a 6 at least once in two rolls of a die?

    a. $1/3$

    b. $1/36$

    c. $1/6$

    d. $1/12$

    e. $11/36$

42. What are the coordinates of the focus of the parabola $y = -9x^2$?

    a. $(-3, 0)$

    b. $\left(-\frac{1}{36}, 0\right)$

    c. $(0, -3)$

    d. $\left(-3, -\frac{1}{36}\right)$

    e. $\left(0, -\frac{1}{36}\right)$

43. An equilateral triangle has a perimeter of 18 feet. If a square whose sides have the same length as one side of the triangle is built, what will be the area of the square?

    a. 6 square feet

    b. 36 square feet

    c. 256 square feet

    d. 1000 square feet

    e. 324 square feet

44. In a group of 20 men, the median weight is 180 pounds and the range is 30 pounds. If each man gains 10 pounds, which of the following would be true?

    a. The median weight will increase, and the range will remain the same.

    b. The median weight and range will both remain the same.

    c. The median weight will stay the same, and the range will increase.

    d. The median weight and range will both increase.

    e. The median weight will increase, and the range will decrease.

45. For the following similar triangles, what are the values of x and y (rounded to one decimal place)?

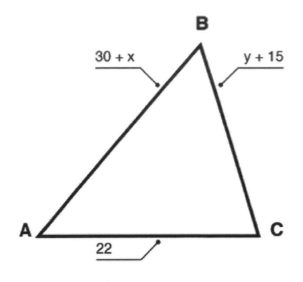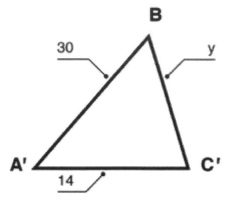

a. $x = 16.5, y = 25.1$
b. $x = 19.5, y = 24.1$
c. $x = 17.1, y = 26.3$
d. $x = 26.3, y = 17.1$
e. $x = 24.1, y = 19.5$

46. On Monday, Robert mopped the floor in 4 hours. On Tuesday, he did it in 3 hours. If on Monday, his average rate of mopping was p sq. ft. per hour, what was his average rate on Tuesday?

a. $\frac{4}{3}p$ sq. ft. per hour

b. $\frac{3}{4}p$ sq. ft. per hour

c. $\frac{5}{4}p$ sq. ft. per hour

d. $p + 1$ sq. ft. per hour

e. $\frac{1}{3}p$ sq. ft. per hour

47. Which of the following inequalities is equivalent to $3 - \frac{1}{2}x \geq 2$?

a. $x \geq 2$
b. $x \leq 2$
c. $x \geq 1$
d. $x \leq 1$
e. $x \leq -2$

48. For which of the following are $x = 4$ and $x = -4$ solutions?

a. $x^2 + 16 = 0$
b. $x^2 + 4x - 4 = 0$
c. $x^2 - 2x - 2 = 0$
d. $x^2 - x - 16 = 0$
e. $x^2 - 16 = 0$

49. What are the center and radius of a circle with equation $4x^2 + 4y^2 - 16x - 24y + 51 = 0$?
    a. Center (3, 2) and radius ½
    b. Center (2, 3) and radius ½
    c. Center (3, 2) and radius ¼
    d. Center (2, 3) and radius ¼
    e. Center (2, 2) and radius ¼

50. If the ordered pair $(-3, -4)$ is reflected over the x-axis, what's the new ordered pair?
    a. $(-3, -4)$
    b. $(3, -4)$
    c. $(3, 4)$
    d. $(-3, 4)$
    e. $(-4, -3)$

51. A triangle has sides with lengths 3, 3, and 10. Which of the following is true?
    a. It is a right triangle.
    b. It is an isosceles triangle.
    c. It cannot be a triangle.
    d. It is an equilateral triangle.
    e. It is an acute triangle.

52. The triangle shown below is a right triangle. What's the value of x?

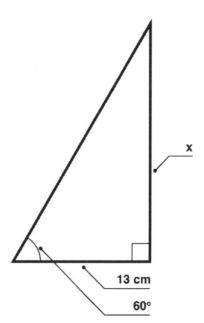

    a. $x = 1.73$
    b. $x = 0.57$
    c. $x = 13$
    d. $x = 14.73$
    e. $x = 22.49$

53. Ten students take a test. Five students get a 50. Four students get a 70. If the average score is 55, what was the last student's score?

    a. 20

    b. 40

    c. 50

    d. 60

    e. 62

54. What is the solution for the equation $\tan(x) + 1 = 0$, where $0 \leq x < 2\pi$?

    a. $x = \frac{3\pi}{4}, \frac{5\pi}{4}$

    b. $x = \frac{3\pi}{4}, \frac{\pi}{4}$

    c. $x = \frac{5\pi}{4}, \frac{7\pi}{4}$

    d. $x = \frac{3\pi}{4}, \frac{7\pi}{4}$

    e. $x = \frac{5\pi}{4}, \frac{\pi}{4}$

55. A company invests $50,000 in a building where they can produce saws. If the cost of producing one saw is $40, then which function expresses the amount of money the company pays? The variable y is the money paid and x is the number of saws produced.

    a. $y = 50{,}000x + 40$

    b. $y + 40 = x - 50{,}000$

    c. $y = 40x - 50{,}000$

    d. $y = 40x + 50{,}000$

    e. $y = 4x + 50{,}000$

56. A pair of dice is thrown, and the sum of the two scores is calculated. What's the expected value of the roll?

    a. 5

    b. 6

    c. 7

    d. 8

    e. 9

57. A line passes through the point (1, 2) and crosses the y-axis at $y = 1$. Which of the following is an equation for this line?

    a. $y = 2x$

    b. $y = x + 1$

    c. $x + y = 1$

    d. $y = \frac{x}{2} - 2$

    e. $y = x - 1$

59. $(4x^2y^4)^{\frac{3}{2}}$ can be simplified to which of the following?

a. $8x^3y^6$

b. $4x^{\frac{5}{2}}y$

c. $4xy$

d. $32x^{\frac{7}{2}}y^{\frac{11}{2}}$

e. x^3y^6

60. A ball is thrown from the top of a high hill, so that the height of the ball as a function of time is $h(t) = -16t^2 + 4t + 6$, in feet. What is the maximum height of the ball in feet?

a. 6

b. 6.25

c. 6.5

d. 6.75

e. 6.8

Answer Explanations

1. D: This problem can be solved using basic arithmetic. Xavier starts with 20 apples, then gives his sister half, so 20 divided by 2.

$$\frac{20}{2} = 10$$

He then gives his neighbor 6, so 6 is subtracted from 10.

$$10 - 6 = 4$$

Lastly, he uses ¾ of his apples to make an apple pie, so to find remaining apples, the first step is to subtract ¾ from one and then multiply the difference by 4.

$$\left(1 - \frac{3}{4}\right) \times 4 = ?$$

$$\left(\frac{4}{4} - \frac{3}{4}\right) \times 4 = ?$$

$$\left(\frac{1}{4}\right) \times 4 = 1$$

2. B: The determinant of a 2 x 2 matrix is $ad - bc$. The calculation is -4(-1) – 2(3) = 4 – 6 = -2.

3. B: Since $850 is the price *after* a 20% discount, $850 represents 80% of the original price. To determine the original price, set up a proportion with the ratio of the sale price (850) to original price (unknown) equal to the ratio of sale percentage:

$$\frac{850}{x} = \frac{80}{100}$$

(where *x* represents the unknown original price)

To solve a proportion, cross-multiply the numerators and denominators and set the products equal to each other: (850)(100) = (80)(x). Multiplying each side results in the equation 85,000 = 80x.

To solve for *x*, divide both sides by 80:

$$\frac{85,000}{80} = \frac{80x}{80}$$

resulting in *x* = 1062.5. Remember that *x* represents the original price. Subtracting the sale price from the original price ($1062.50 – $850) indicates that Frank saved $212.50.

4. A: Because the volume of the given sphere is 288π cubic meters, this means $\frac{4}{3}\pi r^3 = 288\pi$. This equation is solved for r to obtain a radius of 6 meters. The formula for the surface area of a sphere is $4\pi r^2$, so if $r = 6$ in this formula, the surface area is 144π square meters.

5. C: The first step in solving this problem is expressing the result in fraction form. Separate this problem first by solving the division operation of the last two fractions. When dividing one fraction by another, invert or flip the second fraction and then multiply the numerator and denominator.

$$\frac{7}{10} \times \frac{2}{1} = \frac{14}{10}$$

Next, multiply the first fraction with this value:

$$\frac{3}{5} \times \frac{14}{10} = \frac{42}{50}$$

Decimals are expressions of 1 or 100%, so multiply both the numerator and denominator by 2 to get the fraction as an expression of 100.

$$\frac{42}{50} \times \frac{2}{2} = \frac{84}{100}$$

In decimal form, this would be expressed as 0.84.

6. B: Start by squaring both sides to get $1 + x = 16$. Then subtract 1 from both sides to get $x = 15$.

7. C: $y = 40x + 300$. In this scenario, the variables are the number of sales and Karen's weekly pay. The weekly pay depends on the number of sales. Therefore, weekly pay is the dependent variable (y) and the number of sales is the independent variable (x). Each pair of values from the table can be written as an ordered pair (x, y): (2,380), (7,580), (4,460), (8,620). The ordered pairs can be substituted into the equations to see which creates true statements (both sides equal) for each pair. Even if one ordered pair produces equal values for a given equation, the other three ordered pairs must be checked. The only equation which is true for all four ordered pairs is $y = 40x + 300$:

$$380 = 40(2) + 300 \rightarrow 380 = 380$$

$$580 = 40(7) + 300 \rightarrow 580 = 580$$

$$460 = 40(4) + 300 \rightarrow 460 = 460$$

$$620 = 40(8) + 300 \rightarrow 620 = 620$$

8. E: To find the average of a set of values, add the values together and then divide by the total number of values. In this case, include the unknown value of what Dwayne needs to score on his next test, in order to solve it.

$$\frac{78 + 92 + 83 + 97 + x}{5} = 90$$

Add the unknown value to the new average total, which is 5. Then multiply each side by 5 to simplify the equation, resulting in:

$$78 + 92 + 83 + 97 + x = 450$$

$$350 + x = 450$$

$$x = 100$$

Dwayne would need to get a perfect score of 100 in order to get an average of at least 90.

Test this answer by substituting back into the original formula.

$$\frac{78 + 92 + 83 + 97 + 100}{5} = 90$$

9. B: The domain is all possible input values, or x-values. For this equation, the domain is every number greater than or equal to zero. There are no negative numbers in the domain because taking the square root of a negative number results in an imaginary number.

10. E: The augmented matrix that represents the system of equations has dimensions 4 x 3 because there are three equations with three unknowns. The coefficients of the variables make up the first three columns, and the last column is made up of the numbers to the right of the equals sign. This system can be solved by reducing the matrix to row-echelon form, where the last column gives the solution for the unknown variables.

11. B: There are two zeros for the function: $x = 0, -2$. The zeros can be found several ways, but this particular equation can be factored into $f(x) = x(x^2 + 4x + 4) = x(x + 2)(x + 2)$. By setting each factor equal to zero and solving for x, there are two solutions. On a graph these zeros can be seen where the line crosses the x-axis.

12. D: This problem involves a composition function, where one function is plugged into the other function. In this case, the $f(x)$ function is plugged into the $g(x)$ function for each x-value. The composition equation becomes $g(f(x)) = 2^3 - 3(2^2) - 2(2) + 6$. Simplifying the equation gives the answer $g(f(x)) = 8 - 3(4) - 2(2) + 6 = 8 - 12 - 4 + 6 = -2$.

13. D: This system of equations involves one quadratic function and one linear function, as seen from the degree of each equation. One way to solve this is through substitution. Solving for y in the second equation yields $y = x + 2$. Plugging this equation in for the y of the quadratic equation yields $x^2 - 2x + x + 2 = 8$. Simplifying the equation, it becomes $x^2 - x + 2 = 8$. Setting this equal to zero and factoring, it becomes $x^2 - x - 6 = 0 = (x - 3)(x + 2)$. Solving these two factors for x gives the zeros $x = 3, -2$. To find the y-value for the point, each number can be plugged in to either original equation. Solving each one for y yields the points $(3, 5)$ and $(-2, 0)$.

14. D: The expression is simplified by collecting like terms. Terms with the same variable and exponent are like terms, and their coefficients can be added.

15. A: Finding the product means distributing one polynomial onto the other. Each term in the first must be multiplied by each term in the second. Then, like terms can be collected. Multiplying the factors yields the expression $20x^3 + 4x^2 + 24x - 40x^2 - 8x - 48$. Collecting like terms means adding the x^2 terms and adding the x terms. The final answer after simplifying the expression is $20x^3 - 36x^2 + 16x - 48$.

16. E: Finding the zeros for a function by factoring is done by setting the equation equal to zero, then completely factoring. Since there was a common x for each term in the provided equation, that is factored out first. Then the quadratic that is left can be factored into two binomials: $(x + 1)(x - 4)$. Setting each factor equation equal to zero and solving for x yields three zeros.

17 D: The probability of picking the winner of the race is:

$$\frac{1}{4} \left(\frac{number\ of\ favorable\ outcomes}{number\ of\ total\ outcomes} \right)$$

Assuming the winner was picked on the first selection, three horses remain from which to choose the runner-up (these are dependent events). Therefore, the probability of picking the runner-up is $\frac{1}{3}$. To determine the probability of multiple events, the probability of each event is multiplied:

$$\frac{1}{4} \times \frac{1}{3} = \frac{1}{12}$$

18. E: The equation can be solved by factoring the numerator into $(x + 6)(x - 5)$. Since that same factor exists on top and bottom, that factor $(x - 5)$ cancels. This leaves the equation $x + 6 = 11$. Solving the equation gives the answer $x = 5$. When this value is plugged into the equation, it yields a zero in the denominator of the fraction. Since this is undefined, there is no solution.

19. D: This problem can be solved by using unit conversion. The initial units are miles per minute. The final units need to be feet per second. Converting miles to feet uses the equivalence statement 1 mile = 5,280 feet. Converting minutes to seconds uses the equivalence statement 1 minute = 60 seconds. Setting up the ratios to convert the units is shown in the following equation

$$\frac{72\ miles}{90\ minutes} * \frac{1\ minute}{60\ seconds} * \frac{5280\ feet}{1\ mile} = 70.4 \text{ feet per second.}$$

The initial units cancel out, and the new units are left.

20. B: $\frac{5}{2} \div \frac{1}{3} = \frac{5}{2} \times \frac{3}{1} = \frac{15}{2} = 7.5.$

21. A: The graph contains four turning points (where the curve changes from rising to falling or vice versa). This indicates that the degree of the function (highest exponent for the variable) is 5, eliminating Choices C, D, and e. The y-intercepts of the functions can be determined by substituting 0 for x and finding the value of y. The function for Choice A has a y-intercept of 9, and the function for Choice B has a y-intercept of -9. Therefore, Choice B is eliminated.

22. D: This problem can be solved by setting up a proportion involving the given information and the unknown value. The proportion is:

$$\frac{21 \, pages}{4 \, nights} = \frac{140 \, pages}{x \, nights}$$

Solving the proportion by cross-multiplying, the equation becomes $21x = 4 * 140$, where $x = 26.67$. Since it is not an exact number of nights, the answer is rounded up to 27 nights. Twenty-six nights would not give Sarah enough time.

23. D: The slope from this equation is 50, and it is interpreted as the cost per gigabyte used. Since the g-value represents number of gigabytes and the equation is set equal to the cost in dollars, the slope relates these two values. For every gigabyte used on the phone, the bill goes up 50 dollars.

24. C: Graphing the function $y = \cos(x)$ shows that the curve starts at $(0, 1)$, has an amplitude of 2, and a period of 2π. This same curve can be constructed using the sine graph, by shifting the graph to the left $\frac{\pi}{2}$ units. This equation is in the form $y = \sin(x + \frac{\pi}{2})$.

25. D: The shape of the scatterplot is a parabola (U-shaped). This eliminates Choices A (a linear equation that produces a straight line) and C and E (both are an exponential equation, which produce a smooth curve upward or downward). The value of a for a quadratic function in standard form ($y = ax^2 + bx + c$) indicates whether the parabola opens up (U-shaped) or opens down (upside-down U). A negative value for a produces a parabola that opens down; therefore, Choice B can also be eliminated.

26. C: II and III are the only true statements. If graphed this line would have a positive correlation, which make statement I false. Also, if the price of oil increases by $8 per barrel then gas price would increase by $.035(8) = \$0.28$ per gallon. This make statement IV false as well.

27. E: First, find the area of the second house. The area is $A = l \, x \, w = 33 \times 50 = 1,650$ square feet. Then use the area formula to determine what length gives the first house an area of 1,650 square feet. So, $1,650 = 22 \times l, l = \frac{1,650}{22} = 75$ feet. Then, use the formula for perimeter to get:

$$75 + 75 + 22 + 22 = 194 \text{ feet.}$$

28. B: This can be determined by finding the length and width of the shaded region. The length can be found using the length of the top rectangle which is 18 inches, then subtracting the extra length of 4 inches and 1 inch. This means the length of the shaded region is 13 inches. Next, the width can be determined using the 6 inch measurement and subtracting the 2 inch measurement. This means that the width is 4 inches. Thus, the area is $13 \times 4 = 52$ sq. inches.

29. A: First solve for x, y, and z. So, $3x = 24, x = 8, 6y = 24, y = 4$, and $-2z = 24, z = -12$. This means the equation would be $4(8)(4) + (-12)$, which equals 116.

30. D: If $n = 2^2, n = 4$, and $m = 4^2 = 16$. This means that $m^n = 16^4$. This is the same as 2^{16}.

31. B: The y-intercept of an equation is found where the x-value is zero. Plugging zero into the equation for x allows the first two terms to cancel out, leaving -4.

32. D: Dividing rational expressions follows the same rule as dividing fractions. The division is changed to multiplication, and the reciprocal is found in the second fraction. This turns the expression into:

$$\frac{5x^3}{3x^2} * \frac{3y^9}{25}$$

Multiplying across and simplifying, the final expression is $\frac{xy^8}{5}$.

33. D: The midpoint formula should be used.

$$M = \left(\frac{x_1 + x_2}{2}, \frac{y_1 + y_2}{2}\right) = \left(\frac{-1 + 3}{2}, \frac{2 + (-6)}{2}\right) = (1, -2)$$

34. B: The inscribed rectangle is 9 X 12 inches. First find the length of AC using the Pythagorean Theorem. So, $9^2 + 12^2 = c^2$, where c is the length of AC in this case. This means that AC = 15 inches. This means the diameter of the circle is 15 inches. This can be used to find the area of the entire circle. The formula is πr^2. So, $3.14(7.5)^2 = 176.6$ sq. inches. Then take the area of the rectangle away to find just the area of the shaded region. This is $176.6 - 108 = 68.6$.

35. C: A die has an equal chance for each outcome. Since it has six sides, each outcome has a probability of $\frac{1}{6}$. The chance of a 1 or a 2 is therefore:

$$\frac{1}{6} + \frac{1}{6} = \frac{1}{3}.$$

36. A: The slope is given by:

$$m = \frac{y_2 - y_1}{x_2 - x_1} = \frac{0 - 4}{0 - (-3)} = -\frac{4}{3}.$$

37. B: The table shows values that are increasing exponentially. The differences between the inputs are the same, while the differences in the outputs are changing by a factor of 2. The values in the table can be modeled by the equation $f(x) = 2^x$.

38. C: The formula for continually compounded interest is $A = Pe^{rt}$. Plugging in the given values to find the total amount in the account yields the equation $A = 2000e^{0.05*8} = 2983.65$.

39. E: The sample space is made up of $8 + 7 + 6 + 5 = 26$ balls. The probability of pulling each individual ball is $1/26$. Since there are 7 yellow balls, the probability of pulling a yellow ball is $7/26$.

40. B: For the first card drawn, the probability of a King being pulled is $4/52$. Since this card isn't replaced, if a King is drawn first, the probability of a King being drawn second is $3/51$. The probability of a King being drawn in both the first and second draw is the product of the two probabilities: $4/52$ x $3/51 = 12/2652$ which, divided by 12, equals $1/221$.

41. E: The addition rule is necessary to determine the probability because a 6 can be rolled on either roll of the die. The rule used is $P(A \text{ or } B) = P(A) + P(B) - P(A \text{ and } B)$. The probability of a 6 being individually rolled is $1/6$ and the probability of a 6 being rolled twice is $1/6 \cdot 1/6 = 1/36$. Therefore, the probability that a 6 is rolled at least once is $1/6 + 1/6 - 1/36 = 11/36$

42. E: A parabola of the form $y = \frac{1}{4f}x^2$ has a focus $(0, f)$. Because $y = -9x^2$, set $-9 = \frac{1}{4f}$. Solving this equation for f results in $f = -\frac{1}{36}$. Therefore, the coordinates of the focus are $\left(0, -\frac{1}{36}\right)$.

43. B: An equilateral triangle has three sides of equal length, so if the total perimeter is 18 feet, each side must be 6 feet long. A square with sides of 6 feet will have an area of $6^2 = 36$ square feet.

44. A: If each man gains 10 pounds, every original data point will increase by 10 pounds. Therefore, the man with the original median will still have the median value, but that value will increase by 10. The smallest value and largest value will also increase by 10 and, therefore, the difference between the two won't change. The range does not change in value and, thus, remains the same.

45. C: Because the triangles are similar, the lengths of the corresponding sides are proportional. Therefore:

$$\frac{30 + x}{30} = \frac{22}{14} = \frac{y + 15}{y}$$

This results in the equation $14(30 + x) = 22 \cdot 30$ which, when solved, gives $x = 17.1$. The proportion also results in the equation $14(y + 15) = 22y$ which, when solved, gives $y = 26.3$.

46. A: Robert accomplished his task on Tuesday in ¾ the time compared to Monday. He must have worked 4/3 as fast.

47. B: To simplify this inequality, subtract 3 from both sides to get:

$$-\frac{1}{2}x \geq -1$$

Then, multiply both sides by -2 (remembering this flips the direction of the inequality) to get $x \leq 2$.

48. E: There are two ways to approach this problem. Each value can be substituted into each equation. Choice *A* can be eliminated, since $4^2 + 16 = 32$. Choice *B* can be eliminated, since $4^2 + 4 \cdot 4 - 4 = 28$. Choice *C* can be eliminated, since $4^2 - 2 \cdot 4 - 2 = 6$. But, plugging in either value into $x^2 - 16$ gives

$$(\pm 4)^2 - 16 = 16 - 16 = 0.$$

49. B: The technique of completing the square must be used to change $4x^2 + 4y^2 - 16x - 24y + 51 = 0$ into the standard equation of a circle. First, the constant must be moved to the right-hand side of the equals sign, and each term must be divided by the coefficient of the x^2 term (which is 4). The x and y terms must be grouped together to obtain:

$$x^2 - 4x + y^2 - 6y = -\frac{51}{4}$$

Next, the process of completing the square must be completed for each variable. This gives:

$$(x^2 - 4x + 4) + (y^2 - 6y + 9) = -\frac{51}{4} + 4 + 9$$

The equation can be written as:

$$(x - 2)^2 + (y - 3)^2 = \frac{1}{4}$$

Therefore, the center of the circle is (2, 3) and the radius is $\sqrt{1/4} = 1/2$.

50. D: When an ordered pair is reflected over an axis, the sign of one of the coordinates must change. When it's reflected over the x-axis, the sign of the y-coordinate must change. The x-value remains the same. Therefore, the new ordered pair is $(-3,\ 4)$.

51. C: Because $3^2 + 3^2$ is not equal to 10^2, it cannot be a right triangle from the converse of the Pythagorean theorem. However, the Triangle Inequality Theorem states that for any triangle, the sum of the lengths of two sides has to be greater than the third side. $3 + 3$ is not larger than 10, and therefore, these sides cannot form a triangle.

52. E: SOHCAHTOA is used to find the missing side length. Because the angle and adjacent side are known, $\tan 60 = \frac{x}{13}$. Making sure to evaluate tangent with an argument in degrees, this equation gives $x = 13 \tan 60 = 13 \cdot 1.73 = 22.49$.

53. A: Let the unknown score be x. The average will be:

$$\frac{5 \cdot 50 + 4 \cdot 70 + x}{10} = \frac{530 + x}{10} = 55$$

Multiply both sides by 10 to get $530 + x = 550$, or $x = 20$.

54. D: Using SOHCAHTOA, tangent is $\frac{y}{x}$ for the special triangles. Since the value needs to be negative one, the angle must be some form of 45 degrees or $\frac{\pi}{4}$. The value is negative in the second and fourth quadrant, so the answer is:

$$\frac{3\pi}{4} \text{ and } \frac{7\pi}{4}$$

55. D: For manufacturing costs, there is a linear relationship between the cost to the company and the number produced, with a y-intercept given by the base cost of acquiring the means of production, and a slope given by the cost to produce one unit. In this case, that base cost is $50,000, while the cost per unit is $40. So, $y = 40x + 50,000$.

56. C: The expected value is equal to the total sum of each product of individual score and probability. There are 36 possible rolls. The probability of rolling a 2 is $\frac{1}{36}$. The probability of rolling a 3 is $\frac{2}{36}$. The probability of rolling a 4 is $\frac{3}{36}$. The probability of rolling a 5 is $\frac{4}{36}$. The probability of rolling a 6 is $\frac{5}{36}$. The probability of rolling a 7 is $\frac{6}{36}$. The probability of rolling an 8 is $\frac{5}{36}$. The probability of rolling a 9 is $\frac{4}{36}$. The probability of rolling a 10 is $\frac{3}{36}$. The probability of rolling an 11 is $\frac{2}{36}$. Finally, the probability of rolling a 12 is $\frac{1}{36}$.

Each possible outcome is multiplied by the probability of it occurring. Like this:

$$2 \times \frac{1}{36} = a$$

$$3 \times \frac{2}{36} = b$$

$$4 \times \frac{3}{36} = c$$

And so forth.

Then all of those results are added together:

$$a + b + c \ldots = expected\ value$$

In this case, it equals 7.

57. B: From the slope-intercept form, $y = mx + b$, it is known that b is the y-intercept, which is 1. Compute the slope as $\frac{2-1}{1-0} = 1$, so the equation should be $y = x + 1$.

58. A: This has the form $t^2 - y^2$, with $t = x^2$ and $y = 4$. It's also known that $t^2 - y^2 = (t + y)(t - y)$, and substituting the values for t and y into the right-hand side gives $(x^2 - 4)(x^2 + 4)$.

59. A: Simplify this to:

$$(4x^2y^4)^{\frac{3}{2}} = 4^{\frac{3}{2}}(x^2)^{\frac{3}{2}}(y^4)^{\frac{3}{2}}$$

$$4^{\frac{3}{2}} = (\sqrt{4})^3 = 2^3 = 8$$

For the other, recall that the exponents must be multiplied, so this yields:

$$8x^{2 \cdot \frac{3}{2}}y^{4 \cdot \frac{3}{2}} = 8x^3y^6.$$

60. B: The independent variable's coordinate at the vertex of a parabola (which is the highest point, when the coefficient of the squared independent variable is negative) is given by:

$$x = -\frac{b}{2a}$$

Substitute and solve for x to get:

$$x = -\frac{4}{2(-16)} = \frac{1}{8}$$

Using this value of x, the maximum height of the ball (y), can be calculated. Substituting x into the equation yields:

$$h(t) = -16\frac{1}{8}^2 + 4\frac{1}{8} + 6 = 6.25$$

ACT Reading Test

What to Expect

The Reading test contains four passages that are 700-800 words in length. These passages represent the content categories of Literature, Humanities, Social Science, and Natural Science. Each passage has 10 multiple-choice questions associated with it. Test takers have 35 minutes to read the passages and answer the questions.

Tips for the Reading Test

- Play to your strengths. Start reading the passage that falls under the category or topic you are must comfortable with. This will boost your confidence and help you move through that portion of the section efficiently. Test takers often struggle with the fast pace of this section, so starting with something most familiar can help ensure you get a good jump on the Reading questions.

- Underline parts while you read. Key details, clues about the author's purpose, etc. may be revealed in the initial skim or read through. Marking these spots will save time finding them once the questions are addressed without needing to interrupt the flow of reading to stop and answer questions.

- Move along. Skim the passage first and then read the questions carefully. Eliminate the answer choices you know are wrong. If you can't figure it out in 30-45 seconds, mark the question and move on. After 9 minutes, move to the next passage in order to stay on pace. At the very end of the section, guess the answers to those questions you could not figure out or ran out of time to answer.

Key Ideas and Details

Central Ideas and Themes

Topic, Main Idea, Supporting Details, and Themes
The **topic** of a text is the overall subject, and the **main idea** more specifically builds on that subject. Consider a paragraph that begins with the following: "The United States government is made of up three branches: executive, judicial, and legislative." If this sentence is divided into its essential components, there is the topic (United States Government) and the main idea (the three branches of government).

A main idea must be supported with details, which usually appear in the form of quotations, paraphrasing, or analysis. Authors should connect details and analysis to the main point. Readers should always be cautious when accepting the validity of an argument and look for logical fallacies, such as slippery slope, straw man, and begging the question. While arguments may seem sound, further analysis often reveals they are flawed. It's okay for a reader to disagree with an author.

It is important to remember that when most authors write, they want to make a point or send a message. This point or the message of a text is known as the **theme**. Authors may state themes explicitly, like in *Aesop's Fables*. More often, especially in modern literature, readers must infer the theme based on textual details. Usually after carefully reading and analyzing an entire text, the theme emerges. Typically, the longer the piece, the more numerous its themes, though often one theme dominates the rest, as evidenced by the author's purposeful revisiting of it throughout the passage.

Identifying Theme or Central Message

The **theme** is the central message of a fictional work, whether that work is structured as prose, drama, or poetry. It is the heart of what an author is trying to say to readers through the writing, and theme is largely conveyed through literary elements and techniques.

In literature, a theme can often be determined by considering the over-arching narrative conflict within the work. Though there are several types of conflicts and several potential themes within them, the following are the most common:

- **Individual against the self**—relevant to themes of self-awareness, internal struggles, pride, coming of age, facing reality, fate, free will, vanity, loss of innocence, loneliness, isolation, fulfillment, failure, and disillusionment

- **Individual against nature**—relevant to themes of knowledge vs. ignorance, nature as beauty, quest for discovery, self-preservation, chaos and order, circle of life, death, and destruction of beauty

- **Individual against society**—relevant to themes of power, beauty, good, evil, war, class struggle, totalitarianism, role of men/women, wealth, corruption, change vs. tradition, capitalism, destruction, heroism, injustice, and racism

- **Individual against another individual**—relevant to themes of hope, loss of love or hope, sacrifice, power, revenge, betrayal, and honor

For example, in Hawthorne's *The Scarlet Letter*, one possible narrative conflict could be the individual against the self, with a relevant theme of internal struggles. This theme is alluded to through characterization—Dimmesdale's moral struggle with his love for Hester and Hester's internal struggles with the truth and her daughter, Pearl. It's also alluded to through plot—Dimmesdale's suicide and Hester helping the very townspeople who initially condemned her.

Sometimes, a text can convey a **message or universal lesson**—a truth or insight that the reader infers from the text, based on analysis of the literary and/or poetic elements. This message is often presented as a statement. For example, a potential message in Shakespeare's *Hamlet* could be "Revenge is what ultimately drives the human soul." This message can be immediately determined through plot and characterization in numerous ways, but it can also be determined through the setting of Norway, which is bordering on war.

How Authors Develop Theme

Authors employ a variety of techniques to present a theme. They may compare or contrast characters, events, places, ideas, or historical or invented settings to speak thematically. They may use analogies, metaphors, similes, allusions, or other literary devices to convey the theme. An author's use of diction, syntax, and tone can also help convey the theme. Authors will often develop themes through the development of characters, use of the setting, repetition of ideas, use of symbols, and through contrasting value systems. Authors of both fiction and nonfiction genres will use a variety of these techniques to develop one or more themes.

Regardless of the literary genre, there are commonalities in how authors, playwrights, and poets develop themes or central ideas.

Authors often do research, the results of which contributes to theme. In prose fiction and drama, this research may include real historical information about the setting the author has chosen or include elements that make fictional characters, settings, and plots seem realistic to the reader. In nonfiction, research is critical since the information contained within this literature must be accurate and, moreover, accurately represented.

In fiction, authors present a narrative conflict that will contribute to the overall theme. In fiction, this conflict may involve the storyline itself and some trouble within characters that needs resolution. In nonfiction, this conflict may be an explanation or commentary on factual people and events.

Authors will sometimes use character motivation to convey theme, such as in the example from *Hamlet* regarding revenge. In fiction, the characters an author creates will think, speak, and act in ways that effectively convey the theme to readers. In nonfiction, the characters are factual, as in a biography, but authors pay particular attention to presenting those motivations to make them clear to readers.

Authors also use literary devices as a means of conveying theme. For example, the use of moon symbolism in Shelley's *Frankenstein* is significant as its phases can be compared to the phases that the Creature undergoes as he struggles with his identity.

The selected point of view can also contribute to a work's theme. The use of first person point of view in a fiction or nonfiction work engages the reader's response differently than third person point of view. The central idea or theme from a first-person narrative may differ from a third-person limited text.

In literary nonfiction, authors usually identify the purpose of their writing, which differs from fiction, where the general purpose is to entertain. The purpose of nonfiction is usually to inform, persuade, or entertain the audience. The stated purpose of a nonfiction text will drive how the central message or theme, if applicable, is presented.

Authors identify an audience for their writing, which is critical in shaping the theme of the work. For example, the audience for J.K. Rowling's *Harry Potter* series would be different than the audience for a biography of George Washington. The audience an author chooses to address is closely tied to the purpose of the work. The choice of an audience also drives the choice of language and level of diction an author uses. Ultimately, the intended audience determines the level to which that subject matter is presented and the complexity of the theme.

Cultural Differences in Themes
Regardless of culture, place, or time, certain themes are universal to the human condition. Because all humans experience certain feelings and engage in similar experiences—birth, death, marriage, friendship, finding meaning, etc.—certain themes span cultures. However, different cultures have different norms and general beliefs concerning these themes. For example, the theme of maturing and crossing from childhood to adulthood is a global theme; however, the literature from one culture might imply that this happens in someone's twenties, while another culture's literature might imply that it happens in the early teenage years.

It's important for the reader to be aware of these differences. Readers must avoid being **ethnocentric**, which means believing the aspects of one's own culture to be superior to those of other cultures.

Summarizing Information Accurately

Summarizing is an effective way to draw a conclusion from a passage. A **summary** is a shortened version of the original text, written by the reader in his or her own words. Focusing on the main points of the original text and including only the relevant details can help readers reach a conclusion. It's important to retain the original meaning of the passage.

Like summarizing, **paraphrasing** can also help a reader fully understand different parts of a text. Paraphrasing calls for the reader to take a small part of the passage and list or describe its main points. However, paraphrasing is more than rewording the original passage; it should be written in the reader's own words, while still retaining the meaning of the original source. This will indicate an understanding of the original source, yet still help the reader expand on his or her interpretation.

Understanding Relationships

Inferences are useful in gaining a deeper understanding of how people, events, and ideas are connected in a passage. Readers can use the same strategies used with general inferences and analyzing texts—paying attention to details and using them to make reasonable guesses about the text—to read between the lines and get a more complete picture of how (and why) characters are thinking, feeling, and acting. Read the following passage from O. Henry's story "The Gift of the Magi":

> One dollar and eighty-seven cents. That was all. And sixty cents of it was in pennies. Pennies saved one and two at a time by bulldozing the grocer and the vegetable man and the butcher until one's cheeks burned with the silent imputation of parsimony that such close dealing implied. Three times Della counted it. One dollar and eighty-seven cents. And the next day would be Christmas.

> There was clearly nothing to do but flop down on the shabby little couch and howl. So Della did it.

These paragraphs introduce the reader to the character Della. Even though the author doesn't include a direct description of Della, the reader can already form a general impression of her personality and emotions. One detail that should stick out to the reader is repetition: "one dollar and eighty-seven cents." This amount is repeated twice in the first paragraph, along with other descriptions of money: "sixty cents of it was in pennies," "pennies saved one and two at a time." The story's preoccupation with money parallels how Della herself is constantly thinking about her finances—"three times Della counted" her meager savings. Already the reader can guess that Della is having money problems. Next, think about her emotions. The first paragraph describes haggling over groceries "until one's cheeks burned"—another way to describe blushing. People tend to blush when they are embarrassed or ashamed, so readers can infer that Della is ashamed by her financial situation. This inference is also supported by the second paragraph, when she flops down and howls on her "shabby little couch." Clearly, she's in distress. Without saying, "Della has no money and is embarrassed to be poor," O. Henry is able to communicate the same impression to readers through his careful inclusion of details.

A character's **motive** is their reason for acting a certain way. Usually, characters are motivated by something that they want. In the passage above, why is Della upset about not having enough money? There's an important detail at the end of the first paragraph: "the next day would be Christmas." Why is money especially important around Christmas? Christmas is a holiday when people exchange gifts. If Della is struggling with money, she's probably also struggling to buy gifts. So a shrewd reader should be able to guess that Della's motivation is wanting to buy a gift for someone—but she's currently unable to afford it, leading to feelings of shame and frustration.

In order to understand characters in a text, readers should keep the following questions in mind:

- What words does the author use to describe the character? Are these words related to any specific emotions or personality traits (for example, characteristics like rude, friendly, unapproachable, or innocent)?

- What does the character say? Does their dialogue seem to be straightforward, or are they hiding some thoughts or emotions?

- What actions can be observed from this character? How do their actions reflect their feelings?

- What does the character want? What do they do to get it?

Drawing Logical Inferences and Conclusions

<u>Making Inferences</u>
Predictions
Some texts use suspense and foreshadowing to captivate readers. For example, an intriguing aspect of murder mysteries is that the reader is never sure of the culprit until the author reveals the individual's identity. Authors often build suspense and add depth and meaning to a work by leaving clues to provide hints or predict future events in the story; this is called foreshadowing. While some instances of foreshadowing are subtle, others are quite obvious.

Inferences
Another way to read actively is to identify examples of inference within text. Making an inference requires the reader to read between the lines and look for what is implied rather than what is directly stated. That is, using information that is known from the text, the reader is able to make a logical assumption about information that is *not* directly stated but is probably true.

Authors employ literary devices such as tone, characterization, and theme to engage the audience by showing details of the story instead of merely telling them. For example, if an author said *Bob is selfish*, there's little left to infer. If the author said, *Bob cheated on his test, ignored his mom's calls, and parked illegally*, the reader can infer Bob is selfish. Authors also make implications through character dialogue, thoughts, effects on others, actions, and looks. Like in life, readers must assemble all the clues to form a complete picture.

Read the following passage:

> "Hey, do you wanna meet my new puppy?" Jonathan asked.
>
> "Oh, I'm sorry but please don't—" Jacinta began to protest, but before she could finish, Jonathan had already opened the passenger side door of his car and a perfect white ball of fur came bouncing towards Jacinta.
>
> "Isn't he the cutest?" beamed Jonathan.
>
> "Yes—achoo!—he's pretty—aaaachooo!!—adora—aaa—aaaachoo!" Jacinta managed to say in between sneezes. "But if you don't mind, I—I—achoo!—need to go inside."

Which of the following can be inferred from Jacinta's reaction to the puppy?
  a. she hates animals
  b. she is allergic to dogs
  c. she prefers cats to dogs
  d. she is angry at Jonathan

An inference requires the reader to consider the information presented and then form their own idea about what is probably true. Based on the details in the passage, what is the best answer to the question? Important details to pay attention to include the tone of Jacinta's dialogue, which is overall polite and apologetic, as well as her reaction itself, which is a long string of sneezes. Answer choices (a) and (d) both express strong emotions ("hates" and "angry") that are not evident in Jacinta's speech or actions. Answer choice (c) mentions cats, but there is nothing in the passage to indicate Jacinta's feelings about cats. Answer choice (b), "she is allergic to dogs," is the most logical choice—based on the fact that she began sneezing as soon as a fluffy dog approached her, it makes sense to guess that Jacinta might be allergic to dogs. So even though Jacinta never directly states, "Sorry, I'm allergic to dogs!" using the clues in the passage, it is still reasonable to guess that this is true.

Making inferences is crucial for readers of literature, because literary texts often avoid presenting complete and direct information to readers about characters' thoughts or feelings, or they present this information in an unclear way, leaving it up to the reader to interpret clues given in the text. In order to make inferences while reading, readers should ask themselves:

- What details are being presented in the text?
- Is there any important information that seems to be missing?
- Based on the information that the author *does* include, what else is probably true?
- Is this inference reasonable based on what is already known?

Conclusions

Active readers should also draw conclusions. When doing so, the reader should ask the following questions: What is this piece about? What does the author believe? Does this piece have merit? Do I believe the author? Would this piece support my argument? The reader should first determine the author's intent. Identify the author's viewpoint and connect relevant evidence to support it. Readers may then move to the most important step: deciding whether to agree and determining whether they are correct. Always read cautiously and critically. Interact with text, and record reactions in the margins. These active reading skills help determine not only what the author thinks, but what the you as the reader thinks.

Determining conclusions requires being an active reader, as a reader must make a prediction and analyze facts to identify a conclusion. A reader should identify key words in a passage to determine the logical conclusion from the information presented. Consider the passage below:

> Lindsay, covered in flour, moved around the kitchen frantically. Her mom yelled from another room, "Lindsay, we're going to be late!

Readers can conclude that Lindsay's next steps are to finish baking, clean herself up, and head off somewhere with her baked goods. It's important to note that the conclusion cannot be verified factually. Many conclusions are not spelled out specifically in the text; thus, they have to be inferred and deduced by the reader.

<u>Evaluating a Passage</u>

Readers draw **conclusions** about what an author has presented. This helps them better understand what the writer has intended to communicate and whether or not they agree with what the author has offered. There are a few ways to determine a logical conclusion, but careful reading is the most important. It's helpful to read a passage a few times, noting details that seem important to the piece. Sometimes, readers arrive at a conclusion that is different than what the writer intended or they may come up with more than one conclusion.

Textual evidence within the details helps readers draw a conclusion about a passage. **Textual evidence** refers to information—facts and examples—that support the main point. Textual evidence will likely come from outside sources and can be in the form of quoted or paraphrased material. In order to draw a conclusion from evidence, it's important to examine the credibility and validity of that evidence as well as how (and if) it relates to the main idea.

If an author presents a differing opinion or a **counterargument**, in order to refute it, the reader should consider how and why this information is being presented. It is meant to strengthen the original argument and shouldn't be confused with the author's intended conclusion, but it should also be considered in the reader's final evaluation.

Sometimes, authors explicitly state the conclusion that they want readers to understand. Alternatively, a conclusion may not be directly stated. In that case, readers must rely on the implications to form a logical conclusion:

> On the way to the bus stop, Michael realized his homework wasn't in his backpack. He ran back to the house to get it and made it back to the bus just in time.

In this example, although it's never explicitly stated, it can be inferred that Michael is a student on his way to school in the morning. When forming a conclusion from implied information, it's important to read the text carefully to find several pieces of evidence in the text to support the conclusion.

Sequential, Comparative, and Cause-Effect Relationships

Ideas within texts should be organized, connected, or related in some way. In sequential relationships, ideas or events have a temporal relationship; they occur in some sort of order. Every passage has a plot, whether it is from a short story, a manual, a newspaper article or editorial, or a history text. And each plot has a logical order, which is also known as a sequence. Some of the most straightforward sequences can be found in technology directions, science experiments, instructional materials, and recipes. These forms of writing list actions that must occur in a proper sequence in order to get sufficient results. Other forms of writing, however, use style and ideas in ways that completely change the sequence of events. Poetry, for instance, may introduce repetitions that make the events seem cyclical. Postmodern writers are famous for experimenting with different concepts of place and time, creating "cut scenes" that distort straightforward sequences and abruptly transport the audience to different contexts or times. Even everyday newspaper articles, editorials, and historical sources may experiment with different sequential forms for stylistic effect.

Most questions that call for test takers to apply their sequential knowledge use key words such as **sequence**, **sequence of events**, or **sequential order** to cue the test taker in to the task at hand. In social studies or history passages, the test questions might employ key words such as **chronology** or **chronological order** to cue the test taker. In some cases, sequence can be found through comprehension techniques. These literal passages number the sequences, or they use key words such as *firstly, secondly, finally, next,* or *then.* The sequences of these stories can be found by rereading the passage and charting these numbers or key words. In most cases, however, readers have to correctly order events through inferential and evaluative reading techniques; they have to place events in a logical order without explicit cues.

Ideas in a text can also have a **comparative** relationship wherein certain qualities are shown to overlap or be the same between two different things. In comparative relationships, similarities are drawn out. Words like *as, like, also, similarly, in the same way,* and *too* are often used.

Passages that have a **cause-and-effect** relationship demonstrate a specific type of connection between ideas events wherein one (or multiple) caused another. Words such as *if, since, because, then,* or *consequently* indicate a relationship.

Understanding the Meaning and Purpose of Transition Words
The writer should act as a guide, showing the reader how all the sentences fit together. Consider this example:

> Seat belts save more lives than any other automobile safety feature. Many studies show that airbags save lives as well. Not all cars have airbags. Many older cars don't. Air bags aren't entirely reliable. Studies show that in 15% of accidents, airbags don't deploy as designed. Seat belt malfunctions are extremely rare.

There's nothing wrong with any of these sentences individually, but together they're disjointed and difficult to follow. The best way for the writer to communicate information is through the use of transition words. Here are examples of transition words and phrases that tie sentences together, enabling a more natural flow:

- To show causality: *as a result, therefore,* and *consequently*
- To compare and contrast: *however, but,* and *on the other hand*
- To introduce examples: *for instance, namely,* and *including*
- To show order of importance: *foremost, primarily, secondly,* and *lastly*

Note: This is not a complete list of transitions. There are many more that can be used; however, most fit into these or similar categories. The point is that the words should clearly show the relationship between sentences, supporting information, and the main idea.

Here is an update to the previous example using transition words. These changes make it easier to read and bring clarity to the writer's points:

> Seat belts save more lives than any other automobile safety feature. Many studies show that airbags save lives as well; however, not all cars have airbags. For instance, some older cars don't. Furthermore, air bags aren't entirely reliable. For example, studies show that in 15% of accidents, airbags don't deploy as designed; but, on the other hand, seat belt malfunctions are extremely rare.

Also, be prepared to analyze whether the writer is using the best transition word or phrase for the situation. Take this sentence for example: "As a result, seat belt malfunctions are extremely rare." This sentence doesn't make sense in the context above because the writer is trying to show the contrast between seat belts and airbags, not the causality.

Craft and Structure

Word and Phrase Meanings

Most experts agree that learning new words is worth the time it takes. It helps readers understand what they are reading, and it expands their vocabularies. An extensive vocabulary improves one's ability to think. When words are added to someone's vocabulary, he or she is better able to make sense of the world.

One of the fastest ways to decode a word is through context. **Context**, or surrounding words, gives clues as to what unknown words mean. Take the following example: *When the students in the classroom teased Johnny, he was so discombobulated that he couldn't finish a simple math problem.* Even though a reader might be unfamiliar with the word *discombobulated*, he or she can use context clues in the sentence to make sense of the word. In this case, it can be deduced that *discombobulated* means confused or distracted.

Although context clues provide a rudimentary understanding of a word, using a dictionary can provide the reader with a more comprehensive meaning of the word. Printed dictionaries list words in alphabetical order, and all versions—including those online—include a word's multiple meanings. Typically, the first definition is the most widely used or known. The second, third, and subsequent entries move toward the more unusual or archaic. Dictionaries also indicate the part(s) of speech of each word, such as noun, verb, adjective, etc.

Dictionaries are not fixed in time. The English language today looks nothing like it did in Shakespeare's time, and Shakespeare's English is vastly different from Chaucer's. The English language is constantly evolving, as evidenced by the deletion of old words and the addition of new ones. *Ginormous* and *bling-bling*, for example, can both be found in *Merriam-Webster's* latest edition, yet they were not found in prior editions.

How Words Affect Tone

Tone refers to the writer's attitude toward the subject matter. For example, the tone conveys how the writer feels about the topic he or she is writing about. A lot of nonfiction writing has a neutral tone, which is an important tone for the writer to take. A neutral tone demonstrates that the writer is presenting a topic impartially and letting the information speak for itself. On the other hand, nonfiction writing can be just as effective and appropriate if the tone isn't neutral. For instance, consider this example:

> Seat belts save more lives than any other automobile safety feature. Many studies show that airbags save lives as well; however, not all cars have airbags. For instance, some older cars don't. Furthermore, air bags aren't entirely reliable. For example, studies show that in 15% of accidents, airbags don't deploy as designed; but, on the other hand, seat belt malfunctions are extremely rare. The number of highway fatalities has plummeted since laws requiring seat belt usage were enacted.

In this passage, the writer mostly chooses to retain a neutral tone when presenting information. If the writer would instead include their own personal experience of losing a friend or family member in a car accident, the tone would change dramatically. The tone would no longer be neutral and would show that the writer has a personal stake in the content, allowing them to interpret the information in a different way. When analyzing tone, consider what the writer is trying to achieve in the text and how they *create* the tone using style.

An author's choice of words—also referred to as **diction**—helps to convey his or her meaning in a particular way. Through diction, an author can convey a particular tone—e.g., a humorous tone, a serious tone—in order to support the thesis in a meaningful way to the reader.

Connotation and Denotation
Connotation is when an author chooses words or phrases that invoke ideas or feelings other than their literal meaning. An example of the use of connotation is the word *cheap*, which suggests something is poor in value or negatively describes a person as reluctant to spend money. When something or someone is described this way, the reader is more inclined to have a particular image or feeling about it or him/her. Thus, connotation can be a very effective language tool in creating emotion and swaying opinion. However, connotations are sometimes hard to pin down because varying emotions can be associated with a word. Generally, though, connotative meanings tend to be fairly consistent within a specific cultural group.

Denotation refers to words or phrases that mean exactly what they say. It is helpful when a writer wants to present hard facts or vocabulary terms with which readers may be unfamiliar. Some examples of denotation are the words *inexpensive* and *frugal*. *Inexpensive* refers to the cost of something, not its value, and *frugal* indicates that a person is conscientiously watching his or her spending. These terms do not elicit the same emotions that *cheap* does.

Authors sometimes choose to use both, but what they choose and when they use it is what critical readers need to differentiate. One method isn't inherently better than the other; however, one may create a better effect, depending upon an author's intent. If, for example, an author's purpose is to inform, to instruct, and to familiarize readers with a difficult subject, his or her use of connotation may be helpful. However, it may also undermine credibility and confuse readers. An author who wants to create a credible, scholarly effect in his or her text would most likely use denotation, which emphasizes literal, factual meaning and examples.

Analyzing an Author's Rhetorical Choices

Authors utilize a wide range of techniques to tell a story or communicate information. Readers should be familiar with the most common of these techniques. Techniques of writing are also known as **rhetorical devices**.

In nonfiction writing, authors employ argumentative techniques to present their opinions to readers in the most convincing way. First of all, persuasive writing usually includes at least one type of **appeal**: an appeal to logic (**logos**), emotion (**pathos**), or credibility and trustworthiness (**ethos**). When writers appeal to logic, they are asking readers to agree with them based on research, evidence, and an established line of reasoning. An author's argument might also appeal to readers' emotions, perhaps by including personal stories and **anecdotes** (a short narrative of a specific event). A final type of appeal— appeal to authority—asks the reader to agree with the author's argument on the basis of their expertise or credentials. Three different approaches to arguing the same opinion are exemplified below:

Logic (Logos)
      Our school should abolish its current ban on cell phone use on campus. This rule was adopted last year as an attempt to reduce class disruptions and help students focus more on their lessons. However, since the rule was enacted, there has been no change

in the number of disciplinary problems in class. Therefore, the rule is ineffective and should be done away with.

The above is an example of an appeal to logic. The author uses evidence to disprove the logic of the school's rule (the rule was supposed to reduce discipline problems; the number of problems has not been reduced; therefore, the rule is not working) and to call for its repeal.

Emotion (Pathos)

An author's argument might also appeal to readers' emotions, perhaps by including personal stories and anecdotes.

The next example presents an appeal to emotion. By sharing the personal anecdote of one student and speaking about emotional topics like family relationships, the author invokes the reader's empathy in asking them to reconsider the school rule.

> Our school should abolish its current ban on cell phone use on campus. If they aren't able to use their phones during the school day, many students feel isolated from their loved ones. For example, last semester, one student's grandmother had a heart attack in the morning. However, because he couldn't use his cell phone, the student didn't know about his grandmother's accident until the end of the day—when she had already passed away and it was too late to say goodbye. By preventing students from contacting their friends and family, our school is placing undue stress and anxiety on students.

Credibility (Ethos)

Finally, an appeal to authority includes a statement from a relevant expert. In this case, the author uses a doctor in the field of education to support the argument. All three examples begin from the same opinion—the school's phone ban needs to change—but rely on different argumentative styles to persuade the reader.

> Our school should abolish its current ban on cell phone use on campus. According to Dr. Bartholomew Everett, a leading educational expert, "Research studies show that cell phone usage has no real impact on student attentiveness. Rather, phones provide a valuable technological resource for learning. Schools need to learn how to integrate this new technology into their curriculum." Rather than banning phones altogether, our school should follow the advice of experts and allow students to use phones as part of their learning.

Figurative Language

Similes and **metaphors** are part of figurative language that are used as rhetorical devices. Both are comparisons between two things, but their formats differ slightly. A simile says that two things are similar and makes a comparison using "like" or "as"—*A* is like *B,* or *A* is as [some characteristic] as *B*— whereas a metaphor states that two things are exactly the same—*A* is *B*. In both cases, similes and metaphors invite the reader to think more deeply about the characteristics of the two subjects and consider where they overlap. Sometimes the poet develops a complex metaphor throughout the entire poem; this is known as an extended metaphor. An example of metaphor can be found in the sentence: "His pillow was a fluffy cloud". An example of simile can be found in the first line of Robert Burns' famous poem:

> My love is like a red, red rose

This is comparison using "like," and the two things being compared are love and a rose. Some characteristics of a rose are that it is fragrant, beautiful, blossoming, colorful, vibrant—by comparing his love to a red, red rose, Burns asks the reader to apply these qualities of a rose to his love. In this way, he implies that his love is also fresh, blossoming, and brilliant.

In addition to rhetorical devices that play on the *meanings* of words, there are also rhetorical devices that use the sounds of words. These devices are most often found in poetry, but may also be found in other types of literature and in nonfiction writing like texts for speeches.

Alliteration and **assonance** are both varieties of sound repetition. Other types of sound repetition include: **anaphora**—repetition that occurs at the beginning of the sentences; **epiphora**—repetition occurring at the end of phrases; antimetabole—repetition of words in a succession; and antiphrasis—a form of denial of an assertion in a text.

Alliteration refers to the repetition of the first sound of each word. Recall Robert Burns' opening line:

> My love is like a red, red rose

This line includes two instances of alliteration: "love" and "like" (repeated *L* sound), as well as "red" and "rose" (repeated *R* sound). Next, assonance refers to the repetition of vowel sounds, and can occur anywhere within a word (not just the opening sound). Here is the opening of a poem by John Keats:

> When I have fears that I may cease to be

> Before my pen has glean'd my teeming brain

Assonance can be found in the words "fears," "cease," "be," "glean'd," and "teeming," all of which stress the long *E* sound. Both alliteration and assonance create a harmony that unifies the writer's language.

Another sound device is **onomatopoeia**—words whose spelling mimics the sound they describe. Words like "crash," "bang," and "sizzle" are all examples of onomatopoeia. Use of onomatopoetic language adds auditory imagery to the text.

Readers are probably most familiar with the technique of using a **pun**. A pun is a play on words, taking advantage of two words that have the same or similar pronunciation. Puns can be found throughout Shakespeare's plays, for instance:

> Now is the winter of our discontent

> Made glorious summer by this son of York

These lines from *Richard III* contain a play on words. Richard III refers to his brother—the newly crowned King Edward IV—as the "son of York," referencing their family heritage from the house of York. However, while drawing a comparison between the political climate and the weather (times of political trouble were the "winter," but now the new king brings "glorious summer"), Richard's use of the word "son" also implies another word with the same pronunciation, "sun"—so Edward IV is also like the sun, bringing light, warmth, and hope to England. Puns are a clever way for writers to suggest two meanings at once.

Analyzing Text Structure

Organizational Structure within Literaryl Texts
Depending on what the author is attempting to accomplish, certain formats or text structures work better than others. For example, a sequence structure might work for narration but not when identifying similarities and differences between dissimilar concepts. Similarly, a comparison-contrast structure is not useful for narration. It's the author's job to put the right information in the correct format.

Readers should be familiar with the five main literary structures:

1. **Sequence** structure (sometimes referred to as the order structure) is when the order of events proceeds in a predictable manner. In many cases, this means the text goes through the plot elements: exposition, rising action, climax, falling action, and resolution. Readers are introduced to characters, setting, and conflict in the exposition. In the rising action, there's an increase in tension and suspense. The climax is the height of tension and the point of no return. Tension decreases during the falling action. In the resolution, any conflicts presented in the exposition are solved, and the story concludes. An informative text that is structured sequentially will often go in order from one step to the next.

2. In the **problem-solution** structure, authors identify a potential problem and suggest a solution. This form of writing is usually divided into two paragraphs and can be found in informational texts. For example, cell phone, cable and satellite providers use this structure in manuals to help customers troubleshoot or identify problems with services or products.

3. When authors want to discuss similarities and differences between separate concepts, they arrange thoughts in a **comparison-contrast** paragraph structure. **Venn diagrams** are an effective graphic organizer for comparison-contrast structures, because they feature two overlapping circles that can be used to organize and group similarities and differences. A comparison-contrast essay organizes one paragraph based on similarities and another based on differences. A comparison-contrast essay can also be arranged with the similarities and differences of individual traits addressed within individual paragraphs. Words such as *however, but*, and *nevertheless* help signal a contrast in ideas.

4. The **descriptive** writing structure is designed to appeal to one's senses. Much like an artist who constructs a painting, good descriptive writing builds an image in the reader's mind by appealing to the five senses: sight, hearing, taste, touch, and smell. However, overly descriptive writing can become tedious; sparse descriptions can make settings and characters seem flat. Good authors strike a balance by applying descriptions only to passages, characters, and settings that are integral to the plot.

5. Passages that use the **cause and effect** structure are simply asking *why* by demonstrating some type of connection between ideas. Words such as *if, since, because, then*, or *consequently* indicate relationship. By switching the order of a complex sentence, the writer can rearrange the emphasis on different clauses. Saying *If Sheryl is late, we'll miss the dance* is different from saying, *We'll miss the dance if Sheryl is late*. One emphasizes Sheryl's tardiness while the other emphasizes missing the dance. Paragraphs can also be arranged in a cause and effect format. Since the format—before and after—is sequential, it is useful when authors wish to discuss the impact of choices. Researchers often apply this paragraph structure to the scientific method.

Organizational Structure within Informational Texts

Informational text is specifically designed to relate factual information, and although it is open to a reader's interpretation and application of the facts, the structure of the presentation is carefully designed to lead the reader to a particular conclusion or central idea. When reading informational text, it is important that readers are able to understand its organizational structure as the structure often directly relates to an author's intent to inform and/or persuade the reader.

The first step in identifying the text's structure is to determine the thesis or main idea. The thesis statement and organization of a work are closely intertwined. A **thesis statement** indicates the writer's purpose and may include the scope and direction of the text. It may be presented at the beginning of a text or at the end, and it may be explicit or implicit.

Once a reader has a grasp of the thesis or main idea of the text, he or she can better determine its organizational structure. Test takers are advised to read informational text passages more than once in order to comprehend the material fully. It is also helpful to examine any text features present in the text including the table of contents, index, glossary, headings, footnotes, and visuals. The analysis of these features and the information presented within them, can offer additional clues about the central idea and structure of a text. The following questions should be asked when considering structure:

- How does the author assemble the parts to make an effective whole argument?
- Is the passage linear in nature and if so, what is the timeline or thread of logic?
- What is the presented order of events, facts, or arguments? Are these effective in contributing to the author's thesis?
- How can the passage be divided into sections? How are they related to each other and to the main idea or thesis?
- What key terms are used to indicate the organization?

Next, test takers should skim the passage, noting the first line or two of each body paragraph—the **topic sentences**—and the conclusion. Key **transitional terms**, such as *on the other hand*, *also*, *because*, *however*, *therefore*, *most importantly*, and *first*, within the text can also signal organizational structure. Based on these clues, readers should then be able to identify what type of organizational structure is being used.

The following organizational structures are most common:

- **Problem/solution**—organized by an analysis/overview of a problem, followed by potential solution(s)

- **Cause/effect**—organized by the effects resulting from a cause or the cause(s) of a particular effect

- **Spatial order**—organized by points that suggest location or direction—e.g., top to bottom, right to left, outside to inside

- **Chronological/sequence order**—organized by points presented to indicate a passage of time or through purposeful steps/stages

- **Comparison/Contrast**—organized by points that indicate similarities and/or differences between two things or concepts

- **Order of importance**—organized by priority of points, often most significant to least significant or vice versa

Authorial Purpose and Perspective

No matter the genre or format, all authors are writing to persuade, inform, entertain, or express feelings. Often, these purposes are blended, with one dominating the rest. It's useful to learn to recognize the author's intent.

Persuasive writing is used to persuade or convince readers of something. It often contains two elements: the argument and the counterargument. The **argument** takes a stance on an issue, while the **counterargument** pokes holes in the opposition's stance. Authors rely on logic, emotion, and writer credibility to persuade readers to agree with them. If readers are opposed to the stance before reading, they are unlikely to adopt that stance. However, those who are undecided or committed to the same stance are more likely to agree with the author.

Informative writing tries to teach or inform. Workplace manuals, instructor lessons, statistical reports and cookbooks are examples of informative texts. Informative writing is usually based on facts and is often without emotion and persuasion. Informative texts generally contain statistics, charts, and graphs. Although most informative texts lack a persuasive agenda, readers must examine the text carefully to determine whether one exists within a given passage.

Stories or **narratives** are designed to entertain. When people go to the movies, they often want to escape for a few hours, not necessarily to think critically. **Entertaining** writing is designed to delight and engage the reader. However, sometimes this type of writing can be woven into more serious materials, such as persuasive or informative writing, to hook the reader before transitioning into a more scholarly discussion.

Emotional writing works to evoke the reader's feelings, such as anger, euphoria, or sadness. The connection between reader and author is an attempt to cause the reader to share the author's intended emotion or tone. Sometimes, in order to make a text more poignant, the author simply wants readers to feel the emotions that the author has felt. Other times, the author attempts to persuade or manipulate the reader into adopting their stance. While it's okay to sympathize with the author, readers should be aware of the individual's underlying intent.

Characters' Point of View

Point of view is another important writing device to consider. In fiction writing, **point of view** refers to who tells the story or from whose perspective readers are observing as they read. In nonfiction writing, the **point of view** refers to whether the author refers to himself or herself, his or her readers, or chooses not to refer to either. Whether fiction or nonfiction, the author carefully considers the impact the perspective will have on the purpose and main point of the writing.

- **First-person** point of view: The story is told from the writer's perspective. In fiction, this would mean that the main character is also the narrator. First-person point of view is easily recognized by the use of personal pronouns such as *I, me, we, us, our, my*, and *myself*.

- **Third-person** point of view: In a more formal essay, this would be an appropriate perspective because the focus should be on the subject matter, not the writer or the reader. Third-person point of view is recognized by the use of the pronouns *he, she, they*, and *it*. In fiction writing, third person point of view has a few variations.

    - ○ ***Third-person limited*** point of view refers to a story told by a narrator who has access to the thoughts and feelings of just one character.

    - ○ In **third-person omniscient** point of view, the narrator has access to the thoughts and feelings of all the characters.

    - ○ In **third-person objective** point of view, the narrator is like a fly on the wall and can see and hear what the characters do and say but does not have access to their thoughts and feelings.

- **Second-person** point of view: This point of view isn't commonly used in fiction or nonfiction writing because it directly addresses the reader using the pronouns *you, your*, and *yourself*. Second-person perspective is more appropriate in direct communication, such as business letters or emails.

Point of View	Pronouns used
First person	I, me, we, us, our, my, myself
Second person	You, your, yourself
Third person	He, she, it, they

Interpreting Authorial Decisions Rhetorically

There are a few ways for readers to engage actively with the text, such as making inferences and predictions. An **inference** refers to a point that is implied (as opposed to directly-stated) by the evidence presented:

> Bradley packed up all of the items from his desk in a box and said goodbye to his coworkers for the last time.

From this sentence, although it is not directly stated, readers can infer that Bradley is leaving his job. It's necessary to use inference in order to draw conclusions about the meaning of a passage. When making an inference about a passage, it's important to rely only on the information that is provided in the text itself. This helps readers ensure that their conclusions are valid.

Readers will also find themselves making predictions when reading a passage or paragraph. **Predictions** are guesses about what's going to happen next. This is a natural tendency, especially when reading a good story or watching a suspenseful movie. It's fun to try to figure out how it will end. Authors intentionally use suspenseful language and situations to keep readers interested:

A cat darted across the street just as the car came careening around the curve.

One unfortunate prediction might be that the car will hit the cat. Of course, predictions aren't always accurate, so it's important to read carefully to the end of the text to determine the accuracy of one's predictions.

Readers should pay attention to the **sequence**, or the order in which details are laid out in the text, as this can be important to understanding its meaning as a whole. Writers will often use transitional words to help the reader understand the order of events and to stay on track. Words like *next, then, after*, and *finally* show that the order of events is important to the author. In some cases, the author omits these transitional words, and the sequence is implied. Authors may even purposely present the information out of order to make an impact or have an effect on the reader. An example might be when a narrative writer uses **flashback** to reveal information.

Drawing conclusions is also important when actively reading a passage. **Hedge phrases** such as *will, might, probably*, and *appear to be* are used by writers who want to cover their bases and make sure to show there are exceptions to their statements. **Absolute phrasing**, such as *always* and *never*, should be carefully considered, as the use of these words and their intended meanings are often incorrect.

Differentiating Between Various Perspectives and Sources of Information

Primary sources contain firsthand documentation of a historical event or era. Primary sources are provided by people who have experienced an the era or event. Primary sources capture a specific moment, context, or era in history. They are valued as eyewitness accounts and personal perspectives. Examples include diaries, memoirs, journals, letters, interviews, photographs, context-specific artwork, government documents, constitutions, newspapers, personal items, libraries, and archives. Another example of a primary source is the Declaration of Independence. This historical document captures the revolutionary sentiment of an era in American history.

Authors of secondary sources write about events, contexts, and eras in history with a relative amount of experiential, geographic, or temporal distance. Normally, secondary source authors aren't firsthand witnesses. In some cases, they may have experienced an event, but they are offering secondhand, retrospective accounts of their experience. All scholars and historians produce secondary sources—they gather primary source information and synthesize it for a new generation of students. Monographs, biographies, magazine articles, scholarly journals, theses, dissertations, textbooks, and encyclopedias are all secondary sources. In some rare instances, secondary sources become so enmeshed in their era of inquiry that they later become primary sources for future scholars and analysts.

Both primary and secondary sources of information are useful. They both offer invaluable insight that helps the writer learn more about the subject matter. However, researchers are cautioned to examine the information closely and to consider the time period as well as the cultural, political, and social climate in which accounts were given. Learning to distinguish between reliable sources of information and questionable accounts is paramount to a quality research report.

<u>Identifying the Appropriate Source for Locating Information</u>
With a wealth of information at people's fingertips in this digital age, it's important to know not only the type of information one is looking for, but also in what medium he or she is most likely to find it. Information needs to be specific and reliable. For example, if someone is repairing a car, an encyclopedia would be mostly useless. While an encyclopedia might include information about cars, an owner's manual will contain the specific information needed for repairs. Information must also be reliable or credible so that it can be trusted. A well-known newspaper may have reliable information, but a peer-reviewed journal article will have likely gone through a more rigorous check for validity. Determining **bias** can be helpful in determining credibility. If the information source (person, organization, or company) has something to gain from the reader forming a certain view on a topic, it's likely the information is skewed. For example, if trying to find the unemployment rate, the Bureau of Labor Statistics is a more credible source than a politician's speech.

Primary sources are best defined as records or items that serve as evidence of periods of history. To be considered primary, the source documents or objects must have been created during the time period in which they reference. Examples include diaries, newspaper articles, speeches, government documents, photographs, and historical artifacts. In today's digital age, primary sources, which were once in print, are often embedded in secondary sources. **Secondary sources**—such as websites, history books, databases, or reviews—contain analysis or commentary on primary sources. Secondary sources borrow information from primary sources through the process of quoting, summarizing, or paraphrasing.

Today's students often complete research online through **electronic sources**. Electronic sources offer advantages over print, and can be accessed on virtually any computer, where libraries or other research centers are limited to fixed locations and specific catalogs. Electronic sources are also efficient and yield massive amounts of data in seconds. The user can tailor a search based on key words, publication years, and article length. Lastly, many **databases** provide the user with instant citations, saving the user the trouble of manually assembling sources for a bibliography.

Although electronic sources yield powerful results, researchers must use caution. While there are many reputable and reliable sources on the internet, just as many are unreliable or biased sources. It's up to the researcher to examine and verify the reliability of sources. *Wikipedia*, for example, may or may not be accurate, depending on the contributor. Many databases, such as *EBSCO* or *SIRS*, offer peer-reviewed articles, meaning the publications have been reviewed for the quality and accuracy of their content.

<u>Text Credibility</u>
Credible sources are important when drawing conclusions because readers need to be able to trust what they are reading. Authors should always use credible sources to help gain the trust of their readers. A text is **credible** when it is believable and the author is objective and unbiased. If readers do not trust authors' words, they may simply dismiss the text completely. For example, if an author writes a persuasive essay, he or she is outwardly trying to sway readers' opinions to align with his or her own, providing readers with the liberty to do what they please with the text. Readers may agree or disagree with the author, which may, in turn, lead them to believe that the author is credible or not credible. Also, readers should keep in mind the source of the text. If readers review a journal about astronomy, would a more reliable source be a NASA employee or a plumber? Overall, text credibility is important when drawing conclusions because readers want reliable sources that support the decisions they have made about the author's ideas.

Integration of Knowledge and Ideas

Understanding Authors' Claims

The goal of most persuasive and informative texts is to make a claim and support it with evidence. A **claim** is a statement made as though it is fact. Many claims are opinions; for example, "stealing is wrong." While this is generally true, it is arguable, meaning it is capable of being challenged. An initial reaction to "stealing is wrong" might be to agree; however, there may be circumstances in which it is warranted. If it is necessary for the survival of an individual or their loved ones (i.e., if they are starving and cannot afford to eat), then this assertion becomes morally ambiguous. While it may still be illegal, whether it is "wrong" is unclear.

When an assertion is made within a text, it is typically reinforced with supporting details as is exemplified in the following passage:

> The extinction of the dinosaurs has been a hot debate amongst scientists since the discovery of fossils in the eighteenth century. Numerous theories were developed in explanation, including extreme climate change, an epidemic of disease, or changes in the atmosphere. It wasn't until the late 1970s that a young geochemist, named Walter Alvarez, noticed significant changes in the soil layers of limestone he was studying in Italy. The layers contained fossilized remains of millions of small organisms within the layer that corresponded with the same period in which the dinosaurs lived. He noticed that the soil layer directly above this layer was suddenly devoid of any trace of these organisms. The soil layer directly above *this* layer was filled with an entirely new species of organisms. It seemed the first species had disappeared at the exact same time as the dinosaurs!

> With the help of his father, Walter Alvarez analyzed the soil layer between the extinct species and the new species and realized this layer was filled with an abnormal amount of *iridium* – a substance that is abundant in meteorites but almost never found on Earth. Unlike other elements in the fossil record, which take a long time to deposit, the iridium had been laid down very abruptly. The layer also contained high levels of soot, enough to account for all of the earth's forests burning to the ground at the same time. This lead scientists to create the best-supported theory that the tiny organisms, as well as the dinosaurs and countless other species, had been destroyed by a giant asteroid that had slammed into Earth, raining tons of iridium down on the planet from a giant cosmic cloud.

Supporting Claims

Before embarking on answering these questions, readers should summarize each. This will help in locating the supporting evidence. These summaries can be written down or completed mentally; full sentences are not necessary.

Paragraph 1: Layer of limestone shows that a species of organisms disappeared at same time as the dinosaurs

Paragraph 2: Layer had high amounts of iridium and soot – scientists believe dinosaurs destroyed by asteroid.

Simply by summarizing the text, it has been plainly outlined where there will be answers to relevant questions. Although there are often claims already embedded within an educational text, a claim will most likely be given, but the evidence to support it will need to be located. Take this example question:

Q: What evidence within the text best supports the theory that the dinosaurs became extinct because of an asteroid?

The claim here is that the <u>dinosaurs went extinct because of an asteroid</u>. Because the text is already outlined in the summaries, it is easy to see that the evidence supporting this theory is in the second paragraph:

With the help of his father, they analyzed the soil layer between the extinct species and the new species and realized <u>this layer was filled with an abnormal amount of *iridium*</u> – a substance that is <u>abundant is meteorites</u> but almost never found on Earth. Unlike other elements in the fossil record, which takes a long time to deposit, the iridium had been laid down very abruptly. <u>The layer also contained high levels of soot</u>, enough to account for all of the earth's forests burning to the ground at the same time. <u>This lead scientists to create the best-supported theory</u> that the tiny organisms, as well as the dinosaurs and countless other species, had been <u>destroyed by a giant asteroid</u> that had slammed into Earth, <u>raining tons of iridium down on the planet</u> from a giant cosmic cloud.

Now that the evidence within the text that best supports the theory has been located, the answer choices can be evaluated:
a. Changes in climate and atmosphere caused an asteroid to crash into Earth
b. Walter and Luis Alvarez studied limestone with fossilized organisms
c. A soil layer lacking organisms that existed at the same time as the dinosaurs showed low levels of iridium
d. A soil layer lacking organisms that existed at the same time as the dinosaurs showed high levels of iridium

Answer choice (a) is clearly false as there is nothing within the text that claims that climate changes caused an asteroid to crash into Earth. This kind of answer choice displays an incorrect use of detail. Although the passage may have contained the words "change," "climate," and "atmosphere," these terms were manipulated to form an erroneous answer.

Answer choice (b) is incorrect because while the scientists did study limestone with fossilized organisms, and in doing so they discovered evidence that led to the formation of the theory, this is not the actual evidence itself. This is an example of an out-of-scope answer choice: a true statement that may or may not have been in the passage, but that isn't the whole answer or isn't the point.

Answer choice (c) is incorrect because it is the opposite of the correct answer. Assuming the second paragraph was summarized correctly, it is already known that the soil layer contained *high* levels of iridium, not low levels. Even if the paragraph was not summarized that way, the final sentence states that "tons of iridium rained down on the planet." So, answer choice (c) is false.

Answer choice (d) is correct because it matches the evidence found in the second paragraph.

Differentiating Between Facts and Opinions

Fact and Opinion, Biases, and Stereotypes

It is important to distinguish between facts and opinions when reading a piece of writing. When an author presents **facts**, such as statistics or data, readers should be able to check those facts to verify that they are accurate. When authors share their own thoughts and feelings about a subject, they are expressing their **opinions**.

Authors often use words like *think, feel, believe,* or *in my opinion* when expressing an opinion, but these words won't always appear in an opinion piece, especially if it is formally written. An author's opinion may be backed up by facts, which gives it more credibility, but that opinion should not be taken as fact. A critical reader should be suspect of an author's opinion, especially if it is only supported by other opinions.

Fact	Opinion
There are nine innings in a game of baseball.	Baseball games run too long.
James Garfield was assassinated on July 2, 1881.	James Garfield was a good president.
McDonald's® has stores in 118 countries.	McDonald's® has the best hamburgers.

Critical readers examine the facts used to support an author's argument. They check the facts against other sources to be sure those facts are correct. They also check the validity of the sources used to be sure those sources are credible, academic, and/or peer-reviewed. When an author uses another person's opinion to support his or her argument, even if it is an expert's opinion, it is still only an opinion and should not be taken as fact. A strong argument uses valid, measurable facts to support ideas. Even then, the reader may disagree with the argument.

An authoritative argument may use the facts to sway the reader. In the example of global warming, many experts differ in their opinions of which alternative fuels can be used to aid in offsetting it. Because of this, a writer may choose to only use the information and experts' opinions that supports his or her viewpoint. For example, if the argument is that wind energy is the best solution, the author will use facts that support this idea. That same author may leave out relevant facts on solar energy. The way the author uses facts can influence the reader, so it's important to consider the facts being used, how those facts are being presented, and what information might be left out.

Authors can also demonstrate **bias** if they ignore an opposing viewpoint or present their side in an unbalanced way. A strong argument considers the opposition and finds a way to refute it. Critical readers should look for an unfair or one-sided presentation of the argument and be skeptical, as a bias may be present. Even if this bias is unintentional, if it exists in the writing, the reader should be wary of the validity of the argument.

Readers should also look for the use of stereotypes that refer to specific groups. **Stereotypes** are often negative connotations about a person or place and should always be avoided. When a critical reader finds stereotypes in a piece of writing, he or she should immediately be critical of the argument and consider the validity of anything the author presents. Stereotypes reveal a flaw in the writer's thinking and may suggest a lack of knowledge or understanding about the subject.

Using Evidence to Make Connections Between Different Texts

When analyzing two or more texts, there are several different aspects that need to be considered, particularly the styles (or the artful way in which the authors use diction to deliver a theme), points of view, and types of argument. In order to do so, one should compare and contrast the following elements between the texts:

- Style: narrative, persuasive, descriptive, informative, etc.
- Tone: sarcastic, angry, somber, humorous, etc.
- Sentence structure: simple (1 clause) compound (2 clauses), complex-compound (3 clauses)
- Punctuation choice: question marks, exclamation points, periods, dashes, etc.
- Point of view: first person, second person, third person
- Paragraph structure: long, short, both, differences between the two
- Organizational structure: compare/contrast, problem/solution, chronological, etc.

The following two passages concern the theme of death and are presented to demonstrate how to evaluate the above elements:

Passage I

Death occurs in several stages. The first stage is the pre-active stage, which occurs a few days to weeks before death, in which the desire to eat and drink decreases, and the person may feel restless, irritable, and anxious. The second stage is the active stage, where the skin begins to cool, breathing becomes difficult as the lungs become congested (known as the "death rattle"), and the person loses control of their bodily fluids.

Once death occurs, there are also two stages. The first is clinical death, when the heart stops pumping blood and breathing ceases. This stage lasts approximately 4-6 minutes, and during this time, it is possible for a victim to be resuscitated via CPR or a defibrillator. After 6 minutes however, the oxygen stores within the brain begin to deplete, and the victim enters biological death. This is the point of no return, as the cells of the brain and vital organs begin to die, a process that is irreversible.

Passage II

It was her sister Josephine who told her, in broken sentences; veiled hints that revealed in half concealing. Her husband's friend Richards was there, too, near her. It was he who had been in the newspaper office when intelligence of the railroad disaster was received, with Brently Mallard's name leading the list of "killed." He had only taken the time to assure himself of its truth by a second telegram, and had hastened to forestall any less careful, less tender friend in bearing the sad message.

She did not hear the story as many women have heard the same, with a paralyzed inability to accept its significance. She wept at once, with sudden, wild abandonment, in her sister's arms. When the storm of grief had spent itself she went away to her room alone. She would have no one follow her.

There stood, facing the open window, a comfortable, roomy armchair. Into this she sank, pressed down by a physical exhaustion that haunted her body and seemed to reach into her soul.

Excerpt from "The Story of an Hour" by Kate Chopin

Now, using the outline above, the similarities and differences between the three passages are considered:

1. **Style:** Passage I is an expository style, presenting purely factual evidence on death, completely devoid of emotion. Passage II is a narrative style, where the theme of death is presented to us by the reaction of the loved ones involved. This narrative style is full of emotional language and imagery.

2. **Tone:** Passage I has no emotionally-charged words of any kind, and seems to view death simply as a process that happens, neither welcoming nor fearing it. The tone in this passage, therefore, is neutral. Passage II does not have a neutral tone—it uses words like "disaster," "killed," "sad," "wept," "wild abandonment," and "physical exhaustion," implying an anxiety toward the theme of death.

3. **Sentence Structure:** Passage I contains many complex-compound sentences, which are used to accommodate lots of information. The structure of these sentences contributes to the overall informative nature of the selection. Passage II has several compound sentences and complex sentences on their own. It's also marked by the use of many commas in a single sentence, separating modifying words. Perhaps this variety is meant to match the sporadic emotion of the character's discovery of her husband's death.

4. **Punctuation Choice:** Passage I uses only commas and periods, which adds to the overall neutral tone of the selection. Passage II mostly uses commas and periods, and then one semicolon. Again, the excess of commas and semicolon in the first sentence may be said to mirror the character's anxiety.

5. **Point of View:** Passage I uses third-person point of view, as it avoids any first- or second-person pronouns. Passage II also uses third-person point of view, as the story is being told by a narrator about characters separate from the narrator.

6. **Paragraph Structure:** The first passage is told in an objective way, and each paragraph is focused on the topic brought up in the first sentence. The second passage has no specific topic per paragraph. It is organized in a sequential way, so the paragraphs flow into the next in a chronological order.

7. **Organizational Structure:** The structure of Passage I is told in a very objective, organized way. The first paragraph tells of the stages before death, and the second paragraph tells of the stages after death. The second passage is told in chronological order, as a sequence of events, like in a fictional story.

When analyzing the different structures, it may be helpful to make a table and use single words to compare and contrast the texts:

Elements	Passage I	Passage II
Style	Expository	Narrative
Tone	Neutral	Emotional
Sentence Structure	Long	Long/Sporadic
Punctuation Choice	.	. and ,
Point of View	Third	Third
Paragraph Structure	Focused	Sequential
Organizational Structure	Objective/Logical	Chronological

The main differences between the two selections are style, tone, and structure. Possibly the most noticeable difference is the style and tone, as one tone is more neutral, and the other tone is more emotional. This is due to the word choice used and how each passage treats the topic of death. These are only a handful of the endless possible interpretations the reader could make.

Analyzing How Authors Construct Arguments

Constructing Arguments Through Evidence

Using only one form of supporting evidence is not nearly as effective as using a variety to support a claim. Presenting only a list of statistics can be boring to the reader but providing a true story that's both interesting and humanizing helps. In addition, one example isn't always enough to prove the writer's larger point, so combining it with other examples in the writing is extremely effective. Thus, when reading a passage, readers should not just look for a single form of supporting evidence.

For example, although most people can't argue with the statement, "Seat belts save lives", its impact on the reader is much greater when supported by additional content. The writer can support this idea by:

- Providing statistics on the rate of highway fatalities alongside statistics of estimated seat belt usage.

- Explaining the science behind car accidents and what happens to a passenger who doesn't use a seat belt.

- Offering anecdotal evidence or true stories from reliable sources on how seat belts prevent fatal injuries in car crashes.

Another key aspect of supporting evidence is a **reliable source**. Does the writer include the source of the information? If so, is the source well-known and trustworthy? Is there a potential for bias? For example, a seat belt study done by a seat belt manufacturer may have its own agenda to promote.

<u>Logical Sequence</u>
Even if the writer includes plenty of information to support his or her point, the writing is only effective when the information is in a logical order. **Logical sequencing** is really just common sense, but it's an important writing technique. First, the writer should introduce the main idea, whether for a paragraph, a section, or the entire text. Then he or she should present evidence to support the main idea by using transitional language. This shows the reader how the information relates to the main idea and to the sentences around it. The writer should then take time to interpret the information, making sure necessary connections are obvious to the reader. Finally, the writer can summarize the information in the closing section.

NOTE: Although most writing follows this pattern, it isn't a set rule. Sometimes writers change the order for effect. For example, the writer can begin with a surprising piece of supporting information to grab the reader's attention, and then transition to the main idea. Thus, if a passage doesn't follow the logical order, readers should not immediately assume it's wrong. However, most writing that has a nontraditional beginning usually settles into a logical sequence.

Evaluating Reasoning and Evidence

<u>Making Generalizations Based on Evidence</u>
One way to make generalizations is to look for main topics. When doing so, pay particular attention to any titles, headlines, or opening statements made by the author. Topic sentences or repetitive ideas can be clues in gleaning inferred ideas. For example, if a passage contains the phrase *DNA testing, while some consider it infallible, is an inherently flawed technique,* the test taker can infer the rest of the passage will contain information that points to DNA testing's infallibility.

The test taker may be asked to make a generalization based on prior knowledge but may also be asked to make predictions based on new ideas. For example, the test taker may have no prior knowledge of DNA other than its genetic property to replicate. However, if the reader is given passages on the flaws of DNA testing with enough factual evidence, the test taker may arrive at the inferred conclusion or generalization that the author does not support the infallibility of DNA testing in all identification cases.

When making generalizations, it is important to remember that the critical thinking process involved must be fluid and open to change. While a reader may infer an idea from a main topic, general statement, or other clues, they must be open to receiving new information within a particular passage. New ideas presented by an author may require the test taker to alter a generalization. Similarly, when asked questions that require making an inference, it's important to read the entire test passage and all of the answer options. Often, a test taker will need to refine a generalization based on new ideas that may be presented within the text itself.

Textual evidence within the details helps readers draw a conclusion about a passage. **Textual evidence** refers to information—facts and examples that support the main point. Textual evidence will likely come from outside sources and can be in the form of quoted or paraphrased material. In order to draw a conclusion from evidence, it's important to examine the credibility and validity of that evidence as well as how (and if) it relates to the main idea.

If an author presents a differing opinion or a **counterargument** in order to refute it, the reader should consider how and why this information is being presented. It is meant to strengthen the original argument and shouldn't be confused with the author's intended conclusion, but it should also be considered in the reader's final evaluation.

The Steps of an Argument

Strong arguments tend to follow a fairly defined format. In the introduction, background information regarding the problem is shared, the implications of the issue, and the author's thesis or claims. Supporting evidence is then presented in the body paragraphs, along with the counterargument, which then gets refuted with specific evidence. Lastly, in the conclusion, the author summarizes the points and claims again.

Evidence Used to Support a Claim or Conclusion

Premises are the why, and **conclusions** are the what. Stated differently, premises are the evidence or facts supporting why the conclusion is logical and valid. ACT Reading questions do not require evaluation of the factual accuracy of the arguments; instead, the questions evaluate the test taker's ability to assess an argument's logical strength. For example, John eats all red food. Apples are red. Therefore, John eats apples. This argument is logically sound, despite having no factual basis in reality. Below is an example of a practice argument.

> Julie is an American track athlete. She's the star of the number one collegiate team in the country. Her times are consistently at the top of national rankings. Julie is extremely likely to represent the United States at the upcoming Olympics.

In this example, the conclusion, or the *what*, is that she will likely be on the American Olympic team. The author supports this conclusion with two premises. First, Julie is the star of an elite track team. Second, she runs some of the best times of the country. This is the *why* behind the conclusion. The following builds off this basic argument:

> Julie is an American track athlete. She's the star of the number one collegiate team in the country. Her times are consistently at the top of national rankings. Julie is extremely likely to represent the United States at the upcoming Olympics. Julie will continue to develop after the Olympic trials. She will be a frontrunner for the gold. Julie is likely to become a world-famous track star.

These additions to the argument make the conclusion different. Now, the conclusion is that Julie is likely to become a world-famous track star. The previous conclusion, Julie will likely be on the Olympic team, functions as a **sub-conclusion** in this argument. Like conclusions, premises must adequately support sub-conclusions. However, sub-conclusions function like premises, since sub-conclusions also support the overall conclusion.

Determining Whether Evidence is Relevant and Sufficient

A **hasty generalization** involves an argument relying on insufficient statistical data or inaccurately generalizing. One common generalization occurs when a group of individuals under observation have some quality or attribute that is asserted to be universal or true for a much larger number of people than actually documented. Here's an example of a hasty generalization:

> A man smokes a lot of cigarettes, but so did his grandfather. The grandfather smoked nearly two packs per day since his World War II service until he died at ninety years of age. Continuing to smoke cigarettes will clearly not impact the grandson's long-term health.

This argument is a hasty generalization because it assumes that one person's addiction and lack of consequences will naturally be reflected in a different individual. There is no reasonable justification for such extrapolation. It is common knowledge that any smoking is detrimental to everyone's health. The fact that the man's grandfather smoked two packs per day and lived a long life has no logical connection with the grandson engaging in similar behavior. The hasty generalization doesn't take into account other reasons behind the grandfather's longevity. Nor does the author offer evidence that might support the idea that the man would share a similar lifetime if he smokes. It might be different if the author stated that the man's family shares some genetic trait rendering them immune to the effects of tar and chemicals on the lungs. If this were in the argument, we would assume it as truth, like everything else in the Reading Through Language Arts section, and find the generalization to be valid rather than hasty. Of course, this is not the case in our example.

Determining Whether a Statement Is or Is Not Supported

The basic tenant of reading comprehension is the ability to read and understand text. One way to understand text is to look for information that supports the author's main idea, topic, or position statement. This information may be factual or it may be based on the author's opinion. This section will focus on the test taker's ability to identify factual information, as opposed to opinionated bias. The ACT will ask test takers to read passages containing factual information, and then logically relate those passages by drawing conclusions based on evidence.

In order to identify factual information within one or more text passages, begin by looking for statements of fact. Factual statements can be either true or false. Identifying factual statements as opposed to opinion statements is important in demonstrating full command of evidence in reading. For example, the statement *The temperature outside was unbearably hot* may seem like a fact; however, it's not. While anyone can point to a temperature gauge as factual evidence, the statement itself reflects only an opinion. Some people may find the temperature unbearably hot. Others may find it comfortably warm. Thus, the sentence, *The temperature outside was unbearably hot,* reflects the opinion of the author who found it unbearable. If the text passage followed up the sentence with atmospheric conditions indicating heat indices above 140 degrees Fahrenheit, then the reader knows there is factual information that supports the author's assertion of *unbearably hot*.

In looking for information that can be proven or disproven, it's helpful to scan for dates, numbers, timelines, equations, statistics, and other similar data within any given text passage. These types of indicators will point to proven particulars. For example, the statement, *The temperature outside was unbearably hot on that summer day, July 10, 1913,* most likely indicates factual information, even if the reader is unaware that this is the hottest day on record in the United States. Be careful when reading biased words from an author. Biased words indicate opinion, as opposed to fact. See the list of biased words below and keep in mind that it's not an inclusive list:

- Good/bad
- Great/greatest
- Better/best/worst
- Amazing
- Terrible/bad/awful
- Beautiful/handsome/ugly
- More/most
- Exciting/dull/boring
- Favorite
- Very
- Probably/should/seem/possibly

Remember, most of what is written is actually opinion or carefully worded information that seems like fact when it isn't. To say, *duplicating DNA results is not cost-effective* sounds like it could be a scientific fact, but it isn't. Factual information can be verified through independent sources.

The simplest type of test question may provide a text passage, then ask the test taker to distinguish the correct factual supporting statement that best answers the corresponding question on the test. However, be aware that most questions may ask the test taker to read more than one text passage and identify which answer best supports an author's topic. While the ability to identify factual information is critical, these types of questions require the test taker to identify chunks of details, and then relate them to one another.

Assessing Whether an Argument is Valid

Although different from conditions and If/Then Statements, **reasonableness** is another important foundational concept. Evaluating an argument for reasonableness and validity entails evaluating the evidence presented by the author to justify their conclusions. Everything contained in the argument should be considered, but remember to ignore outside biases, judgments, and knowledge. For the purposes of this test, the test taker is a one-person jury at a criminal trial using a standard of reasonableness under the circumstances presented by the argument.

These arguments are encountered on a daily basis through social media, entertainment, and cable news. An example is:

> Although many believe it to be a natural occurrence, some believe that the red tide that occurs in Florida each year may actually be a result of human sewage and agricultural runoff. However, it is arguable that both natural and human factors contribute to this annual phenomenon. On one hand, the red tide has been occurring every year since the time of explorers like Cabeza de Vaca in the 1500's. On the other hand, the red tide seems to be getting worse each year, and scientists from the Florida Fish & Wildlife Conservation say the bacteria found inside the tide feed off of nutrients found in fertilizer runoff.

The author's conclusion is that both natural phenomena and human activity contribute to the red tide that happens annually in Florida. The author backs this information up by historical data to prove the natural occurrence of the red tide, and then again with scientific data to back up the human contribution to the red tide. Both of these statements are examples of the premises in the argument. Evaluating the strength of the logical connection between the premises and conclusion is how reasonableness is determined. Another example is:

> The local railroad is a disaster. Tickets are exorbitantly priced, bathrooms leak, and the floor is sticky.

The author is clearly unhappy with the railroad service. They cite three examples of why they believe the railroad to be a disaster. An argument more familiar to everyday life is:

> Alexandra said the movie she just saw was amazing. We should go see it tonight.

Although not immediately apparent, this is an argument. The author is making the argument that they should go see the movie. This conclusion is based on the premise that Alexandra said the movie was amazing. There's an inferred note that Alexandra is knowledgeable on the subject, and she's credible enough to prompt her friends to go see the movie. This seems like a reasonable argument. A less reasonable argument is:

> Alexandra is a film student, and she's written the perfect romantic comedy script. We should put our life savings toward its production as an investment in our future.

The author's conclusion is that they should invest their life savings into the production of a movie, and it is justified by referencing Alexandra's credibility and current work. However, the premises are entirely too weak to support the conclusion. Alexandra is only a film *student*, and the script is seemingly her first work. This is not enough evidence to justify investing one's life savings in the film's success.

Assumptions in an Argument

Think of assumptions as unwritten premises. Although they never explicitly appear in the argument, the author is relying on it to defend the argument, just like a premise. Assumptions are the most important part of an argument that will never appear in an argument.

An argument in the abstract is: The author concludes Z based on W and X premises. But the W and X premises actually depend on the unmentioned assumption of Y. Therefore, what the author is really saying is that, X, W, and Y make Z correct, but Y is assumed.

People assume all of the time. Assumptions and inferences allow the human mind to process the constant flow of information. Many assumptions underlie even the most basic arguments. However, in the world of Legal Reasoning arguments, assumptions must be avoided. An argument must be fully presented to be valid; relying on an assumption is considered weak. The test requires that test takers identify these underlying assumptions. One example is:

> Peyton Manning is the most over-rated quarterback of all time. He lost more big games than anyone else. Plus, he allegedly assaulted his female trainer in college. Peyton clearly shouldn't make the Hall of Fame.

The author certainly relies on a lot of assumptions. A few assumptions are:

- Peyton Manning plays quarterback.

- He is considered to be a great quarterback by at least some people.

- He played in many big games.

- Allegations and past settlements without any admission of guilt from over a decade ago can be relied upon as evidence against Hall of Fame acceptance.

- The Hall of Fame voters factor in off-the-field incidents, even if true.

- The best players should make the Hall of Fame.

- Losing big games negates, at least in part, the achievement of making it to those big games

- Peyton Manning is retired, and people will vote on whether he makes the Hall of Fame at some point in the future.

The author is relying on all of these assumptions. Some are clearly more important to his argument than others. In fact, disproving a necessary assumption can destroy a premise and possibly an entire conclusion. For example, what if the Hall of Fame did not factor in any of the off-the-field incidents? Then the alleged assault no longer factors into the argument. Even worse, what if making the big games actually was more important than losing those games in the eyes of the Hall of Fame voters? Then the whole conclusion falls apart. The conclusion is no longer justified if that premise is disproven.

Assumption questions test this exact point by asking the test taker to identify which assumption the argument relies upon. If the author is making numerous assumptions, then the most important *one* assumption must be chosen.

If the author truly relies on an assumption, then the argument will completely fall apart if the assumption isn't true. **Negating** a necessary assumption will *always* make the argument fall apart. This is a universal rule of logic and should be the first thing done in testing answer choices.

Here are some ways that underlying assumptions will appear as questions:

- Which of the following is a hidden assumption that the author makes to advance his argument?
- Which assumption, if true, would support the argument's conclusion (make it more logical)?
- The strength of the argument depends on which of the following?
- Upon which of the following assumptions does the author rely?
- Which assumption does the argument presuppose?

An example is:

> Frank Underwood is a terrible president. The man is a typical spend, spend, spend liberal. His employment program would exponentially increase the annual deficit and pile on the national debt. Not to mention, Underwood is also on the verge of starting a war with Russia.

Upon which of the following assumptions does the author's argument most rely?
a. Frank Underwood is a terrible president.
b. The United States cannot afford Frank Underwood's policy plans without spending more than the country raises in revenue.
c. No spend, spend, spend liberal has ever succeeded as president.
d. Starting a war with Russia is beneficial to the United States.

Use the negation rule to find the correct answer in the choices below.

Choice *A* is not an assumption—it is the author's conclusion. This type of restatement will never be the correct answer, but test it anyway. After negating the choice, what remains is: *Frank Underwood is a fantastic president*. Does this make the argument fall apart? No, it just becomes the new conclusion. The argument is certainly worse since it does not seem reasonable for someone to praise a president for being a spend, spend, spend liberal or raising the national debt; however, the argument still makes *logical* sense. Eliminate this choice.

Choice *B* is certainly an assumption. It underlies the premises that the country cannot afford Underwood's economic plans. When reversed to: *The United States can afford Frank Underwood's policy plans without spending more than the country raises in revenue,* this destroys the argument. If the United States can afford his plans, then the annual deficit and national debt won't increase; therefore, Underwood being a terrible president would only be based on the final premise. The argument is much weaker without the two sentences involving the financials. Keep it as a benchmark while working through the remaining choices.

Choice *C* is irrelevant. The author is not necessarily claiming that all loose-pocket liberals make for bad presidents. His argument specifically pertains to Underwood. Negate it— *Some spend, spend, spend liberals have succeeded as president.* This does not destroy the argument. Some other candidate could have succeeded as president. However, the author is pointing out that those policies would be disastrous considering the rising budget and debt. The author is not making an appeal to historical precedent. Although not a terrible choice, it is certainly weaker than Choice *B*. Eliminate this choice.

Choice *D* is definitely not an assumption made by the author. The author is assuming that a war with Russia is disastrous. Negate it anyway—*Starting a war with Russia is not beneficial for the United States.* This does not destroy the argument; it makes it stronger. Eliminate this choice.

Analyzing Two Arguments and Evaluating the Types of Evidence Used to Support Each Claim
Arguments use evidence and reasoning to support a position or prove a point. Claims are typically controversial and may be faced with some degree of contention. Thus, authors support claims with evidence. Two arguments might present different types of evidence that readers will need to evaluate for merit, worthiness, accuracy, relevance, and impact. Evidence can take on many forms such as numbers (statistics, measurements, numerical data, etc.), expert opinions or quotes, testimonies, anecdotal evidence or stories from individuals, and textual evidence, such as that obtained from documents like diaries, newspapers, and laws.

Practice Test

Fiction

Questions 1 – 10 are based upon the following passage taken from Anne of the Island *by Luisa May Alcott, 1914:*

Chapter XIX

An Interlude

"To think that this is my twentieth birthday, and that I've left my teens behind me forever," said Anne, who was curled up on the hearth-rug with Rusty in her lap, to Aunt Jamesina who was reading in her pet chair. They were alone in the living room. Stella and Priscilla had gone to a committee meeting and Phil was upstairs adorning herself for a party.

"I suppose you feel kind of, sorry" said Aunt Jamesina. "The teens are such a nice part of life. I'm glad I've never gone out of them myself."

Anne laughed.

"You never will, Aunty. You'll be eighteen when you should be a hundred. Yes, I'm sorry, and a little dissatisfied as well. Miss Stacy told me long ago that by the time I was twenty my character would be formed, for good or evil. I don't feel that it's what it should be. It's full of flaws."

"So's everybody's," said Aunt Jamesina cheerfully. "Mine's cracked in a hundred places. Don't worry over it, Anne. Do your duty by God and your neighbor and yourself, and have a good time. That's my philosophy and it's always worked pretty well. Where's Phil off to tonight?"

"She's going to a dance, and she's got the sweetest dress for it—creamy yellow silk and cobwebby lace. It just suits those brown tints of hers."

"There's magic in the words 'silk' and 'lace,' isn't there?" said Aunt Jamesina. "The very sound of them makes me feel like skipping off to a dance. And YELLOW silk. It makes one think of a dress of sunshine. I always wanted a yellow silk dress, but first my mother and then my husband wouldn't hear of it. The very first thing I'm going to do when I get to heaven is to get a yellow silk dress."

Amid Anne's peal of laughter Phil came downstairs, trailing clouds of glory, and surveyed herself in the long oval mirror on the wall.

"A flattering looking glass is a promoter of amiability," she said. "The one in my room does certainly make me green. Do I look pretty nice, Anne?"

"Do you really know how pretty you are, Phil?" asked Anne, in honest admiration.

"Of course I do. What are looking glasses and men for? That wasn't what I meant. Are all my ends tucked in? Is my skirt straight? And would this rose look better lower down?"

"Everything is just right, and that southwest dimple of yours is lovely."

"Anne, there's one thing in particular I like about you—you're so ungrudging. There isn't a particle of envy in you."

"Why should she be envious?" demanded Aunt Jamesina. "She's not quite as goodlooking as you, maybe, but she's got a far handsomer nose."

"I know it," conceded Phil.

"My nose always has been a great comfort to me," confessed Anne.

"And I love the way your hair grows on your forehead, Anne. But as for noses, mine is a dreadful worry to me. I know by the time I'm forty it will be Byrney. What do you think I'll look like when I'm forty, Anne?"

"Like an old, matronly, married woman," teased Anne.

"I won't," said Phil, sitting down comfortably to wait for her escort. "Joseph, you calico beastie, don't you dare jump on my lap. I won't go to a dance all over cat hairs. No, Anne, I WON'T look matronly. But no doubt I'll be married."

"To Alec or Alonzo?" asked Anne.

"To one of them, I suppose," sighed Phil, "if I can ever decide which."

"It shouldn't be hard to decide," scolded Aunt Jamesina.

"I was born a see-saw Aunty, and nothing can ever prevent me from teetering."

"You ought to be more levelheaded, Philippa."

"It's best to be levelheaded, of course," agreed Philippa, "but you miss lots of fun. As for Alec and Alonzo, if you knew them you'd understand why it's difficult to choose between them. They're equally nice."

"Marr Holworthy then. You can't find a fault with him."

"No, he would do if he wasn't poor. I must marry a rich man, Aunt Jamesina. That—and good looks—is an indispensable qualification. I'd marry Gilbert Blythe if he were rich."

"Oh, would you?" said Anne, rather viciously.

"We don't like that idea a little bit, although we don't want Gilbert ourselves, oh, no," mocked Phil. "But don't let's talk of disagreeable subjects. I'll have to marry sometime, I suppose, but I shall put off the evil day as long as I can."

"You mustn't marry anybody you don't love, Phil, when all's said and done," said Aunt Jamesina.

"'Oh, hearts that loved in the good old way

Have been out o' the fashion this many a day.'"

224

trilled Phil mockingly. "There's the carriage. I fly—Bi-bi, you two old-fashioned darlings."

1. Phil primarily wants a husband who is:
   a. her true love.
   b. age appropriate.
   c. rich and handsome.
   d. honest and kind.

2. Which of the following events occurred first in the passage?
   a. Phil comes downstairs and enters the living room.
   b. Aunt Jamesina tells Anne about her philosophy of life.
   c. Anne asks Phil what she thinks of Marr Holworthy.
   d. Phil yells at the cat.

3. What does Aunt Jamesina mean when she says, "There's magic in the words 'silk' and 'lace'"?
   a. The words conjure happy thoughts, like dancing and sunshine.
   b. The words describe Phil's creamy yellow silk and cobwebby lace dress.
   c. The words are a reminder that husbands don't want their wives to be happy.
   d. The words fit together like lyrics in a magical song.

4. Which of the following statements BEST describes Phil's attitude toward marriage?
   a. Phil is unemotional and practical in her thoughts about marriage.
   b. Phil is excited to marry her one true love.
   c. Phil doubts she'll ever get married.
   d. Phil doesn't care who she marries.

5. What does Phil mean when she says the looking glass in her room makes her "green"?
   a. The looking glass makes her skin appear green in color.
   b. The looking glass makes her look ugly.
   c. Seeing her reflection in the looking glass gives her pleasure.
   d. Seeing her reflection in the looking glass makes her sick.

6. The following lines of dialogue appear at the end of the passage: "It's best to be levelheaded, of course," agreed Philippa, "but you miss lots of fun." Which of the following statements best paraphrases this sentence in context?
   a. "Obviously I should be more sensible," conceded Philippa, but "I truly enjoy dating a variety of men."
   b. "It's best to be excitable, of course," agreed Philippa, "but I don't want to miss out on the fun."
   c. "I should be more pragmatic," countered Philippa, "but I'm afraid of wasting away my youth."
   d. "I do need to be more rational," admitted Philippa, "but I only care about marrying into wealth."

7. Phil refers to herself as a "see-saw" because she is:
   a. uncertain about what she should wear to the dance.
   b. doubting her love for Marr Holworthy.
   c. hesitant about marrying for money.
   d. indecisive about whom to marry.

8. Compared to Phil, Aunt Jamesina's views on marriage are:
    a. less idealistic.
    b. less vicious.
    c. more tied to love.
    d. more superficial.

9. Where are Stella and Priscilla during the events described in the passage?
    a. At a dance
    b. At a committee meeting
    c. In the living room
    d. In the kitchen

10. Based on the passage, which of the following statements best explains why Phil says, "'Oh, hearts that loved in the good old way/Have been out o' the fashion this many a day'"?
    a. She is mocking Aunt Jamesina for getting married young.
    b. She is mocking Aunt Jamesina for coddling Anne.
    c. She is mocking Aunt Jamesina's advice about marrying for love.
    d. She is mocking Aunt Jamesina for not caring about her looks.

Natural Science

Questions 11–20 are based upon the following passage taken from Social Life in the Insect World *by Jean-Henri Fabre, 1911:*

Chapter XII

The Sisyphus Beetle.—The Instinct of Paternity

The duties of paternity are seldom imposed on any but the higher animals. They are most notable in the bird; and the furry peoples acquit themselves honourably. Lower in the scale we find in the father a general indifference as to the fate of the family. Very few insects form exceptions to this rule. Although all are imbued with a mating instinct that is almost frenzied, nearly all, when the passion of the moment is appeased, terminate then and there their domestic relations, and withdraw, indifferent to the brood, which has to look after itself as best it may.

This paternal coldness, which would be odious in the higher walks of animal life, where the weakness of the young demands prolonged assistance, has in the insect world the excuse that the new-born young are comparatively robust, and are able, without help, to fill their mouths and stomachs, provided they find themselves in propitious surroundings. All that the prosperity of the race demands of the Pierides, or Cabbage Butterflies, is that they should deposit their eggs on the leaves of the cabbage; what purpose would be served by the instincts of a father? The botanical instinct of the mother needs no assistance. At the period of laying the father would be in the way. Let him pursue his flirtations elsewhere; the laying of eggs is a serious business.

In the case of the majority of insects the process of education is unknown, or summary in the extreme. The Insect has only to select a grazing-ground upon which its family will establish itself the moment it is hatched; or a site which will allow the young to find their proper sustenance for themselves. There is no need of a father in these various cases. After mating, the discarded male, who is henceforth useless, drags out a lingering existence of a few days, and finally perishes without having given the slightest assistance in the work of installing his offspring.

But matters are not everywhere so primitive as this. There are tribes in which an inheritance is prepared for the family which will assure it both of food and of shelter in advance. The Hymenoptera in particular are past-masters in the provision of cellars, jars, and other utensils in which the honey-paste destined for the young is stored; they are perfect in the art of excavating storehouses of food for their grubs.

This stupendous labour of construction and provisioning, this labour that absorbs the insect's whole life, is the work of the mother only, who wears herself out at her task. The father, intoxicated with sunlight, lies idle on the threshold of the workshop, watching the heroic female at her work, and regards himself as excused from all labour when he has plagued his neighbours a little.

Does he never perform useful work? Why does he not follow the example of the swallows, each of whom brings a fair share of the straw and mortar for the building of the nest and the midges for the young brood? No, he does nothing; perhaps alleging the excuse of his relative weakness. But this is a poor excuse; for to cut out little circles from a leaf, to rake a little cotton from a downy plant, or to gather a little mortar from a muddy spot, would hardly be a task beyond his powers. He might very well collaborate, at least as labourer; he could at least gather together the materials for the more intelligent mother to place in position. The true motive of his idleness is ineptitude.

It is a curious thing that the Hymenoptera, the most skilful of all industrial insects, know nothing of paternal labour. The male of the genus, in whom we should expect the requirements of the young to develop the highest aptitudes, is as useless as a butterfly, whose family costs so little to establish. The actual distribution of instinct upsets our most reasonable previsions.

It upsets our expectations so completely that we are surprised to find in the dung-beetle the noble prerogative which is lacking in the bee tribe. The mates of several species of dung-beetle keep house together and know the worth of mutual labour. Consider the male and female Geotrupes, which prepare together the patrimony of their larvæ; in their case the father assists his companion with the pressure of his robust body in the manufacture of their balls of compressed nutriment. These domestic habits are astonishing amidst the general isolation.

11. Which of the following statements BEST describes the usual paternal relationship between insects and their offspring?
    a. Most male insects are usually too weak to help raise their offspring.
    b. Most male insects prepare balls of compressed nutriments for their offspring.
    c. Most male insects prepare an inheritance for their offspring.
    d. Most male insects have no relationship with their offspring.

12. Why does the narrator describe Hymenoptera as being less "primitive" than other insects?
    a. Hymenoptera deposit their eggs on the leaves of the cabbage.
    b. Hymenoptera gather food and find shelter for their offspring.
    c. Hymenoptera hatch their offspring near a preselected grazing-ground.
    d. Hymenoptera' mates contribute equally while preparing for their offspring.

13. In the second paragraph, "propitious surroundings" MOST likely means:
    a. an isolated habitat.
    b. a tightknit community.
    c. an area with food.
    d. a cellar full of honey-paste.

14. Why does the narrator mention "the example of the swallows"?
    a. It serves as an example of another type of insect with an uncommon distribution of labor based on sex.
    b. It serves as an example of how animals gather materials to build nests.
    c. It serves as a counter-example of how some raise their brood through adulthood.
    d. It serves as a counter-example to the labor distribution between male and female Hymenoptera.

15. Compared to other insects, dung-beetles are unique because:
    a. the females lay the eggs, and the males prepare their offspring's inheritance by themselves.
    b. the males and females both help prepare for their offspring.
    c. the males are too inept to contribute anything to their offspring.
    d. both the males and females are indifferent to their offspring.

16. Which of the following statements is the most logical conclusion that can be drawn from the passage?
    a. Geotrupes' ball of compressed nutriments are extremely similar to the honey-paste cellars left by the Hymenoptera.
    b. Geotrupes' preparation for their broods stands in sharp contrast to what's observed amongst bee tribes.
    c. Insects prepare for their incoming broods in a variety of different ways, but dung-beetles are the most remarkable due to their equitable distribution of labor between the sexes.
    d. Unlike other insects, male Geotrupes play a far more important role than their female partners in regards to preparing for their brood.

17. For the majority of insects, the males:
    a. excavate storehouses of food.
    b. gather materials for the mother to put in position.
    c. lay the eggs.
    d. die shortly after mating.

18. Compared to higher animals, insects' offspring are generally better suited for survival due to their ability:
    a. to move around and feed themselves.
    b. to build a protective nest.
    c. to collect and store food.
    d. to fly away from predators.

19. How does the narrator characterize the male Hymenoptera's role in leaving an "inheritance" for their offspring?
    a. The male is too weak to help its partner prepare the inheritance.
    b. The male contributes equally to preparing the inheritance.
    c. The male watches its partner and follows her example.
    d. The male is inept and does not assist its partner in preparing the inheritance.

20. Which of the following statements best summarizes the passage's main point?
   a. Unlike higher animals, new-born insects can move around and feed themselves.
   b. Similar to higher animals, most insects provide their offspring with an inheritance of shelter and food.
   c. Insects don't prepare for their brood in the same way as higher animals, and female insects typically shoulder the bulk of the work.
   d. Female insects are significantly stronger than their male counterparts, which is why all insects have an inequitable distribution of labor.

Social Science

Questions 21–30 are based on the following passages taken from Bradford's History of 'Plimouth Plantation' *by William Bradford, 1898:*

2. Chap.

Of their departure into Holland and their troubls ther aboute, with some of the many difficulties they found and mete withall.

An°. 1608.

Being thus constrained to leave their native soyle and countrie, their lands & livings, and all their freinds & famillier acquaintance, it was much, and thought marvelous by many. But to goe into a countrie they knew not (but by hearsay), wher they must [16]learne a new language, and get their livings they knew not how, it being a dear place, & subjecte to ye misseries of warr, it was by many thought an adventure almost desperate, a case intolerable, & a misserie worse than death. Yet [8] this was not all, for though they could not stay, yet were ye not suffered to goe, but ye ports and havens were shut against them, so as they were faine to seeke secrete means of conveance, & to bribe & fee ye mariners, & give exterordinarie rates for their passages.

Ther was a large companie of them purposed to get passage at Boston in Lincoln-shire, and for that end had hired a shipe wholy to them selves, & made agreement with the maister to be ready at a certaine day, and take them and their goods in, at a conveniente place, wher they accordingly would all attende [17]in readines. So after long waiting, & large expences, though he kepte not day with them, yet he came at length & tooke them in, in ye night. But when he had them & their goods abord, he betrayed them, haveing before hand complotted with ye serchers & other officers so to doe; who tooke them, and put them into open boats, & ther rifled & ransaked them, searching them to their shirts for money, yea even ye women furder then became modestie; and then caried them back into ye towne, & made them a spectackle & wonder to the multitude, which came flocking on all sids to behould them. Being thus first, by the chatch-poule officers, rifled, & stripte of their money, books, and much other goods, they were presented to ye magestrates, and messengers sente to informe ye lords of ye Counsell of them; and so they were comited to ward. Indeed ye magestrats used them courteously, and shewed them what favour they could; but could not deliver them, till order came from ye Counsell-table. But ye issue was that after a months imprisonmente, ye greatest parte were dismiste, & sent to y^eplaces from whence they came; but 7. of ye principall were still kept in prison, and bound over to ye Assises.

The nexte spring after, ther was another attempte made by some of these & others, to get over at an other place. And it so fell out, that they light of a Dutchman at Hull, having a ship of his owne belonging [18]to Zealand; they made agreemente with him, and acquainted [9] him with their condition, hoping to find more faithfullnes in him, then in ye former of their owne nation. He bad them not fear, for he would doe well enough. He was by appointment to take them in betweene Grimsbe & Hull, wher was a large comone a good way distante from any towne. Now aganst the prefixed time, the women & children, with ye goods, were sent to ye place in a small barke, which they had hired for y^t end; and ye men were to meete them by land. But it so fell out, that they were ther a day before ye shipe came, & ye sea being rough, and ye women very sicke, prevailed with ye seamen to put into a creeke hardby, wher they lay on ground at lowwater. The nexte morning ye shipe came, but they were fast, & could not stir till aboute noone. In ye mean time, ye shipe maister, perceiveing how ye matter was, sente his boate to be getting ye men abord whom he saw ready, walking aboute ye shore. But after ye first boat full was gott abord, & she was ready to goe for more, the m^r espied a greate company, both horse & foote, with bills, & gunes, & other weapons; for ye countrie was raised to take them. Y^e Dutch-man seeing y^t, swore his countries oath, "sacremente," and having ye wind faire, waiged his Ancor, hoysed sayles, & away. But y^{e}poore men which were gott abord, were in great distress for their wives and children, which they saw thus to be [19]taken, and were left destitute of their helps; and them selves also, not having a cloath to shifte them with, more then they had on their baks, & some scarce a peney aboute them, all they had being abord ye barke. It drew tears from their eyes, and any thing they had they would have given to have been a shore againe; but all in vaine, ther was no remedy, they must thus sadly part.

21. Which of the following was NOT a difficulty faced by the group of travelers?
    a. They didn't know the new country's language.
    b. They weren't allowed to bring their wives or children to the new country.
    c. They didn't know how to make a living in the new country.
    d. Ships charged exorbitant rates for the voyage to the new country.

22. The Dutchman's "sacramente" was:
    a. a prayer.
    b. an oath.
    c. a ritual.
    d. a promise.

23. What went wrong with the ship hired at Boston in Lincoln-shire?
    a. The women got sick due to the rough seas.
    b. The men were separated from their wives and children.
    c. The group couldn't get out of jail in time to board the ship.
    d. The shipmaster betrayed them.

24. Based on the passage, why did the men leave their wives and children?
    a. Armed government officials arrived on the shore.
    b. The government refused to let them out of prison.
    c. The sea was too rough to risk going back for them.
    d. The women were too sick to make the voyage.

25. Ships charged the group of travelers extra fees because:
    a. they were a vulnerable minority group.
    b. the voyage was particularly long and dangerous.
    c. the government outlawed their departure.
    d. they were wealthy enough to afford it.

26. Based on the passage, which of the following statements BEST describes how the government treated the group of travelers?
    a. The government expelled them from their homeland.
    b. The government persecuted the group due to their different religious beliefs.
    c. The government valued the women and children more than the men.
    d. The government repeatedly tried to stop them from leaving.

27. Which of the following events occurred first?
    a. Some of the group's members were kept in prison and sent to the Assises.
    b. Government officials embarrassed the group by parading them through town.
    c. The men cried after getting separated from their wives and children.
    d. The women became sick due to the rough seas.

28. Which of the following statements best summarizes the second paragraph?
    a. The shipmaster's betrayal led to incredible hardship for the group, including public embarrassment and imprisonment.
    b. The group was imprisoned, and they received better treatment from the magistrates than the lords of the counsel.
    c. The women's sickness led to the government officials discovering, seizing, and imprisoning the group.
    d. While some of the group members were released, others were kept in prison and sent to the Assises.

29. Which of the following statements can reasonably be inferred from the men's reaction at the end of the passage?
    a. The men would have to pay even more exorbitant fees and bribes to bring their wives and children to the commune.
    b. The men were more upset by the loss of their possessions than the separation from their wives and children.
    c. The Dutch shipmaster betrayed them by sailing away instead of attempting to rescue the women and children.
    d. There was a strong likelihood that the men wouldn't see their wives and children for a long time.

30. How did the wives and children become separated from the men?
    a. They were still in prison when the ship set sail.
    b They got sick, forcing their boat to take a detour, and they didn't board the ship in time.
    c. They were on a separate boat, and the captain of their boat betrayed them.
    d. They were pulled off course by strong winds, so they didn't reach the agreed upon meeting place in time.

Humanities

Questions 31–40 are based on the following two passages:

Passage I

Taken from Ten Great Religions: An Essay in Comparative Theology *by James Freeman Clarke, 1899.*

7. Influence of Egypt on Judaism and Christianity.

How much of the doctrine and ritual of Egypt were imported into Judaism by Moses is a question by no means easy to settle.

That some of the ritualism to which the Jews were accustomed in Egypt should have been imported into their new ceremonial, is quite in accordance with human nature. Christianity, also, has taken up many of the customs of heathenism. The rite of circumcision was probably adopted by the Jews from the Egyptians, who received it from the natives of Africa. Livingstone has found it among the tribes south of the Zambesi, and thinks this custom there cannot be traced to any Mohammedan source. Prichard believes it, in Egypt, to have been a relic of ancient African customs. It still exists in Ethiopia and Abyssinia. In Egypt it existed far earlier than the time of Abraham, as appears by ancient mummies. Herodotus tells us that the custom existed from the earliest times among the Egyptians and Ethiopians, and was adopted from them by the Syrians of Palestine. Those who regard this rite as instituted by a Divine command may still believe that it already existed among the Jews, just as baptism existed among them before Jesus commanded his disciples to baptize. Both in Egypt and among the Jews it was connected with a feeling of superiority. The circumcised were distinguished from others by a higher religious position. It is difficult to trace the origin of sentiments so alien to our own ways of thought; but the hygienic explanation seems hardly adequate. It may have been a sign of the devotion of the generative power to the service of God, and have been the first step out of the untamed license of the passions, among the Africans.

Such facts as these make it highly probable that Moses allowed in his ritual many ceremonies borrowed from the Egyptian worship.

All the vast range of Egyptian wisdom has gone, and disappeared from the surface of the earth, for it was only a religion of the priests, who kept the truth to themselves and did not venture to communicate it to the people. Only truth is immortal,—open, frank, manly truth. Confucius was true; he did not know much, but he told all he knew. Buddha told all he knew. Moses told all he heard. So they and their works continue, being built on faith in men.

Passage II

Taken from Jewish Theology: Systematically and Historically Considered *by Dr. K. Kohler, 1918.*

Chapter II. What is Judaism?

Owing to this twofold nature of a universal religious truth and at the same time a mission intrusted to a specially selected nation or race, Judaism offers in a sense the sharpest contrasts imaginable, which render it an enigma to the student of religion and history, and make him often incapable of impartial judgment. On the one hand, it shows the most tenacious adherence to forms originally intended to preserve the Jewish people in its priestly sanctity and

232

separateness, and thereby also to keep its religious truths pure and free from encroachments. On the other hand, it manifests a mighty impulse to come into close touch with the various civilized nations, partly in order to disseminate among them its sublime truths, appealing alike to mind and heart, partly to clarify and deepen those truths by assimilating the wisdom and culture of these very nations. Thus the spirit of separatism and of universalism work in opposite directions. Still, however hostile the two elements may appear, they emanate from the same source. For the Jewish people, unlike any other civilization of antiquity, entered history with the proud claim that it possessed a truth destined to become some day the property of mankind, and its three thousand years of history have verified this claim.

Israel's relation to the world thus became a double one. Its priestly world-mission gave rise to all those laws and customs which were to separate it from its idolatrous surroundings, and this occasioned the charge of hostility to the nations. The accusation of Jewish misanthropy occurred as early as the Balaam and Haman stories. As the separation continued through the centuries, a deep-seated Jew-hatred sprang up, first in Alexandria and Rome, then becoming a consuming fire throughout Christendom, unquenched through the ages and bursting forth anew, even from the midst of would-be liberals. In contrast to this, Israel's prophetic ideal of a humanity united in justice and peace gave to history a new meaning and a larger outlook, kindling in the souls of all truly great leaders and teachers, seers and sages of mankind a love and longing for the broadening of humanity which opened new avenues of progress and liberty. Moreover, by its conception of man as the image of God and its teaching of righteousness as the true path of life, Israel's Law established a new standard of human worth and put the imprint of Jewish idealism upon the entire Aryan civilization.

31. Compared to ancient Egypt's religion, Judaism is:
    a. more separatist.
    b. more universalist.
    c. less prophetic.
    d. less tenacious.

32. In both ancient Egypt's religion and Judaism, circumcision was associated with:
    a. the Balaam and Haman stories.
    b. taming passion.
    c. the teachings of Confucius.
    d. a feeling of superiority.

33. Which of the following statements describe a major difference in the attitudes of ancient Egyptian and Jewish religious leaders?
    a. Ancient Egyptian religious leaders jealously guarded their truths, while Jewish religious leaders were more open to disseminating their truths.
    b. Ancient Egyptian religious leaders were eager to share their truths to Judaism, while Jewish religious leaders passed their truths all over the world.
    c. Ancient Egyptian religious leaders shared their truths with the public, while Jewish religious leaders kept their truths to themselves.
    d. Ancient Egyptian religious leaders converted new followers by force, while Jewish religious leaders used their truths to recruit new followers.

34. Which of the following statements best describes the different impacts Judaism and ancient Egypt's religion had on "Aryan civilization"?
    a. Ancient Egypt's religion influenced Judaism, and Judaism influenced Aryan civilization.
    b. Judaism influenced ancient Egypt's religion, and both religions influenced Aryan civilization.
    c. Judaism influenced Aryan civilization, but ancient Egypt's religion had a greater direct impact.
    d. Both religions influenced Aryan civilization, but neither approaches Buddha's impact.

35. Where did a "deep-seated Jew-hatred" first occur?
    a. Palestine
    b. Christendom
    c. Alexandria and Rome
    d. Egypt

36. Both passages agree that:
    a. religious truths exist.
    b. priestly sanctity is the most important part of religion.
    c. all organized religion can be traced back to Africa.
    d. Judaism is an enigma.

37. Why has ancient Egypt's religion "disappeared from the surface of the earth"?
    a. Scholars discovered that ancient Egypt's religious truths were historically inaccurate.
    b. All of the ancient Egyptians converted to Judaism.
    c. Egyptian priests kept the religion a secret, refusing to share it with the public.
    d. Confucius, Buddha, and Moses spoiled the ancient Egyptian religion's secrets.

38. "Israel's prophetic ideal" is:
    a. a duty to assimilate wisdom and culture.
    b. a spirit of separatism.
    c. a rejection of Jewish misanthropy.
    d. a humanity united in justice and peace.

39. While the first passage mostly focuses on the influence of ancient Egypt's religion on Judaism, the second passage focuses on:
    a. understanding the entire Aryan civilization.
    b. explaining the twofold nature of Judaism.
    c. tracing Judaism back to its historical source.
    d. challenging Judaism's truths.

40. Based on the information contained in both passages, which of the following events MOST likely occurred first?
    a. Africans begin practicing the rite of circumcision.
    b. Ancient Egypt's religion disappears.
    c. Jesus commands his disciples to baptize.
    d. Anti-Semitism spreads throughout Christendom.

Answer Explanations

Fiction

1. C: Phil primarily wants a husband who is rich and handsome. When explaining why she doesn't want to marry Marr Holworthy, Phil says, "I must marry a rich man, Aunt Jamesina. That—and good looks—is an indispensable qualification." Aunt Jamesina advises her to marry based on love, but Phil mocks that advice; therefore, Choice A is incorrect. Choices B and D are also incorrect because Phil never explicitly incudes age, honesty, or kindness as qualifications for a husband. She is prioritizing wealth and good looks, so everything else is secondary. Thus, Choice C is the correct answer.

2. B: Aunt Jamesina describes her philosophy of life—"Do your duty by God and your neighbor and yourself, and have a good time"– to Anne before Phil joins the conversation. Phil comes downstairs and enters the living room shortly after this occurs; therefore, Choice A is incorrect. Phil yells at Joseph the cat during the conversation right before the women discuss Phil's suitors; therefore, Choice D is incorrect. Marr Holworthy is discussed at the very end of the passage; therefore, Choice C is incorrect. Thus, Choice B is the correct answer.

3. A: Aunt Jamesina says, "There's magic in the words 'silk' and 'lace'" at the beginning of the passage before Phil joins the conversation. She's describing happy thoughts, and she specifically mentions dancing and sunshine. Although Phil's creamy yellow silk and cobwebby lace dress is what prompts Aunt Jamesina's comment, she is talking about how those two words make her feel, not the dress itself; therefore, Choice B is incorrect. Aunt Jamesina mentions that her husband wouldn't let her wear a yellow silk dress, but that unhappy memory is not why she thinks those words are magic; therefore, Choice C is incorrect. Aunt Jamesina never compares the words to lyrics in a song, so Choice D must also be incorrect. Thus, Choice A is the correct answer.

4. A: Phil is unemotional and practical in her thoughts about marriage. While Anne and Aunt Jamesina want her to marry someone she loves, Phil rejects this line of thinking as old-fashioned; therefore, Choice B is incorrect. Choice C is incorrect because at one point Phil says, "But no doubt I'll be married." Phil very much cares about who she marries because she wants a rich and handsome husband; therefore, Choice D is incorrect. Compared to Anne and Aunt Jamesina's views, Phil's desire to marry for money and looks is an unemotional and practical approach to marriage. Thus, Choice A is the correct answer.

5. C: Phil's reflection in the looking glass gives her pleasure. Before she mentions how the looking glass makes her green, Phil says, "A flattering looking glass is a promoter of amiability." Amiability means having pleasant qualities, and based on context, we can infer that Phil thinks her looking glass is flattering. Choice A is incorrect because it's too literal. Anne doesn't think the mirror literally makes her body or clothes look green. In addition, Anne is clearly using "green" with a positive connotation, which is inconsistent with ugliness or sickness; therefore, Choices B and D are both incorrect. Thus, Choice C is the correct answer.

6. A: The first half of the sentence is agreeing with Aunt Jamesina's advice on being levelheaded, while the second half explains how Phil prioritizes having fun. Based on context, "fun" is referring to dating a variety of men. For Choice A, sensible and conceded are synonyms for levelheaded and agreed, respectively, and the second half matches the sentiment contained in the original sentence. Excitable is an antonym for levelheaded, so Choice B must be incorrect. While pragmatic is a synonym for levelheaded, countered carries the opposite meaning of agreed; therefore, Choice C is incorrect.

Likewise, in Choice *D*, rational is a synonym for levelheaded, but the second half of the sentence is different than the original. Phil cares about wealth and looks, and fun refers to dating multiple rich and good looking men; therefore, Choice *D* is incorrect. Thus, Choice *A* is the correct answer.

7. D: Phil refers to herself as a "see-saw" because she is indecisive about who to marry. This comment appears at the end of the passage when the women are discussing Alec and Alonzo. Phil can't make up her mind as to who she loves, which is why she calls herself a "see-saw." Although Phil does ask the other women about her dress, that's not related to the "see-saw" comment; therefore, Choice *A* is incorrect. Choices *B* and *C* are each contradicted by the passage. Phil flatly rejects Marr Holworthy for being poor, and she has zero hesitation about marrying for money; therefore, Choices *B* and *C* are both incorrect. Thus, Choice *D* is the correct answer.

8. C: While Phil wants to marry a rich and good-looking man, Aunt Jamesina tells Phil not to marry someone she doesn't love at the end of the passage. If anything, Aunt Jamesina is more idealistic than Phil, not less, so Choice *A* is incorrect. In addition, Aunt Jamesina's views on marriage aren't vicious; therefore, Choice *B* is incorrect. Phil is more superficial than Aunt Jamesina, so Choice *D* is incorrect. Thus, Choice *C* is the correct answer.

9. B: The first paragraph states that Stella and Priscilla are at a committee meeting. Only Phil is going to the dance; therefore, Choice *A* is incorrect. There are no characters in the kitchen; therefore, Choice *D* is incorrect. Anne, Aunt Jamesina, and Phil are talking in the living room, and Stella and Priscilla never enter to join the conversation because they're at a committee meeting; therefore, Choice *C* is incorrect. Thus, Choice *B* is the correct answer.

10. C: Phil trills those lines in a mocking tone after Aunt Jamesina advises her to marry for love at the end of the passage. She does so to mock marrying for love as old fashioned. Although Aunt Jamesina defends Anne earlier in the conversation, she's not coddling her; therefore, Choice *B* is incorrect. Choices *A* and *D* are not referenced anywhere in the passage, and therefore, they are both incorrect. Thus, Choice *C* is the correct answer.

Natural Science

11. D: The first two paragraphs describe how most male insects have no relationship with their offspring. After mating occurs, the male terminates the relationship and acts with a cold indifference toward the offspring. The sixth paragraph explains that the reason for this paternal coldness is ineptitude, not weakness; therefore, Choice *A* is incorrect. Gathering balls of compressed nutriments is unique to Geotrupes, not most insects, so Choice *B* is incorrect. Only a few tribes of insects leave an inheritance for their offspring; therefore, Choice *C* is incorrect. Thus, Choice *D* is the correct answer.

12. B: The fourth paragraph describes how Hymenoptera are less primitive than most insects because they leave an inheritance for their offspring. The inheritance includes both food and shelter. Pierides deposit eggs on leaves of cabbage, not Hymenoptera, so Choice *A* is incorrect. Most insects preselect a grazing-ground, so that's not unique to Hymenoptera; therefore, Choice *C* is incorrect. The fifth, sixth, and seventh paragraphs characterize the male Hymenoptera as being extremely unhelpful and not equal contributors, so Choice *D* is incorrect. Thus, Choice *B* is the correct answer.

13. C: Propitious means favorable, and the phrase "propitious surroundings" comes right after the narrator describes how most young insects can feed themselves. So, the propitious surroundings must be related to food. Although Choice *D* lists a specific food source, honey-paste is only mentioned in reference to Hymenoptera, not most insects, so it is incorrect. Likewise, isolated habits are only mentioned in connection with Geotrupes; therefore, Choice *A* is incorrect. The passage doesn't mention tightknit communities, so Choice *B* must be incorrect. Thus, Choice *C* is the correct answer.

14. D: The example of the swallows can be found in the sixth paragraph, which describes how Hymenoptera are too inept to help prepare an inheritance for their offspring. In contrast, both sexes of swallows contribute to building a nest for their young brood. So, the example of the swallows is a counter-example to the labor distribution between male and female Hymenoptera. The example of the swallows occurs before an example of insects with an uncommon distribution of labor based on sex; therefore, Choice *A* is incorrect. In addition, the example is more about mutual labor than simply building nests, so Choice *B* is incorrect. The narrator doesn't mention if swallows raise their brood through adulthood; therefore, Choice *C* is incorrect. Thus, Choice *D* is the correct answer.

15. B: Based on the information contained in the last paragraph, dung-beetles are unique because the males and females both help prepare for their offspring. Dung-beetles "keep house together and know the worth of mutual labour," and the father specifically helps produce the balls of compressed nutriment. Choice *A* does not accurately describe the dung-beetles' labor distribution, so it must be incorrect. Choice *C* describes Hymenoptera, not dung-beetles; therefore, Choice *C* is incorrect. Choice *D* is a false statement, so it's also incorrect. Thus, Choice *B* is the correct answer.

16. C: The passage discusses a variety of different insects' preparations for their brood. In addition, a special emphasis is placed on the distribution of labor between the sexes, and Geotrupes are highlighted as an exceptional example of an insect with an equitable distribution of labor. Choice *C* is a logical conclusion because it best ties those concepts together. Choice *A* is a true statement. However, it does not reference the distribution of labor, which is the most critical part of the passage; therefore, Choice *A* is incorrect. Choice *B* is paraphrasing the final paragraph's topic sentence, and bees aren't mentioned anywhere else in the passage; therefore, Choice *B* is incorrect. Choice *D* is incorrect because male Geotrupes don't play a far more important role than their female partners. The males' role is remarkable because it's equitable. Thus, Choice *C* is the correct answer.

17. D: In the third paragraph, the narrator claims that most male insects survive for only a few days after mating. Only a few insects excavate storehouses of food, like the Hymenoptera and dung-beetles; therefore, Choice *A* is incorrect. The narrator mentions gathering materials for the mother to put in position as an example of how the male Hymenoptera could contribute if they wanted to. However, most male insects don't do that, so Choice *B* is incorrect. The passage never says that any male insects lay the eggs; therefore, Choice *C* is incorrect. Thus, Choice *D* is the correct answer.

18. A: In the second paragraph, the narrator describes how young insects are "robust" and can "fill their mouths and stomach," which is unlike higher animals. Most insects only preselect a grazing-ground and don't build nests; therefore, Choice *B* is incorrect. Only a few insects, like Hymenoptera and dung-beetles, collect and store food, so Choice *C* is incorrect. The passage never mentions insects flying away from predators; therefore, Choice *D* is incorrect. Thus, Choice *A* is the correct answer.

19. D: The narrator characterizes the male Hymenoptera's role in leaving an inheritance as inept and unhelpful in the fifth, sixth, and seventh paragraphs. While the narrator mentions weakness as a possible explanation for the male's laziness, he claims there's a stronger case for ineptitude; therefore, Choice A is incorrect. Choices B and C are contradicted by the passage, so they are both incorrect. The male Hymenoptera doesn't contribute anything or follow their partner's example. Thus, Choice D is the correct answer.

20. C: The passage repeatedly compares insects to higher animals, particularly in regard to the distribution of labor when preparing for offspring. The examples of different insect species highlight the distribution of labor based on sex, and female insects generally do more work than their male partners, which is different than higher animals. Choice A is a true statement, and it's the reason why insects and higher animals prepare for their offspring in different ways. However, it's not broad enough to be the main point because it doesn't reference the preparations or distribution of labor, so Choice A is incorrect. Choice B is contradicted by the passage, and therefore, it is incorrect. Likewise, Choice D is factually incorrect. The narrator specifically mentions that male insects' indifference is the cause of the inequitable distribution of labor, not relative weakness; therefore, Choice D is incorrect. Thus, Choice C is the correct answer.

Social Science

21. B: The first paragraph explains the difficulties facing the group of travelers. Language and making a living are listed in the second sentence, so Choices A and C are both incorrect. Extra fees and exorbitant rates are described in the first paragraph's final sentence; therefore, Choice D is incorrect. Although the men were later separated from their wives and children, that separation was due to a problem with logistics. There was no prohibition specifically against bringing their wives and children. The entire group was legally barred from leaving the country. Thus, Choice B is the correct answer.

22. B: The Dutchman's swears his "sacramente" near the end of the third paragraph, and the preceding phrase describes it as "his countries oath." Although "sacramente" sounds like a religious prayer or ritual, it's specifically described as an oath; therefore, Choices A and C are both incorrect. The Dutchman promises to take the group to the commune, but that's not what the "sacramente" is specifically referencing; therefore, Choice D is also incorrect. Thus, Choice B is the correct answer.

23. D: The ship hired at Boston in Lincoln-shire is the group's first attempt to flee their homeland, and it's described in the second paragraph. After the group reached an agreement with the shipmaster, he betrayed them to the government, which led to government officials arresting the group. The women didn't become sick or get separated until their second attempt at fleeing, so Choices A and B are both incorrect. Following the first shipmaster's betrayal, the group did go to jail, but their imprisonment occurred after their first attempt to leave went wrong; therefore, Choice C is incorrect. Thus, Choice D is the correct answer.

24. A: After the men boarded the ship, armed government officials arrived on the shore. Rather than risk everyone getting caught, the Dutch shipmaster raised the anchor, hoisted the sails, and took off. So, even though the men were moved to tears by the separation, there was nothing they could do. The government refused to let some of the group's member out of prison, but that's not what caused the separation; therefore, Choice B is incorrect. Choices C and D are factually incorrect based on the information contained in the third paragraph, and therefore, they are incorrect. Thus, Choice A is the correct answer.

25. C: Ships charged the group of travelers extra fees because the government outlawed their departure. The first paragraph says that the government barred them from the ports and havens, so they needed to find a secret passage out of the country. As helping the group was illegal, ships charged them extra fees in exchange for taking on that risk. The passage doesn't state why the group is being persecuted; therefore, Choice A is incorrect. Choice B is incorrect because the passage doesn't mention whether the voyage was particularly long or dangerous. While the government does seize property from the group, it's unclear whether the group is particularly wealthy; therefore, Choice D is incorrect. Thus, Choice C is the correct answer.

26. D: The government repeatedly tried to stop the group from leaving. Government officials prohibited the group from entering the ports, arrested the group after their first shipmaster's betrayal, imprisoned the group for attempting to leave, and sent armed soldiers to thwart their second attempt. The government did the opposite of expelling the group; therefore, Choice A is incorrect. It's unclear why the government is persecuting the group, so Choice B is incorrect. Although the government does ultimately capture the women and children, it's because they're the only people left on the shore, not because the government values them more; therefore, Choice C is incorrect. Thus, Choice D is the correct answer.

27. B: Following the first shipmaster's betrayal, the group was arrested, and the government officials paraded them through the street to embarrass them. The group's imprisonment occurred after the embarrassing parade; therefore, Choice A is incorrect. The men cried and the women became sick during the group's second attempt at fleeing their homeland. This occurs after the embarrassing parade through town and subsequent imprisonment; therefore, Choices C and D are both incorrect. Thus, Choice B is the correct answer.

28. A: The second paragraph begins with the group reaching an agreement with a shipmaster at Boston in Lincoln-shire. The rest of the paragraph describes the shipmaster's betrayal, government officials parading the group through the town in an embarrassing way, and the group being imprisoned. The group did receive better treatment from the magistrates than the lords of the counsel while in prison, but Choice B only describes the end of the paragraph, so it is incorrect. The women don't get sick until the third paragraph; therefore, Choice C is incorrect. Choice D is incorrect because it only summarizes the second paragraph's last sentence. Thus, Choice A is the correct answer.

29. D: At the end of the passage, the men were brought to tears after armed government officials arrested their wives and children. Given that the group had already been imprisoned for attempting to flee their homeland, it's reasonable to infer that their wives and children would receive the same or worse treatment. As such, there was a strong likelihood that the men wouldn't see their wives and children for a long time. If their wives and children ever had a third chance to escape, the men would likely have to pay even more exorbitant fees and bribes. However, the men are crying because they knew there might never be another chance for escape, not because of those potential fees, so Choice A is incorrect. The passage does mention how the men lost their possessions as well, but the forced separation was the more traumatic event; therefore, Choice B is incorrect. The Dutch shipmaster didn't betray the group. A rescue attempt would have been in vain, so his only option was to sail away; therefore Choice C is incorrect. Thus, Choice D is the correct answer.

30. B: The wives and children became separated from the men after the women got sick on the way to the meeting place. As a result, the women's boat took a detour, and they weren't ready in time to board the ship before armed government officials arrived on the shore. While some of the group's members were still in prison, many of the wives and children intended to make the voyage; therefore, Choice *A* is incorrect. The captain of the second ship never betrayed them, so Choice *C* is incorrect. The group took a detour due to the women getting sick, not because of strong winds, so Choice *D* is incorrect. Thus, Choice *B* is the correct answer.

Humanities

31. B: Compared to ancient Egypt's religion, Judaism is more universalist. The second passage describes how Judaism is both separatist and universalist. Separatism refers to priestly sanctity and keeping their religious truths pure and free from encroachment. As described in the first passage's final paragraph, ancient Egypt's religion was very separatist because only the priests knew the religion's truths. As such, ancient Egypt's religion was actually more separatist than Judaism; therefore, Choice *A* is incorrect. Only Judaism is described as prophetic, so it's unlikely Judaism is less prophetic than ancient Egypt's religion; therefore, Choice *C* is incorrect. Tenacious doesn't make sense as a point of comparison, so Choice *D* is incorrect. Thus, Choice *B* is the correct answer.

32. D: Ancient Egyptians and Jews practiced the rite of circumcision, and according to the first passage, both religions believed it was connected with a feeling of superiority. The Balaam and Haman stories are related to accusations of Jewish misanthropy, not the rite of circumcision, so Choice *A* is incorrect. The first passage says Africans might have started practicing circumcision to tame passion, but that was not why the ancient Egyptians and Jews started doing it; therefore, Choice *B* is incorrect. Neither passage connects the teachings of Confucius to circumcision, so Choice *C* is incorrect. Thus, Choice *D* is the correct answer.

33. A: Based on the first passage's final paragraph, we know that ancient Egyptian priests closely guarded their religious truths, and the second passage claims that Jews feel a duty to share their religious truths with the world. While the first passage claims that ancient Egypt's religion influenced Judaism, it doesn't say that Egyptian priests actively shared their truths with Jews or the world; therefore, Choices *B* and *C* are incorrect. If anything, it says the opposite. Choice *D* is incorrect because neither passage describes ancient Egyptian religious leaders recruiting new followers by force. Thus, Choice *A* is the correct answer.

34. A: The first passage claims that ancient Egypt's religion influenced Judaism, and the second passage claims that Judaism influenced the entire Aryan civilization. Neither passage claims that Judaism influenced ancient Egypt's religion, so Choice *B* is incorrect. Ancient Egypt's religion impacted Aryan civilization indirectly, mostly through its influence on Judaism; therefore, Choice *C* is incorrect. Information related to Buddha's influence on the Aryan civilization is not contained in either passage, so Choice *D* is incorrect. Thus, Choice *A* is the correct answer.

35. C: The second passage's second paragraph explains how Jewish separatism led to accusations of Jewish misanthropy. As a result, the accusations of Jewish misanthropy caused the spread of a deep-seated Jew-hatred, which first began in Alexandria and Rome. The hatred spread throughout Christendom after it began in Alexandria and Rome; therefore, Choice *B* is incorrect. Palestine and Egypt are not mentioned in connection to the spread of deep-seated Jew-hatred in either passage; therefore, Choices *A* and *D* are incorrect. Thus, Choice *C* is the correct answer.

36. A: Both passages agree that religious truths exist. The first passage's last paragraph describes truth as immortal, which is how ancient Egypt's religious truths were passed on to other religions. The second passage repeatedly claims that Judaism holds religious truths that have shaped the modern world. The first passage criticizes priestly sanctity, so Choice *B* is incorrect. While the first passage does discuss Africa's influence on ancient Egypt's religion and Judaism, it doesn't claim that all organized religion can be traced back to Africa; therefore, Choice *C* is incorrect. The second passage says Judaism can be an enigma for students of religion and history, but neither passage argued that Judaism is enigmatic; therefore, Choice *D* is incorrect. Thus, Choice *A* is the correct answer.

37. C: The first passage's final paragraph explains that ancient Egypt's religion disappeared because Egyptian priests kept the religion a secret, refusing to share it with the public. Neither passage claims that scholars proved ancient Egypt's religious truths to be historically inaccurate; therefore, Choice *A* is incorrect. Likewise, the passages don't indicate whether all of the ancient Egyptians converted to Judaism; therefore, Choice *B* is incorrect. Although Confucius, Buddha, and Moses shared what they knew of ancient Egypt's religion, that's not why the religion eventually disappeared; therefore, Choice *D* is incorrect. Thus, Choice *C* is the correct answer.

38. D: The second passage's second paragraph describes Israel's prophetic ideal as humanity united in justice and peace, and then claims this ideal led to more progress and liberty in Aryan civilization. While the second passage describes Judaism's duty to assimilate wisdom and culture, that duty isn't part of Israel's prophetic ideal; therefore, Choice *A* is incorrect. Similarly, the second passage states that Judaism contains a spirit of separatism, but it's unrelated to the prophetic ideal; therefore, Choice *B* is incorrect. Judaism rejects Jewish misanthropy, which led to the spread of anti-Semitism throughout Christendom, so Choice *C* is incorrect. Thus, Choice *D* is the correct answer.

39. B: While the first passage mostly focuses on the influence of ancient Egypt's religion on Judaism, the second passage focuses on explaining the twofold nature of Judaism. The second passage's first paragraph defines that twofold nature—separatism and universalism—and the second paragraph explains the historical ramifications for both of these aspects. The second passage claims that Judaism influenced the entire Aryan civilization, but that's not the passage's main focus; therefore, Choice *A* is incorrect. The second passage also doesn't contain a lot of information about Judaism's historical sources, so Choice *C* is incorrect. Additionally, the second passage celebrates and never challenges Judaism's claims to religious truth; therefore, Choice *D* is incorrect. Thus, Choice *B* is the correct answer.

40. A: According to the first passage, Africans practiced the rite of circumcision before the ancient Egyptians and Jews. As such, this must have occurred before ancient Egypt's religion disappeared; therefore, Choice *B* is incorrect. Because ancient Egypt's religion predates Judaism and Christianity, we can infer that Africans practiced circumcision before Jesus commanded his disciples to baptize; therefore, Choice *C* is incorrect. Likewise, Africans practiced circumcision before anti-Semitism spread through Christendom, so Choice *D* is incorrect. Thus, Choice *A* is the correct answer.

ACT Science Test

Interpretation of Data

Manipulating and Analyzing Scientific Data Presented in Scientific Tables, Graphs, and Diagrams

Observations made during a scientific experiment are organized and presented as data. Data can be collected in a variety of ways, depending on the purpose of the experiment. In testing how light exposure affects plant growth, for example, the data collected would be changes in the height of the plant relative to the amount of light it received. The easiest way to organize collected data is to use a **data table**.

A data table always contains a title that relates the two variables in the experiment. Each column or row must contain the units of measurement in the heading only. See the below example (note: this is not actual data).

Plant Growth During Time Exposed to Light (130 Watts)	
Time (Hours)	Height (cm)
0	3.2
192	5.0
480	7.9
720	12.1

Data must be presented in a concise, coherent way. Most data are presented in graph form. The fundamental rule for creating a graph based on data is that the independent variable (i.e., amount of time exposed to light) is on the x-axis, and the dependent variable (i.e., height of plant) is on the y-axis.

There are many types of graphs that a person may choose to use depending on which best represents the data. Bar graphs, line graphs, scatterplots, and pie charts are among some of the most common graphics; these, and others, will be discussed in a subsequent section.

Recognizing Trends in Data

The most common relationship examined in an experiment is between two variables (independent and dependent), most often referred to as x and y. The independent variable (x) is displayed on the horizontal axis of a coordinate plane, and the dependent variable (y) is displayed on the vertical axis. The placement of the variables in this way provides a visual representation of what happens to y when x is manipulated. In analyzing trends, x is used to predict y, and since y is the result of x, then x comes before y in time. For example, in the experiment on plant growth, the hours the plant was exposed to light had to happen before growth could occur.

When analyzing the relationship between the variables, scientists will consider the following questions:

- Does y increase or decrease with x, or does it do both?

- If it increases or decreases, how fast does it change?

- Does y stay steady through certain values of x, or does it jump dramatically from one value to the other?

- Is there a strong relationship? If given a value of *x*, can one predict what will happen to *y*?

If, in general, *y* increases as *x* increases, or *y* decreases and *x* decreases, it is known as a **positive correlation**. The data from the plant experiment show a positive correlation—as time exposed to light (*x*) increases, plant growth (*y*) increases. If the variables trend in the opposite direction of each other— that is, if *y* increases as *x* decreases, or vice versa—it is called a **negative correlation**. If there doesn't seem to be any visible pattern to the relationship, it is referred to as **no** or **zero correlation**.

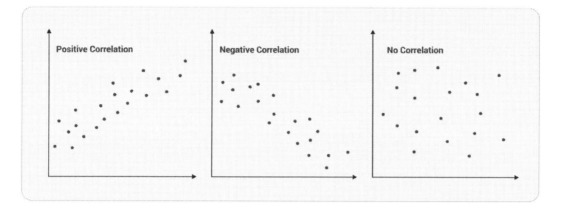

Experiments that show positive or negative correlation within their data indicate that the variables are related. This allows scientists to make predictions based on the data.

The center of a set of data (statistical values) can be represented by its mean, median, or mode. These are sometimes referred to as measures of central tendency.

Mean
The first property that can be defined for this set of data is the **mean**. This is the same as average. To find the mean, add up all the data points, then divide by the total number of data points. For example, suppose that in a class of 10 students, the scores on a test were 50, 60, 65, 65, 75, 80, 85, 85, 90, 100. Therefore, the average test score will be:

$$\frac{50 + 60 + 65 + 65 + 75 + 80 + 85 + 85 + 90 + 100}{10} = 75.5$$

The mean is a useful number if the distribution of data is normal (more on this later), which roughly means that the frequency of different outcomes has a single peak and is roughly equally distributed on both sides of that peak. However, it is less useful in some cases where the data might be split or where there are some **outliers**. Outliers are data points that are far from the rest of the data. For example, suppose there are 10 executives and 90 employees at a company. The executives make $1000 per hour, and the employees make $10 per hour.

Therefore, the average pay rate will be:

$$\frac{\$1000 \times 11 + \$10 \times 90}{100} = \$119 \; per \; hour$$

In this case, this average is not very descriptive since it's not close to the actual pay of the executives *or* the employees.

Median

Another useful measurement is the **median**. In a data set, the median is the point in the middle. The middle refers to the point where half the data comes before it and half comes after, when the data is recorded in numerical order. For instance, these are the speeds of the fastball of a pitcher during the last inning that he pitched (in order from least to greatest):

$$90, 92, 93, 93, 95, 96, 97, 97, 97$$

There are nine total numbers, so the middle or **median** number is the 5th one, which is 95.

In cases where the number of data points is an even number, then the average of the two middle points is taken. In the previous example of test scores, the two middle points are 75 and 80. Since there is no single point, the average of these two scores needs to be found. The average is:

$$\frac{75 + 80}{2} = 77.5$$

The median is generally a good value to use if there are a few outliers in the data. It prevents those outliers from affecting the "middle" value as much as when using the mean.

Since an outlier is a data point that is far from most of the other data points in a data set, this means an outlier also is any point that is far from the median of the data set. The outliers can have a substantial effect on the mean of a data set, but usually do not change the median or mode, or do not change them by a large quantity. For example, consider the data set (3, 5, 6, 6, 6, 8). This has a median of 6 and a mode of 6, with a mean of $\frac{34}{6} \approx 5.67$. Now, suppose a new data point of 1000 is added so that the data set is now (3, 5, 6, 6, 6, 8, 1000). This does not change the median or mode, which are both still 6. However, the average is now $\frac{1034}{7}$, which is approximately 147.7. In this case, the median and mode will be better descriptions for most of the data points.

The reason for outliers in a given data set is a complicated problem. It is sometimes the result of an error by the experimenter, but often they are perfectly valid data points that must be taken into consideration.

Mode

One additional measure to define for *X* is the **mode.** This is the data point that appears most frequently. If two or more data points all tie for the most frequent appearance, then each of them is considered a mode. In the case of the test scores, where the numbers were 50, 60, 65, 65, 75, 80, 85, 85, 90, 100, there are two modes: 65 and 85.

Estimating Data Points

Regression lines can be used to estimate data points not already given. For example, if an equation of a line is found that fit the temperature and beach visitor data set, its input is the average daily temperature and its output is the projected number of visitors. Thus, the number of beach visitors on a 100-degree day can be estimated. The output is a data point on the regression line, and the number of daily visitors is expected to be greater than on a 96-degree day because the regression line has a positive slope.

Interpreting the Regression Line

The formula for a regression line is $y = mx + b$, where m is the slope and b is the *y*-intercept. Both the slope and *y*-intercept are found in the **Method of Least Squares**, which is the process of finding the equation of the line through minimizing residuals. The slope represents the rate of change in y as x gets larger. Therefore, because y is the dependent variable, the slope actually provides the predicted values given the independent variable. The y-intercept is the predicted value for when the independent variable equals zero. In the temperature example, the y-intercept is the expected number of beach visitors for a very cold average daily temperature of zero degrees.

Correlation Coefficient

The **correlation coefficient** (r) measures the association between two variables. Its value is between -1 and 1, where -1 represents a perfect negative linear relationship, 0 represents no relationship, and 1 represents a perfect positive linear relationship. A **negative linear relationship** means that as x values increase, y values decrease. A **positive linear relationship** means that as x values increase, y values increase. The formula for computing the correlation coefficient is:

$$r = \frac{n(\sum xy) - (\sum x)(\sum y)}{\sqrt{n(\sum x^2) - (\sum x)^2}\sqrt{n(\sum y^2) - (\Sigma y)^2}}$$

n is the number of data points.

Both Microsoft Excel® and a graphing calculator can evaluate this easily once the data points are entered. A correlation greater than 0.8 or less than -0.8 is classified as "strong" while a correlation between -0.5 and 0.5 is classified as "weak."

Correlation Versus Causation

Correlation and causation have two different meanings. If two values are correlated, there is an association between them. However, correlation doesn't necessarily mean that one variable causes the other. **Causation** (or "cause and effect") occurs when one variable causes the other. Average daily temperature and number of beachgoers are correlated and have causation. If the temperature increases, the change in weather causes more people to go to the beach. However, alcoholism and smoking are correlated but don't have causation. The more someone drinks the more likely they are to smoke, but drinking alcohol doesn't cause someone to smoke.

Translating Tabular Data into Graphs

Tables provide an informative, organized way to look at the data that is collected from a scientific experiment. They contain every piece of data that is collected and organize it into categories. Graphs are useful tools for translating data presented in tables into a more visual presentation so that trends and results can be seen more readily. Depending on the type of data being collected, different types of graphs should be constructed.

Pie charts show relative parts of a whole group. For example, if you wanted to observe the breakdown, or proportion, of different eye colors in a classroom, you could make a table to record the data, count the number of people with each eye color, enter the data in the table, and then create a pie chart.

Eye color	Number of students
Blue	5
Green	8
Brown	12
Total	*25*

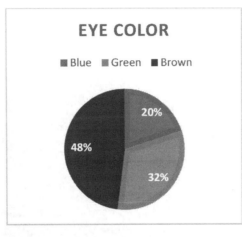

Bar graphs are useful for comparing different items in a related category, where only one variable is changing and being recorded. For example, the amount of interleukin-1β (IL-1β) that is secreted from cultured cells at a certain time point is recorded with different treatments.

	Cells alone	Cells + 1 ng/ml dexamethasone	Cells + 10 ng/ml dexamethasone
IL-1β (ng/ml)	35	15	5

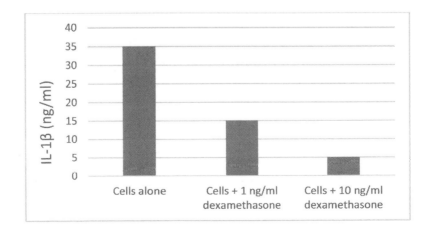

Line graphs are useful for showing changes over time or for a data set that has two changing variables. For example, Scientist A wants to see if a chemical reaction is exothermic, or releases heat, and takes the temperature of her solution every 15 minutes for two hours.

Time (min)	Temperature (°C)
0	22
15	22
30	25
45	30
60	37
75	37
90	35
105	33
120	31

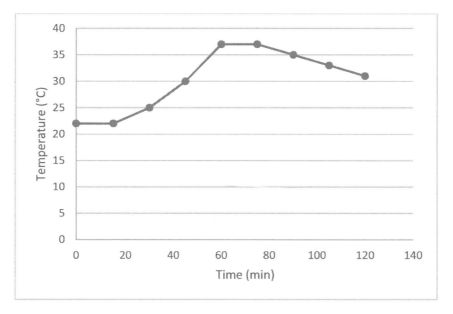

When turning tabular data into any type of graph, the variables must be translated over to the axes of the graph and then the scale of the graph is set. For example, for the line graph above dealing with temperature, the time was set as the *x* variable and the temperature was set as the *y* variable. For temperature, each major gridline was designated as a 5-degree increment. After that, data points from the table were plotted one at a time and then connected to help visualize the results.

Interpolating and Extrapolating

When collecting scientific data, it is often impossible to collect every single data point of interest. Therefore, scientists need to make reasonable, educated guesses to determine the values of the untested data points. For values that fall between the collected data, they use **interpolation**, and for values that fall outside of the collected data, they use **extrapolation**. When the data that is collected is plotted on a graph, the points can be connected using a mathematical and statistical method called **curve fitting**. Curve fitting uses the known data points to construct a curve that fits the trend of the values. Using the continuous points of this curve, missing data points can be interpolated or extrapolated.

For example, Scientist A wants to determine how rapidly her test cells are doubling in number. She can count them every two hours while she is in the lab but will not be able to count them overnight. She can create a graph with points for every two hours that she counts them and can fit a curve to interpolate the number of cells between the two-hour readings and the longer overnight period. She can also extend the curve to extrapolate how many cells she would have after another day.

Time (hrs.)	Number of cells (10^3)
0	1
2	1.25
4	2
6	3
16	16
18	24
20	32
22	48
24	64

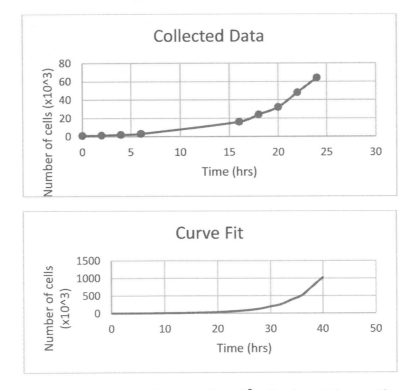

She can interpolate that there were approximately 10×10^3 cells after 13 hours. She can extrapolate that after 30 hours, there were 200×10^3 cells, since it appeared that the number of cells doubled every four hours.

Reasoning Mathematically

Two types of mathematical reasoning that are often used to interpret scientific data are deductive and inductive reasoning. Deductive reasoning starts with a hypothesis, follows steps, and uses specific observations to draw a logical conclusion. The scientific method is an example of deductive reasoning because it starts with a hypothesis and then uses many observations and experimenting to draw a conclusion about the hypothesis. In deductive reasoning, a general premise is proposed, a second premise is made, and then an inference is made about the theory. For example, Sarah reads that when red blood cells are moon-shaped instead of flat and round, the person can have an iron deficiency in their blood. She analyzes a blood sample and finds that Patient A has lower iron levels than normal. She concludes that Patient A has moon-shaped red blood cells.

Inductive reasoning makes general conclusions based on specific observations. A specific set of data is collected and then a conclusion is drawn about the greater, general population. For example, Bill pulls three coins out of a bag. All three coins are quarters. He then induces that the entire bag contains only quarters.

Scientific Investigation

Experimental Tools, Procedures, and Design

Designing a Science Investigation

Human beings are, by nature, very curious. Long before the scientific method was established, people have been making observations and predicting outcomes, manipulating the physical world to create extraordinary things—from the first man-made fire in 6000 B.C.E. to the satellite that orbited Pluto in 2016. Although the history of the scientific method is sporadic and attributed to many different people, it remains the most reliable way to obtain and utilize knowledge about the observable universe. Designing a science investigation is based on the scientific method, which consists of the following steps:

- Make an observation
- Create a question
- Form a hypothesis
- Conduct an experiment
- Collect and analyze data
- Form a conclusion

The first step is to identify a problem based on an observation—the who, what, when, where, why, and how. An **observation** is the analysis of information using basic human senses: sight, sound, touch, taste, and smell. Observations can be two different types—qualitative or quantitative. A **qualitative observation** describes what is being observed, such as the color of a house or the smell of a flower. **Quantitative observations** measure what is being observed, such as the number of windows on a house or the intensity of a flower's smell on a scale of 1–5.

Observations lead to the identification of a problem, also called an **inference**. For example, if a fire truck is barreling down a busy street, the inferences could be:

- There's a fire.
- Someone is hurt.
- Some kid pulled the fire alarm at a local school.

Inferences are logical predictions based on experience or education that lead to the formation of a hypothesis.

Forming and Testing a Hypothesis
A hypothesis is a testable explanation of an observed scenario and is presented in the form of a statement. It's an attempt to answer a question based on an observation, and it allows a scientist to predict an outcome. A hypothesis makes assumptions on the relationship between two different variables, and answers the question: "If I do this, what happens to that?"

In order to form a hypothesis, there must be an independent variable and a dependent variable that can be measured. The **independent variable** is the variable that is manipulated, and the **dependent variable** is the result of the change.

For example, suppose a student wants to know how light affects plant growth. Based upon what he or she already knows, the student proposes (hypothesizes) that the more light to which a plant is exposed, the faster it will grow.

- Observation: Plants exposed to lots of light seem to grow taller.
- Question: Will plants grow faster if there's more light available?
- Hypothesis: The more light the plant has, the faster it will grow.
- Independent variable: The amount of time exposed to light (able to be manipulated)
- Dependent variable: Plant growth (the result of the manipulation)

Once a hypothesis has been formed, it must be tested to determine whether it's true or false. (How to test a hypothesis is described in a subsequent section.) After it has been tested and validated as true over and over, then a hypothesis can develop into a theory, model, or law.

Experimental Design
To test a hypothesis, one must conduct a carefully designed experiment. There are four basic requirements that must be present for an experiment to be valid:

- A control
- Variables
- A constant
- Repeated and collected data

The control is a standard to which the resultant findings are compared. It's the baseline measurement that allows for scientists to determine whether the results are positive or negative. For the example of light affecting plant growth, the control may be a plant that receives no light at all.

The independent variable is manipulated (a good way to remember this is I manipulate the Independent variable), and the dependent variable is the result of changes to the independent variable. In the plant example, the independent variable is the amount of time exposed to light, and the dependent variable is the resulting growth (or lack thereof) of the plant. For this experiment, there may be three plants—one that receives a minimal amount of light, the control, and one that receives a lot of light.

Finally, there must be constants in an experiment. A constant is an element of the experiment that remains unchanged. Constants are extremely important in minimizing inconsistencies within the experiment that may lead to results outside the parameters of the hypothesis. For example, some constants in the above case are that all plants receive the same amount of water, all plants are potted in the same kind of soil, the species of the plant used in each condition is the same, and the plants are stored at the same temperature. If, for instance, the plants received different amounts of water as well as light, it would be impossible to tell whether the plants responded to changes in water or light.

Once the experiment begins, a disciplined scientist must always record the observations in meticulous detail, usually in a journal. A good journal includes dates, times, and exact values of both variables and constants. Upon reading this journal, a different scientist should be able to clearly understand the experiment and recreate it exactly. The journal includes all collected data, or any observed changes. In this case, the data is rates of plant growth, as well as any other phenomena that occurred as a result of the experiment. A well-designed experiment also includes repetition in order to get the most accurate possible readings and to account for any errors, so several trials may be conducted.

Even in the presence of diligent constants, there are an infinite number of reasons that an experiment can (and will) go wrong, known as sources of error. All experimental results are inherently accepted as imperfect, if ever so slightly, because experiments are conducted by human beings, and no instrument can measure anything perfectly. The goal of scientists is to minimize those errors to the best of their ability.

Identifying Controls and Variables

In an experiment, variables are the key to analyzing data, especially when data is in a graph or table. Variables can represent anything, including objects, conditions, events, and amounts of time.

Covariance is a general term referring to how two variables move in relation to each other. Take for example an employee that gets paid by the hour. For them, hours worked and total pay have a positive covariance. As hours worked increases, so does pay.

Constant variables remain unchanged by the scientist across all trials. Because they are held constant for all groups in an experiment, they aren't being measured in the experiment, and they are usually ignored. Constants can either be controlled by the scientist directly like the nutrition, water, and sunlight given to plants, or they can be selected by the scientist specifically for an experiment like using a certain animal species or choosing to investigate only people of a certain age group.

Independent variables are also controlled by the scientist, but they are the same only for each group or trial in the experiment. Each group might be composed of students that all have the same color of car or each trial may be run on different soda brands. The independent variable of an experiment is what is being indirectly tested because it causes change in the dependent variables.

Dependent variables experience change caused by the independent variable and are what is being measured or observed. For example, college acceptance rates could be a dependent variable of an experiment that sorted a large sample of high school students by an independent variable such as test scores. In this experiment, the scientist groups the high school students by the independent variable (test scores) to see how it affects the dependent variable (their college acceptance rates).

Note that most variables can be held constant in one experiment but independent or dependent in another. For example, when testing how well a fertilizer aids plant growth, its amount of sunlight should be held constant for each group of plants, but if the experiment is being done to determine the proper amount of sunlight a plant should have, the amount of sunlight is an independent variable because it is necessarily changed for each group of plants.

Comparing, Extending, and Modifying Experiments

Predicting the Results of Additional Trials

Science is amazing in that it actually allows people to predict the future and see into the past with a certain degree of accuracy. Using numerical correlations created from quantitative data, one can see in a general way what will happen to *y* when something happens to *x*.

The best way to get a useful overview of quantitative data to facilitate predictions is to use a scatter plot, which plots each data point individually. As shown above, there may be slight fluctuations from the correlation line, so one may not be able to predict what happens with *every* change, but he or she will be able to have a general idea of what is going to happen to *y* with a change in *x*. To demonstrate, the graph with a line of best fit created from the plant growth experiment is below.

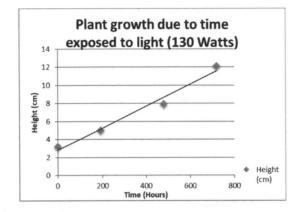

Using the trend line within the data, one can estimate what will happen to plant growth at a given length of time exposed to light. For example, it can be estimated that with 700 hours of time, the plant is expected to grow to a height of about 11 cm. The plant may not grow to exactly 11 cm, but it will likely grow to about that height based on previous data. This process allows scientists to draw conclusions based on data.

Identifying and Improving Hypotheses for Science Investigations

When presented with fundamental, scientific concepts, it is important to read for understanding. The most basic skill in achieving this literacy is to understand the concept of hypothesis and moreover, to be able to identify it in a particular passage. A **hypothesis** is a proposed idea that needs further investigation in order to be proven true or false. While it can be considered an educated guess, a hypothesis goes more in depth in its attempt to explain something that is not currently accepted within scientific theory. It requires further experimentation and data gathering to test its validity and is subject to change, based on scientifically conducted test results. Being able to read a science passage and understand its main purpose, including any hypotheses, helps the test taker understand data-driven evidence. It helps the test taker to be able to correctly answer questions about the science excerpt they are asked to read.

When reading to identify a hypothesis, a test taker should ask, "What is the passage trying to establish? What is the passage's main idea? What evidence does the passage contain that either supports or refutes this idea?" Asking oneself these questions will help identify a hypothesis. Additionally, hypotheses are logical statements that are testable, and use very precise language.

Review the following hypothesis example:

> Consuming excess sugar in the form of beverages has a greater impact on childhood obesity and subsequent weight gain than excessive sugar from food.

While this is likely a true statement, it is still only a conceptual idea in a text passage regarding sugar consumption in childhood obesity, unless the passage also contains tested data that either proves or disproves the statement. A test taker could expect the rest of the passage to cite data proving that children who drink empty calories and don't exercise will, in fact, be obese.

A hypothesis goes further in that, given its ability to be proven or disproven, it may result in further hypotheses that require extended research. For example, the hypothesis regarding sugar consumption in drinks, after undergoing rigorous testing, may lead scientists to state another hypothesis such as the following:

> Consuming excess sugar in the form of beverages as opposed to food items is a habit found in mostly sedentary children.

This new, working hypothesis further focuses not just on the source of an excess of calories, but tries an "educated guess" that empty caloric intake has a direct, subsequent impact on physical behavior.

The data-driven chart below is similar to an illustration a test taker might see in relation to the hypothesis on sugar consumption in children:

Behaviors of Healthy and Unhealthy Kids

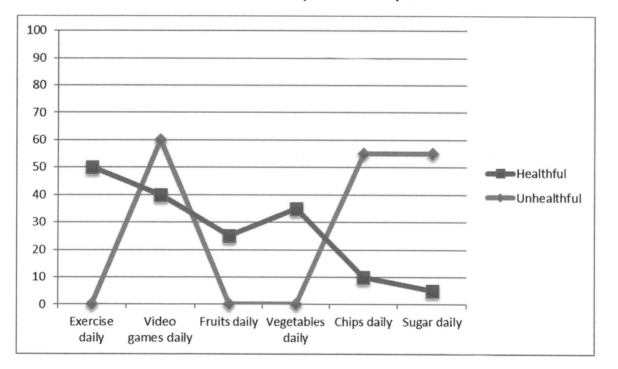

While this guide will address other data-driven passages a test taker could expect to see within a given science excerpt, note that the hypothesis regarding childhood sugar intake and rate of exercise has undergone scientific examination and yielded results that support its truth.

When reading a science passage to determine its hypothesis, a test taker should look for a concept that attempts to explain a phenomenon, is testable, logical, precisely worded, and yields data-driven results. The test taker should scan the presented passage for any word or data-driven clues that will help identify the hypothesis, and then be able to correctly answer test questions regarding the hypothesis based on their critical thinking skills.

Identifying Possible Errors in a Science Investigation and Changing the Design to Correct Them

For a hypothesis to be proven true or false, all experiments are subject to multiple trials in order to verify accuracy and precision. A measurement is **accurate** if the observed value is close to the "true value." For example, if someone measured the pH of water at 6.9, this measurement would be considered accurate (the pH of water is 7). On the other hand, a measurement is **precise** if the measurements are consistent—that is, if they are reproducible. If someone had a series of values for a pH of water that were 6.9, 7.0, 7.2, and 7.3, their measurements would not be precise. However, if all measured values were 6.9, or the average of these values was 6.9 with a small range, then their measurements would be precise. Measurements can fall into the following categories:

- Both accurate and precise
- Accurate but not precise
- Precise but not accurate
- Neither accurate nor precise

The accuracy and precision of observed values most frequently correspond to the amount of error present in the experiment. Aside from general carelessness, there are two primary types of error: random and systematic. **Random errors** are unpredictable variations in the experiment that occur by chance. They can be difficult to detect, but they can often be nullified using a statistical analysis and minimized by taking repeated measurements and taking an average. **Systematic errors** occur when there are imperfections in the design of the experiment itself—usually errors that affect the accuracy of the measurements. These errors can be minimized by using the most accurate equipment available and by taking proper care of instruments and measuring techniques. Common examples of error are listed below.

Random	Systematic
Environmental factors (random changes in vibration, temperature, humidity, etc.)	Poorly maintained instruments
Differences in instrument use among scientists	Old or out-of-date instruments
Errors in judgment—can be affected by state of mind	Faulty calibration of instruments
	Reading the instruments at an angle (parallax error) or other faulty reading errors
Incorrectly recorded observations	Not accounting for lag time

The most basic method to account for the possibility of errors is to take an average (also called a **mean**) of all observed values. To do so, one must divide the number of measurements taken from the sum of all measurements.

$$\frac{Sum\ of\ Measurements}{Total\ \#\ of\ Measurements}$$

For the above example of the pH values, the average is calculated by finding the sum of the pH values ascertained and dividing by the number of values recorded.

$$\frac{6.9 + 7.0 + 7.2 + 7.3}{4} = 7.1$$

The more observations recorded, the greater the precision. It's important to first assess the accuracy of measurements before proceeding to collect multiple trials of data. If a particular trial results in measurements that are vastly different from the average, it may indicate that a random or systematic error occurred during the trial. When this happens, a scientist might decide to "throw out" the trial and run the experiment again.

<u>Identifying the Strengths and Weaknesses of Different Types of Science Investigations</u>
In order to address the strengths and weaknesses of different types of scientific investigations, ACT test takers must first strengthen their capacity for scientific literacy and numeracy. It is important to familiarize oneself with methods for decoding highly specialized scientific terms, formulas, and symbols. Additionally, test takers can take the following suggestions to help identify unique weaknesses and strengths in different types of scientific investigations:

- Using critical analysis, test takers begin asking questions about the accuracy of the methods used to collect, analyze, and display data. They should carefully look at text and graphics that show scientific findings.

- Test takers should determine whether or not the words, data, and symbols provided by the author actually offer information that is relevant for testing a hypothesis or making an inference.

- When two or more passages on the same topic are offered, test takers should cross-analyze the findings to determine what data is accurate or relevant and which findings are most objective.

- Although scientific research strives for objectivity, test takers should highlight any subjective biases that may be embedded in a text. In particular, they should be aware of certain historical or ethical biases that might appear.

- Test takers should double check for any computational inaccuracies.

- Test takers should make suggestions for better ways to present the findings in both texts and visual images.

Evaluation of Models, Inferences, and Experimental Results

Judging the Validity of Scientific Information

Valid science information must have sufficient , credible, accurate evidence that fully support the claims and conclusions. Critical readers examine the facts and evidence used to support an author's claim. They check the facts against other sources to be sure those facts are correct. They also check the validity of the sources used to be sure those sources are credible, academic, and/or peer-reviewed. Consider that when an informative science passage uses another person's opinion to support their argument, even if it is an expert's opinion, it is still only an opinion and should not be taken as fact. A trustworthy study or science report uses valid, measurable facts to support ideas. Even then, the reader may disagree with the argument as it may be rooted in their personal beliefs.

An authoritative argument may use the facts to sway the reader. For example, in a paper on global warming, many experts differ in their opinions of what alternative fuels can be used to aid in offsetting it. Because of this, a writer may choose to only use the information and expert opinion that supports their viewpoint.

Students must be able to distinguish between reliable and unreliable sources in order to develop a well-written research report. When choosing print sources, typically published works that have been edited and clearly identify the author or authors are considered credible sources. Peer-reviewed journals and research conducted by scholars are likewise considered to be credible sources of information.

When deciding on what Internet sources to use, it is also a sound practice for researchers to look closely at each website's universal resource locator, the *URL*. Generally speaking, websites with .edu, .gov, or .org as the Top Level Domain are considered reliable, but the researcher must still question any possible political or social bias. Personal blogs, tweets, personal websites, online forums, and any site that clearly demonstrates bias, strong opinions, or persuasive language are considered unreliable sources.

Science is often a process of checks and balances, andACT students are expected to carry out this process of checks and balances as they analyze and compare information that differs between various science sources. Science demands a high degree of communication, which, in turn, demands a high degree of scientific literacy and numeracy.ACT students must be prepared to analyze the different data and written conclusions of various texts. Contrary to popular belief, science is not an authoritarian field—scientific worldviews and inquiries can be wrong. It is more fruitful to think of science as a living library that is shaped by the complex activities carried out by different groups in different places. This living library is filled with ideas that are shaped by various sources and methods of research. The explanations, inferences, and discussions carried out by scientists are filled with facts that may be flawed or biased. Science, like any other field, cannot completely escape bias. Even though science is meant to be objective, its findings can still lend themselves to biases.

Thus, it is important forACT students to get in the practice of not only making sense of information that differs between various science sources, but also to begin synthesizing this information into a unique worldview. The peer review process is also necessary to ensure checks and balances within the scientific field. The key to making this happen while taking theACT is to maintain an acute awareness of when and where information or data differs. Pay close attention to the ways in which each scientist uses specific words or data to back their overall conclusions.

Below are some key reasons why data and interpretations can differ:

- Historical bias
- Cultural bias
- Interpretation or personal bias
- Lack of implementation and data collection fidelity
- Different data collection approaches
- Different data collection and data analysis tools
- Weak hypotheses
- Compounding variables
- Failure to recognize certain variables

- User error
- Changes in the environment between two studies
- Computation or statistical errors
- Interpretive blind spots
- Lack of understanding of context or environment

Formulating Conclusions and Predictions Based on Scientific Information

Deciding Whether Conclusions are Supported by Data

Drawing conclusions is the process of analyzing patterns in data and determining whether the relationship is **causal**, meaning that one variable is the cause of the change in the other. There are many correlations that aren't casual, such as a city where alcohol sales increase as crime increases. Although there's a positive correlation between the two, crime may not be the factor that causes an increase in alcohol sales. There could be other factors, such as an increase in unemployment, which increases both alcohol sales and crime rates. Although crime and alcohol sales are positively correlated, they aren't causally correlated.

For this reason, it's important for scientists to carefully design their experiments with all the appropriate constants to ensure that the relationships are causal. If a relationship is determined to be causal by isolating the variables from all other factors, only then can conclusions be drawn based on data. In the plant growth experiment, the conclusion is that light affects plant growth, because the data shows they are causally correlated since the two variables were entirely isolated.

Making Conclusions Based on Data

The Science section of the ACT will contain one data-driven science passage that require the test taker to examine evidence within a particular type of graphic. The test taker will then be required to interpret the data and answer questions demonstrating their ability to draw logical conclusions.

In general, there are two types of data: qualitative and quantitative. Science passages may contain both, but simply put, **quantitative** data is reflected numerically and qualitative is not. **Qualitative** data is based on its qualities. In other words, qualitative data tends to present information more in subjective generalities (for example, relating to size or appearance). Quantitative data is based on numerical findings such as percentages. Quantitative data will be described in numerical terms. While both types of data are valid, the test taker will more likely be faced with having to interpret quantitative data through one or more graphic(s), and then be required to answer questions regarding the numerical data. A test taker should take the time to learn the skills it takes to interpret quantitative data so that they can make sound conclusions.

An example of a line graph is as follows:

Cell Phone Use in Kiteville, 2000-2006

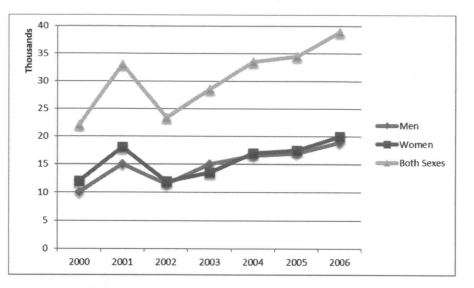

A **line graph** presents quantitative data on both horizontal (side to side) and vertical (up and down) axes. It requires the test taker to examine information across varying data points. When reading a line graph, a test taker should pay attention to any headings, as these indicate a title for the data it contains. In the above example, the test taker can anticipate the line graph contains numerical data regarding the use of cellphones during a certain time period. From there, a test taker should carefully read any outlying words or phrases that will help determine the meaning of data within the horizontal and vertical axes. In this example, the vertical axis displays the total number of people in increments of 5,000. Horizontally, the graph displays yearly markers, and the reader can assume the data presented accounts for a full calendar year. In addition, the line graph also defines its data points by shapes. Some data points represent the number of men. Some data points represent the number of women, and a third type of data point represents the number of both sexes combined.

A test taker may be asked to read and interpret the graph's data, then answer questions about it. For example, the test may ask, *In which year did men seem to decrease cellphone use?* then require the test taker to select the correct answer. Similarly, the test taker may encounter a question such as *Which year yielded the highest number of cellphone users overall?* The test taker should be able to identify the correct answer as 2006.

A **bar graph** presents quantitative data through the use of lines or rectangles. The height and length of these lines or rectangles corresponds to contain numerical data. The data presented may represent information over time, showing shaded data over time or over other defined parameters. A bar graph will also utilize horizontal and vertical axes.

An example of a bar graph is as follows:

Population Growth in Major U.S. Cities

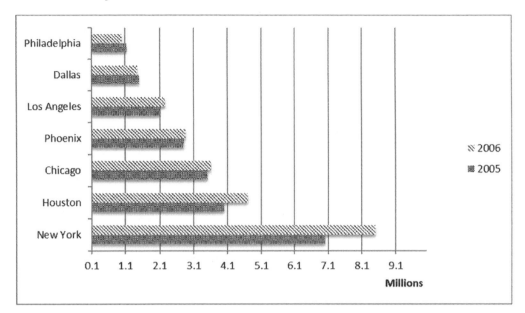

Reading the data in a bar graph is similar to the skills needed to read a line graph. The test taker should read and comprehend all heading information, as well as information provided along the horizontal and vertical axes. Note that the graph pertains to the population of some major U.S. cities. The "values" of these cities can be found along the left side of the graph, along the vertical axis. The population values can be found along the horizontal axes. Notice how the graph uses shaded bars to depict the change in population over time, as the heading indicates. Therefore, when the test taker is asked a question such as, *Which major U.S. city experienced the greatest amount of population growth during the depicted two year cycle,* the reader should be able to determine a correct answer of New York. It is important to pay particular attention to color, length, data points, and both axes, as well as any outlying header information in order to be able to answer graph-like test questions.

A **circle graph** presents quantitative data in the form of a circle (also sometimes referred to as a **pie chart**). The same principles apply: the test taker should look for numerical data within the confines of the circle itself but also note any outlying information that may be included in a header, footer, or to the side of the circle. A circle graph will not depict horizontal or vertical axis information but will instead rely on the reader's ability to visually take note of segmented circle pieces and apply information accordingly.

An example of a circle graph is as follows:

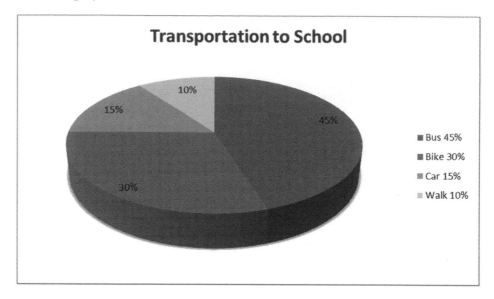

Notice the heading "Transportation to School." This should indicate to the test taker that the topic of the circle graph is how people traditionally get to school. To the right of the graph, the reader should comprehend that the data percentages contained within it directly correspond to the method of transportation. In this graph, the data is represented through the use shades and pattern. Each transportation method has its own shade. For example, if the test taker was then asked, *Which method of school transportation is most widely utilized,* the reader should be able to identify school bus as the correct answer.

Be wary of test questions that ask test takers to draw conclusions based on information that is not present. For example, it is not possible to determine, given the parameters of this circle graph, whether the population presented is of a particular gender or ethnic group. This graph does not represent data from a particular city or school district. It does not distinguish between student grade levels and, although the reader could infer that the typical student must be of driving age if cars are included, this is not necessarily the case. Elementary school students may rely on parents or others to drive them by personal methods. Therefore, do not read too much into data that is not presented. Only rely on the quantitative data that is presented in order to answer questions.

A **scatter plot** or **scatter diagram** is a graph that depicts quantitative data across plotted points. It will involve at least two sets of data.

It will also involve horizontal and vertical axes.

An example of a scatter plot is as follows:

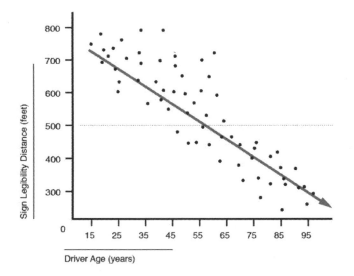

The skills needed to address a scatter plot are essentially the same as in other graph examples. Note any topic headings, as well as horizontal or vertical axis information. In the sample above, the reader can determine the data addresses a driver's ability to correctly and legibly read road signs as related to their age. Again, note the information that is absent. The test taker is not given the data to assess a time period, location, or driver gender. It simply requires the reader to note an approximate age to the ability to correctly identify road signs from a distance measured in feet. Notice that the overall graph also displays a trend. In this case, the data indicates a negative one and possibly supports the hypothesis that as a driver ages, their ability to correctly read a road sign at over 500 feet tends to decline over time. If the test taker were to be asked, *At what approximation in feet does a sixteen-year-old driver correctly see and read a street sign,* the answer would be the option closest to 500 feet.

Reading and examining scientific data in excerpts involves all of a reader's contextual reading, data interpretation, drawing logical conclusions based only on the information presented, and their application of critical thinking skills across a set of interpretive questions. Thorough comprehension and attention to detail is necessary to achieve test success.

Determining Which Explanation for a Scientific Phenomenon is Supported by New Findings
Finding Evidence that Supports a Finding
Science is one of the most objective, straightforward fields of study. Thus, it is no surprise that scientists and science articles are focused on **evidence**. When reading science passages, test takers are sometimes asked to find supporting evidence that reinforces a particular finding. A **finding** in science is a result of the investigation; it is what scientists find out. The majority of science passages tend to avoid opinions; instead, they focus on facts. Although no results are infallible just because the texts are scientific, most results are quantified. Quantified results mean they are expressed in numbers or measurements. Thus, when in doubt, go straight to the data, or numbers, that are offered. Sometimes data is embedded in the text; other times it appears in charts, tables, or graphs. These tools use numbers to demonstrate the patterns discussed in scientific texts, and they help readers to visualize concrete patterns. In order to find evidence to support a finding in scientific passage, all test takers should try collecting and analyzing

the relevant data offered. Regardless of whether the data is coming from the text or a graph, it is helpful when making conclusions.

The following steps are helpful for identifying evidence that supports a finding in a science passage:

- Apply critical analysis and critical thinking by asking the right questions.
- Determine the weight of the information by figuring out its relevance.
- Identify trends in the numbers.
- Make inferences.
- Determine the most appropriate methods for either quantifying or communicating inferences.

Types of Passages and Tips

The ACT science exam tests analytical skills associated with interpreting scientific principles of the natural world. The content may be from biology, the earth sciences, chemistry, or physics. The test presents scientific concepts in the form of passages of three different formats. A total of 40 multiple-choice questions related to the passage are to be completed in 35 minutes.

Test-takers are often surprised to discover that detailed knowledge of science content isn't required to achieve success on the ACT science test. In fact, the test is designed to determine how well an individual is able to analyze, compare, and generalize information. For example, the test doesn't seek to determine if one possesses an extensive knowledge of elephant biology. Instead, the exam might ask one to compare two scientists' differing opinions about elephant communication. In this case, the test taker is *not* required to possess any knowledge about elephants or the manner in which they communicate. All of the information needed to answer the questions will be presented in the passage. The test taker must read the passage, compare the differing hypotheses, analyze the graphical information, and generate conclusions.

Three Types of Passages

Data Representation
Scientific data will be presented in tables, graphs, diagrams, or models. These passages account for 30% to 40% of the ACT Science Test. These passages typically contain 5 or 6 questions designed to test one's ability to interpret scientific data represented in a graphical format instead of written text. These questions do *not* necessarily examine scientific content knowledge (e.g., the equation for photosynthesis); rather, they test students' ability to interpret raw data represented in a table or graph. Therefore, it's possible to do well on this portion of the exam without a detailed understanding of the scientific topic at hand. Questions may ask for factual information, identification of data trends, or graph calculations. For example:

- Based on the attached graph, how did Study 1 differ from Study 2?
- What is the nature of the relationship between Experiment 1 and Experiment 2?
- What is *x* at the given *y*-value?

These passages account for 45% to 55% of the ACT Science Test. Passages present the design, implementation, and conclusion of various scientific experiments. These passages typically contain 5 or 6 questions designed to test one's ability to identify the following:

- What question is the experiment trying to answer?
- What is the researcher's predicted answer to the question?
- How did the researchers test the hypotheses?
- Based on data obtained from the experiments, was the prediction correct?
- What would happen if . . .?
- 2 X 2 Matrix questions: "Yes, because . . ." or "No, because . . ."

Conflicting viewpoints
This section will present a disagreement between two scientists about a specific scientific hypothesis or concept. These passages account for 15% to 20% of the ACT Science Test. The opinions of each researcher are presented in two separate passages. There are two formats for these questions. The test taker must demonstrate an understanding of the content or compare and contrast the main differences between the two opinions. For example:

- Based on the data presented by Scientist 1, which of the following is correct?
- What is the main difference between the conclusions of Expert A and Expert B?

Elements of Science Passages

Short answer questions
Short answer questions are usually one to five words long and require the reader to recall basic facts presented in the passage.

An example answer choice: "Research group #1 finished last."

Long answer questions
Long answer questions are composed of one to three sentences that require the reader to make comparisons, summaries, generalizations, or conclusions about the passage.

An example answer choice: "Scientist 2 disagreed with Scientist 1 on the effects of Bisphenol A pollution and its presumed correlation to birth defects in mice and humans. Scientist 2 proposes that current environmental Bisphenol A levels are not sufficient to cause adverse effects on human health."

Fact questions
Fact questions are the most basic type of question on the test. They ask the reader to recall a specific term, definition, number, or meaning.

An example question/answer: "Which of the following organisms was present in fresh water samples from Pond #1?"
   a. Water flea
   b. Dragonfly nymph
   c. Snail
   d. Tadpole

<u>Graphics</u>
There are several different types of graphics used in the ACT Science Test to represent the passage data. There will be at least one of each of the following types included in the test: tables, illustrative diagrams, bar graphs, scatter plots, line graphs, and region graphs. Most ACT Science passages will include two or more of these graphics.

The **illustrative diagram** provides a graphic representation or picture of some process. Questions may address specific details of the process depicted in the graphic. For example, "At which stage of the sliding filament theory of muscle contraction does the physical length of the fibers shorten (and contract)?"

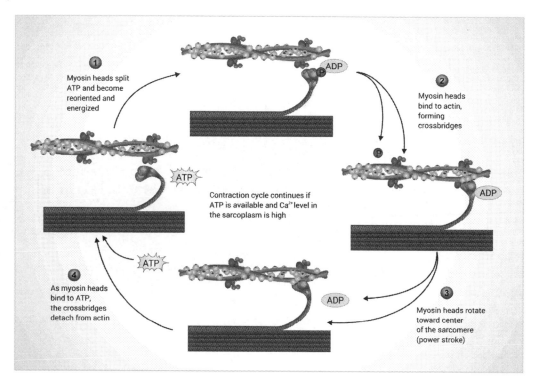

Bar graphs depict the passage data as parallel lines of varying heights. ACT bar graphs will be printed in black and white. Data may be oriented vertically or horizontally. Questions may ask, "During the fall season, in what habitat do bears spend the most time?"

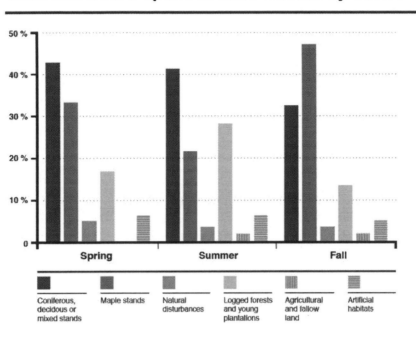

Bar graphs can also be horizontal, like the graph below.

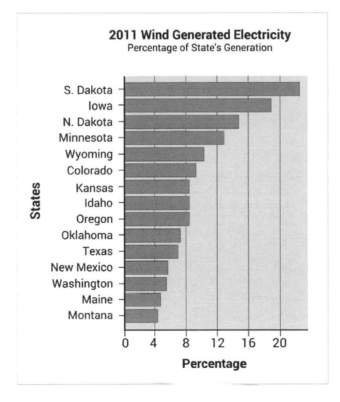

Scatter plots provide a visual representation of the passage data along the x- and y-axes. This representation indicates the nature of the relationship between the two variables. It is important to note that correlation doesn't equal causation. The relationship may be linear, curvilinear, positive, negative, inverse, or there may be no relationship. Questions may ask "What is the relationship between x and y?"

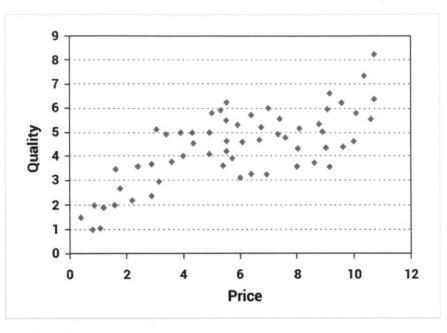

Line graphs are scatter plots that compare and contrast the relationships between two or more data sets. The horizontal axis represents the passage data sets that are compared over time. The vertical axis is the scale for measurement of that data. The scale points are equidistant from one another. There will always be a title for the line graph. Questions related to line graphs might ask," Which of the following conclusions is supported by the provided graph of tropical storms?"

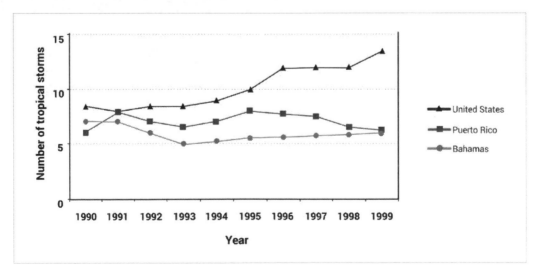

A **region graph** is a visual representation of the passage data set used to display the properties of a given substance under different conditions or at different points in time. Questions relating to this graph may ask, "According to the figure, what is the temperature range associated with liquid nitrogen?"

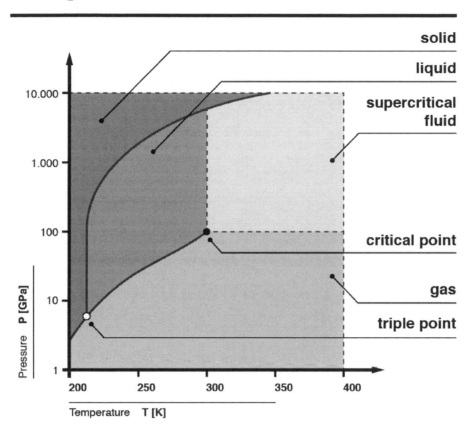

Nitrogen Phases

ACT Science Test tables present passage data sets in tabular form. The **independent variable** is positioned on the left side, while the **dependent variable** is on the right side of the table. The content of ACT Science tables is always discussed in the corresponding passage. Knowledge of all table content isn't required.

Sample Table for Analysis

| Data type | Seismic sources | | | | | | | |
| | Individual faults | | | | | | Area/volume sources | |
	Location	Activity	Length	Dip	Depth	Style	Area	Depth
Geological/Remote Sensing								
Detailed mapping	X	X	X	X		X		
Geomorphic data	X	X	X			X	X	
Quaternary surface rupture	X	X	X			X		
Fault trenching data	X	X		X		X		
Paleoliquefaction data	X	X					X	
Borehole data	X	X		X		X		
Aerial photography	X	X	X					
Low sun-angle photography	X	X	X					
Stellite imagery	X		X				X	
Regional structure	X			X		X	X	
Balanced Cross Section	X			X	X		X	
Geophysical/Geodetic								
Regional potential field data	X		X				X	X
Local potential field data	X		X	X	X	X		
High resolution reflection data	X	X		X		X		
Standard reflexing data	X			X		X		
Deep crustal reflection data	X			X	X		X	X
Tectonic geodetic/strain data	X	X		X	X	X	X	X
Reginal stress data						X	X	
Seismological								
Reflected crustal phase data								X
Pre-instrumental earthquake data	X	X			X	X	X	
Teleseismic earthquake data							X	
Regional network seismicity data	X	X	X	X	X		X	X
Local network seismicity data	X	X	X	X	X			X
Focal mechanism data				X		X		

Answer Choice Elimination Techniques

The ability to quickly and effectively eliminate incorrect answer choices is one of the most important skills to develop before sitting for the exam. The following tips and strategies are designed to help in this effort.

First, test takers should look for answer choices that make absolute "all-or-nothing" statements, as they are usually incorrect answers. Key word clues to incorrect answer choices include: always, never, everyone, no one, all, must, and none. An example of a possible incorrect answer choice is provided below:

"The use of antibiotics should be discontinued indefinitely as they are always over-prescribed."

An example of a possible correct answer choice:

"The use of antibiotics should be closely monitored by physician review boards in order to prevent the rise of drug-resistant bacteria."

Test takers should look for unreasonable, awkward, or irrational answer choices and they should pay special attention to irrelevant information that isn't mentioned in the passage. If the answer choice relates to an idea or position that isn't clearly presented in the passage, it's likely incorrect.

Answer choices that seem too broad or generic and also those that are very narrow or specific are also important to note. For example, if a question relates to a summarization of the passage, test takers should look for answers that encompass a broad representation of the presented ideas, facts, concepts, etc. On the other hand, if a question asks about a specific word, number, data point, etc. the correct answer will likely be more narrow or specific.

Highly Technical Questions

The goal of the ACT Science Test is to measure scientific reasoning skills, not scientific content knowledge. Therefore, candidates shouldn't "cram" for this section using complex scientific concepts from textbooks or online courses. Instead, they should focus on understanding the format of the exam and the manner in which ideas are presented and questions are asked.

Example question about two scientists' conflicting viewpoints:

Scientist 1: Reproductive success in red-tailed hawks has been drastically reduced as a consequence of widespread release of endocrine-disrupting chemicals such as dichloro-diphenyl-trichloroethane (DDT).

Scientist 2: The reproductive fitness of red-tailed hawks is only mildly reduced by the weak effects of DDT, but it is highly sensitive to another class of chemicals called polychlorinated biphenyls (PCBs).

Considering the two viewpoints of the passage, which of the following statements is true?
a. Red-tailed hawks are an endangered species due the effects of over-hunting and the release of toxic chemicals such as DDT and PCBs.
b. PCBs must not be the cause of red-tailed hawk reproductive problems because polychlorinated biphenyls do not affect female reproductive organs.
c. Scientist 2 proposes that PCBs are likely the cause of red-tailed hawk reproductive problems since DDT is only mildly toxic.
d. DDT is a persistent organic pesticide and should be avoided.

Answer A: INCORRECT. This answer is irrational. Neither scientist mentioned anything about hunting or red-tailed hawks being endangered.

Answer B: INCORRECT. This answer is also irrational. Neither scientist proposes that PCBs do not affect female reproductive organs

Answer C: CORRECT. This answer makes the most sense. It's true that Scientist 2 believes that PCBs cause reproductive problems in red-tailed hawks because DDT is only mildly toxic.

Answer D: INCORRECT. This answer is very narrow and specific. The phrase "persistent organic pesticide" isn't mentioned at all in the passage.

Again, the reader didn't need to know anything about dichloro-diphenyl-trichloroethane, polychlorinated biphenyls, red-tailed hawks, reproductive biology, or endocrine-disrupting chemicals to answer the question correctly. Instead, the test taker must consider both viewpoints and make comparisons or generalizations between the two.

Time Management

Using time efficiently is a critical factor for success on the ACT Science Test. Test takers may find the following strategies to be helpful when preparing for the exam:

- There are 40 questions and only 35 minutes, which leaves about 50 seconds for each question. This may seem daunting; however, it's important to consider that multiple questions apply to a single passage, graph, etc. Therefore, it may be possible to answer some in less than 50 seconds, leaving extra time for more demanding questions.

- It's important to read the entire passage before answering the questions and to consider all facts, conflicting viewpoints, hypotheses, conclusions, opinions, etc.

- Be sure to review only the information presented in the passages, as the questions will relate solely to this content.

- Don't get stuck on difficult questions. The exam is designed with a mix of easy and hard questions. Make sure to get all the easy ones answered, and then go back to focus on more difficult questions.

- Try to quickly eliminate answer choices that are obviously incorrect.

General Tips for Success

Before taking the exam, successful test takers practice answering questions from all of the different formats. Being able to quickly identify what one is being asked to do saves valuable time.

Test takers should read each passage completely and make notes or underline important information, such as:

- What is the hypothesis of an experiment?
- What is the result of the experiment?
- What is the experimental question?
- What information led to the researcher's viewpoint?
- What is the main difference between the two experiments?
- What is the main difference of opinion between two researchers?

Test takers should be mindful of the time. There are 40 questions that must be completed in 35 minutes. It is recommended that test takers quickly look at the questions before reading the associated passage. This will provide a general idea of which parts of the passage to read carefully. Test takers should answer all of the questions.

Practice Questions

Passage I

Questions 1-5 pertain to the following information:

Worldwide, fungal infections of the lung account for significant mortality in individuals with compromised immune function. Three of the most common infecting agents are *Aspergillus, Histoplasma*, and *Candida*. Successful treatment of infections caused by these agents depends on an early and accurate diagnosis. Three tests used to identify specific markers for these mold species include ELISA (enzyme-linked immunosorbent assay), GM Assay (Galactomannan Assay), and PCR (polymerase chain reaction).

Two important characteristics of these tests include sensitivity and specificity. Sensitivity relates to the probability that the test will identify the presence of the infecting agent, resulting in a true positive result. Higher sensitivity equals fewer false-positive results. Specificity relates to the probability that if the test doesn't detect the infecting agent, the test is truly negative for that agent. Higher specificity equals fewer false-negatives.

Figure 1 shows the timeline for the process of infection from exposure to the pathogen to recovery or death.

Figure 1:
Natural History of the Process of Infection

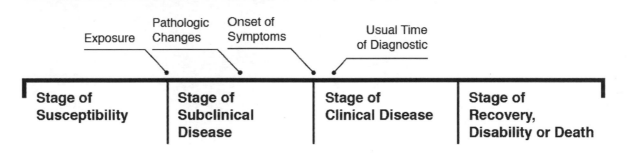

272

Figure 2 (below) shows the sensitivity and specificity for ELISA, GM assay and PCR related to the diagnosis of infection by *Aspergillus*, *Histoplasma* and *Candida*.

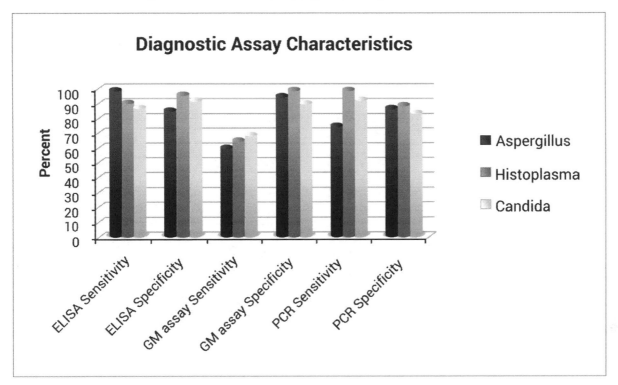

The table below identifies the process of infection in days from exposure for each of the species.

Process of Infection - Days Since Pathogen Exposure			
	Aspergillus	Histoplasma	Candida
Sub-clinical Disease	Day 90	Day 28	Day 7
Detection Possible	Day 118	Day 90	Day 45
Symptoms Appear	Day 145	Day100	Day 120

Figure 3 (below) identifies the point at which each test can detect the organism. Time is measured in days from the time an individual is exposed to the pathogen.

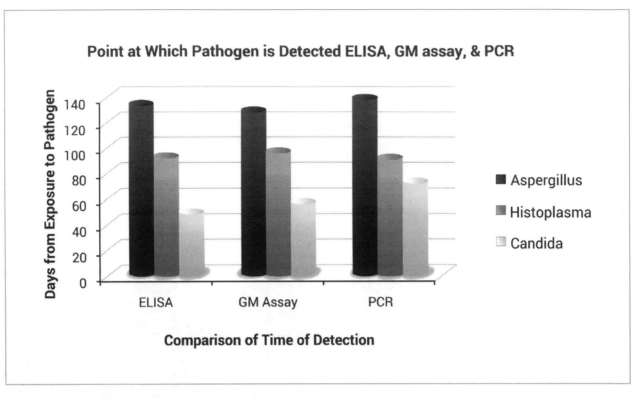

Point at Which Pathogen is Detected ELISA, GM assay, & PCR

Comparison of Time of Detection

1. Which of the following statements is supported by Figure 2?
    a. For *Candida*, the GM assay will provide the most reliable results.
    b. ELISA testing for *Aspergillus* is the most specific of the three tests.
    c. PCR is the most sensitive method for testing *Histoplasma*.
    d. True positive rates were greater than 75% for all three testing methods.

2. In reference to the table and Figure 3, which pathogen can be detected earlier in the disease process, and by which method?
    a. *Candida* by PCR testing
    b. *Aspergillus* by ELISA testing
    c. *Candida* by GM assay
    d. *Histoplasma* by PCR testing

3. In reference to Figure 2, which statement is correct?
    a. There is a 20% probability that ELISA testing will NOT correctly identify the presence of *Histoplasma*.
    b. When GM assay testing for *Candida* is conducted, there is a 31% probability that it will NOT be identified if the organism is present.
    c. The probability that GM assay testing for *Aspergillus* will correctly identify the presence of the organism is 99%.
    d. The false-negative probabilities for each of the three testing methods identified in Figure 2 indicate that the organism will be detected when present less than 70% of the time.

4. Physicians caring for individuals with suspected *Histoplasma* infections order diagnostic testing prior to instituting treatment. PCR testing results will not be available for 10 days. GM assay results can be obtained more quickly. The physicians opt to wait for the PCR testing. Choose the best possible rationale for that decision.

a. The treatment will be the same regardless of the test results.

b. The individual was not exhibiting any disease symptoms.

c. The probability of PCR testing identifying the presence of the organism is greater than the GM assay.

d. The subclinical disease phase for *Histoplasma* is more than 100 days.

5. Referencing the data in Figures 2 and 3, if ELISA testing costs twice as much as PCR testing, why might it still be the best choice to test for *Candida*?

a. ELISA testing detects the presence of *Candida* sooner than PCR testing.

b. ELISA testing has fewer false-positives than PCR testing.

c. There is only a 69% probability that PCR testing will correctly identify the presence of *Candida*.

d. PCR testing is less sensitive than ELISA testing for *Candida*.

Passage II

Questions 6-12 pertain to the following information:

Scientists disagree about the cause of Bovine Spongiform Encephalopathy (BSE), also known as "mad cow disease." Two scientists discuss different explanations about the cause of the disease.

Scientist 1

Mad cow disease is a condition that results in the deterioration of brain and spinal cord tissue. This deterioration manifests as sponge-like defects or holes that result in irreversible damage to the brain. The cause of this damage is widely accepted to be the result of an infectious type of protein, called a prion. Normal prions are located in the cell wall of the central nervous system and function to preserve the myelin sheath around the nerves. Prions are capable of turning normal proteins into other prions by a process that is still unclear, thereby causing the proteins to be "refolded" in abnormal and harmful configurations. Unlike viruses and bacteria, the harmful prions possibly don't contain DNA or RNA, based on the observation of infected tissues in the laboratory that remain infected after immersion in formaldehyde or exposure to ultraviolet light. The transformation from normal to abnormal protein structure and function in a given individual is thought to occur as the result of proteins that are genetically weak or abnormally prone to mutation, or through transmission from another host through food, drugs or organ transplants from infected animals. The abnormal prions also don't trigger an immune response. After prions accumulate in large enough numbers, they form damaging conglomerations that result in the sponge-like holes in tissues, which eventually cause the loss of proper brain function and death.

Figure 1 depicts formation of abnormal prions that results from the abnormal (right) folding of amino acids.

Figure 1:
Configurations of Normal and Abnormal Prions

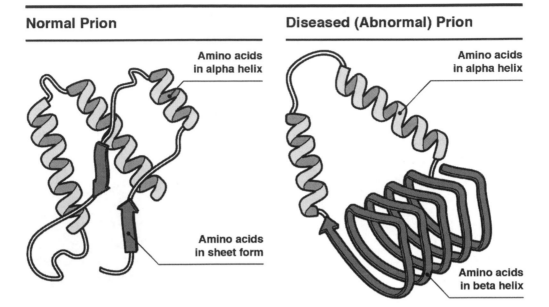

Normal Prion — Amino acids in alpha helix; Amino acids in sheet form

Diseased (Abnormal) Prion — Amino acids in alpha helix; Amino acids in beta helix

Scientist 2

The degeneration of brain tissue in animals afflicted with mad cow disease is widely considered to be the result of prion proteins. This theory fails to consider other possible causes, such as viruses. Recent studies have shown that infected tissues often contain small particles that match the size and density of viruses. In order to demonstrate that these viral particles are the cause of mad cow disease, researchers used chemicals to inactivate the viruses. When the damaged, inactivated viruses were introduced into healthy tissue, no mad cow disease symptoms were observed. This result indicates that viruses are likely the cause of mad cow disease. In addition, when the infected particles from an infected animal are used to infect a different species, the resulting particles are identical to the original particles. If the infecting agent was a protein, the particles would not be identical because proteins are species-specific. Instead, the infective agent is viewed as some form of a virus that has its own DNA or RNA configuration and can reproduce identical infective particles.

6. Which statement below best characterizes the main difference in the scientists' opinions?
    a. The existence of species-specific proteins
    b. Transmission rates of mad cow disease
    c. The conversion process of normal proteins into prions
    d. The underlying cause of mad cow disease

7. Which of the following statements is INCORRECT?
   a. Scientist 2 proposes that viruses aren't the cause of mad cow disease because chemicals inactivated the viruses.
   b. Scientist 1 suggests that infectious proteins called prions are the cause of mad cow disease.
   c. Scientist 1 indicates that the damaging conglomerations formed by prions eventually result in death.
   d. Scientist 2 reports that infected tissues often contain particles that match the size profile of viruses.

8. which of the following is true according to Scientist 1?
   a. Normal proteins accumulate in large numbers to produce damaging conglomerations.
   b. Prions can change normal proteins into prions.
   c. Species-specific DNA sequences of infected tissues indicate that proteins cause mad cow disease.
   d. Prions are present only in the peripheral nervous system of mammals.

9. Which of the following statements would be consistent with the views of BOTH scientists?
   a. Resulting tissue damage is reversible.
   b. The infecting agent is composed of sheets of amino acids in an alpha helix configuration.
   c. Species-specific DNA can be isolated from infected tissue.
   d. Cross-species transmission of the illness is possible.

10. How does the "conglomeration" described in the passage affect function?
    a. Synapses are delayed
    b. Sponge-like tissue formations occur
    c. Space-occupying lesions compress the nerves
    d. The blood supply to surrounding tissues is decreased

11. What evidence best supports the views of Scientist 2?
    a. Species-specific DNA is present in the infected particles.
    b. Prions are present in the cell membrane.
    c. Prions can trigger an immune response.
    d. The infected particles were inactivated and didn't cause disease.

12. Which of the following statements is supported by this passage?
    a. Scientist 1 favors the claim that viruses are the cause of mad cow disease.
    b. Prions are a type of infectious virus.
    c. The process that results in the formation of the abnormal prion is unclear.
    d. Mad cow disease is caused by normal proteins.

Passage III

Questions 13-17 pertain to the following information:

Scientists have long been interested in the effect of sleep deprivation on overeating and obesity in humans. Recently, scientists discovered that increased levels of the endocannabinoid 2-Arachidonoylglycerol (2-AG) in the human body is related to overeating. The endocannabinoids play an important role in memory, mood, the reward system, and metabolic processes including glucose metabolism and generation of energy. The endocannabinoid receptors CB1-R and CB2-R are protein receptors located on the cell membrane in the brain, the spinal cord and, to a lesser extent, in the peripheral neurons and the organs of the immune system. The two principal endogenous endocannabinoids are AEA (Anandamide) and 2-Arachidonoylglycerol (2-AG). The endocannabinoids can affect the body's response to chronic stress, mediate the pain response, decrease GI motility, and lessen the inflammatory response in some cancers.

Figure 1 (below) identifies the chemical structure of the endogenous cannabinoids including 2-AG.

Figure 1:
Chemical Structure of Common Endogenous Cannabinoids

The Five-Best known Endocannabinoids Showing the Common 19 - C Backbone Structure and specific R-group Constituents

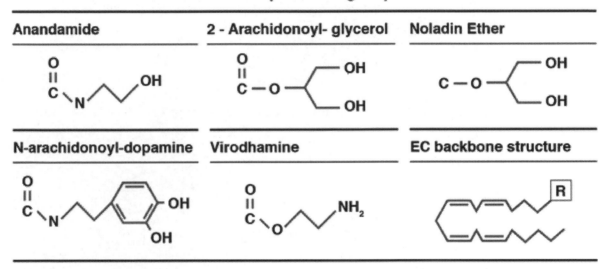

Recent research has also examined the relationship between sleep deprivation and the levels of 2-AG present in blood, as these conditions relate to obesity. The circadian fluctuations of 2-AG are well-known. Levels normally increase in late afternoon and evening. This physiological increase is thought to contribute to late-day snacking behaviors even after adequate calories have been consumed. The relationship between sleep deprivation and 2-AG appears to relate to the effect of 2-AG on the stress response, represented by sleep deprivation in this study. In order to examine this relationship, university scientists conducted an experiment to identify the influence of injections of 2-AG and sleep deprivation on overeating in a population of non-obese male and female participants that ranged in age from 20 – 40 years old. To accomplish this, human research subjects (participants) were allowed to eat their favorite junk foods in addition to consuming sufficient calories each day. All of the participants were injected daily with a solution of either sterile normal saline or 2-AG. Daily weight gain was recorded for the three treatment groups that included: participants A - E who received sterile normal saline injections, participants F - J who received 2-AG injections, and participants K - O who received 2-AG injections and were limited to 4.5 hours of sleep each night for 7 nights. The results of the three trials are shown below.

Figure 2 identifies the daily weight gain (in grams) of participants receiving sterile normal saline injections.

Daily Weight Gain for Patients Receiving Sterile Normal Saline Injections

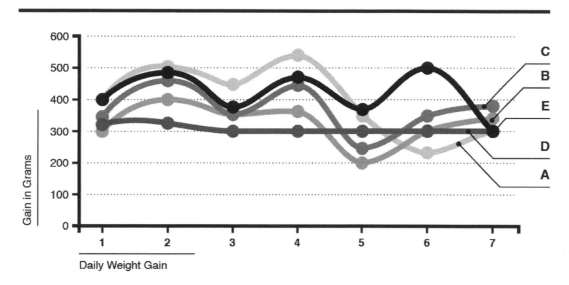

Figure 3 identifies the daily weight gain for participants receiving 2-AG injections.

Figure 3:

Daily Weight Gain for Participants Receiving Daily 2-AG Injections

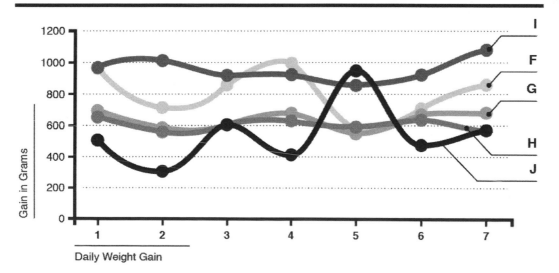

Figure 4 identifies the daily weight gain for participants receiving daily injections of 2-AG who were also limited to 4.5 hours sleep per night for 7 consecutive nights.

Figure 4:

Daily Weight Gain for Participants Receiving Daily 2-AG Injections Who Were Limited to 4.5 Hours of Sleep Per Night for 7 Consecutive Nights

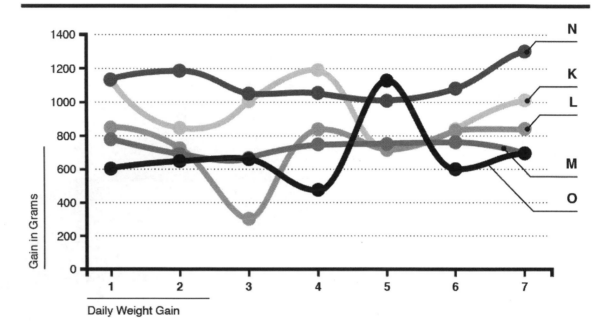

Figure 5 (below) identifies the participants' average daily weight gain by trial.

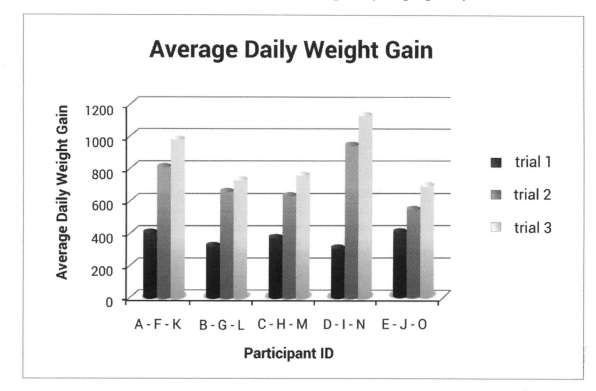

13. What was the main hypothesis for this study?
    a. 2-AG injections combined with sleep deprivation will result in weight gain.
    b. 2-AG injections will increase food intake beyond satiety.
    c. Sleep deprivation will result in weight gain.
    d. The placebo effect of the sterile normal saline will influence eating behavior.

14. Do the study results support the hypothesis? Choose the best answer.
    a. No, participants in trials 1 and 3 all gained weight.
    b. Yes, participants in trial 1 gained more weight daily than participants in trial 3.
    c. No, the average weight gain of participants in trial 2 and trial 3 was the same.
    d. Yes, all trial 3 participants gained more weight than trial 1 participants.

15. Describe the study results for participants D and H.
    a. Participant H gained more than one pound each day.
    b. Weight gain for each participant was inconsistent with the study hypothesis.
    c. There was significant fluctuation in the daily weight gain for both participants.
    d. Participant D's average daily weight was two times participant H's average daily weight gain.

16. According to the researchers, which of the following best describes the influence of sleep deprivation on eating behaviors?
    a. The total number of sleep hours is unrelated to the degree of body stress.
    b. Sleep deprivation stimulates the release of endogenous cannabinoids that may increase food intake.
    c. Deprivation of any variety triggers the hunger response.
    d. Sleep deprivation increases eating behaviors in the early morning hours.

17. According to the passage, how does 2-AG influence eating behaviors?

a. Circadian fluctuations result in increased levels of 2-AG in the afternoon and evening.

b. Endogenous cannabinoids like 2-AG increase gastric motility, which stimulates the hunger response.

c. The sedation that results from the presence of 2-AG limits food intake.

d. Endogenous cannabinoids block the opioid system, which decreases food-seeking behaviors.

Passage IV

Questions 18-22 pertain to the following passage:

A national wholesale nursery commissioned research to conduct a cost/benefit analysis of replacing existing fluorescent grow lighting systems with newer LED lighting systems. LEDs (light-emitting diodes) are composed of various semi-conductor materials that allow the flow of current in one direction. This means that LEDs emit light in a predictable range, unlike conventional lighting systems that give off heat and light in all directions. The wavelength of light of a single LED is determined by the properties of the specific semi-conductor. For instance, the indium gallium nitride system is used for blue, green, and cyan LEDs. As a result, growing systems can be individualized for the specific wavelength requirements for different plant species. In addition, LEDs don't emit significant amounts of heat compared to broadband systems, so plant hydration can be controlled more efficiently.

Figure 1 identifies the visible spectrum with the wavelength expressed in nanometers.

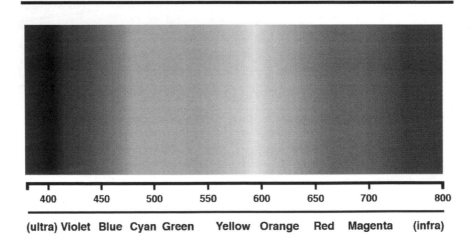

Figure 1:
The Visible Spectrum (Wavelength in Nanometers)

400   450   500   550   600   650   700   800

(ultra) Violet Blue Cyan Green   Yellow Orange   Red   Magenta   (infra)

Figure 2 (below) identifies the absorption rates of different wavelengths of light.

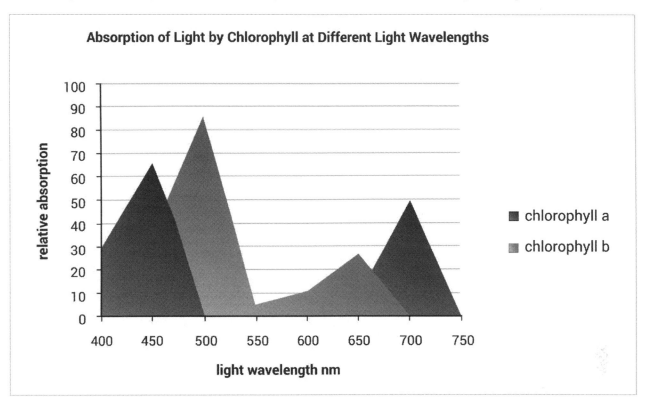

Researchers conducted three trials and hypothesized that LEDs would result in greater growth rates than conventional lighting or white light. They also hypothesized that using a combination of red, blue, green, and yellow wavelengths in the LED lighting system would result in a greater growth rate than using red or blue wavelengths alone. Although green and yellow wavelengths are largely reflected by the plant (Figure 2), the absorption rate is sufficient to make a modest contribution to plant growth. Fifteen Impatiens walleriana seed samples were planted in the same growing medium. Temperature, hydration, and light intensity were held constant. Plant height in millimeters was recorded as follows.

Figure 3 identifies the plant growth rate in millimeters with light wavelengths of 440 nanometers.

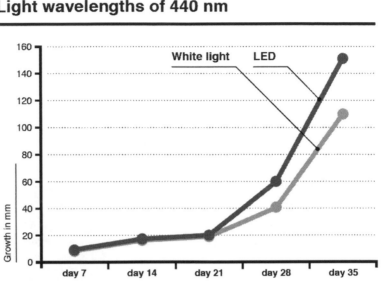

Figure 3:
Plant Growth Rate (mm) with Light wavelengths of 440 nm

Figure 4 (below) identifies the plant growth rate in mm with light wavelengths of 650 nanometers.

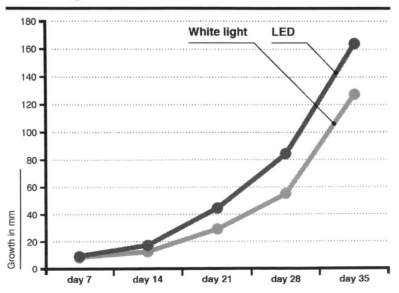

Figure 4:
Plant Growth Rate (mm) with Light wavelengths of 650 nm

Figure 5 (below) identifies the plant growth rate in millimeters with combined light wavelengths of 440, 550, and 650 nanometers.

Figure 5:
Plant Growth Rate (mm) with Combined Light wavelengths of 440, 550, and 650 nm

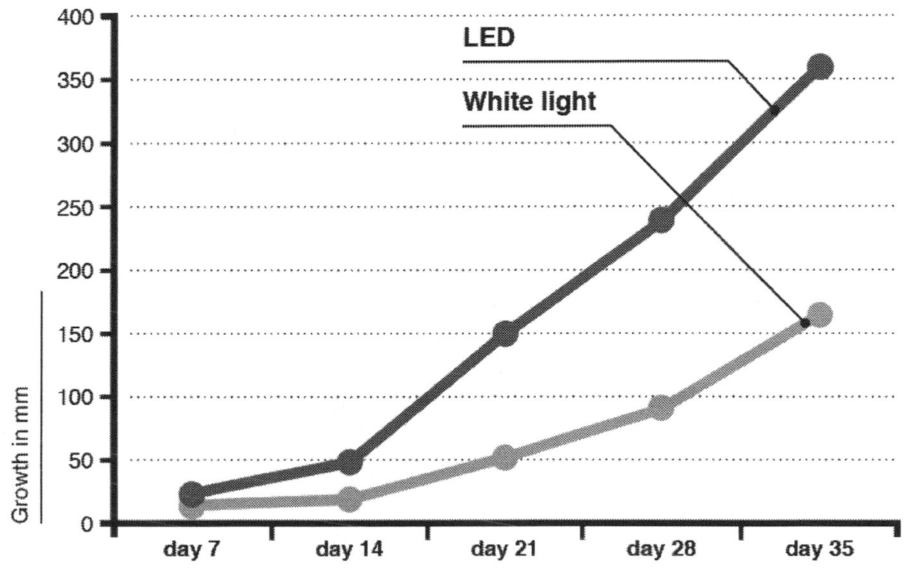

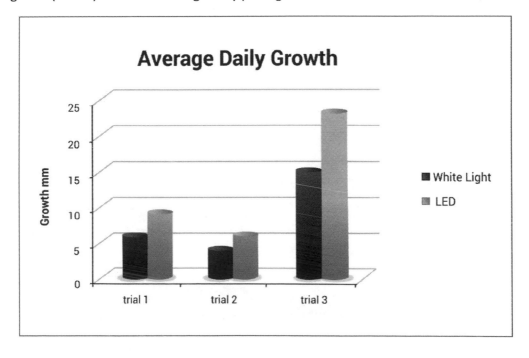

Figure 6 (below) identifies average daily plant growth rate in millimeters.

18. If the minimum plant height required for packaging a plant for sale is 150 millimeters, based on plant growth, how much sooner will the LED plants be packaged compared to the white light plants?
    a. 14 days
    b. 21 days
    c. 35 days
    d. 42 days

19. Plants reflect green and yellow light wavelengths. Do the results of the three trials support the view that plants also absorb and use green and yellow light wavelengths for growth?
    a. Yes, green and yellow light wavelengths were responsible for plant growth in trial 3.
    b. No, white light alone was responsible for measurable plant growth.
    c. Yes, the growth rates in trial 3 were greater than the rates in trials 1 and 2.
    d. No, only the red and blue wavelengths were effective in stimulating plant growth.

20. When did the greatest rate of growth occur for both groups in trial 1 and trial 2?
    a. From 7 days to 14 days
    b. From 28 days to 35 days
    c. From 21 days to 28 days
    d. From 14 days to 21 days

21. If an LED lighting system costs twice as much as a white light system, based only on the average daily growth rate as noted above, would it be a wise investment?
    a. No, because multiple different semi-conductors would be necessary.
    b. Yes, growth rates are better with LEDs.
    c. No, the LED average daily growth rate was not two times greater than the white light rate.
    d. Yes, LEDs use less electricity and water.

22. If the researchers conducted an additional trial, trial 4, to measure the effect of green and yellow wavelengths on plant growth, what would be the probable result?
    a. The growth rate would exceed trial 1.
    b. The growth rate would equal trial 3.
    c. The growth rate would be the same as trial 2.
    d. The growth rate would be less than trial 1 or trial 2.

Passage V

Questions 23-28 pertain to the following passage:

Mangoes are a tropical fruit that grow on trees native to Southern Asia called the *Mangifera*. Mangoes are now grown in most frost-free tropical and subtropical locations around the world. India and China harvest the greatest numbers of mangoes. A major problem the mango industry faces each year is the destruction of fruit after harvest. This destruction is the result of spoilage or rotting that occurs during long shipping and storage times.

To prevent the spoilage of mangoes, fruits are stored and shipped in climate-controlled containers. Ideally, mangoes should be stored at around 5 °C, which is about the same temperature as a home refrigerator. Although storage at 5 °C is highly effective at preventing spoilage, the monetary costs associated with maintaining this temperature during long shipping times are prohibitive.

Fruit companies spend large amounts of money to learn about the underlying cause of spoilage and possible methods to prevent loss of their product. Anthracnose, an infection that causes mango decay, is caused by *Colletotrichum,* a type of fungus that has been identified as a major contributor to mango spoilage. This fungus, which may remain dormant on green fruit, grows on the surface of the mango and can penetrate the skin and cause spoilage. The infection first appears during the flowering period as small black dots that progress to dark brown or black areas as ripening occurs. Humidity and excessive rainfall increase the severity of this infection. Previous studies established that colony sizes smaller than 35 millimeters after 4 weeks of travel resulted in acceptable amounts of spoilage.

Currently, several additional pre-treatment measures aimed at prevention are employed to slow decay of the fruit from the harvest to the marketplace. Industry researchers examined the individual and collective benefits of two of these processes, including post-harvest hot water treatment and air cooling at varied transport temperatures in order to identify optimum post-harvest procedures.

Table 1 identifies the observed mango decay in millimeters at 5 °C, 7.5 °C, and 10 °C with two pre-treatment processes over time measured in days since harvest of the fruit.

Table 1: Days Since Harvest

	2	4	6	8	10	12	14	16	18	20	22	24	26	28
5° C														
Water	1	4	7	9	11	12	14	19	22	23	25	27	28	30
Air	0	2	3	6	8	9	11	12	13	15	16	17	18	19
7.5°C														
Water	2	3	4	5	6	8	9	11	12	13	14	15	16	27
Air	0	2	5	6	7	9	10	15	22	23	24	27	32	39
10°C														
Water	2	3	5	7	8	11	12	14	22	35	42	44	47	62
Air	1	2	4	6	7	9	10	15	19	23	27	29	35	44

Figure 1 (below) identifies the observed mango decay of fruit stored at 5 °C measured in millimeters, with two pretreatment processes, over time measured in days since harvest of the fruit.

Figure 1:
5 °C Mango Decay Rates

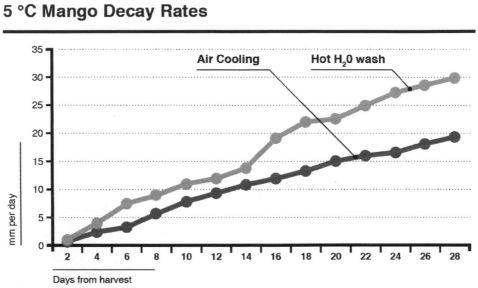

Figures 2 (below) identifies the observed mango decay of fruit stored at 7.5 °C, measured in millimeters, with two pretreatment processes, over time measured in days since harvest of the fruit.

Figure 2:
7.5 °C Mango Decay Rates

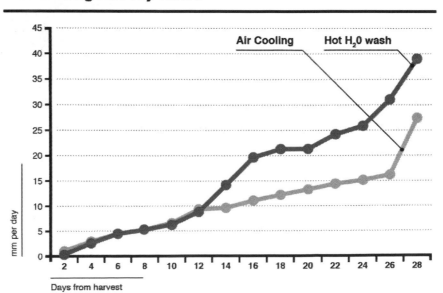

Figures 3 (below) identifies the observed mango decay of fruit stored at 10 °C measured in millimeters, with two pretreatment processes, over time measured in days since harvest of the fruit.

Figures 3:
10 °C Mango Decay Rates

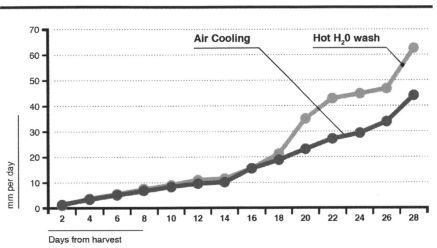

Figure 4 (below) identifies fruit decay measured in millimeters at 5 °C, 7.5 °C, and 10 °C with the combined pre-treatments over 28 days.

Figure 4:
Mango Decay Rates at 5 °C, 7.5 °C, and 10 °C with the Combined Pre-Treatments (Air Cooling & Water Bath)

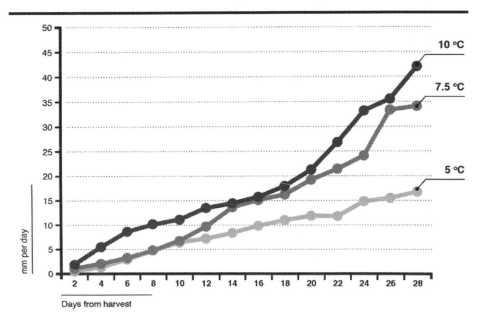

23. According to the passage above, which of the following statements is false?
   a. The optimal temperature for storing mangos is 5 °C.
   b. Anacardiaceae Magnifera is responsible for mango spoilage.
   c. Storing fruit at 5 °C is costly.
   d. Long distance shipping is a critical factor in mango spoilage.

24. If the mangoes were shipped from India to the U.S., and the trip was expected to take 20 days, which model would be best according to the data in Table 1?
   a. The 10 °C model, because fungal levels were acceptable for both pre-treatments.
   b. The 5 °C, model because it's more cost-effective.
   c. The 7.5 °C model, because this temperature is less expensive to maintain, and the fungal levels were acceptable.
   d. No single model is better than the other two models.

25. According to Figures 1 – 3 above, the largest one-day increase in fruit decay occurred under which conditions?
   a. Air cooling at 10 °C
   b. Hot water wash at 10 °C
   c. Air cooling at 7.5 °C
   d. Hot water wash at 7.5 °C

26. Which pre-treatment method reached unacceptable fungal levels first?
   a. Hot water wash at 7.5 °C
   b. Air cooling at 5 °C
   c. Hot water wash at 10 °C
   d. Air cooling at 10 °C

27. The researchers were attempting to identify the best shipping conditions for mangoes for a 28-day trip from harvest to market. Referencing Figures 1 - 4, which conditions would be the most cost-effective?
   a. Air cooling pre-treatment at 5 °C
   b. Air cooling and hot water wash pre-treatment at 5 °C
   c. Hot water wash pre-treatment at 7.5 °C
   d. Air cooling at 10 °C

28. Shipping mangoes at 5 °C is costly. According to the researchers' findings, is shipping mangoes at 5 °C more cost effective than 7.5 °C for trips lasting more than 28 days when combined air cooling and hot water wash treatments are applied?
   a. Yes, shipping at 7.5 °C combined with both pre-treatments resulted in an unacceptable fungal infection rate.
   b. Yes, fungal infection rates were below 35 mm for both pre-treatments 5 °C.
   c. No, air cooling pre-treatment was acceptable at 10 °C, and it's less expensive to ship fruit at 10 °C.
   d. No, hot water wash rates were lower than air cooling at 5 °C.

Passage VI

Questions 29-34 pertain to the following passage:

Scientists recently discovered that circadian rhythms help regulate sugar consumption by brown adipose tissue. The results of this study suggest that circadian rhythms and fat cells work together to warm the body in preparation for early morning activities involving cold weather. A circadian rhythm refers to life processes controlled by an internal "biological clock" that maintains a 24-hour rhythm. Sleep is controlled by one's circadian rhythm. To initiate sleep, the circadian rhythm stimulates the pineal gland to release the hormone melatonin, which causes sleepiness. Importantly, the circadian rhythm discerns when to begin the process of sleep based on the time of day. During the daytime, sunlight stimulates special cells within the eye, photosensitive retinal ganglion cells, which, in turn, allow the "biological clock" to keep track of how many hours of sunlight there are in a given day.

Brown adipose tissue (BAT) is a type of fat that plays an important role in thermogenesis, a process that generates heat. In humans and other mammals, there are two basic types of thermogenesis: shivering thermogenesis and non-shivering thermogenesis. Shivering thermogenesis involves physical movements, such as shaky hands or clattering teeth. Heat is produced as a result of energy being burned during physical activity. Non-shivering thermogenesis doesn't require physical activity; instead, it utilizes brown adipose tissue to generate heat. Brown fat cells appear dark because they contain large numbers of mitochondria, the organelles that burn sugar to produce energy and heat.

Researchers know that brown adipose tissue (BAT) is essential for maintaining body temperature. A new discovery in humans has shown that circadian rhythms cause BAT to consume more sugar in the early-morning hours. This spike in sugar consumption causes more heat to be produced in BAT. Scientists propose that our human ancestors could have benefited from extra body heat during cold hunts in the morning.

Perhaps more significantly, these new findings may suggest a role for BAT in the prevention of Type 2 Diabetes. Two important questions remain; to what degree does BAT affect blood glucose levels, and is it possible to increase BAT in a given individual? The demonstrated increase in sugar consumption and heat production of BAT is thought to be related to insulin-sensitivity. To examine the first question, researchers conducted three trials to examine the relationship between brown fat and blood glucose levels at different points in the day. PET scanning was used to estimate total body brown fat in 18 non-diabetic participants. Total body brown fat expressed as a proportion of total body fat (either 5%, 10%, or 20%) was the basis for group selection. The researchers hypothesized that the blood glucose levels would be inversely related to the percentage of BAT. Resulting data is included below.

Figure 1 (below) identifies the circadian cycle of blood glucose.

Figure 1:
Normal Circadian Plasma Glucose Levels

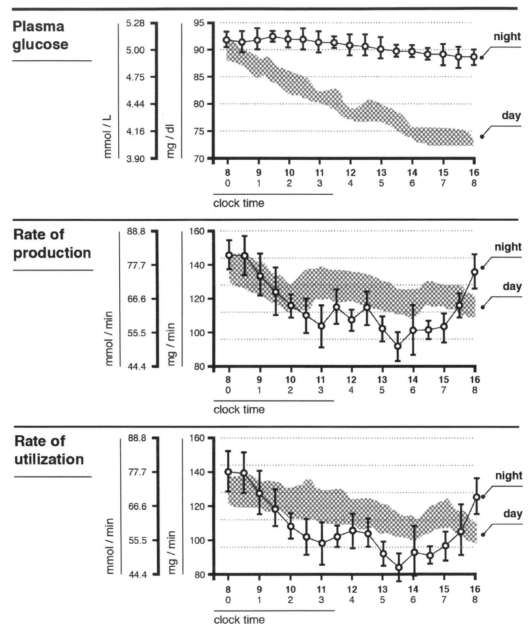

Figure 2 (below) identifies the resulting blood glucose measurements for participants with 5% total brown body fat.

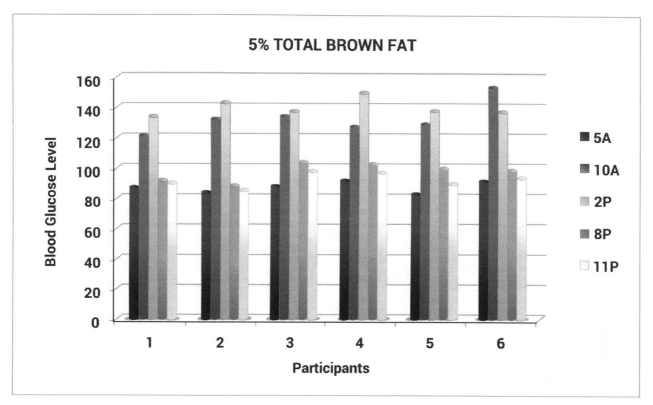

Figure 3 (below) identifies the resulting blood glucose measurements for participants with 10% total brown body fat.

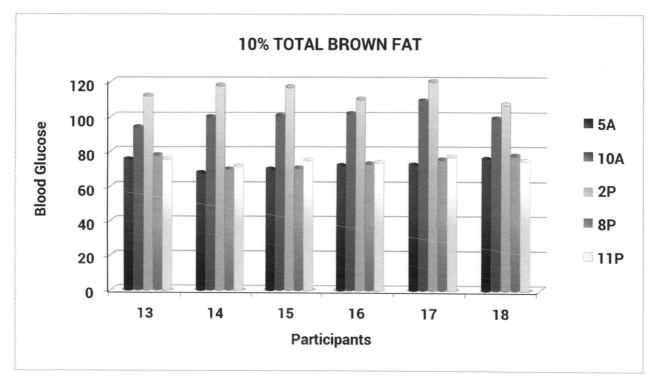

Figure 4 (below) identifies the resulting blood glucose measurements for participants with 20% total brown body fat.

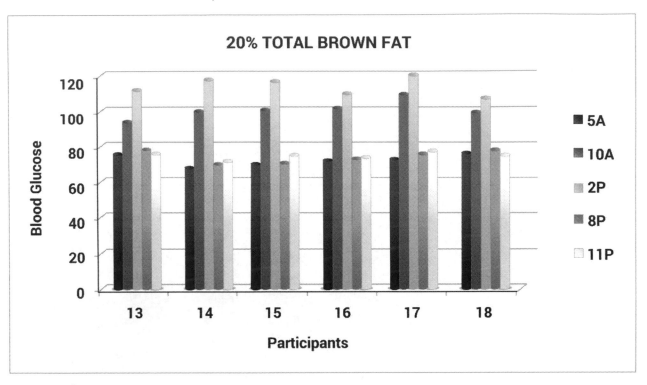

Figure 5 (below) identifies the average blood glucose measurements for the three trials.

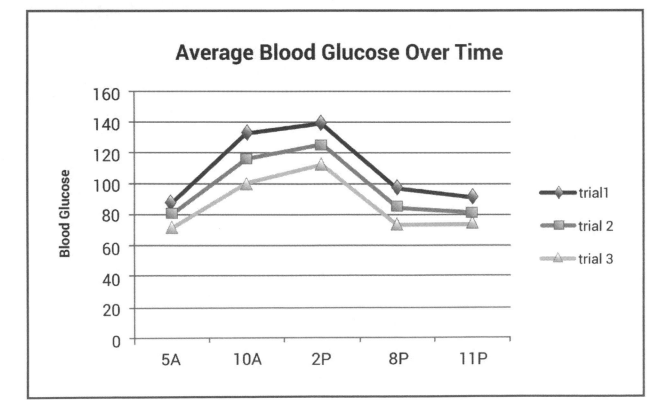

29. Which of the following describes the relationship of the research results in Figure 5?
    a. Positive correlation among the three trials
    b. Curvilinear relationship
    c. Weak negative relationship
    d. No demonstrated relationship

30. Which of the following statements concerning mitochondria is INCORRECT?
    a. Mitochondrial function is diminished in the presence of elevated blood glucose levels.
    b. Mitochondria are responsible for the color of brown fat.
    c. Mitochondria are capable of reproduction in response to energy needs.
    d. Mitochondria are responsible for binding oxygen in mature red blood cells.

31. According to Figure 5, participants' blood sugars were highest at what time of day?
    a. 5 a.m., because heat is generated early in the morning
    b. 8 p.m., because the participants ate less for dinner than lunch
    c. 11 p.m., because brown adipose tissue is not active at night
    d. 2 p.m., because the effects of the early-morning activity of the brown adipose tissue had diminished

32. Circadian rhythms control sleep by doing which of the following?
    a. Stimulating the pineal gland to release ganglia
    b. Stimulating the release of melatonin
    c. Suppressing shivering during cold mornings
    d. Instructing brown adipose tissue to release sugar

33. Which Participant in trial 1 had the highest average blood sugar for the group?
    a. 1
    b. 3
    c. 4
    d. 6

34. Is the data in Figure 5 consistent with the daytime plasma glucose trend in Figure 1?
    a. Yes, Figure 5 blood glucose readings declined from a morning to afternoon.
    b. No, blood glucose readings peaked at 2 p.m..
    c. Yes, morning glucose readings were higher in group 1.
    d. No, nighttime levels fluctuated between 100 and 110.

Passage VII

Questions 35-40 pertain to the following passage:

A biome is a major terrestrial or aquatic environment that supports diverse life forms. Freshwater biomes—including lakes, streams and rivers, and wetlands—account for 0.01% of the Earth's fresh water. Collectively, they are home to 6% of all recognized species. Standing water bodies may vary in size from small ponds to the Great Lakes. Plant life in lakes is specific to the zone of the lake that provides the optimal habitat for a specific species, based on the depth of the water as it relates to light. The photic layer is the shallower layer where light is available for photosynthesis. The aphotic layer is deeper, and the levels of sunlight are too low for photosynthesis. The benthic layer is the bottom-most layer, and its inhabitants are nourished by materials from the photic layer. Light-sensitive cyanobacteria and microscopic algae are two forms of phytoplankton that exist in lakes. As a result of nitrogen and phosphorous from agriculture and sewage run-off, algae residing near the surface can multiply abnormally so that available light is diminished to other species. Oxygen supplies may also be reduced when large numbers of algae die.

Recently, concerns have been raised about the effects of agriculture and commercial development on the quality of national freshwater bodies. In order to estimate the effect of human impact on freshwater, researchers examined plant life from the aphotic layer of three freshwater lakes of approximately the same size located in three different environments. Lake A was located in a remote forested area of western Montana. Lake B was located in central Kansas. Lake C was located in a medium-size city on the west coast of Florida. The researchers hypothesized that the microscopic algae and cyanobacteria populations from Lake A would approach appropriate levels for the size of the lake. They also hypothesized that the remaining two samples would reveal abnormal levels of the phytoplankton. In addition, the researchers measured the concentration of algae at different depths at four different times in another lake identified as having abnormal algae growth. These measurements attempted to identify the point at which light absorption in the photic layer was no longer sufficient for the growth of organisms in the aphotic layer. Resulting data is identified below.

Figure 1 (below) illustrates the zones of the freshwater lake.

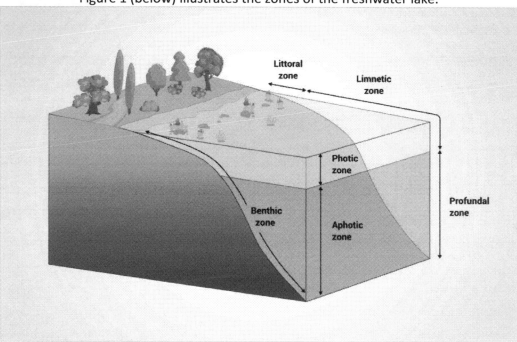

Figure 2 (below) identifies algae and cyanobacteria levels in parts per million for Lake A over six measurements.

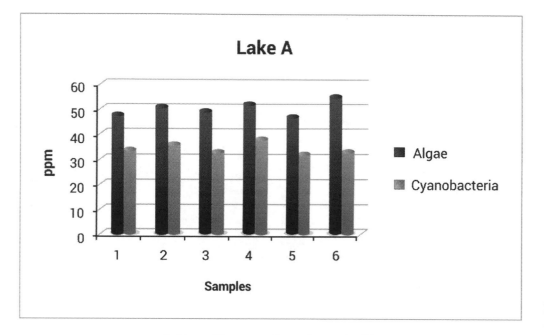

normal: Algae 50 p.p.m. Cyanobacteria 35 p.p.m.

Figure 3 (below) identifies algae and cyanobacteria levels in parts per million for Lake B over six measurements.

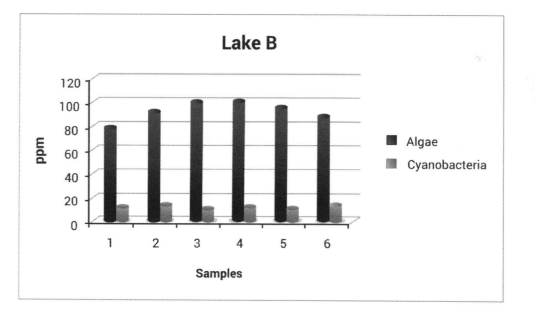

normal: Algae 50 p.p.m. Cyanobacteria 35 p.p.m.

Figure 4 (below) identifies algae and cyanobacteria levels in parts per million for Lake C over six measurements.

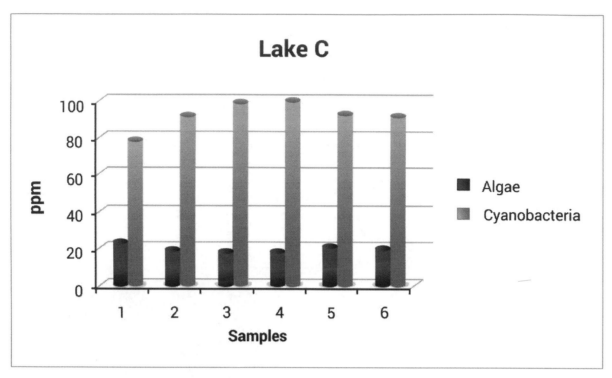

normal: Algae 50 p.p.m. Cyanobacteria 35 p.p.m.

Figure 5 (below) identifies cyanobacteria levels at different depths over time.

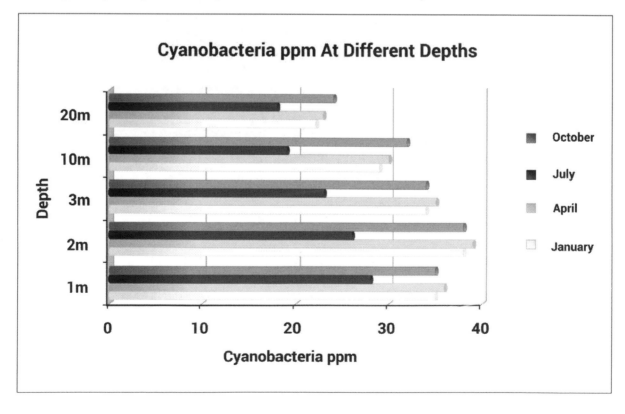

35. Based on Figure 2, was the researchers' hypothesis confirmed?
    a. No, the phytoplankton levels were not elevated in the first trial.
    b. Yes, the phytoplankton levels were raised above normal in each sample.
    c. No, the Lake A numbers were normal.
    d. Yes, algae levels were above normal in Lake C.

36. In Lake B, cyanobacteria were decreased and algae were increased. Which of the following is a possible explanation for this finding?
    a. The overgrowth of algae decreased the light energy available for cyanobacteria growth.
    b. Lake B experienced severe flooding, causing the water levels in the lake to rise above normal.
    c. Agricultural chemical residue depleted the food source for cyanobacteria.
    d. Cyanobacteria cannot survive in the cold winter weather in Lake B.

37. What common factor might explain the results for Lake B and Lake C?
    a. Population concentration
    b. Average humidity of the locations
    c. Average heat index
    d. Excess nitrogen and phosphorous in the ground water

38. As algae levels increase above normal, what happens to organisms in the aphotic level?
    a. Growth is limited but sustained.
    b. Species eventually die due to decreased oxygenation.
    c. Cyanobacteria increase to unsafe levels.
    d. Aerobic bacteria multiply.

39. Referencing Figures 2 and 3, which environment would favor organisms in the benthic layer of the corresponding lake?
    a. Figure 4, because the cyanobacteria are protective.
    b. Figure 3, because increased numbers of Algae provide more light.
    c. Figure 4, because cyanobacteria are able to survive.
    d. Figure 3, because the levels of both species are normal.

40. Which of the following statements is supported by the data in Figure 5?
    a. Algae growth is greater in July than April.
    b. Cyanobacteria can't exist at 20 meters in this lake.
    c. There's insufficient light in the aphotic layer at 3 meters to support algae growth.
    d. Cyanobacteria growth rates are independent of algae growth at 1 meter.

Answer Explanations

1. C: There is a 99% probability of PCR testing identifying *Histoplasma*. GM assay was more specific for identifying *Aspergillus,* 95% to 85%. True positive is defined by sensitivity. The sensitivity of GM assay testing is less than 70%.

2. D: *Histoplasma* is detectable 90 days from exposure. PCR testing is able to detect *Histoplasma* 91 days from exposure—one day after sufficient organisms exist for detection. *Candida* is detectable 45 days from exposure. PCR testing is able to detect *Candida* 72 days from exposure—27 days after a sufficient number of organisms exist for detection. *Aspergillus* is detectable 118 days from exposure. ELISA testing is able to detect *Aspergillus* 134 days from exposure—16 days after a sufficient number of organisms exist for detection. *Candida* is detectable 45 days from exposure. GM assay testing is able to detect *Candida* 56 days from exposure—11 days after a sufficient number of organisms exist for detection.

3. B: The probability that the GM assay will identify *Candida* is 69%. Therefore, there's a 31% probability that it won't be identified. ELISA sensitivity and specificity for *Histoplasma* are both greater than 80%. False-negative probabilities are represented by the specificity of a given testing method. The sensitivity and specificity for GM assay testing for *Aspergillus* is 9% and 96% respectively. All testing methods had greater than 90% specificity for the organisms.

4. C: The sensitivity of PCR testing for *Histoplasma* is 99%, and the test can identify the organism one day after it reaches a detectable colony size. The sensitivity for GM assay testing for *Histoplasma* is 65%. If physicians rely on GM assay testing, they may determine that the individual doesn't have the *Histoplasma* infection. Treatment will depend on the presence or absence of the infection as indicated by testing. Waiting for PCR testing is based on the sensitivity of the test, not the individual's current symptoms. The subclinical phase of *Histoplasma* is 28 days.

5. A: ELISA testing detects *Candida* three days after the organism is present in sufficient numbers to be recognized. PCR detects the organism more than three weeks after it is first detectable. ELISA testing sensitivity for *Candida* is 87% and PCR testing is 92%. However, the ability to identify the presence of the organism earlier in the process of infection (allowing early intervention) outweighs the differences in the probability of identifying the presence of the organism. There's a 92% probability that PCR testing will identify the presence of *Candida*. PCR testing is more sensitive than ELISA: 92% versus 87%

6. D: The main difference in the scientists' opinions is related to the cause of mad cow disease. The existence of species-specific proteins was used by Scientist 2 to support viral infection as the cause of the disease. Transmission rates of the disease and the conversion of normal proteins to prions were not debated in the passage.

7. A: Scientist 2 proposed that viruses were the cause of mad cow disease because chemicals inactivated the viruses. The remaining choices are correct.

8. B: According to Scientist 1, abnormal prions are capable of "refolding" normal proteins in harmful prions. Abnormal proteins accumulate to produce the damaging conglomerations. Scientist 2 didn't find species-specific DNA and used this fact to support viruses as the cause of mad cow disease. According to Scientist 1, prions are located in the central nervous system, not the peripheral nervous system.

9. D: Mad cow disease can be spread between animal species and from animals to humans through consumption of diseased animal products. The resulting damage to the central nervous system is irreversible and will eventually cause the death of the animal. Scientist 2 would not agree that the infecting agent contained amino acids, as they form proteins, and Scientist 2 believes that a virus causes the disease. Scientist 2 demonstrated that the infected tissue of animals that were infected by a different species didn't contain species-specific DNA, which would have been the expected outcome if the infecting agent were a protein.

10. C: The accumulated masses of abnormal prions eventually form sponge-like holes in the brain and spinal cord that result in death. The passage doesn't mention the effects of the synapses, nerves, or blood supply.

11. D: The absence of disease resulting from the inactivated viral particles best supports the views of Scientist 2. There were no species-specific DNA sequences found in the infected particles. Scientist 2 didn't support the existence of prions as the cause of mad cow disease.

12. C: The actual process of "refolding" the normal protein into the abnormal protein isn't clear from this passage. Scientist 1 claims that prions cause the disease. Prions are an abnormal protein, not a virus. Scientist 1 claims that mad cow disease is caused by abnormal proteins.

13. C: The main hypothesis for this study involved the influence of 2-AG levels combined with sleep deprivation on eating behaviors. The combination of the two conditions, not each one separately, constitutes the main hypothesis. The passage didn't discuss a placebo effect in the normal saline injection group.

14. D: The study results support the hypothesis because the participants who received 1-AG injections and were sleep deprived gained more weight than participants who received sterile normal saline injections. The remaining choices do not support the hypothesis.

15. A: Participant H gained more than 1 pound (450g) per day. There was little fluctuation in the day-to-day weight gain for each participant. Participant H in trial 2 gained more weight than participant D in trial 1.

16. B: Sleep deprivation increases the levels and duration of action of 2-AG, an endogenous cannabinoid, especially in the late afternoon. The stress effect increases with the degree of sleep deprivation. The passage doesn't discuss a relationship between sleep deprivation and the hunger response. Eating behaviors are increased in late afternoon as a result of the extended duration of 2-AG action.

17. A: Circadian fluctuations increase the levels of 2-AG during the afternoon and evening. This increase is believed to stimulate food intake beyond the point of satiety. Endogenous cannabinoids decrease gastric motility. 2-AG may have a calming effect on mood, but food intake is still increased in the presence of afternoon and evening levels of 2-AG. Endogenous cannabinoids work with the opioid system to mediate the pain response, not food-seeking behaviors.

18. A: In trial 3, the plants grown with the combined-wavelength LED's reached 150 millimeters by day 21. The plants grown with white light reached 160 millimeters by day 35.

19. C: In trial 3, with LED lighting that included green and yellow wavelengths, plant growth was greater than trial 1 or trial 2 with either blue or red wavelengths. However, from the available information, it can only be said that green and yellow wavelengths *contributed to* plant growth in trial 3, but not that green and yellow wavelengths *alone* were responsible for plant growth in trial 3. There was plant growth in all lighting conditions.

20. B: In trial 1, from day 28 to day 35, white light growth increased by 71 millimeters, and red light increased by 78 millimeters. In trial 2, from day 28 to day 35, white light growth increased by 71 millimeters, and blue light increased by 78 millimeters.

21. C: The average daily growth with LED lighting was not twice the white light average daily growth. LED systems did result in better growth rates and they do require less water and electricity. However, the question is based on recorded average daily growth, and that rate was not double the white light rate.

22. D: The passage says that green and yellow wavelengths are reflected by the plant. Therefore, it's expected that those wavelengths would result in slower growth than the blue or red wavelengths, which are absorbed.

23. B: *Anacardiaceae Magnifera* is the genus and family name for the mango. The *Colletotrichum* fungus causes the spoilage. The remaining choices are correct.

24. C: According to Table 1, at 20 days, the fungal level at 7.5 °C was the same as the fungal level at 5 °C. Because the 7.5 °C temperature is less expensive than the 5 °C temperature, the 7.5°C model is best. The 10°C model is less expensive than the 7.5 °C, but fungal levels are greater. Only the 7.5 °C and 5 °C models had acceptable fungal levels at 20 days.

25. B: The hot water wash pre-treatment fungal level increased by 15 millimeters from day 26 to day 28 at 10 °C. It was the single largest one-day increase across the trials. Air cooling at 10 °C increased by 5 millimeters from day 14 to day 16. Air cooling at 7.5 °C increased by 7 millimeters from day 26 to day 28. Hot water wash at 7.5 °C increased 11 millimeters from day 26 to day 28.

26. C: The hot water wash fungal level at 10 °C reached 35 millimeters on day 20. The maximum fungal level for air cooling at 5 °C was 19 millimeters, and at 10 °C, 35 millimeters on day 26. The maximum fungal level for hot water at 7.5 °C was 36 millimeters on day 28.

27. C: The fungal levels were acceptable with the hot water wash at 7.5 °C, and the 7.5 °C temperature is less expensive to maintain. Air cooling and hot water wash pre-treatment at 5 °C resulted in acceptable fungal levels, but the 5 °C temperature is costlier. Fungal levels were not acceptable at 28 days at 10 °C.

28. B: Shipping mangoes at 5 °C is costly, but for the 28-day trip, the fungal levels were only acceptable in the 5 °C model. Air cooling fungal rates at 5 °C were lower than the hot water wash rates, but each was acceptable. Fungal rates at 7.5 °C and 10 °C were unacceptable.

29. A: The correlation was positive, because when one variable increased, the other increased, and when one variable decreased, the other decreased. There are two forms for a curvilinear relationship. In one curvilinear relationship, when variable 1 increases, a second variable increases as well, but only to a certain point, and then variable 2 decreases as variable 1 continues to increase. In the other form, variable 1 increases while variable 2 decreases to a certain point, after which both variables increase. In a negative relationship, high values for one variable are associated with low values for the second variable.

30. D: Mitochondrial activity is suppressed by elevated blood glucose levels. Mitochondria use sugar to produce cellular energy, and the presence of large numbers of mitochondria in BAT gives BAT a brownish color. Mitochondria contain DNA and can reproduce additional mitochondria when additional energy is required. In the body, mature red blood cells are the only cells that don't contain mitochondria.

31. D: Blood sugars for all groups identified in Figure 5 were highest at 2 p.m.

32. B: Circadian rhythms control sleep by stimulating the release of melatonin from the pineal gland. Ganglia are nerve cells, not hormones, that affect sleep. BAT doesn't release sugar; it utilizes sugar for heat production. Shivering on cold mornings is a desirable form of thermogenesis but isn't associated with sleep.

33. D: The average blood sugar for participant 6 was 115. Participant 1 was 105, participant 3 was 112, and participant 4 was 82.

34. B: The daytime blood glucose levels in Figure 1 decreased as the day progressed. The blood glucose levels in Figure 5 peaked for the day at 2 p.m. Night blood glucose levels didn't reach 100. Group I's levels are irrelevant to the question.

35. A: Based only on Figure 2, the researchers' hypothesis wasn't confirmed. Subsequent trials confirmed the hypothesis.

36. A: Increased algae levels can block sunlight, limiting growth of species inhabiting lower zones. The passage doesn't identify the effects of rainfall or cold temperatures on phytoplankton growth, so Choices *B* and *D* are incorrect. The passage identifies the effect of phosphorous and nitrogen residue on algae growth, but not as a food source for cyanobacteria.

37. D: The passage identifies freshwater contamination by phosphorous and nitrogen as the most common cause of algae overgrowth. Population density would be more common in Florida than Kansas.

38. B: As algae levels increase above normal, organisms in the aphotic level plants don't receive adequate light for normal growth and oxygen levels are decreased, resulting in the death of oxygen-dependent species.

39. C: Algae block the sunlight, which limits growth.

40. A: Algae growth was greater in July, which limited the amount of light reaching the lower zones of the lake, decreasing the levels of cyanobacteria. Cyanobacteria existed in less-than-normal concentrations at 20 meters, but there were measurable levels of the organisms. Algae growth at 3 meters wasn't measured. The passage states that cyanobacteria growth is associated with algae growth, not independent of algae growth.

ACT Writing Test

For some people, a writing test can seem very intimidating, perhaps even as scary as public speaking. However, with a little planning and practice, there's no reason to be afraid. Let's look at some strategies to help test takers do their best.

What to Expect

The test contains a topic followed by three possible viewpoints. Read everything carefully and brainstorm an opinion on the topic. Then, write an essay that clearly evaluates all three viewpoints and states and supports the opinion using relevant facts and personal experiences along with creativity and critical thinking.

The assignment must be completed within a 30-minute time frame. Thirty minutes may not seem like a lot of time, but it is sufficient for organizing thoughts and putting the best words forward. Keep in mind that there is no right or wrong answer to the writing test. The important thing is to approach the response in an organized, clear, and direct way. In other words, be sure the writing makes sense.

So, how is that done?

Before the Big Day

Practice. Practice. Practice. While the concept of practice may seem unappealing, it is important to be aware of its value. Just as skills in any sport will likely improve with practice, creating sample writings will exercise "writing muscles" and will likely elevate skills and proficiency. Any kind of writing practice is advantageous, but essay writing is particularly relevant.

It also helps to be aware of how long it takes to comprehend and complete an essay assignment such as the ACT Test to determine if it is necessary to work faster.

Another tip is to ask others for their opinion. Feedback is a very important tool for becoming aware of strengths and weaknesses. Ultimately, the best opportunity for success is to work on being both a reader and a writer.

Keys to Good Writing

Use proper grammar, spelling, punctuation, and other formal writing techniques. This isn't an email or a text to send to friends with *lol* and *l8r,* where the only punctuation marks are in emojis, and the only capital letters are for shouting. There's nothing wrong with typing that way in a text, but this is a different kind of writing. It's closer to a speech, so start thinking more formally about how to express thoughts.

Explain thoughts in an organized way. Writers shouldn't assume that readers share the same knowledge or thoughts. It is necessary to explain the opinion that an idea is "bad" or "good," even if it seems obvious. Make sure the reasons are relevant and consistent—writing won't be credible if an argument contradicts a previous statement.

On Test Day

Brainstorm

Don't just start writing! Writing lacks direction if thoughts and ideas aren't organized first. So, before writing a single sentence of the opening paragraph, take a few minutes to **brainstorm**. Write down anything and everything related to the topic. Don't filter out anything, no matter how silly it might seem; it's impossible to know what ideas might grow into a full argument. It might be a good idea to use the scratch paper provided to jot down ideas and organize them, grouping similar ideas together. At this point, keep in mind that the people scoring the test will be looking for variety, creativity, and imagination—in the examples, in the ways the points are made, and especially in the perspectives.

While forming thoughts on the topic, imagine someone who disagrees. What arguments would that person make? How would he or she see the topic? Write down those ideas. Keep in mind that there are often many ways to justify the same position. So, imagine people who may agree but for completely different reasons, and write down what they might say as well. Including diverse viewpoints will show a well-rounded understanding of the topic.

Lastly, when brainstorming, don't forget that, although covering multiple viewpoints is key to good writing, truly *great* writing comes from bringing personal experience to the content. If the topic can be related to something personal (and still make a relevant, organized point), the writing will be more memorable—and probably earn a higher score.

Inventory

Keep brainstorming until the ideas stop flowing (but keep an eye on the clock—don't go over five minutes, or it may be difficult to get the actual writing done). Then, take a deep breath, and look at the ideas. Look for those that have a lot of information and strategies to support them, even if they're not the most exciting ones. At this point, it may be necessary to start cutting ideas that don't have enough material to back them up.

An **angle**, or pattern, should start to emerge—a common theme to pull the most promising ideas together. Keep this overarching direction in mind while deciding what to keep and what to drop. Once again, good writing comes from having well-developed and supported ideas, but *great* writing finds a way to connect all those ideas into a single big idea.

Organize

After deciding what written material to use, start putting it all in order. Look for ideas that flow logically. Seek out similarities or differences that draw certain thoughts together into a natural sequence. If one area looks weak or needs more support, either come up with some convincing evidence to strengthen it or take it out. Don't include anything that can't be backed up or that doesn't fit in the flow of the main idea.

Manage the Clock

Don't let the clock be the enemy. By now, it should be possible to see how many points there are and how much time is left. Do some simple math to figure out how much time there is to develop each idea. Don't forget to leave some time to review and proofread the writing (proofreading will be covered later).

Write

After all the preparation work is done, writers should have a clear idea of what they want to say. Keep in mind that there are certain things the scorers are looking for to show that the writing is well-thought-out. Also, be sure to write legibly, as the score could be lowered if the handwriting is poor.

Introduction
The opening paragraph is the **introduction**. It should include the following basic components:

- **A short restatement of the topic.** Don't just copy the writing prompt; rephrase it to suit the ideas. Make it look like the topic was created to make the points.

- **A personal opinion, or a statement of the overall big theme.** This will help set up the reader to understand how the smaller ideas fit into the big picture.

- **Smaller ideas.** They will serve as road maps for the audience. Telling readers how to navigate the ideas is like letting them see a "movie trailer" for the writing. They'll know what the writing is about, and they'll be interested to see how the ideas are developed.

Body
This is the meat of the writing and what all the brainstorming time has been spent preparing for. But by now, the ideas aren't bouncing around; they're neatly lined up, in order, ready to be released on the page. So, start writing!

Don't rush. With all these ideas, it's easy to start rushing to get them all down at once. This can lead to long, complicated, hard-to-follow sentences with lots of ideas crammed in. That's not good writing. Remember, hard work went into organizing the thoughts, and all the ideas are there. So, slow down. Make each point, one at a time, in the clearest, most direct way possible. Look for ways to connect ideas. Transition sentences that lead from one concept to another are a great way to provide flow and can prevent the writing from sounding like a collection of unrelated statements.

Conclusion
All the points have been made, developed, and connected to one another. Now it's time to write a **conclusion**. Conclusions sometimes seem silly and repetitive, but they really do serve an important purpose. State the opinion again and the main reasons behind it. Revisit the big idea here, and possibly restate the small ideas in a very basic way. Don't go through the details again—that's already been done. Also, don't present any *new* information or ideas in the conclusion. Simply summarize what's been said and wrap it up into a neat package for the reader.

Proofread

Everyone makes mistakes in the heat of writing on an exam: a misspelled word, a sentence that doesn't make sense, or a paragraph that seems disjointed and confusing. Be sure to leave a few minutes (at the end) to go back and reread the writing. Read slowly, trying to hear the words. It may feel silly, but moving the lips will help internalize the flow and make it easier to catch writing problems. Most mistakes are quick fixes, and any writer will be glad to have gone back and corrected them.

Also, be sure to delete any notes left while working through the assignment or any text from the brainstorming session. The formatting (indented paragraphs, for example) should be consistent. Leave readers with a document that looks appealing and "clean"—without mistakes—before they read a single word.

Final Thoughts

When time runs out, it will probably feel like there was room for improvement. That's normal. In fact, scorers understand the difficulties of creating organized, coherent writing in a timed situation under pressure. No one expects the writing to be perfect. With that in mind, here are some ideas for test takers to consider while working through the writing test:

- **Don't panic**. This is doable. Stop if it feels like brain overload is setting in and drawing a blank is imminent. Take a deep breath and remember the process. Don't force it. It's even okay to stop for a 30-second "mental vacation" to clear the mind.

- **Make the clock work**. Brainstorming and dividing the task into smaller chunks allows for viewing the remaining time in the least stressful way. If writing an entire essay in 30 minutes is overwhelming, just focus on finishing the next paragraph.

- **Don't try to impress anyone**. Don't use fancy words just because they're familiar—writers shouldn't use any word that they're not 100 percent sure about. Also, don't add more writing just to make the essay longer. What's important is clear, organized writing. If the ideas have been brainstormed, developed, and written in a logical order, it will be possible to put a lot of meaning into very few words.

In the end, by following these procedures, writing an easy-to-follow and well-thought-out response on the test should be no trouble. Remember: This can be done!

Good luck, and good writing!

Writing Prompt

Writing

Directions

Write an organized, coherent essay about the passage below. In your essay, make sure you:

- Clearly state your own opinion on the issue and analyze the relationships between your perspective and at least one other perspective
- Develop and support your ideas with evidence
- Organize your ideas logically
- Communicate your ideas in standard English

Prompt

People who share their lives on social media sites are edging into dangerous territory. Social media sites such as Facebook, Instagram, and Snapchat are black holes for those easily addicted to validation and acceptance. Society should be wary of allowing their kids to have open access to social media sites.

Perspectives

1. Although there are many negative side effects to social media, such as predatory accounts, cyberbullying, and identity theft, there are many positive sides to social media as well. Carrying around information 24/7 has its perks and can't be all bad—in fact, we are a society thriving on technology and connection.

2. People should take care to stay away from social media and get their validation and acceptance from entities that truly matter, like from themselves or a higher being. Being outside and getting exercise is a good alternative to staring at a screen all day. Those who get out and expand their worlds will definitely experience happier lives.

3. People should not be afraid of social media when it's able to bring so much opportunity to society. Staying in touch with family and friends, supporting political cries, and creating business opportunities are just some of the ways social media is beneficial to the community.

Dear ACT Test Taker,

We would like to start by thanking you for purchasing this study guide for your ACT exam. We hope that we exceeded your expectations.

Our goal in creating this study guide was to cover all of the topics that you will see on the test. We also strove to make our practice questions as similar as possible to what you will encounter on test day. With that being said, if you found something that you feel was not up to your standards, please send us an email and let us know.

We would also like to let you know about other books in our catalog that may interest you.

SAT

This can be found on Amazon: amazon.com/dp/1628455217

ACCUPLACER

amazon.com/dp/162845492X

TSI

amazon.com/dp/162845511X

SAT Math 1

amazon.com/dp/1628454717

AP Biology

amazon.com/dp/1628454989

We have study guides in a wide variety of fields. If the one you are looking for isn't listed above, then try searching for it on Amazon or send us an email.

Thanks Again and Happy Testing!
Product Development Team
info@studyguideteam.com

Interested in buying more than 10 copies of our product? Contact us about bulk discounts:

bulkorders@studyguideteam.com

FREE Test Taking Tips DVD Offer

To help us better serve you, we have developed a Test Taking Tips DVD that we would like to give you for FREE. **This DVD covers world-class test taking tips that you can use to be even more successful when you are taking your test.**

All that we ask is that you email us your feedback about your study guide. Please let us know what you thought about it – whether that is good, bad or indifferent.

To get your **FREE Test Taking Tips DVD**, email freedvd@studyguideteam.com with "FREE DVD" in the subject line and the following information in the body of the email:

     a. The title of your study guide.

     b. Your product rating on a scale of 1-5, with 5 being the highest rating.

     c. Your feedback about the study guide. What did you think of it?

     d. Your full name and shipping address to send your free DVD.

If you have any questions or concerns, please don't hesitate to contact us at freedvd@studyguideteam.com.

Thanks again!

Made in the USA
San Bernardino, CA
07 February 2019